MAUDE ADAMS

MAUDE ADAMS

*Idol of American
Theater, 1872–1953*

by ARMOND FIELDS

McFarland & Company, Inc., Publishers
Jefferson, North Carolina, and London

LIBRARY OF CONGRESS CATALOGUING-IN-PUBLICATION DATA

Fields, Armond, 1930–
Maude Adams : idol of American theater,
1872–1953 / by Armond Fields.
p.   cm.
Includes bibliographical references and index.

ISBN 0-7864-1927-X (softcover : 50# alkaline paper) ∞

1. Adams, Maude, 1872–1953.   2. Actors—
United States—Biography.   I. Title.
PN2287.A4F54   2004   792.02'8'092 — dc22   2004010483

British Library cataloguing data are available

Cover photograph: Undated portrait of Maude Adams (detail),
Museum of the City of New York

Manufactured in the United States of America

McFarland & Company, Inc., Publishers
Box 611, Jefferson, North Carolina 28640
www.mcfarlandpub.com

Acknowledgments

I am grateful to the following people for making their archives available to me and for their guidance in completing my research.

John Ahouse, University of Southern California Special Collections
Marty Jacobs, The Museum of the City of New York
Annette Fern, Houghton Library, Harvard University
Betty Sanchez, Cenacle Central Archives
Bobbi Burk, Stephens College archivist
Maren Jeppsen, Utah State Historical Society
New York Public Library, Performing Arts Division
Princeton University Library, Rare Books and Special Collections
General Electric Archives, Schenectady, New York
University of Utah
Chicago Historical Society
San Francisco Public Library, Historical Center
California Historical Society
San Francisco Performing Arts Library and Museum
Nevada Historical Society
Oregon Historical Society

Special recognition also goes to my intrepid researchers: Mary Jane McIntire, geneologist extraordinaire; Emily Kelley; Donna Radz; Giao Luong; Ned Comstock; and Dr. Dan Gardner. To John Farrell, my editor, my thanks for another job well done.

My wife, Sara, has been especially helpful. Her insights and interpretations of Maude Adams decidedly strengthened this book. My love and gratitude for her continuing efforts on my behalf.

Contents

Introduction

"I'm youth, I'm joy! I'm a little bird that has broken out of its egg," sang Maude Adams in her role as "Peter Pan, The Boy Who Wouldn't Grow Up." She was starring in J.M. Barrie's stage play in its first American production. The play quickly swept the country.

Thanks to the play's success, Maude Adams became the essence of Peter and captured the admiration of thousands of parents and children. Hundreds of admirers crowded the stage door to see, even touch, Peter. Maude never disappointed them.

At one crucial point in the play, when Captain Hook had poisoned Tinker Bell, Maude lightly skipped to the front of the stage and appealed directly to the audience, since only they could save Tinker. "Do you believe in fairies?" she called out. And, at every performance, the audience shouted, "Yes, we believe in fairies!"

Peter Pan was an amusing, exciting, adventurous tale, full of fantasy. Adults and children alike were entranced with the play. Barrie's story was an invention and a vision combined into one enchanting theatrical production. Yet, the play also represented a miniature world of Maude's personal and theatrical life.

As a baby, Maude was introduced to the theater by her actress mother, Annie Adams. Annie promoted her daughter's career at the cost of her own hopes and ambitions. Maude appeared in many children's parts since nearly every melodrama of the time contained such roles. Maude led the life of a performer, experiencing the strain of touring along with the delights of audience approval. School and personal life were sacrificed because they interfered with the theater.

With the guardianship of her mother and of impresario Charles Frohman, Maude became a reigning star of the New York stage. Frohman insisted that his performers dedicate themselves to the stage. Because of her unswerving commitment to acting, Maude became one of Frohman's favorite actresses.

It was not surprising that this young woman, a Broadway star, had difficulty separating the fantasy world of the stage from her real life. To protect her fragile psyche, Maude chose to withdraw from the public eye.

When rest and relaxation were needed, Maude frequently retreated to live in a convent.

Maude remained a private person throughout her life, sharing her encounters, trials, tribulations, and successes with only a select group of companions. At the height of her phenomenal career, she retired from the stage.

In the meantime, Maude remained active away from the public eye. She collaborated with the scientists at General Electric to perfect her innovations for stage lighting; she attempted to write and produce movies; she taught drama and produced plays at a small Midwestern college.

Maude died in obscurity. Today, few people are aware that she was Broadway's most scintillating actress during the early decades of the twentieth century. Few recognize that her acting methods and production techniques provided the foundations for dramatic art for successive performers and producers. Fewer still are aware that Maude was the one who introduced to this country an imaginative story that has become a symbol for America's love of fantasy.

No performer could emulate the "Boy Who Wouldn't Grow Up" as Maude portrayed the role, because no one was able to imbue it with her sensitivity, desire, and passion. Peter Pan was not only a stage role for Maude; it was an extension of her personal view of life.

The era in which Maude lived was one of the theater's most innovative periods. Audiences idolized Maude because she was the most talented and recognized interpreter of the dramatic stage.

This story of Maude Adams seeks to tell about her life experiences and her dramatic genius as they influenced each other throughout her long and successful career. It will explore and attempt to understand the mysteries that surrounded this enigmatic woman.

1

The Adams Heritage

The story of Maude Adams begins with the landing of the *Mayflower* in 1620.

John Howland, Maude's ancestor, was a passenger on that illustrious ship.[1] A signer of the Mayflower Compact at Cape Cod, Howland played an important role in establishing a settlement for the Pilgrims. According to Governor Bradford's log, Howland had been sent out to find a promising spot to settle, although a storm very likely determined the Pilgrims' landing at Plymouth.

Howland was active on the governor's council and served as a selectman. A sturdy, hard-working man, Howland lived until he was eighty years of age. He produced only daughters, however, so the family name was quickly lost. Howland also had the dubious distinction of being the only passenger to fall overboard during the *Mayflower's* trip across the Atlantic.

Some historians and biographers have claimed that Maude was also related to U.S. presidents John Adams and John Quincy Adams, but genealogical research reveals no such connection.

Maude was one of the ninth generation in descent from John Howland. She was a member of the Society of Mayflower Descendants, having number 1634 in that Society and 5049 in the General Society. Maude officially joined the Society in May 1919, although she had probably known of her ancestry since she was a girl. Interestingly, Maude never chose to advertise the *Mayflower* affiliation during her theatrical career; and it is likely that most people were not aware of her ancestry. Another well-known actress of the period, Lillian Russell, also was a descendant of John Howland.

Over the generations, the Adams family moved from Massachusetts to Vermont and later traveled on to Ohio and Ontario, Canada, in search of better farmland and more lucrative markets. As pioneers, they followed the wave of early immigrants across the wilderness as the country annexed new Western territories.

Maude's grandfather, Barnabas Lathrop Adams, called Barney, was born May 28, 1812, in Bastard Township, Leeds, Ontario, Canada.[2] Barnabas's father, Joshua

Adams, had been born in Rutland, Vermont, after which the family moved to Canada. The census listed them as farmers.

Barnabas migrated to Iowa from Ontario because he had been told that excellent, cheap farm land was readily available. On June 22, 1846, at age thirty-four, Barnabas married Julia Ann Barker, a twenty-year-old woman, daughter of the leading farmer in the community of Montrose, Iowa. The first of their eight children was born a year later.

While still residing in Canada, Barnabas had been persuaded to join the Mormon Church by friend and proselytizer David Moore. After his marriage, he and Julia moved to Navoo, Illinois, the site of a growing Mormon community.

In 1840, because Illinois was engaged in a hotly contested state election, local legislators welcomed Mormon settlers from the East with open arms, each hoping they would join his particular party. The Mormons were led by Joseph Smith. Stephen A. Douglas, the state's most prominent politician, befriended Smith and openly supported the Mormon cause, although probably for political rather than religious reasons.[3]

For the site of his new settlement, Smith had chosen a bleak-looking stretch of farmland, left unweeded, near a deserted village that had once been an experimental community. Sponsored by Douglas and John C. Bennett, Quartermaster of the State of Illinois, a unique charter for the town of Navoo was passed by the legislature. The charter ensured that the leaders of the settlement could initiate their own laws for local governance. Immigration from as far away as England quickly filled the community, where both work and food were plentiful.

During early 1847, Barnabas brought his wife and child to Navoo. But instead of a thriving town, Julia found community members preparing for a mass exodus west. "Outsiders" were killing the Mormons and burning their homes. This religious prejudice had become so hateful that the Mormons felt compelled to leave. Then, Joseph Smith was mysteriously murdered, and the Navoo charter was repealed by the state legislature.

The Mormons appointed a new leader, Brigham Young, to lead them out of Navoo. Barnabas immediately volunteered his services for the journey westward. He sent his wife, now pregnant, and his child back to Iowa to await his call to join him when a new settlement had been established. Julia did not know if she would ever see her husband again.

In July 1847, after a long and arduous trek across uncharted territory, the Brigham Young company entered the Great Salt Basin, where they decided that this expanse of semi-desert would be their future settlement. During the long trek, Barnabas had served as night guard, watching over the cattle that were left to graze while the pioneers slept. Because of his knowledge of using streams to facilitate logging, Barnabas was particularly helpful when wagons were required to ford streams.

Shortly afterward, Barnabas returned to Iowa, gathered up his wife, child, and all the household goods that could be packed in a prairie schooner, and made his way back to the Salt Lake Basin. They were among the fortunate few who successfully completed the weary hundreds of miles through snowstorms, across rivers, and over mountain ranges to their goal.

What awaited the family was a log cabin with buffalo robes fitted over the windows and door to deflect the desert winds, a hard dirt floor, and a minimum of furniture. Armed men stood constant guard against Indian incursions. Nonetheless, Little Cottonwood Canyon, their home, had abundant water and fertile farmland and was situated quite near the new settlement. Less than a month after the family's arrival, in January 1848, Julia gave birth to her second daughter, Asenath Ann Adams, later nicknamed Annie.[4]

Barnabas and Julia had eight children in all, the two girls and six boys. In keeping with the Mormon faith, Barnabas married two other women. Wife #2, Hannah Grove Chase, had five children, three girls and two boys. Wife #3, Ellen Nelson, had one boy. Barnabas married her when he was fifty-three, four years before his death. Asenath Ann Adams shared the home with thirteen siblings, covering a twenty-year age span.

Annie later recalled that, as a child, she had constantly been warned about roaming mountain lions and coyotes. She remembered her father's going to work in the fields armed. She remembered the scourge of locusts that devastated their crops one season.[5]

"Play-acting," as it was called, had already been introduced into the Mormon community before Annie was born. Under Joseph Smith's guidance, a brass band had been founded in Navoo; and a dramatic society periodically performed plays—only humorous ones, as decreed by Smith. Under Smith's aegis, a theater and dance hall had been built. Thomas A. Lyne, an actor who had converted to the Church, moved to Navoo and began producing plays. So popular were the productions that even Brigham Young appeared in them. However, the exodus west and the extensive efforts needed to develop the new community made amusement a low priority.

Once settled in Salt Lake, the inhabitants reinstituted Friday night dances, as promoted by Brigham Young, who believed such events were important for the welfare of the community. According to Annie, one of her first public appearances, a reading, occurred at one of these Friday socials.

About the time Annie was five years old, the first real play was produced in Salt Lake City. Called "Pizarro," it was put on at the Social Hall, a building set aside primarily for amusements. Social Hall was the first theater west of the Missouri River. It quickly became a center for dramas, concerts, public lectures, and sessions for the territorial legislature. In 1850, the Deseret Musical and Dramatic Association was formed. A play, "Robert Macaire," was presented at the Social Hall, just recently built. It was here that little Annie expressed interest in acting as she witnessed the various local productions.[6]

"Pizarro" was professionally staged, produced and acted by several men who later went on to theatrical careers outside the territory. Due to the success of the performances, Brigham Young proposed the erection of a theater, a radical suggestion that almost split the community. Some argued that the theater represented a symbol of

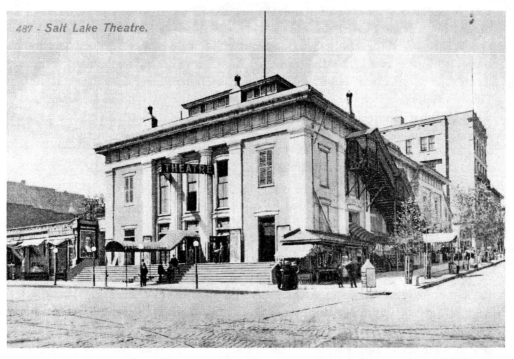

487 - Salt Lake Theatre.

The Salt Lake Theater was the city's premier venue for popular and dramatic entertainment. When it opened, the theater was said to have been the most modern west of the Rockies. Annie appeared in many local productions there, as did Maude years later when she was on tour. (Used by permission, Utah State Historical Society, all rights reserved)

society's impurities; others maintained that the new temple should be completed first. Nevertheless, Young prevailed and, underwritten by a Church fund, construction of the theater began. It was named the Salt Lake Theater and became one of the most modern playhouses in the West.

According to Church records, nearly every person able to work helped in building the theater. Trees from Cottonwood Canyon, cut and hauled by Barnabas and his men, supplied the timber to erect the building. For their efforts, workers received "admissions" to the plays when the theater was completed.

A gala ceremony preceded opening night. On March 8, 1862, two plays were presented, "The Pride of the Market" and "State Secrets." While box seats were sold for seventy-five cents each, any items of value were taken in exchange for admittance, from produce of all kinds to articles of clothing. Such exchanges went on for years; even visiting performers often came away with bushels of food in lieu of money. In an inaugural speech in front of the theater, Young cemented the notion that the theater was "an adjunct to the Church and never a factor against it."[7]

The theater seated 1,500 people. It was lit by oil burners and boasted red velvet-lined boxes, each with red velvet-cushioned chairs. It was said that the acoustics in the theater were perfect. A large stage featured the latest in backdrop machinery, imported from Denver. There were even individual dressing rooms for performers, although water was only available in a common trough backstage. Brigham Young had his own box, with his own special armchair, and always wore his hat during performances. Married women wore the traditional poke bonnets to the theater; young women and girls were allowed to attend in more fashionable hats.

When Annie's own family began to realize that she had an affinity for acting, she was allowed to appear in several plays put on by her school. It was said that "she created a sensation." One of Annie's teachers suggested to Barnabas that Annie had dramatic ability. Would he allow her to appear on the stage? Because of his reluctance toward a "suspect" profession, Barnabas was hesitant to give his approval. Finally he agreed to a hearing with the managers of the theater and allowed Annie to audition for them. "I remember that hearing as if it were yesterday," Annie recalled. "I was given a part from 'Ernest Maltravers' to read. Caine and Clawson (theater managers) and all other members of the company who happened to be present went to the back of the theater. Then, high and dry on the stage, I read as I had never read before." The result could not have been more exciting for the young woman. The managers promised her a role that they believed she could handle, in a play about to be staged.

A week later, Annie was cast as Grace Otis, a minor role in "Solon Shingle, or The People's Lawyer." It was 1865. Annie was seventeen years old, and her career as an actress was about to be launched.[8] "I knew there were many others waiting for my place," she remembered, "so I began studying. The first winter I lived at home, and Brigham Young's private carriage called for and delivered me." Young had all the ladies in the cast escorted to and from the theater, even during rehearsals.

"The next winter I lived in town with Aunt Polly Angell. My board and room was paid by the theater (although performers received no regular salary), and I was given one annual pass which I gave to the woman who did my laundry."

From that moment, the secrets of the backstage were revealed to Annie: the costuming room, with its long rows of colorful dresses and suits; the make-up room, complete with mysterious jars and tubes to be applied to the face; the set room, where every era of history had an appropriate backdrop; the barber shop; and, of course, the dressing rooms themselves, where performers prepared for their stage entrances. She discovered that, just before each performance, all of the performers had to pass muster under the exacting eye of the stage manager before they could appear in front of the audience.

Rehearsals had their own rituals. The company assembled to hear the play read by the stage manager, performers impatiently awaiting the moment they would be given the assigned parts. All the parts, copied meticulously by the manager, were laid out on a table, each part with the name of the actor written above the name of the character he or she was to play. Each time Annie wondered excitedly what role management had given her. She was never disappointed.

The real test came when a well-known star visited Salt Lake City appearing in one of his or her signature plays. It was usual to supply the visiting artist with the best talent from the local dramatic company in support. A local actress's highest point of artistry was reached when she was chosen for the supporting company. Despite having played on the stage for only seven months, Annie was assigned leading parts. For the next five years, Annie became the leading lady in numerous productions at the theater and a well-known figure in the community.

At the same time that seventeen-year-old Annie Adams was appearing as a star attraction at the Salt Lake Theater, James H. Kiscadden was roaming various mining towns in search of that ever-evasive bonanza.

James's father, also called James, had come from Ireland during the latter part of the eighteenth century to take advantage of the free farming land available in Ohio. His wife, Rebecca Stuart Ewing, had also come from Ireland; but there is no evidence to indicate whether they were married in Ireland or the U.S. In 1819, the first of their seven children was born in Ohio. James was the last child, born on May 24, 1836, in Clark County, Ohio. Little is known of his early years. He left home while a teenager to make his fortune prospecting at the newly opened gold and silver lodes discovered across the mountainous West.[9]

At age twenty-four, James was employed as a bookkeeper in Leavenworth, Kansas, possibly working for his brother, William. Although he had no formal schooling, he could read and write and was good with numbers. Two years later, he again was attracted to a new ore find at Grasshopper Creek, Montana Territory, in the Northern Rockies. On his way there, he was told of an even richer strike at Alder Gulch, seventy-five miles to the east, and decided to go there instead. Apparently, the adventure netted little for James.

In the summer of 1863, James was in Virginia City, where he and his brother William built a stone structure, the first stone building in town, to house their grocery business. Less than a year later, they sold the building and two lots for $8,000.[10]

In early 1864, James was in the northern reaches of the Montana territory, having partnered with seven men to found a town "at the mouth of the Marias for the great city of the Northwest."[11] Several months later, a charter for Ophir Town was approved by territory officials. For unknown reasons, however, development was never carried out; and James returned to Virginia City.

At the time, Virginia City was being harassed by outlaws, robbers, and killers who focused on the highways leading to the town, the routes usually taken by prospectors to bring their ore to local banks. Led by a colorful and controversial sheriff, Henry Plummer, a Vigilance Committee was formed to deal with the miscreants. During its first few months of existence, several outlaws were publicly hanged; and, for a while, the town seemed to settle down.

Enter one Joseph A. Slade, a former station-tender on the Overland Trail.[12] When Slade arrived in town, he was accompanied by his beautiful young wife, Maria Virginia, who was rumored to have been a prostitute. He also ran a string of horses. Slade had the reputation of being "a bad drunk" and his wife had "a vicious temper."

On a beautiful day in March 1864, when the roads finally opened due to the spring thaw, Slade rode into Virginia City from his ranch, got roaring drunk and proceeded to terrorize the townsfolk. After beating up several people and destroying a milk wagon, he harassed two respected merchants. First, he entered the Kiscadden store. James, familiar with Slade and his wife from Alder Gulch, attempted to persuade the marauding man to return to his ranch. On his way out of town, Slade stopped to insult another local merchant and ostentatiously threatened him with a gun.

Quickly, the Vigilance Committee was called out and gathered to confront Slade. They took away his gun, tied him up, and informed him he had one hour to live. Suddenly sober, Slade begged to be freed, pledging that he would never drink again. No one listened to his pleas. When the hour was up, a desperately struggling Slade was carried to a scaffold behind the Virginia Hotel and summarily hanged. James, a witness to the hanging, cut down Slade's lifeless body.

Shortly afterward, having been told of the events by friends from town, Maria Virginia Slade rode into Virginia City. Everyone stayed as far away as possible from her, not knowing what she might do. So intense was her anger that she refused to permit burial of her husband in Virginia City, nor anywhere in Montana Territory. Instead, she had an elegant casket made and lined with tin. Slade's body was placed inside, and the casket was filled with alcohol. Several months later, the casket was carried by wagon to Salt Lake City, 400 miles away, for burial. Driving the wagon to Utah, and accompanying Maria Virginia, was James Kiscadden.

Less than a month after Slade's hanging, Virginia and James Kiscadden were married by the Chief Justice of the Montana Territory. They moved to Salt Lake City.

A year later, the couple separated, Maria Virginia going to take up residence in St. Louis, never to see her husband again. It was not until 1868, however, that James requested a divorce from the court. On October 29, 1868, a divorce was granted, the claim being spousal desertion.[13] At the time, James was working for his brother, William, who was president of the Miner's National Bank. James collected gold and silver ore from the various mining sites.

There, it was recorded that James entered a court order to collect on an $1,800 promissory note given to him by Henry Standish, one of the partners of the ill-fated Ophir Town venture. In 1868, the court answered in favor of James and he found himself $1,800 richer. The amount was twice what local merchants might earn in two years. The money left James with a comfortable bank account with which to pursue his interests in the city.

Meanwhile, at the age of twenty, Annie Adams had become a leading actress at the Salt Lake Theater. It was exhilarating but not all fun, as Annie related in her autobiography. "I worked my brain and nervous system into shreds. Plays were being changed every night or two, and long speeches were the rule. One had to be letter-perfect. There were few rehearsals in which to build one's part."[14] Her situation was made even more complicated since two handsome men were actively seeking her attention.

Both James H. Kiscadden and Jack O'Neil attended the theater practically every evening to watch Annie's performances. Kiscadden was a dashing, tall, slender, and daring man, well dressed, but with a dubious reputation garnered from his mining

"The Marble Bride" was one of the first plays in which Annie Adams was allowed to appear.
She was eighteen years old. Manager Clawson had to persuade Annie's father, Barnabas,
that his daughter had acting talent.

days and Virginia City escapades. O'Neil was much like Kiscadden, a self-styled soldier of fortune and adventurer. Both were Gentile, which made them aliens in the Mormon city. When they attended the theater, they were forced to sit in the "Gentile section," thus able to keep a steely eye on one another, while both admired Annie.

Kiscadden did a better job of wooing Annie, and it soon became obvious that she preferred him over O'Neil. Barnabas, however, was against both men. Not only did he not want Annie to marry a Gentile, but he also must have been aware of Kiscadden's past adventures. Certainly, he believed Kiscadden unfit to marry his daughter, no matter her feelings for this worldly, personable man. In spite of Barnabas's remonstrances, the tender friendship appeared to be maturing quickly. Barnabas firmly believed he had to "protect" his daughter from this non-believer.

With dispatch, Barnabas informed the theater that Annie would no longer be available, since she was about to leave Salt Lake City. In spite of her protestations, Barnabas promptly shipped Annie to her maternal grandparents, Platt and Thankful Banker, in Clark County, Missouri, in order to "save" his daughter. The move not only separated her from Kiscadden; it also cut short her theatrical career. Annie was inconsolable.

Like the typical ending of a melodrama, however, a surprising event reunited Annie and James. On June 2, 1869, Barnabas died unexpectedly, felled by a heart attack. While lifting the bed of a wagon he injured himself internally. He afterwards complained of a pain in the chest. He continued working, believing it was not serious. Several days later, he sat down to dinner; and while he was eating he fell to the floor. When he was raised up, Barnabas gasped twice and died. A large funeral was conducted, led by Brigham Young, honoring this humble, industrious man for his years of devotion to the cause.[15]

Unhesitatingly, immediately after the funeral, James traveled to visit Annie and convince her to marry him. Since they could not be married in Salt Lake City because the Mormons forbade marriage to Gentiles, they were married in Clark County, Missouri, on August 15, 1869. Shortly afterward, the couple returned to Salt Lake City to take up residence next door to Annie's mother. As was not unusual at the time, James and Annie shared the home with several of her brothers and sisters.

The 1870 Census reported that James was unemployed. Annie tended the house and supervised eight children, ranging in age from two to fifteen. There seemed no way she could resume her stage career.

Eventually, James was able to resume his job at his brother's bank; but his particular responsibilities often took him away from home for extended periods of time. In June 1870, Annie became pregnant. Unfortunately, the birth of her twin boys in late February 1871 ended in tragedy, both of them stillborn. Annie was distraught and believed she had to do something to remove herself from an onerous situation.

Since she was forbidden to return to the local theater, she obtained a position at Piper's Opera House, in Virginia City, as a member of the local stock company. A highlight of her brief career there was an appearance playing with the touring star McKee Rankin in a melodrama.

In 1872, when Maude was born, she shared the house with eight other children, most of them her mother's younger siblings. When Annie returned to the stage, little Maude often accompanied her to the theater. (Used by permission, Utah State Historical Society, all rights reserved)

When she was again several months pregnant, Annie returned to Salt Lake City. She was no longer considered a Mormon because she had married a Gentile. Nonetheless, most of the family animosity was set aside; and Annie was looked after by her mother, Julia, during the last few months of her pregnancy. Because of his job, James spent most of his time traveling.

When Annie was about to give birth, a friend was dispatched to ride the twenty-five miles to the Alta mines to tell James he was needed at home. He arrived in time to witness the birth of a healthy girl. She was given the name Maude Ewing Kiscadden.

2

Introduction to the Stage

After Maude's birth, Annie wished to return to the Salt Lake Theater. She believed, however, that her husband would be against the idea. Instead of confronting her husband regarding her ambition, she persuaded a friend of the family, Jack Langriche, who also happened to be affiliated with the theater, to speak on her behalf. After several long discussions, James reluctantly consented. Annie was immediately reinstated into the local dramatic group to play leading roles, although she had not appeared on stage for several months.

Little Maude often accompanied her mother to the theater. Sometimes, the maid or James brought Maude to the theater at night so the family could walk home together after the performance. Maude seemed attracted to the theater environment, with its bustle of people, bright lights, varicolored costumes and scenery, not to mention the attention she received from performers and backstage personnel. She soon developed the habit of sleeping during the day and remaining awake at night, seemingly accommodating to her mother's working hours.[1]

Maude's first stage appearance occurred accidentally, albeit auspiciously, when she was only nine months old.

At the beginning of the 1873 theatrical season, the local drama company was attempting to deal with the usual early-season oversights and omissions. This particular evening, the property man was surprised by the cast manager's demand for a baby.

The play was "The Lost Child," a farce melodrama, a popular form of stage entertainment at the time. About to take a stroll, a family leaves their baby with a nurse. Once the family has gone, the nurse gives the baby to another woman and departs on other business. The exchange begins a series of "hand-offs" to various people, none of them really knowing what to do with the baby. The baby finally lands on a tray in a restaurant, the very place that the family is dining. Lying on the tray, the baby is presented to its surprised but grateful family.[2]

The "baby" planned for the production usually consisted of the ragdoll variety.

13

At the last moment, however, the stage manager declared he needed a real baby for the play. To satisfy the stage manager's demand, the flustered property man waded into the audience and borrowed a two-month-old infant from an agreeable parent.

During most of the play, the baby endured the various exchanges without a whimper. However, when the plot reached the deciding moment and the baby was to be delivered back to its "family," the otherwise cooperative infant began to kick and scream. Backstage everyone was frantic, including the manager, who now wanted to introduce the ragdoll substitute to complete the scene. Annie and the other performers attempted to quiet the squalling baby, with no success.

Just then, Maude's nurse happened to be preparing her to leave the theater. With little hesitation, Annie turned to the manager. "Here," she exclaimed, "take Maudie," and handed him her child. Reclining on the tray, precisely on cue, Maude Adams was whisked on stage.

The two-month-old baby had been exchanged for nine-month-old Maude. While the people backstage, in their panic, had not considered the discrepancy, the audience quickly recognized the switch and burst into howls of laughter. Maude apparently realized that she had become the center of attention. She sat up on the tray, smiled, and waved her arms toward the footlights. The audience now responded with cheers and applause. The play had been saved, and Maude was introduced to the world of theater.

In early 1874, Annie received an invitation to become a leading member of the stock company at Piper's Opera House in Virginia City. The salary was quite attractive, as was the six-month contract. John Piper was an ex-saloonkeeper who became interested in owning the local theater. By gradually buying into it, he became sole owner in 1868. Thus began a thirty-year career that would dominate theatrical activities in the region. It was Piper's practice to attract his actors by advancing them large sums of money, then withholding any salary until the debt was worked off.[3]

James's business required him to be out-of-town for extended periods of time. Annie believed she had reached the upper limit of an acting career in Salt Lake City, and the new challenge seemed worth pursuing. Maude would accompany Annie on her new engagement.

Piper's Opera House resembled a two-story barn with a wide porch extending across the entire front of the building, highlighted by a series of pillars that supported a roof over the foyer. Glass doors were located under the foyer roof. Inside, seats covered the entire floor, right up to the doors.

When the house was constructed, workers had to dig and blast into solid rock in order to lay a foundation. The stage was built atop the rock, the slope of the hillside providing the stage's elevation. This type of sloping stage was known as a "rake" stage, and its incline served as origin for the theatrical terms "upstage" and "downstage." Though his theater was at first unheated, Piper soon installed stoves for the comfort of patrons, most of whom remained bundled up on cold and windy nights no matter the stoves' output. The ingenious Piper placed the stovepipes so as not to obstruct any patron's view of the stage, an important promotional device.

Like most theaters, Piper's Opera House had a stage covered with advertising from local merchants. Seating consisted of rows of individual chairs that could be easily arranged to suit the entertainment. (California Historical Society, FN-35892))

Backstage equipment was adequate; but there were only minimal accommodations for the performers, and no hot water. If a large cast happened to be performing, actors had to take turns using the dressing rooms. Throughout the theater, lighting consisted of gas lamps. To illuminate the stage, small gas lamps lined the front, which meant that the rear of the stage was always in semidarkness. Consequently, performers always managed to play at the front of the stage, often leaning over the footlights to emphasize their lines.

Like other mining towns, Virginia City supported its own resident company. With the advent of the transcontinental railroad, along which Reno was a stop, the Virginia City spur helped to import traveling headliners from the East. Since melodrama was the prevailing entertainment, a full cast of players was usually needed to support the headliner. Within days, and sometimes hours, the resident company was required to learn the lines of an entire play. Usually, on the morning before the first performance, a full dress rehearsal took place with the headliner to smooth out the presentation. It was a laudable endeavor; yet, more often than not, such rehearsals left much to be desired.

A key member of the resident company was the prompter, essential in assisting performers to recite their lines at the correct moment. Not surprisingly, the prompter became the vital ingredient of any performance. If he were too noticeable, relied on too frequently, the play would be deemed a failure. Otherwise, the audience usually forgave resident company performers' brief lapses of memory. For an accomplished headliner, these gaffes must have been excruciating, although when a star agreed to a tour, such episodes were anticipated, particularly in the West. Indeed, it was in response to these traumas that the phrase "the show must go on" became the mantra for touring headliners.

Annie's addition definitely bolstered the Piper stock company. Not only had she become a reliable actress, she was a quick-read, knew the components of stage blocking, and already had considerable experience with traveling headliners. She immediately fit in and quickly assumed leading roles.

Annie, Maude, and her maid lived in a boardinghouse near the theater. James remained in Salt Lake City, having expressed his displeasure with Annie's decision to work in Virginia City. That such a distance — some 400 miles— prevented him from seeing his little girl surely did not help his disposition. Nonetheless, he seemed to have done nothing to modify the situation.

As had been the case in Salt Lake City, Maude was frequently taken to the theater, where she became quite familiar with the surroundings. As Annie explained her young daughter's behavior: "She would have made an almost perfect stage-child. She slept more quietly in the daytime and seemed more bright and animated at night. She never cried at night, and during the times she was brought to the theater by her nurse, she was always the picture of wide-eyed wonderment."[4] While Annie would not have admitted it at the time, she had already begun plotting a stage career for her infant daughter.

While in Virginia City, Annie and Maude's life followed a professional routine. Annie arose late in the morning, ate a breakfast snack, and spent the remainder of the morning studying her lines. After lunch, a rehearsal took place at the theater, usually directed toward assisting struggling performers or rearranging material to make the play easier to memorize. Annie then took a short nap before eating a light dinner. By 7:00 P.M., she was at the theater to prepare for the evening's performance. She usually returned to the boardinghouse by 11 P.M.

Maude was normally cared for by the maid during the day, although she was often taken to the rehearsal. She and the maid usually appeared at the theater while the performance was in progress, to be met by Annie, and other backstage admirers, at the conclusion of the play. This pattern continued until the fall of 1875, shortly before Maude celebrated her third birthday.

On October 26, 1875, Annie's tenure as leading actress of Piper's stock company came to an abrupt end when fire destroyed more than a square mile of Virginia City, including Piper's Opera House. Luckily, the theater was closed at the time.

Immediately, the enterprising Annie applied for a job at the Bush Street Theater, San Francisco. Thanks to her experience and reputation, she was quickly hired as a member of the stock company, at a starting salary of thirty-five dollars a week.

Shortly after Annie and Maude arrived in San Francisco, James followed and obtained a job as a bookkeeper at Parke and Lacy, distributors of heavy mining machinery, on Montgomery Street. In the city directory, Annie was listed as an actress for Maguire's New Theater. Yet, the name had already been changed to the Bush Street Theater, as Maguire continued his aggressive efforts to gain a monopoly of theaters in the city. The Kiscaddens were living in an apartment at 13 Powell Street, between Union Square and the emerging Chinatown, close to the theater district.

Born of immigrant parents in New York, Tom Maguire rose from hack driver to gambler to saloonkeeper to become one of the West's great impresarios. During the period of his ascendancy, he was called the "Napoleon" of San Francisco theater.[5]

Maguire had followed the westward movement of the '49ers and opened a saloon. In 1850, he opened the Jenny Lind Theater on the second floor of the casino he ran. In 1854, he built Maguire's Opera House, which became the city's leading theater. Maguire frequently traveled

Maude wrote that she loved walking with her father and hearing his stories of the old West. Yet from her first play at age five until James' death when she was eleven, Maude only occasionally lived with him. (The Harvard Theatre Collection, The Houghton Library)

to New York to persuade headliners to visit his theater. He became quite successful in enticing them to play in San Francisco in spite of the ten-day train trip across the country. He claimed to spare no expense in attracting headliners and making his productions the most professional in the West.

For several decades, Maguire dominated the local theater scene, building theaters, managing and producing plays, in effect, determining what San Francisco audiences saw. He seemed to possess an instinct for the theatrical and an intuitive knowledge of what would draw a crowd. His ultimate accomplishment was to manage the Baldwin Theater, which opened in May 1877. The following year, Maguire left San Francisco for New York, where he attempted to enter the theater business, albeit unsuccessfully. In late 1875, when Annie joined the Maguire forces, he owned or managed three theaters in San Francisco.

During the next year and a half, Annie was frequently called upon to appear in melodramas. As a character actress, she had the unique ability to quickly learn new roles, no matter the usual problems associated with resident stock companies. Had she wished, Annie could have appeared continuously in the shows that arrived in San Francisco during the theater season, from September to June. Yet, she was more selective, accepting only those roles she believed she was capable of performing properly. For this reason, she avoided comic opera and Shakespeare. Still, she could always be found in attendance at first-night performances of new shows, often taking Maude with her. When Annie appeared in a play, little Maude was usually found in the wings, watching the entire action of the play. Though she was only three years old, some claimed she could already memorize the lines of a play and repeat them whenever asked.

In spite of Annie's stage successes, James continued to argue against her commitment to the theater. Long debates about the issue changed nothing. One result of this unfinished business was James's increased drinking. During one particularly difficult period, he temporarily moved out of the apartment to a boardinghouse close by. Nonetheless, he would never miss his Sunday walks with Maude, which she recalled in later years as a highlight of her childhood. Maude claimed her father was a great storyteller, recalling his early adventures in the wilderness, as well as reciting stories of the West's development. Among the tales that James might have related to his daughter was that of the fabulous success of Elias Jackson "Lucky" Baldwin.

Baldwin had first arrived in San Francisco in 1853. He began his career by operating livery stables and managing a hotel. Fortunately, Baldwin invested in the first Comstock silver lode near Virginia City and quickly became a millionaire. He was later the first president of the Pacific Stock Exchange, owned vast land holdings in Southern California, and was credited with building the Santa Anita racetrack.

In 1876, Tom Maguire convinced Baldwin to build an elaborate hotel and theater in San Francisco. Located on Market Street, between Powell and Ellis, the hotel was six stories tall and boasted 400 lavish rooms. It was designed in French Renaissance style, with a mansard roof, towers and cornices, and a main cupola from which flags fluttered on momentous occasions. To the natives of San Francisco, the Baldwin Hotel was the most elegant "palace" they had ever seen.

The theater was located in the center of the hotel and seemed a palace in its own right, complete with an ornate bar and billiard room. It had a capacity of 1,700 people and a large stage to accommodate the most extensive of companies. The interior was resplendent with rich mahogany, stained glass, crystal chandeliers, and elaborate, colorful frescoes. Walls and furniture were covered with red velvet and trimmed with gold leaf. The curtain was said to have cost more than $6,000; the chandeliers $1,500 each.

The theater officially opened in March 1876. Maguire acted as manager of the hotel and theater. A young, aspiring actor, David Belasco, was selected as Maguire's assistant. The Baldwin's first attraction was Barry Sullivan in "Richard III." James A. Herne was stage manager; Belasco served as prompter. Although she was reluctant to appear in a Shakespeare play, Annie took a small part in the cast.

Looking for performers to comprise a high-quality stock company at the Baldwin, Maguire carefully selected local actors with whom he was already familiar. They

The Baldwin Theater was considered the most elegant venue in the city and the only place for high-class productions. Theater people like David Belasco, James A. Herne, Tom Maguire, and James O'Neill, father of Eugene O'Neill, began their careers there. (San Francisco History Center, San Francisco Public Library)

were to be available for all the traveling shows Maguire was in the process of book-ing for the future. Demands on the company would be substantial; but the salaries were generous, and the backstage environment the best in the West. With Annie's selection to the stock company, her career was reinvigorated; and she was now earn-ing more than her husband. Yet Annie was even more ecstatic about the chance to place little Maude in the wings of a "fine" theater.

In January 1877, Annie was loaned by Maguire to the Grand Opera House stock company for a series of plays, "Tom Cobb," a farce comedy, and "Chilperic," an Arthurian legend.[6] Both shows played one week. Members of the stock company had only two days to prepare for the second play, while the first play was making its final performances. Such was the life of a typical stock company cast.

When a male headliner arrived from the East, his entourage generally consisted of three people, an advance man, a manager, and a secretary/dresser. As part of the agreement with a theater, the cast would be supplied by its resident stock company. The headliner usually performed a signature play associated with his name. The com-bination of play and name is what constituted his reputation and audience appeal. For example, J.K. Emmet played "Fritz" for more than thirty years, Joseph Jefferson played "Rip Van Winkle" for nearly his entire career, and Edwin Booth always had his "Hamlet." Headliners could earn up to $500 for a week's work, consisting of seven performances, five evenings and two matinees. If the headliner was an outstanding drawing card, his traveling and hotel expenses would be covered, as well.

About a week before the headliner reached town, the advance man and man-ager arrived to take charge of the planning. The advance man was in charge of pub-licity and advertising — newspapers, posters, billboarding, speaking to various social and business groups — to promote the upcoming play. He also had to find out which of the resident company were recognizable enough to include in the advertising. The manager had the task of selecting the cast from the resident company roster and rehearsing them each morning for the entire week preceding the arrival of the head-liner. The script was introduced, and the cast made to go through their paces, although the headliner's part remained blank. Unfortunately, cast turnover was common. Some members dropped out, or were forced out, because of the difficulty of the lines; some balked at the size of the role (too small); still others felt the role did not suit their abilities. Such problems had to be resolved by hiring new performers and integrat-ing them into the play as quickly as possible. During this week of rehearsals, the prompter was the most important person on the stage.

The last performance of the current play was staged on Saturday night. The opening of the new play took place on the following Tuesday night. On Monday morning, the headliner arrived at the theater to engage in a full-scale dress rehearsal of the play. By that time, the cast had to know their lines, cues, and stage blocking. Moreover, under the exacting direction of the headliner, they had to be able to give meaning to their characterizations. If the headliner so desired, rehearsals might con-tinue up to curtain time on Tuesday night. As was the custom at the time, performers were not paid for rehearsal time, only for actual performances.

Everyone awaited the Wednesday morning reviews of the play that appeared in the newspapers. Reviews were crucial to the success or failure of the play. A reviewer would never give an ambiguous review, knowing that journalistic competitors would not hesitate to revel in their own critiques. The headliner was assumed to be a finished actor, one who, of course, knew his or her part intimately. He or she was given the most attention. A good review meant full houses for the remainder of the week. A mediocre or poor review might very well shorten the headliner's stay in the city. The cast also received their share of attention. Certain actors familiar to the critics, like Annie, were singled out as doing their jobs with professionalism or fulfilling their assignments adequately. Those who did not perform well received a sharp put-down or, mercifully, were not mentioned at all. How intrusive the prompter was also had an effect on the review.

Audiences in San Francisco's finer theaters were generally polite, since they represented the better classes. Nonetheless, if a play were well received, cheers, shouts, and applause for curtain calls and speeches would resound in the hall. If a play were performed below expectations, applause would be minimal and the audience would quickly file out of the auditorium.

These unwritten rules of theater behavior were followed as long as the headliner had one role to play and an engagement was scheduled for a week. But what happened when a headliner featured repertory?

Backstage became the most imperious, obsessive, critical, urgent, and nerve-racking environment that ever occupied a theater. Imagine a resident company's having to learn three plays in less than a week. Imagine their not knowing until hours before the opening curtain which play they were to perform that evening. Imagine their being forced to learn a fourth play if one of the original plays received poor reviews. Such episodes occurred often; and only the most flexible, versatile, and professional performers could meet the challenge. Annie Adams was one of those gifted performers.

During May and June 1877, Buffalo Bill and Captain Jack appeared at the Bush Street Theater. They presented three enjoyable plays and attracted large audiences. If they decided to perform only one play for the week, the decision would guarantee a drop in attendance toward the end of the week. Present all three shows on successive nights, and the box-office would be good. Annie supported the headliners in "Life on the Border," "The Red Right Hand," and "Secrets of the Plains" for the three-week engagement.[7] When the Buffalo Bill combination visited San Jose, Sacramento, Virginia City, and Carson City in a single week, before returning to San Francisco, Annie was the leading actress playing opposite Buffalo Bill. At least, she was not required to change her costume for each of the plays.

James had returned to the family from his temporary exile. After almost a year living in a small apartment on Powell Street, the Kiscaddens moved to larger quarters at 131 Montgomery. In spite of his periodic bouts of drinking, James continued to hold his job with Parke and Lacy. The combined earnings for Annie and James allowed them to pay for two maids, one to take care of Maude, the other to handle domestic duties. When Annie worked at the Baldwin Theater, Maude and the maid usually accompanied her to the theater.

In early October 1877, the advance man and manager for J.K. Emmet arrived in San Francisco to select and rehearse stock company members for his play, "Fritz, Our German Cousin."

Joseph Klein Emmet was born in 1841 in St. Louis, Missouri, where he began as a sign painter who prepared sets for local theaters.[8] Gaining a taste for performance, he soon devised his own song-and-dance act. Emmet began his stage career in minstrelsy and, after several years of perfecting his act, moved into variety. Performing as a "Dutch" comedian, he wore a green blouse and cap and wooden shoes, and sang in broken English. In 1870, he first appeared as Fritz, a young man seeking his long-lost sister. The play, which included songs he had written and now performed, made him a star. It also provided him with a vehicle for the remainder of his career, as every few years he introduced a new Fritz adventure. Besides being able to dance and sing, Emmet was also an accomplished musician. These talents, combined with a winning personality, assured him star status on the variety circuit. When "Fritz" came to town, audiences knew they were in for a pleasant evening.

Annie was one of the first performers to be selected to appear in the play. By the end of the first day of auditions, all the roles had been filled. All but one. The script called for the brief appearance of a small boy, his role containing several lines in a scene that included the child's being tied to a revolving millwheel. Yet, no small children could be found to fill the role. When the manager appealed to the stock company members for help, a friend of Annie's suggested little Maude.

"Would you be willing to let Maudie try out for the part?" the manager asked Annie.

"Yes, but…" was her answer. She knew that James would have to be persuaded to allow his daughter to appear on stage. Annie had succeeded in getting James at least to tolerate her own stage ambitions, but she feared he would not willingly let Maude enter into theatrical work.

At the dinner table that evening, Annie asked James to allow Maude to appear in "Fritz." Not surprisingly, James balked at the suggestion. "And let my daughter make a fool of herself?" he exclaimed. When the discussion between Annie and James had reached an impasse, Maude broke in. "Papa, Maudie won't make a fool of herself." She spoke in such a plaintive manner that James could not refuse his daughter. "All right, Maudie," he replied, "you're the general."[9]

The following day, Annie brought Maude to Emmet, who was delighted to see a child audition for the part. He became even more delighted when Maude learned her part in an hour and, during full-dress rehearsals, played it like an "old stager." Emmet, ever the promoter, listed the roles of the entire stock company in the newspapers. Ending the list, in upper case letters, was "Le Petit Maude" as Little Schneider.

At Annie's insistence, and with Emmet's agreement, it was decided to use Adams as Maude's stage name. It sounded more stage-like than Kiskadden. When James was informed of the decision, he sighed in resignation.

The production played at the Bush Street Theater for three weeks. "Fritz," Emmet, and the supporting stock company received excellent reviews. There was no mention of Maude. Nevertheless, her brief role caught the attention of other managers, and Maude's stage career had officially begun.

A week after Emmet's departure, Annie and Maude were cast in a farce-melodrama, "A Bunch of Keys," at the Baldwin Theater. All of the cast members belonged to the resident stock company. Maude had no lines to speak; it was only a walk-on part. The play lasted one week and audience reaction to it was, at best, mediocre. Still, the applause Maude received served as constant reminder of her role in "Fritz" and enhanced her desire for the stage.

Annie, of course, was ecstatic sharing the stage with Maude. On the other hand, James sensed that he had lost his little girl to his wife's ambitions, a belief not conducive to a happy household. In later years, Maude acknowledged that her early appearances on the stage were "a tug of war with her father." She perceived it to be rather in the nature of a dare. Maude wished to prove to her father that she would not make any false or embarrassing steps, that she was unafraid of the stage.

Forty-nine years later, Maude would recall her first stage experience with awe and foreboding. She remembered entering "in a great empty place with huge, dark spaces." She saw a man sitting at a table under the shadows cast by a lighted gas jet. She approached him with great trepidation. "It was there that a part was handed to her," and she was told to learn her lines and be ready to recite them on stage. It had all seemed quite mysterious.[10]

Annie appeared in several plays during the early part of 1878, but five-year-old Maude was not asked to audition for a part until March. Unlike her previous appearances, this would be an important role in a well-known and well-liked melodrama.

James O'Neill (father of Eugene O'Neill) was the Baldwin Theater's leading man and general manager of the stock company. He chose to perform "A Celebrated Case," a popular murder melodrama, as the spring offering at the Baldwin, in between visits from Eastern touring companies. He also planned to have the company tour several nearby cities to improve the play's profitability.

According to the *San Francisco Chronicle*, "A Celebrated Case" was a strong play, with intense situations and "some French ingenuity shown in the construction."

The plot: Jean Renaud helps a dying nobleman, who entrusts him with his papers, family jewels, and money. Knowing that further absence from his regiment will be considered desertion, he nonetheless hurries home to give his wife the valuables. Kissing his wife and little daughter and wishing them goodbye, he returns to his regiment. A villain, who has observed the whole incident, breaks into the Renaud home, confronts the wife, and demands the valuables. The wife resists. In the bedroom, the child hears the scuffling and calls out to her mother. The mother replies: "It is nothing, child. Your father is with me." The wife is murdered and the villain escapes with the valuables. Next day, Jean Renaud is accused of murdering his wife. His child is later brought before the court as the chief witness against him.

Maude, as "Little Adrienne," in "A Celebrated Case." It was her first experience as a member of a touring company. The company played in Sacramento and Virginia City.

The prosecutor addresses little Adrienne: "No doubt your mother told you to always tell the truth?"[11]

"Yes, sir. So did papa."

"Well, tell me. When did you last see your father?"

"You see, I ... . I can't tell."

"Well?"

"Papa told me I must not tell he was at home last night."

"You are very sure you saw him?"

Little Adrienne tells of kissing her father and being put to bed. "But I heard them talking," she adds. "After a little, I thought papa was angry; they talked so loud."

"And what did mamma say?" inquires the prosecutor.

"Mamma cried out, 'Mercy! Mercy! Have mercy!' I wanted to get out. I called."

"Who answered you?"

"Mamma."

"What did she say?"

"She said: Hush, child. Hush! I am with your father."

Renaud is convicted and sent to jail, where he remains for twelve years. His child is adopted by the Colonel of his regiment, who was also his judge. The grown daughter recognizes her father on the regimental grounds and a painful scene of reconciliation ensues. The real murderer is at last discovered when he claims the estate of the nobleman. Renaud is finally exonerated and reunited with his daughter.

Maude was selected to play Adrienne Renaud, the accused father's daughter. It had to have been a difficult role for a girl with little stage experience, especially for one not yet able to read. Annie repeatedly read her daughter the play and Maude's part in it until she had memorized the lines. Then Annie rehearsed Maude on her cues and the kind of voice she was to use in the courtroom scene. When Maude appeared at the company rehearsal, she not only startled the cast with her precise recitation of the lines, she also acted the role with a naturalness rare among children.

"A Celebrated Case" opened at the Baldwin Theater on April 25, 1878, to play only three days. Still, it was an immediate hit; and the theater was crowded every night. Reviews were excellent, and O'Neill was congratulated for presenting such a sophisticated play before local audiences. Among newspaper reports about the play, Maude received her first notice.

> The part of the child was intelligently taken by little Maude Adams, whose child-like and perfectly natural acting entirely captured the sympathetic audience and gained her repeated applause when brought before the curtain by Mr. O'Neill at the end of the act.[12]

Annie did not have a part in the play, but she accompanied Maude to every performance. She also helped her dress; applied her makeup (a first for Maude); and had Maude practice her lines before going on stage.

The brief appearance of the play at the Baldwin had been dictated by the arrival of Mme. Mojeska and her opera entourage. So O'Neill took the entire company to

Sacramento for one week, then to the new Piper's Opera House in Virginia City for another week's engagement. It was Maude's first experience as a member of a touring company.

Since the trip to Sacramento took only a half a day, soon after the company arrived, they gave an evening performance. They were housed in a boardinghouse close to the theater, one that catered to theatrical people. Light breakfasts and early dinners were available to the boarders, and the parlor was stripped of furniture so the company could rehearse. Although the train ride and boardinghouse accommodations were not very comfortable, Maude thoroughly enjoyed the adventure and found everything about it exciting. Sacramento audiences were equally enthusiastic about the play and Maude's part.

The following week, the company traveled to Virginia City to appear at the newly rebuilt Piper's Opera House, which had reopened in January, 1878. Unfortunately, the new theater was inferior to the original; and patrons considered going there an unsatisfactory experience. Piper then widened the stage by two feet on each side and advanced it six feet forward. On the other hand, the wings, where performers were stationed to enter the stage, were reduced in size. Several cubicles had been erected as dressing rooms, but they were far short of those needed for a traveling company. Another building had been built for a scene-painter to prepare backdrops for coming shows, but it was not large enough to accommodate a completed backdrop.

The hall seated 900 patrons. Admission prices were high: ten dollars for a lower box seat; five dollars for an upper box; one dollar for dress circle seats; fifty cents for parquet seats. But all prices were high in a mining town. Cheaper seats could be had on benches and wooden chairs moved into place when needed and removed for dances. The back of the hall was known as "the pig-pen," where spitting privileges prevailed. The new Piper's remained without heat for more than ten months after its opening. When heating was finally installed, the stoves were randomly located, the result being excessive heat for people seated nearby and none for those seated at a distance. In addition, the stovepipes obstructed sight lines. Lighting in the theater was supplied by kerosene lamps and lanterns, distinct fire hazards. In 1883, Piper's Opera House burned to the ground again.

Train travel from Sacramento to Virginia City took almost a full day. After traversing one range of mountains to reach Reno, where a train change was necessary, the trip to Virginia City was all uphill, on dangerously winding track. Upon arrival, for their comfort, the company was housed in a hotel. Due to the limited number of dressing rooms at the theater, performers changed into their costumes at the hotel and walked to the theater. As they walked down the main street toward the theater, townspeople recognized them. Men tipped their hats. Women nodded. Many applauded the performers in respect.

"A Celebrated Case" played to full houses in Virginia City, for a week's receipts of more than $3,250. Yet, with expenses of $700 for train fare, $2,200 for salaries, $200 for an orchestra, and $250 for bill posting and printing, the O'Neill company lost several hundred dollars for its Virginia City engagement.

Piper's Opera House, in Virginia City, was the most imposing building on the main street. However, performers changed into their costumes at the hotel and walked to the theater. After burning down, the theater reopened in 1878, only to be destroyed again by fire in 1883. (California Historical Society, FN-35893)

Back at the Baldwin Theater, the company performed "A Celebrated Case" for two evenings and one matinee, to packed houses, recouping some of O'Neill's losses. Again, a newspaper mentioned that Maude's part "was exceedingly well played by a child so young in years."

Meanwhile, the situation at home had again deteriorated because of James's drinking; and he returned to the nearby boardinghouse where he had stayed before. He visited Annie and Maude on Sundays, but there was no doubt in his mind that not only Annie but now Maude was wed to the theater. What kind of relationship Maude actually developed with her father under the circumstances is unknown. Yet her recollection of him years later proved to be one of love, caring, and respect, a portrait so positive that it bordered on the romantic.

Since most of the local theaters were closed for the summer, Annie spent the time teaching Maude to read and write. At the end of August, they both appeared in "The Romance of a Poor Young Man," at the Baldwin Theater. The play ran for ten days instead of the usual week, since the next company to appear at the Baldwin had been stalled by train trouble. In this play, Maude had a small role and few speaking lines.

Maude's excitement was unbounded when Annie informed her daughter that they had been signed by the Kennedy and Fitzgerald combination to appear in repertory on a tour to Portland, Oregon. If successful, the tour would last a month. Maude eagerly anticipated all the new places, new plays, unknown theaters, and unascertained audiences she could only imagine. James, however, was not pleased with the news, since it represented the longest period yet of separation from his daughter.

Diligently learning roles to perform in new plays, packing for one full month, dreaming of the mysteries of touring yet to be revealed, Maude was already living the life of an actor. With both excitement and anxiety, she waited, impatient for her great adventure to begin.

3

Mastering Her Skills

The fall tour began with a one-night stand at Petaluma's newly built theater, an easy train ride from San Francisco. "The Lady of Lyons," a melodrama already familiar to most audiences, was performed. Maude had a walk-on part, hardly noticed by the audience and not mentioned in the program.

Two days later, members of the Kennedy and Fitzgerald combination boarded a steamer at the San Francisco docks in preparation for an ocean voyage to Portland, Oregon.

In 1878, there were only two routes available to travel from San Francisco to Portland. One route required a train ride to Redding, California, then stagecoach travel over the Siskiyou Mountains into the Wilamette Valley to Salem, Oregon. Finally, another train would carry weary travelers from Salem to Portland. The entire trip took three days and the stagecoach portion was quite hazardous, following winding and occasionally treacherous mountain trails. In contrast, the boat trip was a quick and relatively smooth ride of two days. The price of the trip included a small cabin and meals. Most often, traveling companies chose the steamer because it also afforded them two days for rehearsals. When a company was playing repertory, time for rehearsals was critical. For Maude, her first boat trip was an exciting event, one never to leave her memories. In later years, she looked forward to and thoroughly enjoyed ocean voyages.

The tour also included a brief visit to Salem, where the Oregon State Fair was being celebrated. Evening entertainment was part of the fair spectacle, and companies were given a guarantee in order to persuade them to perform there. While in Salem, the company played "Romeo and Juliet," "Hunchback," "The Lady of Lyons," and "Much Ado About Nothing" on successive evenings. Shakespearean plays were usually condensed and their language modified so audiences could more easily understand them.

Some performers were able to memorize their lines in the short time allotted them, but it was not uncommon to have performers reading from the script while on stage. Mrs. Scott-Siddons, granddaughter of the famous tragedian who had been an adored star on the London stage, and Messrs. Kennedy and Fitzgerald played the leading roles and needed little practice because they had performed the parts so many times. The remainder of the company, however, spent entire days prior to each performance preparing for that evening's presentation. Annie had faced this challenge many times before, had actually appeared in a number of these plays, and was always ready to play her assigned part with confidence. Maude appeared in only "The Lady of Lyons," an undemanding part.

Actors in a touring company like Kennedy and Fitzgerald's had to be competent, efficient, and finished performers. Any actor who was not up to at least fifty parts, including Shakespeare and the most popular farce comedies and melodramas of the day, could not qualify. Yet, even for veterans like Annie, the strain of this life style could be terrifying. Memorizing, rehearsing all day, and preparing one's wardrobe, an actor's life in touring repertory was, as one performer aptly called it, "the most exhausting for the brain and body."

Fifteen hours a day in the theater and eight performances a week contributed to weariness and tension. Frequently, a member of the company would temporarily lose emotional control; and his or her next stage appearance would almost certainly reflect hostility and frustration. When the leading actors laid out a scene — "you stand there; don't cover me; to the left; then you give me my cue" — the cast often became so tense, they just got out of the way and watched. Nevertheless, acting was their job; and performers worked hard at it because they had faith in the importance of their profession.

While on tour, Maude's mind was completely filled with learning dialogue and plot lines and watching performers play their parts. She was also a keen observer of the myriad backstage activities, all of which, in some magical way, seemed to coalesce into a finished production. From the wings, she watched audiences and observed how they reacted to comedy and pathos. This was a life in which one was busy each day "being someone else." When was there time to be a normal little girl? Not when one was on tour, Annie explained to Maude.

The company was appearing at Portland's best and newest theater, the New Market, which had only recently opened. Constructed completely of brick, the theater had cost more than $100,000 to build. The ground floor was used as a public market; the second and third floors housed the theater. Access and egress were difficult. To get to the orchestra seats one had to climb to the third story, then descend a narrow flight of stairs. The gallery did not have a separate exit, which crowded all departing patrons together into the lower-level corridors. One door, on the second level, had been designed specifically for use in case of fire, but it was always locked. Patrons complained that the theater was located in the middle of the wholesale business section, previously unfrequented by locals after dark. In spite of these inconveniences, the theater was heavily patronized by theatergoers from throughout the city. It was not until 1883 that the theater was remodeled.

On the other hand, the proscenium and backstage contained some of the best equipment found in the Northwest. A beautiful velvet curtain adorned the stage. The backstage had plenty of room for scenery and dressing rooms, and the wings had sufficient space for performers. For well-known headliners and their companies, scenery was usually prepared to "dress up" their presentations. For short-term companies, like Kennedy and Fitzgerald, no scenery was available; nor did they carry any. Scenery then consisted of little more than a chair, table, and sofa. The back and side curtains were draped with colored scarves. Only the costumes worn by actors helped the audience identify the era and social class expressed in the play.

For four weeks, Portland audiences were entertained with repertory. Mrs. Scott-Siddons assumed the lead in all of them; playing opposite her were Kennedy and Fitzgerald. Certain company members, like Miss Walters, Miss Lottie Wade, and Mr. Sutherland, were mentioned as having "acquitted themselves" well. Neither Annie nor Maude was mentioned in the advertising or the reviews. In spite of her infrequent stage appearances, Maude was learning a great deal about acting life. As the only child in the company, she received a good deal of attention from other performers, who often shared acting tips with her.

No sooner had Annie and her daughter returned to San Francisco than Maude auditioned for and obtained a part in "Sea of Ice" at the Grand Opera House. The entire company was comprised of local performers. Maude was to play "Little Marie" and had several sentences to recite, which she did creditably. With only average attendance, the play staggered through a single week.

While she was appearing in "Sea of Ice," Maude was asked to appear in a revival of "Uncle Tom's Cabin" (UTC to theater people) one of those classic plays which was revived at least once each theater season. At one time during the early 1880s, more than twenty touring companies were performing their own versions of "Uncle Tom's Cabin."

After a poor showing at the California Theater with an English melodrama, the touring combination of Barton and Lawlor decided to present a sure winner, as any version of UTC seemed to be. According to advertisements, nothing was being spared to make the play a "most elaborate presentation," which included "magnificent scenery" by Voegtlin, the city's most famous set designer, a "great plantation scene," a "wonderful apotheosis," and "a host of real colored vocalists in their jubilee songs and specialties."[1]

Little Maude played an important role as Eva, with Alice Kingsbury, a teenager, as Topsy. The roles were presented in blackface and demanded a "colored" accent, or as close to one as the young performers could simulate. In the *Chronicle* review of the play, Maude and Kingsbury were the only players singled out.[2]

For four days, Annie worked with Maude on her lines and cues, teaching her an appropriate Southern accent and demonstrating examples of the kind of pathos that Maude would have to bring to her role as Eva. When the company held its first full-dress rehearsal, Maude was ready, though nervous about playing such an important part.

"Uncle Tom's Cabin" opened at the California Theater on November 11, 1878, to a full, yet critical, house, since most patrons had already seen versions of the play. Maude celebrated her sixth birthday on the stage. The production obviously satisfied the audience, as reported by the *Chronicle* reviewer.

> The revival of "Uncle Tom's Cabin," with plantation melodies and spectacular effects, was the attraction at this theater last evening. Taken altogether, the well-known drama was played in a most acceptable manner, and its varying phases were received with all due appreciation. The honors of the evening belong to Mr. Welles as "St. Clair," and to little Maude Adams, who played the part of "Eva" in the most charming and affecting manner.[3]

The show played to capacity houses the entire week. Little Maude was now being recognized as a child with stage talent, and theater managers made a note of her abilities for future work.

On December 4, the annual benefit night for the Elks was held at the Grand Opera House. Performers from all local theater companies volunteered to appear in a modified version of "After Dark." Most of the actors read their lines from a script, since no one had any time to rehearse. The actual presentation proved as funny as the script was supposed to be sad. Maude received a round of applause when she appeared on stage. She played a street urchin selling matches with a single line to say: "Box o' lights? Box o' lights, Sir? Cigarlights. Only a penny, Sir." She was applauded again when she left the stage.

This photograph of Maude was probably taken to promote her appearances in San Francisco. Only six years old, she already displayed a stage actress's presence. (The Harvard Theatre Collection, The Houghton Library)

A week later, Francis S. Chanfrau brought his nationally famous character, Kit, to the California Theater.[4] Born in New York in 1824, self-educated, Chanfrau had left the city to work as a ship's carpenter in the West. Upon returning to New York, he took up dramatics and shortly appeared in minor roles at the Bowery Theater. After some years honing his talents, he appeared in "A Glance at New York in 1848," playing the character of Mose, a New York fireman. He performed Mose for nearly twenty years, both in the original play and in its many sequels.

As he aged, so did his characterizations. In 1865, Chanfrau played Sam, an American who sailed to England just in time to triumph over several villains. In 1870, he wrote and acted in "Kit, the Arkansas Traveller," the story of an American pioneer. He played the role until his death in 1884.

At the time of his San Francisco appearance, Chanfrau was a guaranteed box-office hit. Besides "Kit," Chanfrau brought with him "The Octoroon," a story of murder and intrigue on a Southern plantation. Chanfrau planned to present each play for one week. Since he had to recruit the cast for local performances, he promised those selected a short tour of Nevada towns after the current engagement, thereby increasing their earnings from the show. Annie and Maude were among those selected as part of his supporting company.

In "Kit," Maude appeared in the Prologue as Little Alice — every melodrama featured a Prologue to explain the plot and its characters. Little Alice lived with her mother in a small house on the banks of the Mississippi River. As the curtain opened, Maude was the first to speak. "Well, I do declare, if Papa ain't playing again, and the same old tune." Maude now sported a western twang. Enter a villain who had a score to settle with Kit. While Kit was absent, the villain forced Alice and her mother into a boat. As Kit was returning, he saw his wife and child being taken away. End of Prologue; exit Maude.

In "The Octoroon," Maude played Little Paul, a mulatto boy, with a decided colored accent. Again, after the first scene, Little Paul gave way to adult Paul as the story leapt forward twenty years.

Each time Maude was given a new part to learn, Annie took it first and read it over carefully. She then turned the script over to Maude, while she memorized her own lines. When Maude said she had learned her part by heart, Annie went over it with her several times. She then had Maude act the part in their own private rehearsals. Annie watched Maude's every word and gesture and advised her on nuances that would improve the presentation. Maude repeated her part dozens of times more until Annie believed it was satisfactory.

Even though Maude knew her parts as well as any professional, Annie admitted to suffering from "heart throbs" every time Maude performed. "I suppose that is natural," she said, "the anxieties of a mother. How many times I cannot tell, I have stood in the wings with my prompt-book and guided my child mentally, if not orally, through her part."[5] Maude was quickly grasping the fact that acting was serious business; total concentration and commitment were necessary if one wished to excel.

For the entire two weeks of his engagement, Chanfrau attracted large audiences.

In all of the newspaper reviews, Maude received only one short mention. "Little Maude Adams as the 'Alice Redding' of the Prologue, produced a lasting impression."

Chanfrau then took the entire company to Carson City for a run of several days. After that, they traveled to Sacramento during the first week of January, 1879; then only two nights in Virginia City, due to Nevada's declining economy at the time. The *Daily Territorial Enterprise* reported: "He had good crowds and received sincere plaudits." The newspaper also mentioned that Chanfrau had been supported by Annie Adams—she was obviously remembered by Virginia City audiences—and "little Maude Adams, a sweet little child of seven years." In reality, Maude had only turned six in November.

When Annie and Maude returned to San Francisco, Maguire, the Baldwin stock company manager, informed his cast that he had signed them for a two-month, spring-season engagement at the New Market Theater in Portland, Oregon. Their offerings would consist of a repertory of at least seven different plays, most of which the company had already performed, like "A Celebrated Case," "The Octoroon," "Ten Nights in a Bar Room," and "Sea of Ice." Annie was designated the leading actress, and Maude was selected to appear in plays that she had performed before.

Throughout these months of performances, no personal mention of James has been found. He still worked at Parke and Lacy in San Francisco. According to the city directory, however, he was again living in a boardinghouse.

On January 21, 1879, the company arrived in Portland and found, to their surprise, that manager Maguire had also scheduled them to perform several plays to close the New Market's winter season. Rehearsing in earnest, the company played "Arrah Na Pogue" and "Under the Gas Light" to good audiences. Annie starred in both plays and was complimented for her portrayals.

A week later, the New Market Theater opened its spring season in what was advertised as "Baldwin successes," the "great cards of the Baldwin Theater during the past season." Manager Maguire promised that he planned to introduce some of the "greatest attractions in the country" to Portland audiences. Hyperbole, no doubt, but it filled seats. Also included in Maguire's announcement was the fact that "Miss A. Adams and the wonderful child actress, Little Maud, had been engaged to perform. In another section of *The Daily Oregonian*, was an article declaring that:

> The celebrated actress Miss Annie Adams and "Little Maud," the child wonder, arrived last evening on the *Oregon* [steamer], and will, under engagement to Manager Maguire, appear on the commencement of the new season.[6]

To introduce the spring season schedule, Maguire chose "A Celebrated Case." In a large newspaper advertisement, Maguire reported that Annie Adams was to be featured as "the favorite emotion actress." Included was a mention of "Little Maud, the wonderful child-actress." Maguire claimed they were both making their first appearances in the city. (Not true.) Maguire had seen to it that the play would be reproduced in exactly the same way it had appeared in San Francisco, with the same scenery and costumes. Although the production's expense was admittedly high,

Maguire claimed the play would attract large crowds and profitable box-office receipts.

Maguire continued advertising the opening of the spring season as a major entertainment event in Portland which, indeed, it was. Annie and Maude were again featured, with Maguire promoting them almost beyond credibility. Annie had been labeled by Maguire as "an actress of very considerable merit and reputation." Maude, according to the pretentious Maguire, had been "pronounced by dramatic writers of San Francisco, Virginia City, and other places as the most talented and accomplished child on the American stage."[7] Two-thirds of the house were sold out before the first performance.

Much to Maguire's frustration, however, the opening of "A Celebrated Case" had to be postponed one week because Maude had taken ill and had been ordered to bed by the theater physician. Maguire was quite upset by the delay because it meant a loss of box-office revenue and a possible decline in ticket sales. In public announcements, he apologized for the inconvenience and promised patrons that their tickets would be honored for any of the play's dates. The newspaper reviewer added condolences of his own regarding Maude.

The postponement is chiefly to be regretted on Little Maudie's account, and the news of her speedy recovery will be gladly received by every one.[8]

The hazards of touring companies: a little girl playing a minor role could postpone a production for an entire week. Of course, Maguire was even more abashed due to the amount of adver-

Annie Adams had been a starring performer in Salt Lake City before moving to San Francisco. She then became a character actress in stock companies as Maude grew into increasingly demanding parts. Annie closely supervised her daughter's stage career, subjugating her own. (The Harvard Theatre Collection, The Houghton Library)

tising he had already purchased. In his career as manager, he had never before experienced such an episode. Luckily for Maguire, the delay allowed additional time for patrons to buy all of the remaining seats for opening night, as well as most of the seats for the following nights. "As the company has had ample time for rehearsals, a most perfect performance is anticipated," wrote the newspaper's theater critic.

"A Celebrated Case" lived up to its promotional flurry, and little Maude won the hearts of Portland theatergoers. The *Daily Oregonian* reviewer declared boldly that "no piece ever presented in this city can compare in the slightest degree with this powerful drama."

Of little Maude, as young Adrienne, he was even more eloquent.

> Little Maud made her first appearance before a Portland audience. Her acting was simply sublime, and received the hearty and enthusiastic applause of the large and intelligent audience. Her intense emotion left few dry eyes among the spectators.[9]

During the first few years of Maude's appearances, her name was frequently misspelled, the "e" being dropped. In spite of Annie's efforts to correct the problem, the shortened spelling of the name persisted.

Annie appeared in the play proper and assumed the adult role of Adrienne. She, too, received an excellent review.

> Her intense acting is so refreshing that one almost forgets that she is acting. We feel assured in predicting that Miss Adams will be joyfully welcomed by the theatergoing public of this city.[10]

Maguire was ecstatic at box-office receipts and the audience's reactions to Annie and Maude. He immediately began planning for more of the same.

"A Celebrated Case" played to four nights of full houses, all of them S.R.O. When "A Woman of the People" replaced it, further demand for the first play was so pronounced, Maguire had it performed again at a Saturday matinee. The accolades continued. Annie was extolled as "a most perfect actress." Maude was called "most excellent" and singled out for having "carried the audience with her." The matinee audience was reported as having been the largest ever in the theater's history.

A few days later, "The Octoroon" followed. In the opinion of the reviewer, the play had been carried by both Annie and Maude. Annie "played the part of Zoe, the Octoroon, with delicacy of style and fidelity, if we are to judge from the frequent outbursts of applause which her acting provoked."

Maude appeared as the boy Paul. "To say that she did most admirably expresses the general verdict. She received a just recognition from the hands of the audience."[11]

Following the last performance of "The Octoroon," Annie was the recipient of a benefit. As part of the benefit's festivities, there were speeches by Maguire — he would never miss an opportunity to speak before an audience — the mayor, and other local dignitaries, bouquets of flowers that filled the stage, and the presentation to Annie of a diamond ring from "her appreciative audience." It is doubtful that Annie had ever received such loving recognition since first appearing on stage.

"The Danicheffs" was next presented, featuring Annie in the leading role. Yet Maude was in such demand, Maguire felt compelled to put on a special evening presentation of "Ten Nights in a Bar Room," which featured both Annie and Maude. Additional lines were written into Maude's role so she could make a more pronounced appearance on stage.

In "Jesse Brown," Annie acted with a Scottish dialect and sang two songs, one of which was "Should Auld Acquaintance Be Forgot." When the audience called for an encore, they sang along with her. "The emotional qualities of 'Jesse Brown' required intense, realistic acting," reported the reviewer, "in which Miss Adams appears to most special advantage."[12] Maude also appeared in the piece, although briefly. Originally, there had been no part in the play for Maude; but Maguire believed she should make a stage appearance, even a short one, to capitalize on her popularity. Still, she was singled out as playing her part "to perfection."

After a matinee of "The Sea of Ice," near the end of the engagement, Maguire put on a benefit for Maude in his own inimitable fashion. Regarding the benefit, the newspaper announced: "We hope a full house will greet this wonderful child actress on the occasion of her last appearance."[13]

How does one present a benefit performance for a child of six? Along with the usual speeches, each extolling Maude's acting virtues, Annie spoke of her daughter's successful, if brief, career. Maude sang two songs. For a finale, Maude received a necklace from the owner and manager of the theater. It was her first theater gift. Having practiced her remarks with her mother, Maude gave a brief speech, telling the audience that giving pleasure to them surpassed all other rewards. Surely, Maude had not written the speech; but the audience rose from their seats, cheering and applauding.

For Maguire, the engagement had been a huge financial success, beyond anything that he had anticipated or even hoped. The trip back to San Francisco was triumphant, not likely to be forgotten by the cast, particularly by Annie and Maude. Maude had received her first taste of fame, and she found it exhilarating.

In May, back in San Francisco, Annie and Maude appeared in "A Woman of the People," at the Baldwin Theater. Their efforts met with mediocre audiences and mixed reactions. The accolades of Portland were not to be found in their hometown. The reality of being a stock company performer in a city where there were many others tempered the heady thrill of success. Maude quickly discovered that every part, every city, and every audience could be different. Enthusiasm or tepidity could be encountered on any given night for any given play. "Good performers," her mother explained, "have to learn to accept success or failure as they happen."

A brief excursion to Salt Lake City helped to renew Annie and Maude's confidence. Booked for three days at the Salt Lake Theater, they appeared in "A Woman of the People" and "Little Susie." For each performance, the theater was full, particularly with friends and relatives, and mother and daughter received glowing reviews for their efforts. Regarding Annie: "Miss Adam's [sic] appearance was refined and artistic, her acting beautifully pathetic."

For Maude:

Her little daughter, Maud, is a wonder. Like her mother, a born actress, she not only has a prepossessing address, but her elocution is as clear and perfect as her acting is free and unrestrained.[14]

After a brief visit with Julia and relatives, Annie and Maude returned to San Francisco, somewhat richer from their public's patronage.

Manager Maguire could not pass up the opportunity for a capacity house, even for a single evening. Over the weekend of June 23 and 24, he sponsored a benefit for two San Francisco child actresses who had experienced recent successes, Flora Walsh and Maude Adams. At successive matinees, the two girls appeared together in one-act plays, "The Wandering Boys" and "Barney's Courtship," each followed by benefit activities. Along with the two plays, the program included the Loring Club Quartette, athletic demonstrations by members of the Olympic Club, recitations, and "a grand olio by the best professionals in the city," including Annie. It was claimed that "Barney's Courtship" had never before been attempted by children. The two matinees were sellouts, Manager Maguire's promotional artistry scoring again.

On September 13, "Chums," the long awaited play by James A. Herne and David Belasco opened at the Baldwin Theater. Included in the cast were Annie and Maude, playing the part of Little Crystal.

Although Herne and Belasco called their piece "original," considerable debate developed among theatrical authorities as to who had actually written the script and how it had been modified by the current authors of the play. Both Herne and Belasco had become well-known names in San Francisco as actors and managers, but this was their first written dramatic piece. The question being debated was whether "Chums" was legitimately a Herne-Belasco collaboration or, as the San Francisco Chronicle expressed it, the piece might owe its being "to some remote dramatic authority." In spite of the controversy, the play was presented, filled the Baldwin to capacity for its two-week engagement, and established Herne and Belasco as excellent playwrights.

David Belasco was born in 1853 in San Francisco, of Portuguese-Jewish parents.[15] He began his acting career at age twelve and at twenty had become a callboy at one of the local theaters. Continuing his acting career, Belasco had small parts in plays featuring two great actors, John McCullough and Edwin Booth. While playing in Virginia City, he met Dion Boucicault, an icon of melodramatic theater at the time, from whom he learned much about directing and writing. When Belasco returned to San Francisco, Tom Maguire chose him to be his assistant in operating the Baldwin Theater, where James Herne was not only the leading resident actor, but also manager of the stock company.

James A. Herne was born in 1839 in Cohoes, New York, the son of poor, Irish immigrants.[16] At age thirteen, he worked in a brush factory. In spite of his father's admonitions against the theater, James decided on a performing career. He spent several years touring with small companies through major Eastern cities, yet none of this activity seemed to improve his career prospects. Seeking a change of venue, he moved to San Francisco and soon became one of the city's best-known and most versatile actors. It was at the Baldwin Theater that he met David Belasco.

The idea for "Chums" supposedly came from Belasco, who never revealed to Herne that the story had been taken from another contemporary play, "The Mariner's Compass." When the plot of the play was made public, theater people accused both Herne and Belasco of plagiarism, although, at the time, it was common practice to take plots of plays, freely adapt them, and present the adaptation as an original production. It was Belasco's vehement denials of any wrong doing and revelation of the similarities between "Chums" and "The Mariner's Compass" that set people against Belasco. Herne was deeply embarrassed by the accusations and split with Belasco. Nonetheless, the play was well received by audiences wherever it was staged. When the production was moved East, to avoid any lingering doubts as to the play's authenticity, its title was changed to "Heart of Oak."

Flora Walsh (left) and Maude appeared in two one-act plays, "The Wandering Boys" and "Barney's Courtship," at two special benefit matinees put on in their honor by Manager Maguire. Maguire did not overlook any opportunity to attract full houses to the Baldwin Theater. The matinees were sellouts.

The *Chronicle* chastised the co-authors for calling the piece "original"; yet, at the same time, their reviewer called the play excellent.

> The audience was not only large, but enthusiastic, applauding the scenery and calling actors, authors, and scene painter, some or all of them, before the curtain after nearly every act.[17]

The plot: Terry Dennison (Herne) has adopted two wards, a girl, Crystal, and a boy, Ruby. Both Terry and Ruby fall in love with Crystal, who, out of gratitude, agrees to marry Terry, although she really loves Ruby. Terry and Crystal have a daughter, Little Crystal (Maude). When Terry finds out that Crystal and Ruby are in love, he sets out to sea, telling everyone that if he does not return in five years, he should be considered dead.

After six years, a report reveals that Terry's ship has sunk. Crystal and Ruby plan to marry and, to honor Terry's memory, set up a monument in a cemetery. While the marriage ceremony is taking place, Little Crystal meets an old, blind sailor in the churchyard. He is her father, but she is not aware of it. He talks with his child in the shadow of his own monument, finds out what has happened, and dies in the arms of his child, Crystal, and Ruby.

As Little Crystal, Maude had a heartwarming scene with the old, blind sailor, her father, in the churchyard. The scene invariably brought tears to the eyes of the audience, as the little girl attempted to learn about the old sailor and befriended the feeble man before he died.

In the *Chronicle* review of the opening-night performance, Maude was given her share of credit.

> Little Maude Adams is a remarkable child. She is free from the parrot-like delivery and stilted gestures of most infant actresses. She is as natural as can be wished, or expected. The honors of the strong scene at the base of the monument must be conceded to her.[18]

One of the play's distinguished patrons was general and former president U.S. Grant, who was passing through San Francisco after his return from a trip to Australia. Another theater patron was an eighteen-year-old advance agent for Haverly's Minstrels, Charles Frohman, who had just arrived in town to promote his company. He never forgot Maude's performance, astutely recognizing, even through his young, not yet professional eyes, the little girl's stage potential.

The following month, San Francisco's city fathers sponsored an Authors' Carnival, an event lasting nine days at the spacious Mechanic's Pavilion. Thirteen hundred performers from all of the city's theaters took part in the proceedings, ranging from readings to dramatic sketches. Literary tableaux were set up, where the performers, in appropriate costumes, gave their presentations. Adult admissions were fifty cents, children twenty-five cents, the entire proceeds going to the Young Women's Christian Association, the Ladies' Protective and Relief Society, the San Francisco Female Hospital, and the Old Ladies' Home. Annie and Maude participated in the festivities, Annie as a Lady of the Harem in an amusing skit, Maude, dressed as an Indian girl with long pigtails.

Loaned to the California Theater for a Christmas extravaganza, Annie and Maude played important parts in a lavish musical and romantic production of "Seven Sisters." The show included a *corps de ballet*, featuring principal dancers from Europe (or so the advertisement claimed); a high-wire act; a contortionist; a chorus "of highly trained voices"; a *Zouave* drill "by beautiful young ladies"; and a cast headed by George D. Chaplin, a veteran actor. Annie had a small part as one of the sisters, Fascinella. Maude played "Cupid, a well-known spirit, afterwards the Spirit of the Chrysalis." The production played through the Christmas season to large crowds.

Three days after "Seven Sisters" closed, Annie and Maude appeared in "Ten Nights in a Bar Room," a classic melodrama, at the California Theater. Maude played a small part as Little Mary Morgan, the granddaughter of a blind peasant. In the second of the two scenes in which she appeared, Maude was called on to recite a speech to the heroine, after having been coached by her old school-master. She had to give the speech hesitatingly, with parts of it prompted by the old man. Midway through the speech she was to cry out: "I don't know any more. I can't remember the rest." Then, her character was to go on and finish the speech in her own words. It was a complicated part for a child; but Maude carried it off so well, the audience believed she had really forgotten her lines.

On February 2, 1880, Maguire's Baldwin stock company again traveled to Portland, Oregon, anticipating a repeat of the previous year's successes. Featured, of course, were Annie and Maude. The engagement was for six weeks at the New Market Theater, in a repertory of twenty-six plays, or one play every several days. On matinee days, one play was presented in the afternoon and another at the evening performance. Annie appeared in twenty of the plays; Maude appeared in six, one of which, a version of "Little Susie," had been especially written for her. This one-act play was a condensed version of "Out to Nurse," duplicating the scene where Susie was dressed as a boarder, Joey, to confuse her parents. Maude also sang and danced in the play, although her songs and dances were unrelated to the script. In the six plays in which she appeared, Maude played both boy and girl roles.

On the evening of March 2, a complimentary benefit was given for Annie and Maude, at which both would play in condensations of "Hunted Down" and "Out to Nurse." "The entertainment last night at the joint benefit of Miss Adams and Little Maud was the best performance given at New Market during the present season."[19]

Annie "achieved another triumph" and was called by the audience to appear before the curtain at the end of the second act. As for Maude, she "distinguished herself by her graceful, piquant acting, singing and dancing, and was heartily applauded throughout."

Their act had to be repeated at the next matinee, with a full house and similar results.

Theaters closed during the summer because of the heat and guaranteed low attendance. When the new season opened in early September, 1880, Annie had parts in several plays at the Baldwin Theater. When her mother acted alone, Maude stood in the wings to watch the play, paying careful attention to all of its elements. She obtained her next part when the latest London success, starring James O'Neill and Adeline Stanhope, was booked by Manager Maguire into the Baldwin Theater for a September 6 opening. This time, Maude not only had more lines than her mother did, but she was also listed well above her in the program.

The play was "Ninon," a drama that takes place during the most tumultuous part of the French Revolution. Maude had the part of the Dauphin, heir to the throne, a boy's role. Ninon saves the life of the unhappy and frightened Dauphin, stalked by riotous mobs. Later, she reveals herself as a Republican, like the rioters, bent on overthrowing the monarchy. Still, she hides the Dauphin so he can make his escape. Although the part was small, Maude received recognition for her work in the *Chronicle.* "A word of praise is due to the precocious talent of little Maud Adams, to whom was assigned the part of the unhappy Dauphin."[20]

On the last evening of the engagement, a gala performance was given in honor of President Rutherford B. Hayes, General William T. Sherman, and California Governor G.C. Perkins. Maude would remember that particular evening because she was quite nervous appearing before such important dignitaries. In the climax of the play, Ninon hides the Dauphin from the approaching mob. At that performance, just as the mob broke into her quarters, Stanhope, playing Ninon, instead threw the Dauphin into a corner of the sofa and abruptly sat on him, hiding him under her wide skirts, not next to her as had been called for in the script. Stanhope's unexpected and extravagant action quickly cured Maude of any fear she might have displayed in the scene.

The success of "Ninon" persuaded Maguire to tour the play in Sacramento, Stockton, San Jose, and Oakland during the latter part of September. The remainder of the year was equally busy for Annie and Maude, as they appeared in two plays together, and Maude in one play, alone.

One of the two plays was "Fairfax," again starring James O'Neill and Adeline Stanhope. For her part, Annie was paid forty-five dollars; Maude's salary was seven and a half dollars, both for a week's work. "Fairfax" took place in the South and was filled with the usual melodramatic elements—mistaken identity, disguises, murder, escapes, and, ultimately, redemption. "Little Maud Adams," said the program, had the part of "Virgie, age 9, daughter of Fairfax, a widower." She also sang a song.

The second play was a revival of "Rip Van Winkle," starring Robert McWade, a respectable actor following in the footsteps of the venerable Joseph Jefferson, who had played Rip for almost his entire career. In McWade's version, Rip was a vagabond; spirits and dwarfs were prevalent; a wedding occurred; and several boys and girls had dancing parts. Maude appeared in Act One as Little Steenie, Rip's daughter, age 6. Annie had the parts of Alico, Rip's sister, in Act One, and Mistress Alice Knickerbocker in Act Three. The production lasted two weeks, an astonishing run, considering that San Francisco theatergoers were rather tired of the oft-repeated play. Second week box-office receipts were slim.

"The Queen's Evidence," another typical melodrama, was presented at the Standard Theater, December 20, and played into the early days of 1881. Maude had a small part as "Alfred."

During the latter part of 1880, James had moved back home. Only a few months later, he returned to the boardinghouse, the family reconciliation a failure. It had become obvious that the marriage was in jeopardy, although no mention of divorce surfaced. Touring and long hours at the theater separated Annie and Maude from

James, but Annie did not seem to mind. The schedule prevented Maude from seeing her father, except for those supposed long Sunday walks that the adult Maude would later recall.

For several years now, eight-year-old Maude had been living in a make-believe world. Writing for a San Francisco newspaper, an astute observer of the theater wondered whether such a young child could comprehend the difference between the real world and playacting, let alone fully appreciate the decision to become an actress.

4

Touring Adventures

It was the twilight of his theatrical career and John E. Owens was ailing, both physically and financially. In December 1880, to replenish his depleted funds, Owens traveled to San Francisco to present his new play, "The Man From Cattaraugus." San Francisco audiences had always been good to him, and this visit was no different. The play received good reviews and garnered substantial box-office receipts.

Born in 1823, Owens had at one time been a wealthy and popular comic actor.1 He had won acclaim for the portrayal of eccentric characters, particularly garrulous old men. His most notable role was Solon Shingle in "The People's Lawyer," in which he appeared more than 2,000 times. Thanks to Owens, "The People's Lawyer" had become a classic melodrama and was repeated for years by other touring companies. Since there were no copyright laws, any company could present a play that had gained popularity elsewhere. Invariably the play was modified to tailor it to the leading actor's abilities and to his particular audiences. Annie's first stage role had been in "The People's Lawyer."

Owens negotiated a deal with manager Maguire to lease the Baldwin stock company for an engagement in Portland, Oregon, beginning February 11, 1881. It was new territory for Owens but an already profitable location for Maguire. Annie and Maude were included in the package, since they were big favorites in Portland. During the two-week engagement at the New Market Theater, Owens and the company put on a repertory of eight plays. Annie appeared as the leading lady opposite Owens; Maude appeared in only one play, "Self," because she was ill for most of the visit.

Upon arrival in Portland, the Owens company was featured in newspaper articles in addition to advertisements that Owens himself bought to promote the opening. The articles mentioned that Annie and Maude were part of the company and "were well-known to local audiences." Owen's advertising made no mention of any performers but himself.

"The Man From Cattaraugus" received good reviews. "Everything centers on the star," reported the reviewer; but Annie was not overlooked. She was "warmly received and did not disappoint her friends." This pattern continued throughout the engagement, and box-office receipts made the trip a profitable one for Owens.

"Self" was first put on at a matinee, followed by an evening performance. Maude played "Cash Boy" in the store scene. Although she had recovered from her illness, she did not appear in any of the other plays.

This time, neither Annie nor Maude received the kind of attention they had secured during their previous visits to Portland. Owens overwhelmingly promoted himself, in contrast to Maguire, who had promoted Annie and Maude. No matter their past successes, the engagement was an example of the fleeting nature of the recognition audiences gave performers.

Back in San Francisco, a combination of a new script by David Belasco and the arrival of the Wallack company from New York combined to present a play of female treachery, "La Belle Russe!" at the Baldwin Theater. The play opened on July 18 for a two-week engagement. According to reviewers, the circumstances under which the play was performed were odd. The Wallack company, featuring such stars as Osmond Tearle, William Elton, Gerald Eyre, and Miss Ethel Aiden, had originally come West to open their season in September. Normally, theaters were closed for the summer; but Belasco wanted his play to be staged as soon and as often as possible, before it was sent East. He persuaded the Wallack company to put on the play earlier than usual, guaranteeing them a portion of the profits. The play was also Belasco's first as manager, and he wished to present the production with a minimum of competition from other theaters. His gamble turned into sold-out performances for the entire engagement.

Maude was enlisted to play in "La Belle Russe!" taking the role of Little Ray. The play was in four acts, the entire action taking place over one day. No prologues, no long separations in years, a distinct variation from the usual melodrama. The plot: there are two sisters, one good, one bad. The good sister marries an English nobleman. While he loves his wife, he is unable to tolerate his mother's disapproval of the marriage. He enlists in the army and is later reported dead. His mother, remorseful for what she has done, seeks out his widow. The bad twin, upon hearing of this search, takes her sister's place, accompanied by a daughter, Little Ray. Little Ray is welcomed by the nobleman's mother.

Grandmother, her arm around Little Ray: "Look around you, my dear, look around you, my little heiress, for all you can see is your own."[2]

Little Ray: "Oh, how pretty! Oh, Grandmamma! This beautiful place is like Heaven! And are the pretty things I see my own, Gradmamma? For always?"

Grandmother: "Your own forever, little one. Only wait until you see all the pretty new dresses and hats and dolls and picture books. And the gold watch. And the black and white pony,"

Little Ray: "A large gold watch. And a small, black and white pony."

Grandmother: "Go and see the pretty garden you are the mistress of."

Little Ray: "I want to remain here with you. If I go, Grandmamma, may I pick some of the flowers? Oh, I love to pick flowers! Oh, Grandmamma, I never saw you until yesterday, yet I love you as much as though I had known you ever so long. Oh, you dear, good, kind Grandmamma! Good-bye, till I come back."

Little Ray, however, does not return. The real wife reappears with a son, the rightful heir. Little Ray shows no regrets for losing her role as heiress, nor all of its accoutrements, just as long as she can be with her mother.

Local newspapers gave "La Belle Russe!" superb reviews. From the *San Francisco Chronicle*: "It is of a stronger class than 'Forget-Me-Not,' is full of startling scenes, and of an interest that at once thrills and bewilders."[3]

The Call praised Belasco for his writing. "The author has so clearly managed every situation, and infused so bold a story into his work, that the spectator is deeply interested from beginning to end."[4]

All of the main characters received complimentary remarks for their fine acting and "splendid talents." *The Call* was the only newspaper that mentioned Maude. "A very interesting and effective hit indeed was little Maud Adams, the child Ray."

Annie did not appear in the play, but she was in the wings at each performance, prompting her daughter to play the role with feeling.

For Belasco, the production had been a decided triumph, unsullied by previous controversy. Less than a year later, Belasco would move to New York to become a theater manager. It was the beginning of an illustrious, if sometimes debatable, career as manager, playwright, and impresario.

On August 8, Annie and Maude appeared in "Jane Eyre," at the Bush Street Theater, for a two-week engagement. For once, they were listed in newspaper advertisements for the play. The visiting company was led by Charlotte Thompson, who was also responsible for adapting the Bronte novel for the stage. Thompson had been playing this role for a decade and had visited San Francisco seven years earlier with the same presentation. Large audiences attended performances for the entire engagement.

Annie was singled out as playing her character, Mrs. Reed, "with quiet but very mean cruelty." Maude was also recognized for her work as Adele, the *Chronicle* reporting that "Little Maud Adams looked the doll and acted the little woman."[5]

Appearing at the California Theater at the time was W.E. Sheridan in a repertory of his famous roles. Sheridan planned to continue his tour in Portland, Oregon, and attempted to recruit Annie to work in his company. Annie refused because Sheridan would not take Maude along. No matter. Two days later, Annie and Maude were hired to appear again with Charlotte Thompson, in a play written especially for her talents by J.K. Tollatson, "The Planter's Wife."

Thompson excelled at playing oppressed women, and this play was no exception. Owner of a Southern plantation, she was an aggrieved woman struggling with foul circumstances and villainy. The play appealed strongly to audiences, as Thompson's character was at once emotional and vulnerable. While its appeal to the more sophisticated San Francisco audiences was problematic, small-town performances would generate full houses and teary patrons.

"The Planter's Wife" appeared for one week and three days at the Bush Street

Theater. It played to houses not quite full, except at matinees, when the theater was almost entirely populated by women.

The plot was that of a typical melodrama. While working as a governess for Northern family, Edith Gray (Thompson) is cajoled into marrying Daniel Barton, a shady suitor who proposes to his new wife that they rob the family for whom she works. She refuses, and her husband throws her into a dark cell. Escaping her cruel confinement, Edith moves South and becomes a companion to Miss Dora, who is engaged to Albert Graham, a millionaire planter. A letter informs Edith that Barton is dead. Of course, he is not dead. He shows up just as Edith has herself won the heart of Graham and is about to marry him, thus committing bigamy. The scheming Barton attempts to marry Dora and force her to steal a valuable document from Graham's desk. He almost succeeds in persuading Graham that Edith is behind the theft. Ultimately, her innocence is proved; Edith's previous marriage to Barton is found to have been a fraud; Graham reconciles with Edith; and Barton, harshly denounced by all concerned, is thrown out.

Annie played the role of Dora, "again proving what a useful, reliable actress she is." Maude had a minor part as Torrette, a colored servant.

"The Planter's Wife" touring company left San Francisco to begin its meandering tour back East with a series of one-night stands in Oregon, Idaho, and Montana.

There was excitement in the Kiscadden household when Annie received a letter from Thompson hoping that she and Maude could join the company in Helena, Montana, and become permanent members. The tour was planned to continue for another six months; and due to cast defections, Thompson needed to fill slots. That both Annie and Maude would become regular company members for a full season surely was an enticing offer, one rarely available to performers. That they would be able to visit New York, while being paid for their presence, also held decided advantages.

Not surprisingly, James was very upset. He refused to allow Maude to accompany her mother. In spite of his admonitions, Annie was adamant. She was not about to lose the opportunity to go East, where theater careers are made; and Maude had to accompany her. The end result of the argument saw Annie and Maude packing for a long road tour and catching the next train to Helena. It took them three days, with a change in Ogden, Utah, to join the Thompson company. James had not approved his wife's decision but was powerless to prevent it. He had nothing to fall back on but his increasing alcoholism. Leaving her father, Maude would never again see him alive.

An extended tour of several months was very different than one lasting only a few weeks. A performer quickly came to the realization that he or she would not see home for a long time. The more one thought about that fact, the more homesick one became. Yet homesickness was a decided obstacle to good acting; and it had to be overcome if the performer hoped to survive in the profession.

Boredom was the real enemy for any actor on tour. Days and nights of endless travel to small towns, unfamiliar theaters, and enigmatic audiences made performances indistinguishable. Long hours were spent in hotels or boardinghouses waiting for the time to go to the theater. The easy availability of "booze" and gambling were tempting, particularly for veterans of touring who had already "seen it all." Rehearsals were infrequent, since the same play was performed every day. For those who were new to such conditions, organizing a daily routine was imperative. If the company faced a series of one-night stands—common for touring companies visiting small towns— taking care of the essentials of life proved a challenge. More often than not, eating and sleeping were needs fulfilled on the train.

Frequently, performers had to change into their costumes on the train if dressing rooms in the theater were few or nonexistent. If the theater was on the main floor, then dressing rooms were in the basement. Take your pick: next to a boiler that ran your makeup and wilted your costumes or near a door that admitted sub-zero blasts of air. Lighting was so poor that the application of makeup was accomplished more by touch than by sight.

A newcomer to touring was always asked if he or she knew how to do laundry while on a moving train. The answer, of course, was that one was unable to do it. Washday was usually on Sunday, or any day when the company stayed in a town for more than twelve hours. Members of the company maintained their own costumes and supplied their own makeup.

Train travel in the early 1880s provided its own share of adventures. Trains were rarely on time. This was an era of "junctions." Touring required many train changes to reach specific destinations, because of the large number of independent railroads and the dearth of direct connections. It was not uncommon to find a company sitting in a cold station during the early morning hours waiting for their connection. Late trains challenged the ability of the troupe to reach the next theater on time. Some long delays required the company to skip a town in order to get back on schedule. That meant a night's salary lost.

Sleeping on the train in comfort was unpredictable. Some trains had rudimentary sleeping cars; some had only hard seats. The tracks were frequently bumpy, and the cars swayed with each bump. During warm weather, passenger cars were hot and stuffy. Yet opening the windows meant letting in cinders and dust generated by the engine.

Of course, weather often contributed to the success or failure of the company. During the summer, heavy rains washed out tracks; and hot weather buckled them. In winter, snowstorms stranded companies, and cold weather froze wheels and switches. Among superstitious performers, weather conditions were sometimes viewed as conspiratorial, upsetting touring even more than the usual inconveniences faced.

Most cast members had no knowledge of a town's theaters or of its audiences. The first thing the company did upon arriving in a new town was to visit the theater, so they could discover what awaited their performance preparations. Since theater fires were a constant menace, fire escapes were eagerly sought out. If a local bank was closed, the company's business manager would be obliged to carry sacks of coins to the next stop. Some towns had no doctors. If a cast member became ill, the actor performed anyway, because no one could afford not to work, nor could the cast deal with his or her absence. Besides, one never knew what kind or quality of doctor might be available.

Housing was more likely to be barely civilized than minimally comfortable. Noises from the downstairs saloon interrupted sleep. Sagging springs, lumpy mattresses, broken windows, no closets, and no bath were all common. And many places simply refused to accept actors. Eating properly was always a challenge. Most prepared food was bad, nearly all of it fried. Whether or not one could eat at odd hours was determined by the availability of food. The company ate what it could get, when they could get it. Yet, few actors ever had stomach problems. As one theater historian joked, "Actors needed a digestive system made of noncorrosive metal."[6]

Performers were strangers in the towns they visited. Their contact with townspeople was brief. Everyone knew they did not belong. For three hours each night, they were the best-known people in town; the rest of the time it was lonely. The locals often expected performers to be like the characters they played on stage, which could lead to unfortunate consequences. Actors were required to present a good appearance to support the image of their profession. Then, there was that final evaluation made of the touring company: was the play received well or not.

Romantic liaisons within the company were rare, because they created unnecessary tension among members, as well as having an undesirable effect on performance. It was bad for business, and managers dealt with indiscretions quickly. Men were able to pass their spare time more easily than women. They could visit saloons and meet women, which entailed its own risks. Women could shop or take in the local sights; otherwise, they remained on the train or in their sleeping quarters.

Nonetheless, whatever the circumstances, they could easily have been worse. Veteran performers often told tales to uninitiated colleagues about the "horrors" of touring.

Why, then, did performers accept such conditions? First, because these were the only work conditions available; second, for the outside chance of becoming a headliner and earning a good salary. Moreover, the ordeal itself provided benefits for the performer. Having survived every adversity demonstrated that a performer was strong, resilient, and brave. Friendships were formed and experiences shared that offered a sense of mutual professional respect, the kinds of associations upon which acting thrived. Actors returned each season because they had defeated the specters of touring. These opportunities kept alive their desire to entertain and please audiences. After all, that was the ultimate reward for having chosen an acting career.

For nine-year-old Maude, the tour was sometimes monotonous but mostly exciting, the disappointments and delights of everyday performances a revelation in commitment to one's profession. It was the delights to which she paid most attention, since they spelled survival and success. Maude's views of acting were taking form. Her mother provided unrelenting tutelage, twenty-four-hours a day. For all of its difficulties, touring helped develop Maude's acting technique. She learned how to handle tedious repetition of the same part every night by preparing her entrance with little mental games. She refreshed her part by practicing it with differing voices, gestures, and accents. She memorized other performers' parts. She discussed with other members of the company the meaning of the play, which astonished them; such "mature" thoughts coming from a child. She asked her mother to read classical literature to her, and she herself was an avid reader. The training that Maude absorbed on this tour helped to define what a career on stage would demand, and she seemed to delight in its challenges.

The tour took the company through Montana and into Utah, where a three-day engagement in Salt Lake City had been scheduled. As in Annie and Maude's previous visit to the Salt Lake Theater in 1879, the auditorium was crowded with friends and relatives. Advertising in the *Deseret News* featured "America's greatest actress, Charlotte Thompson, supported by a powerful, dramatic company," although no other names were mentioned. The opinion of the newspaper's reviewer heralded the play's local success.

> This is a very good play of a very good class. It has genuine literary merit, is stirring and emotional as well as humorous, and given opportunities for a wide variety of acting.[7]

Among the minor players, Annie was singled out as filling her role "admirably." Maude was not mentioned, although she was roundly applauded each time she entered or departed the stage. There was no time for visiting relatives; after the final performance, the company quickly boarded the train for their next destination.

From Utah, the routing took the company through Colorado, Nebraska, Iowa, and into Illinois for the Christmas season. During this time, the company had played "The Planter's Wife" more than 140 times in fifty towns. Theaters ranged from outdoor tents to nicely-equipped houses. Bad weather had been minimal, and only two performance days were lost. But sickness among company members had been frequent enough to force last-minute cast changes. Some performers, like Annie, played three different parts when the cast was short-handed. Maude's part remained exclusively hers, but several times she was dressed and made-up as an adult to fill in. As the tour continued, parts of the plot were rewritten to inject refreshment and give some members added acting opportunities. As both manager and headliner, Thompson did what she could to retain the company's focus on the play. For Maude, observing how a company was run would pay dividends in the future, when she managed her own cast of players.

The company's first anxious moments occurred when a rumor about Thompson spread through the cast. It was mysteriously reported that she had been seen taking the previous night's box-office receipts and leaving town. Concern dissolved when she appeared at the afternoon rehearsal. A case of mistaken identity.

Another anxious moment arose when it was reported that several male cast members had been arrested for causing a disturbance at a local saloon. The problem was quickly solved by paying a fine to the sheriff and giving him four complimentary tickets for the evening's performance.

At the beginning of 1882, Thompson informed the company that they were unable to obtain booking in New York City and their season would end on February 1, in Providence, Rhode Island. Their last month would consist of one-night stands in New York and Massachusetts. The weather also turned against the company. A blizzard forced them to remain in Erie, Pennsylvania, for three days. Another storm in Massachusetts resulted in the company's arriving late for an evening performance. A patient audience watched them put on the first act at the same time the scenery was being set up.

In Providence, the final three performances were staged with mixed emotions. Some members had already contacted other theaters seeking immediate work; others planned to return home to rest after such an arduous tour, A few, like Annie, looked forward to visiting New York, where they would have an opportunity to call on managers for future assignments.

Following the final performance, the company held a farewell party. They thanked Thompson for holding them together for nearly six months under the most difficult of conditions and for never missing the payment of their weekly salaries. They toasted themselves for having the perseverance to remain with the company. They cheered one another for upholding the values and virtues of their profession. It was a very moving occasion, at which tears and affectionate hugs brought down the final curtain of a remarkable season. Maude never forgot that sentimental celebration; it would later become a special event for her and her own company at the close of their several seasons.

From Providence, Annie and Maude traveled to New York, where they remained for almost two months. The money that they had saved while on tour allowed them the comforts of hotel living and attendance at theaters. Annie made appointments with theater managers to seek employment for herself and Maude — in New York City, they hoped. One of her appointments was with Charles Frohman, who had recently become manager of the Madison Square Theater and a booker of touring shows.

Charles Frohman's move to the Madison Square Theater professionally united the Frohman brothers, Charles, Gustave and Daniel.[8] Together, they went on to establish a new era in the commercial conduct of American theater; it was the dawn of "big business" development, which soon spread across the country. Daniel selected the casts, organized and rehearsed the companies. Gustave was responsible for the road equipment. Charles arranged and booked the tours. All three chose the plays, but Charles's talent for picking winners dominated their selections. Their first success was "Hazel Kirke," a play by Steele Mackaye, which ran 486 nights in New York City and generated substantial profit for the brothers. Based on that overwhelming success, Charles launched his impresario career. At the time Frohman met with Annie and Maude, he already directed several agents and had established a network of theaters in towns not previously considered theatrical centers. He was in the process of perfecting the viability of high-class touring companies and attracting new talent that he would mold into headliners.

Annie and Maude's meeting with Frohman proved inconclusive. He recalled having seen Maude in San Francisco several years before, but he had no work for either of them at the moment. He did suggest that Maude come back "in a few years" to meet with him again. None of their meetings with theater managers produced work for Annie and Maude, nor were any managers encouraging about the future. In late March, mother and daughter headed West, with a planned stop in Salt Lake City.

Annie now believed the time had come for Maude to attend school. She chose the Collegiate Institute, a Presbyterian school in Salt Lake City, as the proper place to enroll her daughter.[9] Maude would stay with her maternal grandmother, whom she loved very much. Along with schooling, Maude would have the opportunity to enjoy her grandmother's farm, to which she seemed most attracted.

Their arrival in Salt Lake City coincided with the beginning of the semi annual conference of the Mormon Church, running from April 5 to 10, 1882. Included in the festivities were stage performances put on by the Home Dramatic Club, of which Annie had once been a member. It took but a few moments to persuade Annie to once again play with them.

Annie stayed in Salt Lake City until August, when she was called by the Baldwin Theater management to return to their stock company. Maude had already begun school, and her grandmother had taken over caring for her, so Annie had no qualms about leaving Maude and returning to San Francisco.

Annie did not live with James. He continued living in a boardinghouse, and she found a small apartment near the theater. Annie discovered that James's drinking had become so serious that he had been arrested several times for disorderly conduct. Holding onto his job had become a tenuous matter. Still, there was no discussion of divorce between the couple. Writing to Maude, Annie made no mention of James or his condition. Annie wrote of her theater activities; Maude spoke of her experiences at school.

On August 26, Annie appeared in "M'liss" at the Baldwin Theater. A week later, she played in "Fairfax" and was reported to have done "artistic work." The *Chronicle* also announced that Annie was attempting to put together a company to perform "The Child Wife" and "Queen of Bohemia," in which she would star. The reviewer doubted that she could accomplish her goals, as she had no financial backing. He proved correct in his assessment.

Several weeks later, Annie joined the Bates Company to perform in two plays, "Camille" and "Under the Gaslight," at the Grand Opera House. When Mrs. Bates decided to tour Oregon and the Northwest, she asked Annie to join her company. Annie accepted the job and left San Francisco in the middle of December. If she saw James before she departed, it was their last encounter while he was alive.

The Bates Company tour took the company to Portland, Tacoma, Spokane, and Seattle. There is no evidence available of how successful the trip may have been, but since it continued for more than a month, the tour seems to have been at least marginally profitable. Annie's reputation in Portland surely must have helped the company attract good audiences.

March 1883, found Annie back in Salt Lake City, where she appeared at the

At ten, Maude was sent to the Collegiate Institute in Salt Lake City to be educated. She stayed for four years. When Annie returned to the theater in San Francisco, Maude followed.

Walker Theater in "Fate," which attracted poor houses, and "Camille," in which she starred and played to good-sized audiences. Of course, she stayed with her mother and Maude. Annie forbade Maude to accompany her to the theater, because she wanted Maude to focus all her energies on her studies.

A week later, Annie assumed the lead in "Pink Dominos," which drew very well for three weeks, so well, in fact, that the company decided to take the play on a short tour of the Northwestern Territories, later to comprise the states of Utah, Montana, Idaho, and Wyoming. It was an ambitious and innocently conceived decision. After several weeks of poorly attended houses, the company returned to Salt Lake City, having lost all the profits they had collected prior to the tour.

Since the Salt Lake Theater season had almost concluded, Annie had no opportunity to apply for new assignments. Instead of returning to San Francisco where she could easily have found work, Annie chose to remain with Maude for the summer. A notice in the *New York Clipper* revealed her situation. "Annie Adams cannot find enough to busy herself in a theatrical way here, and has established a small millinery establishment, by way of diversion."[10]

James Kiscadden died on September 21, 1883. Annie received a dispatch about his death several days later. She first planned to travel to San Francisco to bury him there but decided, instead, to have his body shipped to Salt Lake City. Articles regarding James's death in the *Chronicle* presented a confusing story, although it was obvious that alcoholic excess had been the cause.

> James H. Kiscadden, a circus man, who had been on a protracted spree, was found dead in bed yesterday in his room at the Bonanza lodging house, on Market Street, between 4th and 5th. His remains were removed to the morgue.[11]

The following day, the *Chronicle* published a notice telling of the reason for James's death.

> A physician's certificate has been given in the case of Kiscadden that he died from pneumonia; and the body has been taken away from the morgue, where it had been left under a misapprehension.[12]

In the same issue of the *Chronicle,* James's obituary appeared.

> James H. Kiscadden, September 21, 1883, age 47 years. Body at W.J. Mallory's Embalming Parlor, 733 Mission Street, and will be shipped today (Sunday) at 2 P.M. to Salt Lake City for interment.

The delay in informing Annie of James's death was likely due to the fact that the people with whom he had boarded knew little of his background. Circus man? To the end, James had been employed by Parke and Lacy. Pneumonia? A possible consequence of alcoholism, which, according to his death certificate, had been the specific cause of his death.

James's body arrived on September 28, and he was buried in a Gentile cemetery, following brief services. Annie expressed sadness but seemed to be relieved of the burdens that James had placed on her during the past several years. Maude was disconsolate. Since she spent so little time with him during the last few years of his life, we shall never know her real connection to James. Whether fantasy or reality, what clearly remained with Maude for decades after was a loving image of her father.

5

An Ingenue's Achievements

For almost four years, Maude attended the Salt Lake Collegiate Institute, a Presbyterian school. During this period, she and her mother lived with Julia, Maude's grandmother, who owned a small farm just outside town.

In late 1886, after having been offered a position in the Alcazar Theater stock company, Annie returned to San Francisco to resume her career. By this time, for Maude, schooling had become a thing to be endured; and she was ready to escape from the Institute at a moment's notice. Several months after Annie settled in San Francisco with a steady salary and a small apartment, Maude joined her, having persuaded her mother that pursuing a theatrical career was decidedly more important than school. Nonetheless, prior to rejoining Annie on the professional stage, young Maude's four-year stay in Salt Lake City did help her sharpen her own focus on the theater.

The Salt Lake Collegiate Institute had been founded in 1875, under the auspices of the Presbyterian Church, as an alternative to the overriding local influence of the Mormon Church. Many Gentiles had entered the city in the previous decade, mostly business and commercial people; and they sought their own religious outlets.

The Institute was located near the center of the city in a pleasant neighborhood. The main building was a large, two-story, brick structure. With a seating capacity for 250 students, it provided laboratory and recreation space. Adjacent to the school, another building, called "the Octagon," provided boarding space. A third building had recently become property of the Institute, and the new space was intended for additional school activities. A large and ornate Presbyterian church stood nearby. The families of students were assessed tuition of ten dollars a quarter. For qualified students from needy families, special scholarships were available.

The Institute professed three purposes: to establish a top-ranked school, equal to the best in the U.S.; to prepare students for college; and to give assistance to students who, without financial aid, would be unable to enjoy the advantage of education. Entrance requirements were rigorously maintained by a careful selection process. The school offered a full curriculum, which included art, music, and dramatics. It was equally strong on order, obedience, and self-control. Since a student's moral nature was to be elevated and refined, Bible studies were an important part of the daily exercises.

Maude entered the Institute at the upper elementary level, likely fifth grade. Her classes consisted of reading, spelling, writing, drawing, language, arithmetic, geography, and the mandatory Bible lessons. In high school, she would have been introduced to history, science, foreign languages, and dramatics.

While Annie continued her small millinery business, she occasionally appeared in productions staged by the local Dramatic Association. How Annie justified putting Maude in a Presbyterian school, rather than a Mormon school, is unknown.

Teachers and relatives described the pre-teen Maude as being a slender, almost frail-looking girl. At the same time, her personality was perceived to be strong-willed. She possessed a wistful, quiet face; but when she smiled, observers became aware that she radiated, particularly through her eyes, a subtle sense of determination. She was described as having two long braids of fine, dark brown hair that hung down her back. Her school uniform consisted of long, dark dresses and a sailor's hat. She carried her books in a sack hung over her shoulder. Externally, she resembled an ordinary schoolgirl.

School personnel viewed Maude as shy and self-conscious, sometimes even timid and retiring. Yet, when Friday "recitation" days came, Maude became a favorite performer, regaling her fellow students and their parents with imaginative and expressive poetry readings. On some occasions, she devised a costume to enhance the excitement of the recitation. To recite a poem about a grandmother, she borrowed clothing from Julia and applied makeup to resemble an old woman, complete with a humped back and cackling voice. Maude's principal expressed the belief that she gave "brilliant recitations," yet possessed a "total ignorance of her power."

Although Maude had less formal schooling than her peers, she was more advanced in both reading and math, thanks to her mother's tutoring and the experiences she had already accumulated from her many theater performances. She was perceived as possessing a vivid imagination — having a strong sense of make-believe, teachers said — and being quite observant, not afraid to seek answers when she felt the need. She was quick to learn and an avid reader who especially liked poetry, history, and geography. When Maude was asked who her favorite literary figure was, she unhesitatingly named Joan of Arc. It was a prophetic choice of heroines.

The school principal frequently attempted to dissuade Maude from her desire to become an actress, his argument being that stage life was inherently immoral. Maude rejected his entreaties and continued, even intensified, her interest in theater. Efforts were also made to convert Maude to the Presbyterian religion; but she refused those appeals as well, remarking that the school's efforts in this regard disturbed her.

While studying dramatics, Maude turned her grandmother's attic into a theater where she and her friends put on melodramas. Maude was director, stage manager, and leading lady, using the roles and lines she had learned before as a basis for the improvised play. She was good at mimicking others and did funny imitations. Immediately after seeing a play at the theater, Maude returned home and imitated the various performers, to her family's delight.

Maude took guitar lessons, which developed a skill she continued into adulthood. She also learned to pick out melodies on the piano. Although she had no formal singing instruction, Maude had a pleasant voice and had already demonstrated her vocal abilities in several plays. Maude was observed to sit alone for hours, apparently dreaming of herself as a great actress, as good as her mother, she hoped. Having witnessed certain aspects of the theatrical world, she was already conjuring up greater acting successes for herself.

Although Maude had cousins living nearby and friends at school, she was most devoted to her mother and her grandmother, Julia, to whom she gave the most affection. The fact that adults perceived her as "a far-away child"—the principal declared her "a child apart"—suggested that few other relationships were ever close. On the other hand, so close was Maude to her grandmother that she might interrupt another activity because she felt, at the moment, that not enough time and attention was being given to Julia. For her part, Julia was the force behind Maude's education, as Annie was busy with other responsibilities.

Maude loved Julia's farm, as she did nature. Nearby forests, mountains, and streams could be viewed, and visited, whenever Maude was so inclined. She spent a good deal of time with the farm animals, especially horses and dogs. Although Maude expressed a fear of horses, it did not deter her from mastering the art of riding.

In her autobiography, Annie called the young Maude a beautiful, simple schoolgirl who was an excellent scholar and brilliant in her dramatics. That perception, combined with Annie's influence, did much to direct Maude toward a stage career. When Annie departed for San Francisco to join the Alcazar Theater company, she knew that Maude would not be far behind.

In November, 1886, Annie appeared at Morosco's Amphitheater in "East Lynne." Newspapers duly noted her return to the stage. That play was followed by an engagement at the Baldwin Theater in "Kenneth Gordon," with Annie playing a leading role. Annie had also found a comfortable apartment near the theater district. When she wrote Maude about her activities, Maude became adamant about joining her mother so that she herself might return to the stage. "I want to quit school, Mamma," she declared. "I want to go on stage with you."[1] Maude was on the proverbial next train to San Francisco.

On January 10, 1887, at the Alcazar Theater, fourteen-year-old Maude made her reappearance on stage in "Little Jack Shepard." The play was successfully received by crowded houses and continued for a two-week engagement. There was no mention of Maude in reviews; however, her presence was noted by local managers. Within a week, Maude and Annie were selected to appear in Joseph Grismer's production of "Monte Cristo." Annie had a minor part as Corconte; Maude played the role of Mlle.

The ornate Alcazar Theater competed with the Baldwin for the best in touring companies. Annie and Maude were members of the theater's stock company. (San Francisco History Center, San Francisco Public Library)

Danglars, the daughter of M. Danglars (Frank Mordaunt), one of the leading characters.

"Monte Cristo" opened February 7 at the Alcazar Theater for a four-week engagement. Reviews of the production boasted that "the story is thrilling, the characters very effective, and the scenery lavish." A capacity house on opening night greeted the actors with enthusiasm and demanded many curtain calls. The *San Francisco Chronicle* included the cast along with its review, listing Miss Maude Adams. While Maude was dressed beautifully for the part, she did not have a single line of dialogue. Grismer, however, was so pleased with her appearance and her preparation for the role, he wrote in a line for her to speak.

After the success of "Monte Cristo," Grismer put on "The Wages of Sin" for a week to extend his run at the Alcazar. It was common practice for touring headliners who had attracted good box-office receipts to remain in town with another production, to take advantage of their popularity. Maude was included in the cast, playing a minor role with no speaking lines.

In the middle of May, the melodrama "Harbor Lights" arrived in San Francisco after highly successful engagements back East, particularly in Boston. Local critics liked to boast that both cities—Boston and 'Frisco—had "similar tastes in dramatic matters." The cost of bringing the play to the Alcazar was considerable. Beyond the guarantee paid to the play's producers, Alacazar management claimed to have spent more than $4,000 to mount the show, which demanded heavy sets and novel mechanical effects. They hoped the costs would be made up by selling tickets at advanced prices. The cast list was reported in the *Chronicle* and included Annie but not Maude, although she would be making a short appearance dressed as an old woman.

"Harbor Lights" played to S.R.O. audiences during its three-week engagement. Because of its profitability, the production's manager decided to embark on a short tour of California cities: Los Angeles, Stockton, and San Jose. Both Annie and Maude were members of the touring company. According to reports from each city, the play was an outstanding success. Yet Maude was quite disappointed. She was appearing only in minor parts, with almost no speaking lines. Children's roles had offered more opportunity than ingenue roles, she found; and there were very few ingenue roles in melodramas. In spite of her frustration at not being selected for better parts, Maude persevered. Her time would come, counseled her mother. Annie's advice would prove correct, but not for several months.

During the first few months of the new theater season, which opened in September, Annie appeared in five different plays in successive weeks, all as a member of the Alcazar stock company. There were no parts for Maude in these plays. Still, she accompanied her mother to the theater each night and observed all of the activity, both in front of the footlights and backstage. As practice, she memorized the parts of the leading actresses.

M.B. Curtis was one of those veteran performers who had made a good living playing a unique character in a series of melodramatic adventures. As Sam'l of Posen, a Hebrew role, he had become so familiar that both reviewers and audiences believed he could play no other part. He fooled them all by producing a new play, "Caught in a Corner," in which his Hebrew delineation took on new dimensions of good nature and humor that created instant sympathy with audiences.

"Caught in a Corner" opened at the Alcazar Theater on October 10 for a two-week stay. Advance ticket sales were so strong that it was decided to extend the play another week. Annie had a feature role in the play; and Maude was given an ingenue role, Mary Stuart, that met her every wish.

As usual with a touring headliner, rehearsals began three days before opening and lasted fifteen hours a day. The last rehearsal, the afternoon of the opening evening's performance, was full-dress; and final changes were being made at about the same time that first-nighters were finding their seats. Curtis had food brought in so that no time was wasted. It was quite amusing to Maude to see the entire company, on stage, in costume, eating and practicing their lines at the same time.

The production was an immediate hit even though several reviewers thought the plot a weak one. The story could be more intelligible, said one. Another predicted the play was "not long for this world." Audiences, however, loved Curtis and the play and crowded the theater each night, enthusiastically cheering the company at the end of each act. Curtis garnered most of the accolades for his characterization. Albina de Mer, Mr. Levick, and Charles Mestayer were singled out for their acting. Annie "made a capital Mrs. Wilkins." And in the *Chronicle* review, Maude received a line of praise. "Maude Adams, now an ingenue of considerable ability, showed a decided aptitude for her profession in Mary Stuart."[2]

Other reviewers were positive but more modest in their compliments. "Miss Maude Adams presented a pleasant picture," reported one reviewer, "and with a little more experience will become a valuable adjunct to our local stage."[3] Another said that Maude seemed to be "progressing rapidly." Public comments about her acting surely must have pleased her.

Curtis was so delighted with the box-office results that he took the entire company on a three-week-long tour of California cities, which included three days each in Los Angeles and San Diego, as well as two-day visits to Stockton, Sacramento, Santa Cruz, San Jose, and Oakland. On the way to Los Angeles, Maude celebrated her fifteenth birthday and was feted by the company. Maude observed that, compared to her touring experiences five years earlier, theaters in these cities now had excellent backstage equipment and fully-equipped dressing rooms with hot-and-cold running water. The company was housed in respectable hotels and rode in comfortable passenger trains.

Indeed, touring had changed in the past five years, which made it more financially rewarding for touring productions. These days, headliners took entire companies with them. Not only was this found to be cheaper, but the quality of performances also increased immeasurably, since performers were so familiar with the offerings. That meant there was no need to recruit actors in each city, a great relief for both manager and headliner. It also guaranteed work to actors for an extended period of time. Booking agents were now available for touring companies. They were able to set up and confirm a route that was more economical, efficient, and tightly scheduled.

The railroads had been greatly improved. They were faster and more comfortable and adhered to schedules and junction connections more rigorously. Many long-distance trips offered both sleeping and eating facilities for performers. As theater of all kinds became more acceptable to the general public, performers found they were welcome at better hotels and boardinghouses. Some now even catered to actors, accommodating their services to meet the performers' eccentric schedule.

Of course, some problems still existed. Weather conditions slowed trains and caused touring schedules to be changed. Theaters in small towns still had only primitive facilities. And the fear of a company's being stranded because funds ran out always remained in the minds of performers. Nevertheless, the overall risks of touring had been reduced, to the satisfaction of actors.

During the first three months of 1888, Maude appeared in only one play. "The Silver King" opened at the Alcazar Theater on January 30 for a two-week engagement. Maude played a minor role with a few speaking lines. It was a role to which, according to a reviewer, she was "well fitted." "The Silver King" was a romantic melodrama that had originally played in London, England, where it had been a big hit. Brought to the U.S. and modified to meet local tastes, the play lost much of its comedy and genuineness. Still, for its brief run, the play attracted good houses.

At much the same time, Duncan Harrison, a novice at play writing, wrote and took the lead in a play, "The Paymaster," first presented at San Bernardino, California, on March 15. The play proved surprisingly successful and was quickly moved to the Bush Street Theater in San Francisco for its first big-city test. Since "The Paymaster" carried only a few actors, most of the performers had to be recruited locally. The play called for an ingenue; and Maude was quickly selected for the role of Moyna Sullivan, a maid. Annie was cast in a leading part as Mrs. Helen O'Conner, the hero's mother.

The plot: Robert Emmett O'Conner, lieutenant and paymaster, and Francis Houghton, colonel of the regiment, are in love with the same girl, Ethel Miley. O'Conner succeeds in winning the love of Ethel, much to the chagrin of Houghton, who is soon scheming to thwart their plans. Knowing that O'Conner holds $50,000 to pay the soldiers, Houghton plans to steal the money from O'Conner's office. In the process of breaking into O'Conner's desk, Houghton breaks the point of his knife; and it falls to the floor unnoticed. Houghton charges O'Conner with the crime and has him imprisoned. Meanwhile, Ethel has entered O'Conner's office after the robbery and found the knife point. Curious about it, she carries it away.

With the help of his friend, Larry O'Brien, O'Conner breaks the rusting bars of the jail window and dives into an adjacent river, in sight of Ethel, who is out for a stroll. O'Conner escapes to his mother's home, and a search for him fails. Now that his rival is a fugitive, Houghton renews his pursuit of Ethel, who is sketching on the banks of a lake. She breaks her pencil and asks Houghton for a knife. He gives her his knife and she quickly notices that the point of the blade is missing and that the point she picked up in O'Conner's office fits Houghton's broken blade. In his anger, Houghton throws Ethel into the lake. O'Conner sees his love drowning in the lake, rescues her, and carries her to his home. When she revives, Ethel tells the story of her meeting with Houghton. When Houghton attempts to arrest O'Conner, he himself is imprisoned. O'Conner is exonerated, and he and Ethel are married.

The play's reception in San Francisco far exceeded the anticipated reaction. It attracted full houses for its entire two-week run. Encouraged by the result, Harrison decided to tour the play East toward a possible appearance in New York. To ensure the quality of the company, Harrison attempted to sign all the players to a long-term touring contract. Most of the performers accepted, including Annie and Maude, who viewed the trip as an opportunity to be seen again by Eastern agents and managers. Annie was to be paid forty-five dollars a week; and Maude was to receive twenty-five dollars, the highest salary she had ever been given. Combining their salaries, they were able to save a good portion of their income for later needs, since train fare and housing were to be paid by Harrison. "The Paymaster" might very well be the opportunity Annie had sought to advance her and Maude's careers.

The tour began with several weeks of one-night stands through Oregon, Idaho, and Wyoming, with a two-day visit to Salt Lake City, and, finally, a week's run in Denver. When the

After her return from school, Maude returned to the stage, appearing in ingenue roles. Because there were so few ingenue roles in melodrama, Annie and Maude turned to playing in touring companies. Maude quickly learned that touring was a challenging experience for performers.

company played Salt Lake City, Annie and Maude were entertained by relatives and friends. At the theater, each time they appeared on stage, loud cheers rang out from admirers in the audience. The week's stop in Denver gave the company a chance to relax. Harrison took the opportunity to rehearse new elements he wished to include in the play, among them adding more speaking lines to Maude's part.

Since the theater season was approaching its usual June closing date, Harrison booked only two more engagements, a week's visit in Kansas City and, he hoped, several weeks in Chicago. Yet his plans were almost disrupted by an argument with his leading lady. Harrison was a firm believer in making stage episodes as realistic as possible. The scene in which Ethel is thrown into the lake required that the actress be dumped into a large tank of water. The actress refused to be drenched nightly and balked at continuing with the company. Enter Maude.

As was typical for her, Maude had already memorized the Ethel Miley role. Harrison fired his leading lady and selected Maude to replace her. A little makeup would make her appear older. Nor was Maude afraid to be dunked every night. Directed by Harrison, frantic rehearsals were undertaken to integrate the new leading lady into the flow of the play. Harrison was amazed at how quickly Maude fit into the part and assisted her colleagues in uniting their efforts.

Annie, however, was quite upset and believed that the nightly dunking might jeopardize Maude's health. Instead, she persuaded Harrison to have her replace Maude in the dunking. Dressed as Maude, Annie was thrown into the water. When Ethel was next seen in the arms of O'Conner, she proved to be mysteriously dry, although she had just been rescued from the lake. Apparently the audience noticed neither the switch, nor Ethel's dry clothing.

For Maude, assuming the role of the play's heroine meant not only a boost in visibility and salary, but also the excitement of playing the lead in a popular melodrama. Although she knew the lines perfectly, she practiced them every morning to make her performance that night even better than the previous night's, particularly her expressions of love to the hero. Unfortunately, that dynamic came to an abrupt halt in Kansas City when Harrison, while diving off a rock to save the drowning Ethel, struck the edge of the tank and injured his leg so seriously that he had to retire from the company for several weeks. Maude then had to relearn her cues and expressions to accommodate Harrison's substitute, who had none of the charisma of the original leading man.

On June 11, the company arrived in Chicago, to appear for two weeks at the Grand Opera House. Advertising in the *Sunday Inter Ocean* boasted that the company carried five tons of scenery (for a melodrama to carry that much scenery meant it was a high-class production) and that the play cost $10,000 to produce, an obvious exaggeration. The ad went on to claim:

> See the Great River Scene — 28,000 cubic feet of Real Water!
> See the thrilling rescue!
> See the natural waterfall!
> See the terrific leap of 28 feet 6 inches!

> In San Francisco and other cities of the West, the drama
> has been highly commended and popularly approved and in
> Denver it made a great success.[4]

Listed as leading lady, Ethel Miley, was "Maud Adams."

Although the regular theater season had closed and only the ten-cent variety houses remained open, or perhaps due to that fact, "The Paymaster" attracted full houses and profitable box-office receipts. The play received good reviews, and Harrison was lauded for his skillful writing.

> A well-written, carefully constructed play, with a number of effective, stirring incidents and skillfully contrived situations, "The Paymaster" has an agreeable story and several interesting characters. The play has a uniform strength that holds well to the end, and keeps the attention of the audience.[5]

The *Inter Ocean* reviewer reported that "Miss Maud Adams is pleasing as Ethel Miley." The *Chicago Tribune* wrote: "Miss Maud Adams, who is new to Chicago, was the heroine. She is a gentle and pleasing actress."

The play retained its appeal so well, it was transferred to the Haymarket Theater on the other side of town for another two weeks. On opening night at the Haymarket, the play "drew the largest house of any it has had since it was first shown in this city." The play finally closed its Chicago run on July 14. Since joining the company in San Francisco, Annie and Maude had appeared 120 times; and Maude had played the leading role in fifty-six performances.

To complete a very successful tour, Harrison announced that the company had been booked into Philadelphia for an August 20 opening. Rehearsals would begin August 6 at the Chestnut Street Theater. A visit to New York would follow. Of course, like the rest of the company, Annie and Maude could not have been more pleased. They soon joined other company members on a train to Philadelphia, where they would rest before beginning their new season, not only employed, but with the strong prospect of being booked into high-class Eastern theaters.

When rehearsals began, four new members of the cast were introduced. One of them was a new leading lady, replacing Maude. Harrison and the Eastern managers had conferred and agreed that, given Maude's age, she was too young to play the love interest. Neither Annie nor Maude disputed the decision. Maude herself knew she was too young for the part. Indeed, she believed that she had sometimes acted the role in an unintentionally comical manner. She was hurt but not surprised by the change. Instead, she returned to her earlier role of a maid, expanded with some excellent lines that now highlighted the smaller part.

"The Paymaster" began its second season on August 18, at the Chestnut Street Theater, before a large audience. "The play was received with favor, which increased as the piece progressed," reported the *New York Clipper*. The play next traveled to Baltimore for a profitable week, then on to Pittsburgh, where it enjoyed "fairly good business," before arriving in New York. For Harrison and the company, their success was a daydream come true.

"The Paymaster" opened at the Star Theater on September 17, for a one-week engagement, to a "large and well-pleased house. The melodrama is to be credited with a popular success."[6] For the remainder of the week, full houses were the norm. Maude repeated her role as Moyna Sullivan, the maid, but with many more speaking lines. Nevertheless, no mention of her acting was made by any of the New York reviewers.

During the play's stay in New York, however, a visit to the theater by Charles Frohman, ever on the lookout for more talent, reminded him of his earlier, positive impression of Maude. Frohman was attracted by her charming and professional performance. He noted that he must keep her in mind for a future part.

Leaving New York, the company played weeklong engagements in Buffalo, Jersey City, Williamsburg, and Brooklyn, before returning to New York for another week. In the meantime, Charles Frohman talked to his brother, Daniel, about Maude. He expressed interest in signing Maude but had no immediate openings. Daniel, however, did have available a recently vacated, small role in "Lord Chumly," starring the well-known and venerable headliner, E.H. Southern.

While "The Paymaster" was in Brooklyn, Daniel Frohman approached Annie and Maude. Would Maude be interested in a small part in Southern's play? Could she live on her own, that is, apart from her mother? Could she learn a new role quickly enough to appear in the play within a week? Would fifty dollars a week be a reasonable salary? An excited "yes" to everything Frohman asked was Maude's answer. Since she would not be going along, Annie made Frohman promise that Southern himself would be Maude's guardian while they were on tour.

"Lord Chumly" was currently appearing in Boston and Maude was dispatched there to appear for the first time on October 29. It could not have been a better birthday present for the soon-to-be sixteen-year-old actress. As Jesse Deane, she was replacing Dora Leslie in the cast. Leslie had come to dislike her small role for its lack of opportunity.

None of the Boston newspapers made any mention of the substitution; but the *New York Clipper* offered a cryptic sentence, reporting that "Maud Adams, daughter of Annie Adams, has been engaged for Daniel Frohman's forces."

Edward Hugh Southern, son of the famous British comedian, proved to be a

E.H. Southern claimed that he taught Maude how to laugh. The headliner nicknamed Maude "Mrs. Midget"; she, in turn, called him "Mr. Oldest." Playing with Southern gave Maude valuable experience and gained the attention of producer Charles Frohman.

more versatile actor than his father, not only appearing in Shakespearean plays, but also gaining great popularity in the classic melodramas of the day.[7] Born in New Orleans in 1859, Southern was educated in England. He made his debut in 1879, in one of his father's plays. He toured with the famous actor, John McCullough, for several years, honing his artistic skills. He then became a leading man with Daniel Frohman's Lyceum Theater company, where he remained for ten years. It was during this time that he met Maude. Southern would later claim that he had taught the too-serious young girl to laugh by giving her daily lessons.

For her first rehearsal of "Lord Chumly," Maude appeared at the Hollis Street Theater. She had already memorized the part. In his memoirs, Southern recalled the slim, childish figure, dressed in a summer frock, who arrived on the set. She had little to say, except her lines, but observed everything that transpired on stage. Southern personally directed all rehearsals; and he took it upon himself to practice Maude in her cues, as well as facial and body expressions. He chided Maude for not opening her lips far enough and worked with her to speak more with her mouth and to laugh with an "open gladness." Southern offered classes in laughter, which, interestingly, he considered one of his own artistic shortcomings; and he enlisted Maude to join his group. Maude later recalled that her laughter techniques were, indeed, due to Southern.

Southern also gave company members nicknames. He dubbed Maude "Mrs. Midget," because she was small, elf-like, bashful, elusive, and mysterious. She was also earnest about her work, always ready, and untiring, according to Southern. In turn, Maude called Southern "Mr. Oldest," because he always seemed to be playing old men's roles. The nicknames remained; and, for years, they addressed each other using these titles.

"Lord Chumly" returned to New York and it final weeks at the Lyceum Theater. No sooner had Maude joined the company than its tour ended November 10. Maude had appeared in a total of only thirteen performances. What about her future? Daniel Frohman had not forgotten about Maude, but he had no immediate opportunities for her.

Annie and Maude settled into a simple boardinghouse on West 27th Street, New York City. Annie was still playing in "The Paymaster," which finally closed in January 1889. Now both were unemployed. After several fruitless weeks seeking employment, they were ready to return to San Francisco.

Charles H. Hoyt had begun his career as a "doctor" of scripts, but he quickly became an accomplished and recognized playwright on his own.[8] His latest play, "A Midnight Bell," had first been produced at the Alcazar Theater, San Francisco, on April 4, 1888, about the same time Annie and Maude had joined "The Paymaster" company. Daniel Frohman now suggested that Hoyt consider Annie and Maude for his new Eastern company, and Hoyt quickly sought them out. Rehearsals would begin on February 6, with an opening performance in Buffalo on February 18.

Hoyt was born in Concord, New Hampshire, in 1860. Because of his mother's death and his father's continuous travel, Hoyt spent his early years exploring various employment options. He obtained a job as a humor writer for the *Boston Post*, during which time he developed a friendship with William Harris, a local theater impresario. When Harris needed a vehicle to fill a week at his theater, he asked Hoyt to write a farce and, later, to work on scripts that needed help. Soon, veteran comic actor Willy Edouin asked Hoyt to write him a play; and the result was "A Bunch of Keys," which became an immediate success. That was followed by a series of successful satires on hotels, kidnapping, railroads, and superstitions. By 1888, Hoyt had gained the reputation of being one of the most humorous satirists in theater. "A Midnight Bell" was a comic melodrama about a deacon who confronts a crooked banker.

The play depends, for the most part, on its characters and amusing incidents. It takes place in a small town, so far removed from large urban areas as to be a world unto itself. Few of its inhabitants have ever been to the "big city." Society revolves around the church and the schoolhouse. The old cashier of the bank is the chief businessman of the town and also a combination selectman, school board member, and constable. The first act of the play takes place at the house of the old man; the second, the schoolhouse; the third, a sewing society; and, lastly, a choir rehearsal in the meeting house.

The old man (Thomas Q. Seabrooke) is puffed up with his own importance in town and, with more energy than judgment, gets himself involved in many ludicrous predicaments. A boy (Eugene Canfield), whose ideas of life have been obtained from sensationalist literature, serves as the old man's foil. The clergyman (R.J. Dillon), while not a man of the world, displays a sincere and earnest nature. His younger sister (Maude Adams) has a quick wit, is full of high spirits, yet believes that her position as the minister's sister demands dignity. Nonetheless, every episode in which she seeks to manifest it devolves into fun and mischief. A young lawyer from the city (Frank Lane) is brought in to straighten out a problem in which the bank is involved. While a young schoolteacher (Isabella Coe) is gentle and refined, the rest of the town is filled with gossiping old women and misbehaving children. The amusing side of small town life predominates; its more serious aspects provide a background for the humor. Reviewers quickly recognized the play as a considerable departure from the usual farce- or comedy-melodrama, which, very likely, made the play so popular with audiences.

Annie had the part of an old maid, Lizzie Grout; Maude was cast as Dot Bradbury, the minister's sister. For the role, she appeared in three of the four acts and had many breezy and amusing lines.

"A Midnight Bell" opened at the Bijou Opera House, New York, on March 5, 1889, the house "filled to suffocation with a brilliant audience, eager to give cordial greeting to Charles H. Hoyt's latest production."[9] The play had actually started in Buffalo, February 18, then moved to Baltimore to smooth out the production. Only days before the New York opening, cast changes were made which then demanded extra rehearsals. In fact, the opening had to be delayed a day in order to incorporate the new cast members.

"A Midnight Bell" was an instant hit and played for more than twelve weeks to full and profitable houses. By the fourth week, advance sales were so strong, the play was booked to the end of the season. Each week's reviews spoke of crowded houses and enthusiastic audiences. Messrs. Seabrooke, Canfield, Dillon, Lane, Coe, and Maude Adams "bore off the honors of the production." The twelve weeks, however, had their share of distractions.

Four weeks into the run, it was decided to fit the theater with electricity, an exercise that took several days and many mishaps to accomplish. Lights blinked on and off indiscriminately while the play was being performed; performers endured periods of darkness in the dressing rooms while they were making up; sporadic, unscheduled illuminations of the lobby and marquee occurred, before the new technology finally functioned normally. At the same time, to reduce the cost of salaries, several minor players were fired; and new ones were hired to replace them. Still more rehearsals had to be held to integrate the new performers. Extra matinees were scheduled by the theater manager, to the disgruntlement of the company, because they would not receive extra salary for the increased performances.

Moreover, the notorious Gerry Society invaded one of the performances to question the management for employing "the young girl, Maude Adams," since city law stated that no person under sixteen could perform on stage. Eldridge T. Gerry, head of a private organization, the Gerry Society, a.k.a., the Society for the Prevention of Cruelty to Children, was an evangelical socialite who had been given power by the city government to enforce laws concerning the appearance of underage children on stage. Gerry rose to demand that Maude be removed from the cast. When it was proved that Maude was sixteen, Gerry and his cohorts stomped out of the theater frustrated; and the play continued.

On the positive side, "A Midnight Bell" celebrated its fiftieth performance with complimentary souvenirs; and a 100th performance with signed photographs of the principals, including Maude. In May, the theater manager paid off a $25,000 mortgage for the Bijou, thanks to the overwhelming success of the play. On July 1, at the play's last performance for the season, J.T. Maguire, the theater's treasurer, was given a benefit; and the play's principals were given tokens of appreciation for their stellar efforts. Hoyt was called on stage to make a speech, in which he specifically saluted Maude for the quality of her acting and commitment to the production. The best news was saved for his closing remarks: "A Midnight Bell" would reopen in September to launch a long tour "of the provinces"; and the entire company was asked to return. For performers, this was what they had worked for the entire season. It was not only a compliment to their efforts, but also a vindication of their loyalty and perseverance.

The Adamses' summer was spent in New York, Annie appearing in several plays to earn some needed income and Maude enjoying, for the first time, the sights of the city. Rehearsals were called for September 1. Booking agents had no trouble routing the play across the country now that it had accumulated such a profitable history.

Two months shy of her seventeenth birthday, Maude was appearing in a leading role with a touring company that had already proven its worth. In the three years since returning to the stage, Maude, the teenage actress, had decidedly matured. Now fully aware and quite knowledgeable about what she observed, she could evaluate and analyze details of a play, tearing it apart and rebuilding it to better understand its nuances and the meaning of the role she played. She had developed a practice routine that became an integral part of her daily activities. Working for weeks to understand her part, Maude's entire focus was "to live" the part; and she did so with an increasingly sensitive ability to "feel" the human elements in the story. Maude placed herself in the character's role and imagined how she would act under the same conditions. From that point, she practiced each step, gesture, and expression to make the character come alive. Often, she would adopt the character's personality in her everyday activities, even changing her own speech and physical movements. Other actresses surely went through this process to learn their stage skills, but Maude seemed to make of the process her entire world.

Not surprisingly, there was neither time nor space for anything but the theater. Her social life was minimal, if ever she was allowed by her mother to participate in any activities that presented themselves to stage folk. While, at her age, young men would normally be of interest, Maude shrugged off any attention they might show her. With her mother and stage managers as "protectors," Maude had no apparent interest in becoming friendly with male admirers. Within the structured confines of the play, there were no other opportunities.

Maude was also developing an uncanny understanding of audiences, what they liked and disliked, what stage business they responded to, and what behavior they sought from actors to identify more closely with the hero or heroine.

All of these factors were helping to establish a foundation upon which Maude's acting ability could be developed and nurtured as she headed for stardom. Annie once declared that Maude believed she had to give up everything else to become a successful actress. There is little doubt that Annie had a great deal to do with such a sophisticated and mature articulation from a teenager.

After two weeks of exhaustive rehearsals, the company left the familiar surroundings of New York for Peoria, Illinois, where, on September 11, "A Midnight Bell" began its tour. An S.R.O. crowd greeted them on opening night with shouts for curtain calls and speeches. It reminded the company how genuinely popular their play had become.

For two months, they visited most of the major cities of the Midwest: St. Louis, Kansas City, St. Paul, Minneapolis, Milwaukee, Cleveland, and Pittsburgh. Each city reported "splendid business," "crowded houses," "large audiences," and S.R.O. A few minor casualties: bad weather; a theater that had burnt down the previous week (a decided relief to the cast, who readily admitted to the fear of fire at a theater in which they were appearing); several of the principals' becoming ill from food poisoning.

Maude celebrated her seventeenth birthday in Pittsburgh. The event almost passed unnoticed, even by Maude herself. Yet a loving card from Julia brightened the day, and cast members sang "Happy Birthday" to Maude before the curtain went up.

"A Midnight Bell" came to the Grand Opera House, Chicago, for the last two weeks of November. Reported advance ticket sales assured the company of "significant houses." Newspaper ads declared: "a genuine novelty"; "fresh from a run of five months in New York"; "Hoyt's new departure — a beautiful picture of New England village life." Yet no mention of any performers. The play was now being labeled a comedy-drama, with a distinct plot, full of familiar characters, set in a New England village. While the various characters were described by the reviewers, no actors were specifically named, at least not until the play had been performed for several days. For its two-week engagement in Chicago, the play attracted full houses. "This new piece is original and is not fashioned upon the stereotyped lines of the bucolic drama of the day. "'The Midnight Bell' has a happy, wholesome tone."[10] Of Maude, the reviewer reported: "Miss Maud Adams was chic and charming in the trying role of the minister's sister."

"A Midnight Bell" opened in Boston for the Christmas season, an advantageous booking for any play. Hoyt appeared on opening night and received accolades from the audience after the final curtain. Reviews of the play were excellent and the major performers were singled out for their "fine work." Maude, "as Dot, the minister's sister, gave a charming and dainty character bit." So heavy was the demand for tickets, the play's engagement was extended into January.

The production was scheduled to return to New York in the middle of January

1890; but the theater manager suggested to Hoyt that he delay the opening because of the current competitive climate. Lillian Russell, Margaret Mather, and Julia Marlowe were all starring in their own plays; Richard Mansfield was forcefully elocuting "Richard III"; Eddie Foy was joking in "Bluebird, Jr.," the David Henderson extravaganza; and Gilbert & Sullivan's opening of "The Gondoliers" was attracting huge audiences. Hoyt, however, refused the advice; he had been booked for only a month in New York and wanted to take full advantage of his stage success. "A Midnight Bell"

At age seventeen, Maude appeared in a leading role in "A Midnight Bell," a play by Charles H. Hoyt. She had begun to develop a rigid routine for practicing and performing. The theater had become her entire world. (California Historical Society, FN-35894)

opened at the Bijou Theater on January 13. Hoyt was quickly proven correct in his decision. "A large audience did full justice to the revival of 'A Midnight Bell' evening of 13. Its success was instantaneous."[11]

Included in the *Clipper* review was a short notice about Maude. "Dainty Maude Adams renewed her former success and is certainly one of the most attractive members of the cast."

At one of the performances, in the audience were Daniel Frohman and E.H. Southern, who remarked affirmatively about the acting of "Mrs. Midget." Southern was planning a Western tour for May and June; and he requested that Maude be in his cast. Actually, "A Midnight Bell" was nearing the terminus of its season, scheduled for the end of April. The timing could not have been more propitious for Maude. Before the company departed for Philadelphia, "Mr. Oldest" signed "Mrs. Midget" for his tour, at sixty dollars a week! He planned to perform "Lord Chumly" and "The Highest Bidder." Maude was already familiar with the former; but, this time, she would be given a larger part. Annie was also signed for a part in the play.

For the next few months, "A Midnight Bell" played in and around New York, taking advantage of its decided popularity. Philadelphia; Boston; back to New York for a week; Providence; Harlem; New York again; Washington, D.C.; Newark; and finally Jersey City. When the production appeared in New York for the third time, it was reported that "there were plenty of empty seats." Quietly, the season ended three weeks later. After the play's last performance in Jersey City, a cast party was held to celebrate a highly successful tour of thirty-three cities and 424 performances. Noticeably absent from the festivities were Annie and Maude, on their way to join E.H. Southern, already in the midst of rehearsals.

Lord Chumly appears the fool but is, in reality, a smart and charming man. He is in love with Eleanor Butterworth. Jesse Deane (Maude) is in love with Hugh Butterworth, a lieutenant, and brother of Eleanor Le Sage, a crook. Hugh has been given one thousand pounds that was collected for the widow of a fellow officer. He delivers only two hundred. Lord Chumly decides to live in single rooms so he can pay the remainder to the widow, but he is unable to find her. Much to his surprise, the widow is actually his landlady. It is revealed that Hugh, at the time he held the one thousand pounds, was drugged by Le Sage, who stole the remaining money. Locating the money for its rightful owner is Chumly's challenge; and, once exonerated of the crime, Hugh and Jesse find love together.

After a tedious five-day train trip to Tacoma, Washington, "Lord Chumly" opened on May 6 for a three-day engagement. While on the train, Southern rehearsed the company rigorously, although some observers accused Southern of being more fidgety than efficient, thus taking longer to prepare the play. Since Southern loved to perform, rehearsing seemed to have become an excuse for "doing something," even before the actual performances were given. By the time the company reached the West Coast, they were already exhausted. Tacoma audiences noticed, and it took the company several days to settle down.

When they appeared in Portland, Oregon, at the recently opened Marquam

Grand Theater — a great improvement over the New Market Theater, thought Maude — business was "immense." Then a train trip down to San Francisco for a two-week engagement. Trains now carried passengers up and down the coast, from Vancouver, Canada, to San Diego, California. No more stagecoaches; no more steamers.

The California Theater was filled nightly during the entire run because Southern was such a popular attraction and local playwright David Belasco was "Chumly's" author. The engagement was a financial success, and both Southern and Belasco were given honors for their efforts. Maude appeared only in "Lord Chumly." (There were no ingenue parts in "The Highest Bidder.") Annie appeared in both plays. When the reviews were published, only Maude was mentioned. Said the *Chronicle* reviewer: "She is a San Francisco girl of great promise who was favorably known here before she went East."[12]

From San Francisco, the company began its trek back East. Its next stop was Salt Lake City. Brigham Young's old theater had been torn down; and a new one, the Grand Opera House, had taken its place. (Almost every city claimed a Grand Opera House, even though opera was never presented there.) Maude had not performed in Salt Lake City since she was seven years old. All of the Adamses' relatives and friends filled the theater at every performance — two evenings and a matinee — and applauded each time either one entered or left the stage. Several meals were also presented in their honor. As might be expected, the *Deseret News* gave both actresses glowing reviews.

A stop in Denver, where they played a week "to full houses"; then finally to Omaha, where a three-day visit closed the brief tour. Southern was very pleased with the success of the tour. Daniel Frohman was quite satisfied because the play had been profitable. Maude was delighted because she had played a leading role to everyone's satisfaction.

In March, Daniel Frohman purchased a half-interest in W.H. Gillette's new play, "All the Comforts of Home." Since he was so busy producing other plays, he transferred Gillette's play to his brother, Charles, who had just leased Proctor's Twenty-third Street Theater in New York and needed a play to open the new season. While casting for the play, Daniel reminded his brother about Maude, particularly, what she had contributed to "Lord Chumly" and, before that, to Hoyt's "A Midnight Bell."

Charles Frohman summoned Maude to his office. In his usual direct, sometimes frightening manner, he wanted, almost demanded, that Maude perform in his new play, to open in September. Then, in a more conciliatory tone, he asked, "Would you be interested?"

Thus began an endearing friendship that lasted for twenty-five years.

6

Under Frohman's Tutelage

Until the emergence of Charles Frohman, theatrical managers were mainly perceived as flamboyant "showmen," sporting diamonds, wearing loud clothes, tugging a golden cable for a watch chain, and twirling an ebony, gold-headed cane.

Frohman, in contrast, was a cool-headed, articulate planner who wielded firm control over the plays, performers, and theaters under his aegis. To him, theater was strictly a business, evaluated by profit and loss, successful plays, and the development of star personalities. Not surprising that, in the theatrical world, he was variously known as the "Napoleon of the Drama," the "Little Giant," or the "Mastermind Upstairs." To his friends and associates he was "C.F.," to distinguish him from his almost equally successful brother, "D.F.," Daniel Frohman.

Charles Frohman grew to prominence during the 1880s and 1890s as theater itself became the country's most popular leisure-time phenomenon and firmly established itself as an integral part of the American culture. For Frohman, the story could have been one tailored to reflect the American Dream. Long years of unending hard work, risk-taking and perseverance, at the same time experiencing the business from its lowest to its highest echelons, ultimately gained Frohman his position as a theater impresario. Yet he was perceived as everyone's friend, a man of his word, and the simplest of men in his personal life. He himself shunned publicity — he rarely agreed to have photographs taken — but readily spent thousands of dollars to promote his players and productions. For more than thirty-five years, Charles Frohman was Broadway's most reported upon, envied, and emulated manager.

Meeting the man, observers quickly understood the reasons for his theatrical achievement. He may have been short and stout, but his demeanor conveyed strength and confidence. His smiling, calm face easily cemented friendships, providing assurance and support to those who undertook his projects. His private life was shrouded in mystery. He never married; but rumors suggested that he had liaisons, sometimes with women and sometimes with men. In the public's eye, he seemed to enjoy no other activities except those related to the theater.

He was an autocrat to those whom he employed; his word was law. Yet, he was liberal with money; and if he had faith in a person, that person could have anything he or she wanted. His handshake was a bond; he never had a signed contract with an actor or an author.

Charles Frohman was born on June 17, 1860, the third of three sons, to Henry and Barbara Frohman.[1] His parents were German Jews who had emigrated to the U.S. in 1845. Henry opened a cigar-making factory in Sandusky, Ohio, a town inhabited by German immigrants like himself. Successful as he was as an entrepreneur, Henry aspired to be an actor and organized an amateur theatrical company. He both appeared in and directed the plays of Schiller and other classical German authors.

Because the parents strongly believed in the education of their sons, the two oldest, Daniel and Gustave, were sent to schools in New York. Once Henry realized that the center of commerce for his own occupation lay in New York, in 1864, the entire family moved there. The enterprising Henry located his cigar-making business in the midst of the theater district and his daily customers soon comprised local performers and managers. His commercial neighbor was August Brentano, who began his celebrated bookstore selling European scenarios to American producers.

While his older brothers liked school and were good students, Charles was an impulsive and restless child who preferred street activities to schoolbooks. He was a disappointment to his parents, who had great

By the 1890s, Charles Frohman, "C.F." to his friends and associates, had become the leading impresario in America. His care and attention in developing Maude's career helped make her a star. (Photo: White. Undated. Museum of the City of New York. Gift of Mr. and Mrs. Otis Skinner. 31.101.28)

aspirations for him. Instead, he was put to work in the cigar store, where he met many theater personalities. These encounters inspired him to pursue a career in the theater.

During the early 1870s, at the high point for touring minstrel companies, older brother Gustave was hired as an advance agent for Charles Callender's Georgia Minstrels. At about the same time, Daniel obtained work at the *New York Graphic*, the first illustrated daily newspaper ever published in the United States. Although Charles was only twelve years old at the time, Daniel got him a job in the circulation department of the newspaper, at ten dollars a week.

Within a few years, Gustave rose to become manager of Callender's Minstrels; and he persuaded Daniel to join the company as an advance agent. In the meantime, along with his daytime job at the newspaper, Charles found work in the box office at Hooley's Theater in Brooklyn.

In January, 1877, Gustave got Charles a job as traveling agent for the Dillon touring company, at the salary of twenty-five dollars a week plus hotel expenses. It was Charles's first time on the road; but he quickly learned the art of agenting, which then primarily consisted of advertising and promoting a company prior to its appearance in a town. He quickly mastered the art of gaining friendships among all those who meant business to him. The road experiences exposed Charles to many misadventures: stranded companies; floods; being run out of town; paltry box-office receipts; and drunken actors. Yet, the experiences also taught him the necessity of maintaining control over touring companies and their routes, a piece of the business he later perfected when he took over booking tours. After a season of mixed successes and failures, Charles was glad to return home. Yet, when asked by Daniel whether he wanted to continue in the business, Charles eagerly wanted to know what his next assignment would be.

During the summer of 1878, J.H. Haverly, then the dean of minstrel company managers, bought Callender's Minstrels and melded the company into his own Haverly's Mastodons. Gustave was made manager of the company, Daniel was advance agent, and Charles was hired as treasurer. Charles quickly proved himself to be everyone's confidant and often helped company members get out of trouble. He was also an enterprising treasurer. He bought a large safe that was prominently featured in each town as the company settled into its quarters. Actually, there was little money to put into the safe because Haverly spent everything on touring expenses. When people saw the safe being carried, its appearance made them feel that Haverly's Mastodons were a highly profitable troupe.

The Frohman brothers traveled with Haverly throughout the 1879 and 1880 seasons. In July 1880, the company sailed for London, to bring high-class minstrelsy to English audiences. They played there until Christmas and completed a profitable tour. One innovation that Charles developed there was the posting of colored paper show bills. Charles would not forget the enthusiasm of English audiences, a fact he filed away for future consideration. The opportunities to entertain them seemed unlimited. In 1881, Charles became manager of Haverly's, as his brothers obtained better jobs elsewhere.

Within months, Daniel sought out Charles to save the stranded "Hazel Kirke" Company in San Francisco from disbanding. If he were able to save the company, his salary would be seventy-five dollars a week. Charles not only rescued the company, he booked the previously hapless troupe all the way back to New York.

In 1881, the three Frohman brothers were brought together again when they were hired to operate the new Madison Square Theater, New York City. Located back of the old Fifth Avenue Hotel at Twenty-fourth Street near Broadway, the Madison Square was a beautiful, if small, venue. It had been decorated by Louis Tiffany and possessed a unique double stage — one stage would be prepared while the other was in use — that shortened the usual long intermissions. The theater opened with "Hazel Kirke," which became an instant hit and played for an unprecedented 486 nights to profitable box-office receipts.

Daniel was the theater's first manager; Gustave was director of traveling companies. (At one time, there were eight companies on the road at the same time, all playing "Hazel Kirke.") Charles was Gustave's associate, arranging and booking road tours. For the Frohmans, this launched the era of serious theater business, controlled and operated by serious producers.

It was at the Madison Square Theater that Charles became interested in the actual productions themselves. He watched rehearsals with a critical eye and made suggestions to authors and managers that ultimately improved the productions. His interest in production values soon became an important feature of his management duties.

At the beginning of the 1883-1884 season, Charles became an independent manager. He produced three plays that received good reviews but generated little in the way of profits for him. A year later, a disastrous tour by one of these plays placed him perilously close to bankruptcy. Barely twenty-five years of age, Charles could envision his theatrical career about to be consumed by debt.

Charles then heard of the play "Shenandoah," which had recently opened in Boston. The play had flopped and was about to be abandoned. Charles believed the play had distinct possibilities and quickly obtained its rights. He persuaded the play's author to change portions of it to increase excitement and tension, for example, portraying Sherman's march through Georgia. Charles borrowed money for the revamped production, and "Shenandoah" opened at the Star Theater, New York, on September 9, 1889. The new play was an immediate hit and subsequently went on to a highly profitable tour. Charles was able to pay off all of his debts and retain sufficient funds to invest in several new shows. He was now on his way to becoming the city's premier impresario.

One of the projects to which he was attracted was a new play written by William Gillette, called "All the Comforts of Home." This was to be Maude's first association with Frohman. Of course, Frohman was already familiar with Maude. Given her obvious if yet untrained talent, he envisioned her as a leading lady whose appealing tenderness could capture audiences.

After Maude and Annie had been signed for the play, Frohman began tinkering with the script. Watching rehearsals, he believed a love scene between Maude and the leading man should be inserted. Although the romantic interlude was merely a brief parting at a doorway, it revealed Maude's acting qualities and elicited strong emotional reactions from the audience.

Rehearsals for "All the Comforts of Home" began August 11. After three weeks of intensive work, the production was presented to live audiences at the New Worcester Theater, Worcester, Massachusetts, beginning September 1, for a three-day engagement. Frohman attended these performances, as well as the rehearsals. Whole scenes were changed, lines rewritten, and scenery reworked. Although the local newspaper showed little enthusiasm for the play, the company concentrated on making it a cohesive entity, one with which everyone felt satisfied and confident.

To smooth out the revised production, Frohman had the play presented in Providence, Rhode Island, for another three performances. These appearances proved to everyone that the company had come together. "Splendid business. The show caught on wonderfully," reported the *Clipper* reviewer, who had been following the play during its trials.

"All the Comforts of Home" opened at Proctor's Twenty-third Street Theater, September 8, 1889. The first-nighter audience received the play with cheers and applause for the principals and for author William Gillette, even though he had a hard time recognizing his own work.

The plot: a jealous husband takes his family away for a trip, leaving an impecunious nephew in charge of a large and well-furnished mansion. The nephew, assisted by an extraordinary protégé, rents apartments in the house to a number of peculiar people, all of whom he assures will find "all the comforts of home." These boarders annoy, assist, and misunderstand each other, fall in and out of love, quarrel, and become almost hopelessly mixed up in complications. The comedic features of the play kept audiences constantly laughing.

> Its introduction promises to result to entire profit of Managers Proctor and Turner as well as to Charles Frohman, whose company made their first appearance here, and won well-earned plaudits for the even excellence of their acting.[2]

The reviewer reported that Henry Miller, the leading man, Ida Vernon, M.A. Kennedy, J.C. Buckstone, and "dainty" Maude Adams shared in the night's honors. Maude played the role of Evangeline Bender, an ingenue who believes she is deeply in love with Alfred Hastings (Henry Miller), although he shows no recognition of her feelings because he is in love with another woman.

The play also achieved a goal Frohman had been seeking for some time — the establishment of his first stock company. Operating a stock company had its risks. It demanded good plays, professional actors, and surmounting frequent challenges. Frohman knew he would have to meet these demands if he wished to maintain and develop a stable of performers that would consistently attract receptive audiences.

Frohman's plan was to play "All the Comforts of Home" until October 7, then introduce a new play, "Men and Women," to run the remainder of the season. As skilled as the stock company was, they found it difficult to perform one play eight times a week while, at the same time, daily rehearsing a new play. When the performers complained of the confusion it was causing them, Frohman backed off, to some extent.

Instead of opening the new play early in October, he scheduled it for October 20, thereby giving the performers an additional two weeks to rehearse the new play. It was really no problem at the box office because "All the Comforts of Home" continued to draw excellent crowds. The *Clipper* called the play "an unquestioned success" and attributed the delay of the new play to this fact.

At the same time that the stock company was rehearsing the new play, Frohman was hiring a cast to take "All the Comforts of Home" on tour after it closed in New York. The tour lasted the entire theater season and returned a sizable profit to him. Due to his sophisticated booking abilities, which enabled him to select high-class theaters and give the play substantial promotion, the road company found excellent crowds and reviews at every stop.

Frohman's new production, "Men and Women," was the combined effort of David Belasco and Henry De Mille, an unlikely pair of collaborators. De Mille graduated from Columbia University, after which he joined the Columbia College Grammar School to help write school plays. Scholarly and prim, he possessed a mild disposition. In his work, De Mille was exact and methodical.

Belasco, in contrast, had risen through the hardscrabble ranks of theater production, using every means possible to make a name for himself. He was known to be high-strung and possess a fierce temper.

De Mille wrote his first play, "Duty," a story of overreaching social climbers, which Belasco directed under Daniel Frohman's aegis. Produced in 1883, the play failed. His next play, "The Main Line," a railroad melodrama, was again produced by Daniel Frohman. This time, the play was well received and toured the country for several years. It was then that Daniel Frohman brought De Mille and Belasco together to write plays. At De Mille's summer home, the two devised a writing method that critics viewed, charitably, as awkward and strange.

The results of their labors were tedious and overlong, crowded with an assortment of characters and unrelated action. With only the bare outline of a plot, the pair removed to a theater, where Belasco enacted scenes while De Mille wrote the dialogue. Alternatively, Belasco would describe a scene and ask De Mille to fill in the lines. Dialogue seemed to be dictated by Belasco's acting rather than driven by a unified plot. The finally agreed upon play had all the elements of familiar melodrama, although Belasco would claim it was an original genre.

Their first product, "The Wife," was badly received by reviewers, yet was accepted by audiences because it was well staged and well acted. As De Mille and Belasco reworked the play, shortening it and reducing the number of parts, the play improved. It finished the season, having been performed 239 times, and returned a good profit. Daniel Frohman asked for more of the same, this time to feature the popular E.H. Southern.

The result was "Lord Chumly," a play that was viewed by critics as a patchwork of several other melodramas. When offered the lead role, Southern at first declined, believing that he would be negatively compared to his father. Thanks to Belasco's histrionic persuasiveness, Southern reluctantly agreed to take the role. In the process, he achieved a personal triumph. Again, the play and its authors were castigated by reviewers; but audiences loved the comedy, and it was a season-long success.

A third collaboration, "The Charity Ball," featured a clash of two personalities, a clergyman (good) and his dissolute brother (evil), along with the usual melodramatic elements. By this time, critics tired of needling the authors and admitted the public would likely enjoy the play, which they did.

When Charles took over his brother's contract with De Mille and Belasco, he demanded a play that featured extraordinary male and female characterizations. The plot revolved around a banking scandal that was filled with love scenes and expressions of family togetherness, along with melodramatic elements already employed by the authors in previous plays. "Men and Women" was the play's title, supposedly chosen by Frohman when the authors were unable to agree. Not surprisingly, the play was panned by critics; but audiences loved it because it was beautifully staged and acted.

The duo parted, since Belasco was now preoccupied with making Mrs. Leslie Carter a star. De Mille next created a successful adaptation of "The Lost Paradise," from the German. In 1893, De Mille fell ill with typhoid fever and died before he reached his fortieth birthday. He left two sons, William C. and Cecil B. De Mille. Belasco went on to produce plays heavily laced with realism, although many critics believed his obsession with realism masked his lack of artistry and originality.

"Men and Women" opened at Proctor's Twenty-third Street Theater on October 21, 1890. Since "Men and Women" was being rehearsed at the same time that the company was performing "All the Comforts of Home," October 20 was devoted to its first and only full-dress rehearsal, an event that extended well into the night.

The plot: a young bank cashier misappropriates securities belonging to his bank. In a reckless endeavor to become speedily wealthy for the sake of the woman he loves, he loses everything in speculation. The cashier watches the condemnation of his innocent assistant before the bank examiner and even testifies against him. Not until his wife-to-be informs him that she knows the facts does the guilty cashier accept the handcuffs intended for his assistant and allow himself to be led off to jail.

The play was well received by both reviewers and audiences and quickly built to capacity proportions during its first week. "Delighting audiences," was the *Clipper* report. "Crowded and enthusiastic audiences," said the *New York Times.*

Maude had a small part, playing Dora Prescott, bank cashier William Prescott's sister. The role of William Prescott was played by William Morris (still an actor, several years away from becoming a theatrical agent). Annie played their mother, Mrs. Jane Prescott. Maude was not very pleased with the small part, but she promised herself to do her best. Still, she received no recognition from reviewers.

On December 1, "Men and Women" celebrated its fiftieth performance. The *Clipper* declared that "the comedy drama is running along with splendid success, and large and delighted audiences are the rule."[3] Charles Frohman himself expressed satisfaction now that De Mille and Belasco had shortened the play and added new comedy scenes, at his insistence. Frohman also announced that, at the conclusion of its New York engagement, the company would tour the principal cities, stay out all summer, and travel as far west as San Francisco.

The play's continuing profitability delayed the planned tour. "Men and Women" played its 100th performance on January 12, 1891, and Frohman announced that it would remain in New York until March 7. Several weeks later, the closing date was reported to be March 28. At the play's 150th (February 20) and 200th (March 25) performances, souvenirs were distributed to the attending patrons, who each received photographs of the performers, including Maude. Frohman was so pleased with the results that he postponed William Gillette's new comedy until "Men and Women" could finally vacate Proctor's. When the company at last departed from New York, Frohman outfitted them with a special railway car, complete with eating, sleeping, and lounging facilities.

First stop on the tour was the Grand Opera House, Cincinnati, Ohio, where they "played to great houses, and the engagement was one of the best of the season." In St. Louis, the company "drew crowded audiences." Advance ticket sales were so strong in Chicago, the next engagement, that their run was extended a second week, and then a third.

In Chicago, "Men and Women" received the usual reactions from reviewers for a De Mille-Belasco play.

> De Mille and Belasco have succeeded in giving us a purely American drama, and its turning upon "securities" makes it doubly so. It is a play with a moral and a thrust or two at human justice, but lacks what plays written for stock companies always lack — a central figure around which the interest and admiration of the audience concentrate themselves. The play is admirably staged and costumed, but is too long and too scattered in its interest.[4]

Frank Mordaunt, William Morris, and Miss Sydney Armstrong were singled out as giving excellent performances. Commendable in their comedy lines were Odette Taylor, J.C. Buckstone, M.A. Kennedy, Leslie Allen, and Maude Adams. Maude had finally been mentioned by a reviewer.

Frohman announced that the first week's box-office averaged $1,100 a night, a record for the theater. For the second and third weeks, S.R.O. was the standard at every performance. By the third week, reviewers were talking about the acting qualities of the stock company, citing their artistic excellence, "carefully selected people who work well together and are in every way worthy of the high praise which has been given them."[5]

Before leaving Chicago, Frohman told the company that, if De Mille finished "The Lost Paradise" in time, it would receive its initial presentation in Chicago, due to the audience's enthusiastic response to "Men and Women." A date was not given, but Frohman said the event would be "soon."

Annie and Maude excitedly anticipated the company's next stop, a three-performance engagement in Salt Lake City. Relatives and friends filled the theater. They did not seem to be disappointed, even though neither Annie nor Maude played significant parts. Each time they entered or departed from the stage, they received enthusiastic applause. Relatives filled their dressing room after the performance. Annie and Maude stayed with Julia.

Next stop was San Francisco, where the Adams shared a nervous anticipation, since they had not played in their hometown for several years. The *Chronicle* noted that Maude, although in a minor role, "will have a chance few young actresses have had to show what she can do."

When the play opened at the familiar Baldwin Theater on May 12, the West Coast *Clipper* representative reported:

> "Men and Women" received its first coast production last evening, and it is needless to telegraph that the performance and company achieved a brilliant success and attracted the usual first-nighters in numbers to SRO.[6]

In fact, the engagement was extended a third week with continuous S.R.O. crowds. It was doing so well that Frohman promised to return in a few weeks not only to repeat "Men and Women," but also to introduce another play, "Diplomacy." His announcement came as a complete surprise to the company. It meant rigorous daytime rehearsals to prepare the play. Frohman also informed them that they had three weeks before the play would be introduced. For the first time, the company expressed some ill humor about the situation.

A week's run in Los Angeles turned into two weeks, somewhat relieving the pressure as the cast worked on "Diplomacy." The company wondered why Frohman wanted to change plays in the middle of the tour. Fortunately, they quickly found it was not his intention to do so. Instead, he planned to present both plays in the weeks ahead. He had correctly calculated that it would increase the public's visits to the theater to see the company perform two different plays during one engagement.

The *Los Angeles Times* reviewer spent a good deal of space discussing the skills of the leading members of the stock company, alluding to the fact that, without them, the play would be of average quality. And Maude was mentioned again: "Maude Adams, with her lovely voice, made a pretty little ingenue as Dora."[7]

"Diplomacy" was introduced to San Francisco audiences at the California Theater on June 21, to a crowded house. The play was not new, having been toured in the U.S. for several seasons, though never by such an accomplished stock company. Written by Sardou, the play was easily mastered by intelligent actors, and the plot situations came naturally with no improbabilities. Audiences knew from the beginning what the ending would be, but they remained interested nevertheless. The play offered dramatic contrasts that audiences readily felt and understood. After performing "Men and Women" for so long, the company found that acting "Diplomacy" was a great relief. "The play thoroughly pleased the crowded audience, that remained after the curtain fell to recall the actors, having given them curtain calls on each act."[8]

Maude had the part of Dora in a De Mille–Belasco production, "Men and Women." The play was an immediate success and Maude was singled out as an ingenue with an excellent acting future. (Undated. Museum of the City of New York)

Both Annie and Maude were mentioned for their parts, although not necessarily to their liking.

Annie Adams has done many things better than the Marquise.
Maude Adams would have made a decided hit in Dora if her youth and enthusiasm had not carried her away in the last part of the scene with her husband. The ear-

lier part of her performance was charming, easy, graceful and unaffected, so much so as to promise the very brightest future for her, but she is not mature enough yet to handle such a scene as that with Julian.[9]

This was Maude's largest part and longest review to date. Her potential was being recognized. Still, her experience, performing love scenes, for example, was questioned. It was soon on Frohman's list to see that she be educated in those areas.

After "Diplomacy" was performed for a week, the company returned to "Men and Women" for their second and last week in San Francisco. Back on the road with one-night stands up the coast to Portland, Seattle, Tacoma, and Spokane, where only "Men and Women" was presented. Frohman decided that both plays would only be presented in cities where they spent two or more nights.

Two announcements came from the Frohman office, revealing his plans for the next season. H.C. De Mille had been dispatched to Denver to meet the stock company and begin rehearsals for "The Lost Paradise," the play Frohman promised to introduce in Chicago sometime in August. The other news did not concern the company's current activities. Nevertheless, it was a portent for the troupe, and for Maude in particular.

John Drew, the popular comedy drama headliner who had been associated with Augustin Daly's theater, had been contracted by Charles Frohman.[10] Their agreement was to last several years. The contract would go into effect at the beginning of the 1892-93 season, upon the termination of Drew's arrangement with Daly, which had one more season to run. Frohman stated that he would supply Drew with a number of new plays and an excellent supporting company, by which he meant his stock company. He also promised to supply the star with elaborate stage productions. Moreover, after suitable openings in New York, engagements would be played in all the larger cities where Drew was already popular.

A card game at which Drew had met Frohman for the first time was followed by several meetings during which Drew made clear that he was not "wedded" to Daly. "I'm not bound as a serf," he had said, when asked by Frohman about his commitment to Daly. Frohman quickly made a generous offer to Drew, much larger than anything Daly could counter. With no hesitation, Drew joined the Frohman stable. The decision would turn out to be fortuitous for both Drew and Frohman and, although she was still many months away from earning a principal role, for Maude as well.

The stock company arrived in Chicago on August 1. While en route, they had begun rehearsals for "The Lost Paradise." To take advantage of Chicago's enthusiasm for his stock company, Frohman planned to present "Men and Women" the first week, "Diplomacy" the second week, and introduce "The Lost Paradise" the final week of their engagement. It would also give the company two additional weeks to rehearse "The Lost Paradise."

Frohman had the scenery and costumes sent from New York a week before "Paradise" was to open, so the company could conduct several full-scale rehearsals. During this time, De Mille worked with the company, adjusting dialogue, changing the sequence of scenes, and directing the performers in their respective parts. In his report to Frohman, he noted that Maude was always on time for rehearsals and practiced her part diligently and with all seriousness. Frohman promised to be in Chicago two days before the "Paradise" opening, and De Mille wished to have the play in as perfect order as possible.

Both "Men and Women" and "Diplomacy" attracted good houses at the Columbia Theater. Additional promotional activity for the initial presentation of "The Lost Paradise" created large advance ticket sales and ensured capacity audiences for its one-week appearance.

The new play opened on August 17, 1891. In spite of a very humid night, typical for Chicago in late summer, the heat did not prevent first-nighters from wearing their most expensive finery, complete with furs. It was also quite hot in the theater, and even hotter on stage. Stagehands with towels greeted each performer as he or she left the stage and patted them down before they reentered. By the last act, costumes were sweat-soaked and rumpled; makeup had all but dissolved from the performers' faces. Seated in a box just to the right of the stage were De Mille and Frohman. The eyes of the audience glanced up at them expectantly throughout the entire performance.

The following morning, reviews in Chicago's newspapers surely made De Mille and Frohman beam with satisfaction. From the *Herald*: "Play, author, and company scored an undeniable success."[11] The *Chicago Tribune* spoke glowingly. "A sterling American drama, great of capabilities. Profound motive and a moral which every thoughtful auditor will take home."[12] And the *Chicago Post* boasted of the city as a fertile ground for new theater. "That the time has come for launching high-class dramatic ventures in Chicago was proven last night by the complete success of Henry C. De Mille's new play."[13]

The plot: the hero of the play is Reuben Warner (William Morris, in one of his most accomplished roles). He is superintendent of the Knowlton Iron Works, owned by Andrew Knowlton (Frank Mordaunt). Knowlton lavishes his wealth and love on his daughter Margaret (Sydney Armstrong), who is celebrating her twenty-fourth birthday. In contrast, he pays his men starvation wages; but his daughter is ignorant of all that transpires at the factory. When Ralph Standish (Orrin Johnson), the son of a man for whom Knowlton had worked, proposes, he is accepted by Margaret, although she refuses to kiss him. Standish receives a half-interest in the factory and attempts to take over its operation immediately. When Warner tells Knowlton that the men are about to strike, Knowlton refuses to do anything about the situation. Then Warner declares his love for Margaret, whom he has loved since she was a child. Knowlton insults Warner by telling him he is foolishly attempting to rise above his station, being nothing more than a workman.

Later, Warner discovers in a diary left by the elder Standish that the latter had bequeathed his invention of the Volter dynamo to Warner, his protégé. Thus, Warner has Knowlton in his power. Nonetheless, loving Margaret and anxious to save her from ruin, he destroys pages of the diary but is observed doing so by a female employee of the factory. Then, seen by Standish with diary pages in his hand, Warner is accused by Standish of theft. Warner does not wish Margaret to know he owns the invention that made her father's wealth, so he remains silent under the accusation; and she believes him a thief. After a dramatic confrontation between the workmen and the factory owners, the men walk off their jobs. Margaret shows great compassion for the workers. She breaks her engagement with Standish, then learns of her father's guilt and Warner's nobility. Margaret and Warner are engaged, and the strike is terminated.

Annie had a small part as Knowlton's wife, and her acting was viewed as "acceptable." Maude, as Nell, appeared in a long scene as one of the factory's sickly working girls. The *Inter Ocean* praised her acting as "sweetly sympathetic, like a violet blushing unseen" and followed the compliment by suggested that Maude was "one of the most promising of the rising young actresses of the day."[14]

The *Evening News* wrote an article about the pretty young women featured in the play, one of whom was Maude. She was described as being "sweet" and "not such a baby as she looks" but fitting "the spiritual nature of Nell."[15] Another reviewer took those very features and interpreted them more negatively. "Maude Adams was pathetic and sweet in the little, half-starved factory girl Nell. She is inclined to let go the reins of her emotions, producing a sort of blind staggers known only to excitable actresses."[16]

Interviewed after opening night, Frohman declared that he was so pleased with the new play that "not a single line, scene or situation would be changed" when it was produced in New York. He expressed particular pleasure with the principal performers and, without hesitation, included Maude among them.

After Chicago, "The Lost Paradise" appeared in Milwaukee, St. Paul, and Cincinnati, on its way to an engagement in Boston, where the company would inaugurate the opening of the newly built Columbia Theater. Frohman was going to attend the opening; but a labor strike — it must have seemed ironic to Frohman — delayed final work on the theater. He stayed in New York while the company rested, enjoying their first break since beginning the tour by rehearsing "Men and Women." Frohman had again changed the schedule and decided to run "Men and Women" until the company reached New York.

The *Boston Globe* reported that the play came "with the prestige of 250 nights' run in New York City, besides honors won elsewhere."

> Allowing for the enthusiasm incident to an occasion like that of yesterday, the spontaneous applause so freely bestowed left no doubt of the fact that the audience was thoroughly delighted with the production.[17]

Among all the accolades given the principal actors, Maude received a short, but complimentary comment. "Miss Maud Adams was deliciously sweet and ingenuous as Dora."

Maude celebrated her nineteenth birthday with little fanfare. A simple gift of a necklace from the company and an after-theater dinner marked her last year as an ingenue.

When "Diplomacy" was played a week later, audience reactions were similarly enthusiastic. "The play has sprung at once into popularity," reported the *New York Clipper*, "and with repeated calls by the audience, and speeches by the principals."[18] Frohman had traveled to Boston to see the opening of "Diplomacy," but he had no sooner arrived than he received a cable from New York informing him of his mother's death. At age sixty-five, she had been in ill health for some time. The Frohman brothers and their father attended the simple, private funeral and burial that Mrs. Frohman had requested. Except for the obituary and a brief comment that she was the mother of the Frohman "boys," there was no other mention in the newspapers.

"The Lost Paradise" opened at Proctor's Twenty-third Street Theater, New York, on November 16, to immediate success.

> On the inaugural night the audience was enthusiastic from the start, and Mr. De Mille was justified in making a speech. The drama is strong, even brilliant at times. Its characters are boldly sketched. It is handsomely staged and powerfully acted, the conspicuously good work being contributed by William Morris (who is now a leading actor of recognized ability, and ranking high), Orrin Johnson, Cyril Scott, Maud Adams, Etta Hawkins, C. Leslie Allen, Sydney Armstrong, and Odette Tyler.[19]

Frohman's appraisal of Maude in Chicago and New York provided further evidence for his belief in her growing stardom. His attentive observation of her part as Nell, the consumptive factory girl, led to a rare public comment, with Frohman declaring: "There's big talent in that girl." He also noticed that her interpretation contained an irresistible appeal to women in the audience.

"The Lost Paradise" played its 100th performance on February 2, 1892. The play had proven so prosperous, Frohman decided to let it run in New York until March 5, instead of putting it on tour immediately.

At the same time, Frohman began his promotional announcements about the eagerly anticipated arrival of John Drew to Frohman's forces. Drew would open in October, at Palmer's Theater. He would be moved to the Empire Theater, under construction at Broadway and Fortieth Street, as soon as it was completed. He would be the head of his own company (actually Frohman's stock company). He would tour the country with the most elaborate productions available. He would be supported by the finest actors Frohman could hire. All of this while Drew was still performing under his contract with Augustin Daly.

When they departed from New York, Frohman supplied two specially equipped passenger cars for his company. Their tour was to last three months, ending in Chicago, the site of "The Lost Paradise's" original opening. Crowded houses and profitable box-office receipts supported the company at each engagement.

Chicago newspapers proclaimed the return of the play, spoke of its success everywhere it had appeared, and boasted that it had begun its stage career in their city. "The Lost Paradise," they declared, "is a delightful, impressive, magnetic play."

Above: When Maude's selection to appear with John Drew was announced, the *New York Clipper* put her likeness on its front page in a position of prominence. Maude was nineteen years old.

Left: At the time John Drew joined the Frohman forces, he had already established himself as a leading actor. Frohman planned to use him as the head of a high-class stock company. The impresario's choice of Maude as Drew's co-star began her rise to stardom. (Photo: Sarony. Undated. Museum of the City of New York)

On May 9, the play returned to the Columbia Theater, to "an eager and delighted audience." It remained overwhelmingly appealing for the entire three-week engagement. Advance ticket sales would make the play the most popular in the history of the Columbia.

During the engagement, Maude was singled out for her portrayal of Nell, the factory girl. For a small part, performed by an almost unknown actress, the compliment could not have been more gratifying. "Another striking sketch filled with pathos and a delicate sympathetic charm is that presented by Maude Adams, a young actress imbued with genuine dramatic instincts."[20]

Charles Frohman had left for Europe to further his business interests, the first of many trips as his theater empire grew. Among his various activities, he was to receive the play Alexander Bisson had been preparing for John Drew. Before leaving, he sent a message to Maude that he wished to meet with her on his return to New York. Obviously nervous, Maude wondered what this summons meant.

The meeting was short and sweet. Maude came away thrilled and excited. Typical of the manner in which Frohman announced his plans, the *Clipper* published a statement sent to them from the Frohman office.

> Maude Adams, of Charles Frohman's Stock Co., has been selected to play leading roles with John Drew. Miss Adams has been with Mr. Frohman's Stock Co. for two years, and has done excellent work both in comedy and drama.[21]

7

First Steps to Stardom

Following Charles Frohman's instructions, Maude and John Drew met for the first time in San Francisco where both were playing. Drew was staying at the Baldwin Hotel and was appearing in the theater there. When Maude visited Drew at the Baldwin, it brought back many memories of her childhood days performing, with her mother, in the standard melodramas of the day. This visit was entirely more significant. Maude was meeting with her future leading man, the head of his own company, to determine their compatibility, both on and off the stage. It was with fear and hesitation that she approached the meeting.

Maude found Drew to be an affable man. He seemed kindly, humorous, and respectful to women. His manner quickly put the usually shy young woman at ease, and they engaged in a pleasant conversation. Both promised to work together diligently in their new assignment. The biggest problem they discussed was how to bridge the gap of nineteen years in their ages in love scenes. It would be an artistic challenge.

Drew's initial impression of Maude was that she seemed too frail. He had become accustomed to appearing with leading ladies who were physically larger and stronger, robust women like Ada Rehan. Maude, in her girlish slightness—she was five feet tall and weighed 100 pounds—seemed too fragile to be a leading woman. Yet her expressive face, obvious intelligence, and seriousness of purpose impressed Drew. He recognized that Frohman was undoubtedly correct in selecting Maude. His "frail girl," Drew later acknowledged, never missed a rehearsal or a performance during the five years they worked together.

John Drew was born in 1853 into a famous actor's family. At the age of twenty, he first appeared on stage at his mother's own venue, the Arch Street Theater, in Philadelphia. He was an avid student and a quick read. After several years learning the art of acting, he was asked to come to New York to appear in plays written and produced by Augustin Daly, then one of the city's leading impresarios. Drew debuted in "The Big Bonanza" and immediately was recognized as a potential star. Remaining with Daly, Drew became a headliner playing "high comedy" (drawing room comedy), in such roles as a polished gentleman, roué, guardian, or cultured lover. An actor of striking good looks, he was tall and lean, carried himself with confidence and authority, and had large, heavy-lidded eyes and a drooping black moustache, making him the classic handsome man of the era.

In private life he was a true gentleman, good-natured, funny, and sociable. At the theater he was a serious professional, a consummate actor, and, as Frohman had astutely perceived, the proper person to mentor Maude.

When Charles Frohman chose Maude to co-star with John Drew, he was laying the groundwork for what many historians would later judge to be his greatest achievement. This gentle, charming, delicate, and attractive little girl, who had persevered along the perilous path of melodrama as a child actress, was now at the foot of the steps leading to stardom. It was a story unique in the annals of legitimate theater. As much as Frohman was involved with actors and productions, there was no other instance in which he literally built a star's future.[1]

Maude did not disappoint him. No actress devoted herself to such a rigorous and disciplined life in theater as Maude did during her five years with John Drew. These experiences elicited every nuance and every feature of her acting ability and helped to mature her beyond even the limits of what she herself believed could be done.

Their first play together was "The Masked Ball." Rehearsals began early in August at the Madison Square Theater, with Frohman in attendance nearly every day, doing a good deal of dissecting as the play took shape. Maude had memorized her part beforehand but quickly realized the difference between knowing a part and playing it on stage with real actors. Rehearsals changed line meanings and emotional interpretations. Reactions to actors changed. What seemed funny proved deadly serious, and what seemed solemn turned out to present a comedic situation. Most of all, Maude assimilated the spiritual beauty of meaningful dialogue and body dialectics.

In the play, Maude found one scene particularly difficult to perform. The young wife, Maude, to punish her husband, Drew, for willingly misrepresenting her and her family to her former suitor, pretends to be tipsy. It was a state of being that Maude herself had never before experienced, although she had been witness to drunken people — including actors and very likely her father — who had left a profound impression on her. Maude admitted to the difficulty of the scene and, as she approached performing it, was self-conscious and over-careful.

The scene was rehearsed many times, but Maude could not get it across as she and Frohman desired. There was a fine line between a person's appearing tipsy without actually being so and an actor's effectively conveying that subtle message to an audience. An inflection of the voice, a facial expression, or a sway of the body could spoil spontaneity, and all delicacy would be lost. A flower gave Maude the insight to play the scene with good taste.

At one rehearsal, someone had given Maude a long-stemmed rose. Held at various angles, it tilted in tipsy fashion but did not lose its beauty. Maude took the rose home. Using it as a prop, she rehearsed the scene until the part had been refined to her satisfaction. On stage, the rose helped make Maude's part a success, and it was retained in the final production. Of even greater significance, this was the scene that inspired critics to recognize Maude as a unique and exciting new performer, with a delicate charm all her own.

The play tells the story of a young Frenchman who is compelled to go out of town on business. In his absence, he asks a close friend to call upon a certain young lady whom he has been courting, tell her he loves her, and ask if he may have her hand. The young man claims he has no time to do it himself. The dutiful friend visits the young lady, falls in love with her at first sight, and proposes to her for himself. He is accepted and immediately writes to his friend that the young lady and her family do not possess the qualities necessary for his friend's entering the family, but he says nothing about having married the lady himself.

In her first play with John Drew, "The Masked Ball," Maude electrified the audience by appearing to be tipsy without really being so. Drew knew she was headed for stardom. (San Francisco History Center, San Francisco Public Library)

About the time of the carnival in Nice, the young man returns to France; and complications ensue. The husband does his utmost to keep any knowledge of the marriage away from his friend, especially to prevent a meeting with his wife. Yet, they all attend a masked ball, where the former lovers meet. The young wife learns of her husband's deception and determines to make him suffer. She pretends to a state of inebriation. After the husband apologizes for his behavior and the friends reconcile, the situation is resolved. John Drew played the husband, Dr. Paul Blondet, and Maude his wife, Suzanne Blondet. Annie had a small part as Madelene Beromet, a servant. The comedy was adapted by Clyde Fitch from a French play by Alexander Bisson and Albert Carre.

Part of Frohman's plan to guide Maude through the training process of becoming a star was to make certain that her mother continued to be her stage colleague and familial supervisor. By giving Annie a part in the play, Frohman saw to it that she was at Maude's side both on and off the stage, ensuring her daughter's continued focus on acting.

Once, interviewed by a reporter, Maude admitted to preferring comedic parts to sentimental ones. When she was quoted as disliking being kept in "sniveling parts" for two years, Frohman quickly informed her that she was not to conduct any more interviews; all public statements henceforth would emanate from the Frohman offices. Frohman strongly believed that an actress should keep her personal life, and opinions, remote from the public. "You are not to be interviewed," he informed Maude. "You are not to be quoted. People will wonder at you, yearn for the details of your private life. Let them. It will only spur their interest and their desire for you."[2]

"The Masked Ball" opened at the Davidson Theater, Milwaukee, September 19, 1892. This would be the first of several weeks on the road to "finish" the play before introducing it to New York audiences. The following week, the play was presented at the Columbia Theater, Chicago, where it met with only mixed success. One reviewer reported on "the friendly sentiment" Drew received from the audience. "If there was a fault, it was in the excess of enthusiasm."

In contrast, another reviewer considered the play to be "a trifling work, not in any degree remarkable for brilliancy, nor conspicuously clever." Still another wrote that, while the play was mirthful and had some wit, "it is also burdened with commonplace and unnecessary dullness." It was obvious that Frohman and Fitch had some work to do before opening the play in New York. Long rehearsals were initiated, with changes in dialogue, scene sequences, and action, the performers having to memorize and practice new material almost daily as changes were made.

All reviewers, however, recognized that the play's success or failure hinged upon the performances of its leading actors, namely, John Drew and Maude Adams. For Maude, the comments were both positive and negative. The critic from the *Inter Ocean*, who had once before spoken negatively of Maude's abilities, again cited the "charming and winsome" actress as lacking "the comedy brilliance, dash, and spirit essential to the effective characterization of Suzanne Blondet. She does not meet the important requirements of the part."[3]

Another critic regarded her acting more favorably. "Maude acts with taste, intelligence, and a graceful womanliness," he said, "entering appreciatively into the purpose and nature of the part, and gives a performance that cannot fail to enhance her professional reputation."[4]

In another article, the *Daily News* reviewer took special notice of Maude, identifying her "as one of the charming surprises of the evening." His words had a hint of prophecy.

> Miss Adams touches the subtle character with a deliciously original color. She does not look the part in any one situation. She has an awkward boyish manner and a mild, delicate face which contradicts her intelligent acting, fine voice and brilliant comedy. I think Miss Adams is one of those lasting artists who will grow upon the public and achieve immense popularity; she is so sincere, clear and simple in her methods and plainly intellectual.[5]

Armed with these critical evaluations, Frohman reworked the production for its opening in New York. He was about to introduce to the public two stars under his direction: John Drew, who came with a ready-made reputation and stellar reviews; and Maude Adams, a new and hopefully exciting talent, now to perform before discerning audiences. Among all the people involved with the production, Frohman was the calmest and most confident.

"The Masked Ball" opened at Palmer's Theater, New York, on October 3, 1892. According to the *New York Times* critic, it was "a first night that will be long remembered."

> The piece in which Mr. Drew appeared last night was well chosen. His new manager, Charles Frohman, has shown his usual sagacity in its selection, and in the choice of the actors associated with his star. Two of these, Miss Maude Adams and Mr. Harwood, have parts scarcely less grateful than Drew's, and Miss Adams, by her exceedingly delicate and delightfully humorous treatment of a trying role, fairly shared the honors with the hero of the night.[6]

The usually critical *New York Clipper* reviewer called the play "a pleasant one of success." He went on to predict that the theater "will be crowded nightly."

By the second week of the engagement, Drew had become so popular that audiences demanded he make curtain calls at the end of each act. At the end of Act II, in which Maude "rendered a dangerous scene of mimic tipsiness," she, too, was called before the curtain. Their four-week engagement was extended two more weeks. Advance ticket sales were so brisk that Frohman extended the play's life by moving it to the Standard Theater for an indefinite period, which meant as long as the play continued to fill the theater.

The Standard Theater was selected to show "The Masked Ball" because Frohman's dream, the Empire Theater, had not yet been completed. Indeed, had it not been for his old friend Al Hayman, Frohman's "dream theater" would never have come to fruition.

Hayman had directed Frohman to look at a property uptown for his new theater, since, he believed, that was the direction the theater district was moving. Hayman even suggested that he would build the theater for his friend.

"Where?" asked Frohman excitedly.

"I've got some lots at 40th and Broadway," Hayman replied, "and it's a good site."[7]

The next day, a deal was finalized for the building of the Empire Theater. A construction partnership was formed between Frank Sanger, Al Hayman, and William Harris. They were so confident of Frohman's success that they turned the building over to him without a written contract. Their only enjoinder was that he should do with it as he pleased.

From the moment ground was broken, Frohman spent part of each day watching and supervising the construction of the theater. It was to be his personal gift to the theatrical industry in New York, and he nursed the project along like a proud father.

The Empire Theater officially opened on January 25, 1893. Since it had not been available for "The Masked Ball," Belasco's "The Girl I Left Behind Me" inaugurated the theater. In fact, Drew's company did not play at the Empire until September 1894.

The opening of the Empire Theater further established Frohman's position as Broadway's preeminent producer. It opened a new theater district that within a few years would be crowded with competing venues. Frohman established his offices at the theater, which became the nerve center for his business interests. It was at the Empire that Frohman made his stock company nearly an institution, thanks to his selection of star performers and lavish productions. Any new play presented by the stock company spoke well for its authors. Through the company, Frohman introduced authors such as Oscar Wilde, Henry Guy Carleton, Clyde Fitch, and Arthur Wing Pinero to American audiences.

"The Masked Ball" closed its New York engagement on January 19, 1893, after a highly profitable run of nineteen weeks. Drew had proven his worth as a dramatic headliner. Maude had become a co-star overnight, all because of a long-stemmed rose.

Comfortably ensconced in a special train that Frohman had outfitted for the tour, the company headed for Chicago for a second two-week engagement feeling confident of their success. The *Clipper* reported that "advance sales warrants the prediction of a phenomenally successful sojourn," and that Mr. Drew was "accepted as one of the best light comedians in America." The critic of the *Inter Ocean* even suggested that Maude "is said to give a more finished characterization of Suzanne than she did before."

"The Masked Ball" met with immediate audience approval. Drew's popularity and the play's success in New York guaranteed full houses for the length of the engagement. What was surprising, however, was the *Inter Ocean's* critic, who now fairly gushed with praise over Maude's improved acting.

> Charming Maude Adams has increased the merit of her performance by self pos-
> session that gives more graceful expression to the dainty, delicate, yet joyous comedy
> that was so pleasant a surprise in her work when she first appeared as Suzanne.[8]

He went on to describe both Maude's physical and professional attractiveness.

> "Miss Adams is one of the loveliest young ladies on the stage, the exquisite sweet-
> ness of her face predisposing an audience in her favor. Miss Adams succeeds in con-
> vincing the spectators that the spectacle of a pretty girl slightly inebriated is delightfully
> piquant. Moreover, Miss Adams has a smile to which the most obdurate critic would
> succumb."

A highly successful week in St. Louis preceded a trip to Philadelphia, Drew's hometown, where friends and admirers were preparing a "homecoming to be remembered." Opening at the Broad Street Theater, Drew captivated a full house. "As a prodigal son, who, for a long time had absented himself, John Drew came back to his home making his stellar debut in 'The Masked Ball.'"[9]

Through the third week of the engagement, Drew continued to draw large crowds. His personal magnetism was so huge that the play itself and members of the company were almost forgotten. Maude was briefly mentioned once for her "charming" acting. Nevertheless, the lack of public acknowledgment did not alter her preparations each day. Each morning, Maude rehearsed her part in front of a mirror, practicing her lines in various ways. At each rehearsal, she played her role as if it were opening night. She arrived at the theater two hours before the curtain and spent time wandering through the seats and backstage, as if to absorb the "vibrations" of the theater that surrounded her, before going to her dressing room. There, she rested on a couch, in seeming meditation, before applying her make-up, which was minimal, and putting on her costume.

Before each performance, a long-stemmed rose was delivered to Maude to accompany her "tipsy" scene. Maude kept all the used roses in a box. One evening, the rose was not delivered; and Maude had to resurrect a used rose from the box as a substitute, which caused considerable amusement among the company. Maude herself laughed so much that she found it hard to concentrate on her lines as she waved the limp rose around. Several times, she performed without the rose, just to see if she could do it. Neither the cast nor audiences noticed any difference in her delivery.

The accolades Maude received, especially for the "tipsy" scene, in no way changed her approach to acting. If anything, she plunged more deeply into performance, challenging herself to do even better. Drew observed her commitment and mentioned it to Frohman, who merely smiled at the news.

Drew liked to host small parties after the show, inviting friends and cast members. He attempted to interest Maude in attending them, to encourage her to be "more social." At first, Maude refused, admitting to being shy and self-conscious in social situations. "With your own company?" asked Drew. After several overtures by Drew to draw her into the group, Maude relented; but she usually sat apart, saying little. Nonetheless, Drew vowed to make Maude more sociable.

On the play's 250th performance, April 17, in Philadelphia, a bust of John Drew was given to each member of the audience, and the leading man called for a cast party at a local restaurant. Drew accompanied Maude and her mother to the restaurant. At the party, he made a short speech thanking the cast for their efforts on his behalf. He particularly mentioned Maude's dedicated work and his pleasure in having her as a co-star. Maude was so embarrassed that she fled the room. At her request, Drew never complimented her in public again.

"The Masked Ball" now entered that part of the tour, near the end of the season, when one-night stands dominated the schedule. The season was to end on May 27, and the company had eighteen cities to visit during the final month. With the exception of a week in Washington, D.C., all stops were in New England, in smaller towns. The Taylor Opera House, in Trenton, New Jersey, was the site of the company's final performance. Frohman came down to Trenton to distribute gifts to the cast members and tell them that their tour of "The Masked Ball" would continue in August. Response to the play had been so splendid, Frohman decided to delay the introduction of a new play until early 1894.

Annie and Maude passed the summer in a small cottage on Staten Island. Maude hiked, tended a garden, and read.

In July, the Frohman office announced that John Drew would begin his season in St. Paul, Minnesota, on August 15, continuing his tour with "The Masked Ball." The date was unusually early for season openings, but Frohman wanted to be in theaters before other companies began their tours. Starting out with a premier production would enhance the box-office and garner good reviews earlier than his competitors. That he chose to do so in lesser markets—smaller populations but high-class theaters—made his decision all the more significant. The announcement mentioned that Maude would continue as Drew's co-star.

The early starting date meant that rehearsals had to begin in late July and the company had to be traveling by August 10 to meet the opening date. Rehearsals went smoothly because the play was already familiar; no new cast members were hired, and no script changes were made. Of special interest to Maude, and to Frohman, was her appearance on the cover of the *New York Clipper* on July 29, in an uncommonly fine portrait engraving. It is likely that the Frohman office was responsible, attempting to take advantage of her growing success and, at the same time, enacting Frohman's plan to create a stage image for Maude. A brief biography accompanied the picture, which embellished Maude's early days in the theater. It was Maude's first public recognition in a national theatrical newspaper, and she had to have been pleased.

Instead of St. Paul, on August 25, "The Masked Ball" tour began in Duluth, Minnesota. Why such a small town to inaugurate a tour?

Duluth was a thriving and rich mining town with an excellent theater that attracted all the touring companies. It was located on a main railroad line to the West. And it offered generous box-office guarantees for those willing to appear there. Considering the nature of the town, it attracted a fashionable audience who were sophisticated enough to appreciate an Eastern drawing-room comedy.

Not surprisingly, a crowded house, full of opening-night enthusiasm, met Drew, Maude, and the company and rewarded the performers with twelve curtain calls. Maude's "tipsy" scene elicited much whistling and foot stamping, sometimes so loud that her lines could barely be heard. Just the fact that a young woman would appear to be drunk in public was enough to set off the audience; and when she won her point by presenting it so discreetly, the women in the audience applauded heartily. Frohman had already noticed how Maude captured younger women, as if she delineated each of their personal fantasies.

The tour ran from late August to late December. After visiting eighteen cities during this time, to consistently full houses and profitable box-office receipts, "The Masked Ball" put on its last performance in Boston. The production had been presented more than 400 times, in thirty-six cities, with the same cast, a Frohman feature.

Rehearsals for Drew's new farce comedy, "The Butterflies," began in Newark, December 4, with the hope that the company would be ready to open the play in Boston on December 16. Stress on the company to rehearse one play during the day while performing another one at night took its toll. Not only the confusion of working on two plays at one time, but also the fatigue of traveling fifteen weeks and performing eight shows a week made it difficult for the cast to meet Frohman's schedule. Frohman agreed to an appeal by Drew for a week without performances while rehearsing the new play in Boston. Although actors did not usually earn a salary while in rehearsals, Frohman continued to pay the company, a gracious act of recognition not usually found among producers.

During the last days of fully costumed rehearsals, Frohman came to Boston to supervise the production. The play, however, was not yet ready to be presented to audiences. Instead of delaying the opening, Frohman had the company play "The Masked Ball" to Boston audiences for a week before introducing "The Butterflies."

While Maude continued to be enthusiastic about appearing with the Drew company, she did not care for her role in the new play, believing it to be of lesser significance, with much less emphasis on her characterizations. As one reviewer remarked: "How could one top the "tipsy" role?" Nevertheless, given her professional commitment, she worked as hard to perfect the new part as she had for her role as Suzanne. Still, Maude's role in "The Butterflies" engendered far less commentary from reviewers, other than to note that she played her part well.

In "The Masked Ball," the *Boston Globe's review* of Maude's acting was exemplary.

> Miss Maude Adams, the buoyant, versatile, coquettish Suzanne, gave even a better impersonation of the doctor's wife than she did last season, which is saying a great deal. Piquant, vivacious and natural, her success was immediate.[10]

In contrast, the same reviewer wrote but a sentence of Maude's work in "The Butterflies." "The character of Miriam was very attractive and Miss Adams interpreted it with her cleverness."[11]

The play was written by Henry Gay Carleton, and was considered by critics to be his best play. A comedy, the play was simply a charming description of rather probable events in the everyday life of the class of people whose only object is to enjoy themselves. That the play was performed by the Drew company proved a critical ingredient. "These clever people would be able to make much of anything," declared a local critic.

The story of "The Butterflies" opens in Mr. Hiram Green's (Harry Harwood) residence in Florida, where all the characters meet. Mr. Green has a young daughter, Suzanne (Olive May), and a young son by the name of Barrington (Arthur Byron). A widow, Mrs. Ossian (Annie Adams), is staying at his house, ostensibly to provide companionship for his daughter.

Suzanne is in love with an Englishman, Andrew Strong (Lewis Baker), and Barrington thinks he is in love with Miss Miriam (Maude), the daughter of Mrs. Beverly Stuart-Dodge (Kate Meek). Mrs. Ossian, on the other hand, has a son, Frederick (John Drew), who is in love with Miriam, whom he has rescued from drowning by dragging her from the water by the heels. At this point, the already troubled situation becomes increasingly complicated.

Mrs. Stuart-Dodge, who possesses an exalted sense of herself and her family, wishes to marry her daughter to the richest young man she can catch. Barrington seems to be her objective.

Miriam, however, loves Frederick, though he has no money and is in debt. Mrs. Stuart-Dodge, despite all her pretensions, finds herself in a similar predicament. By coincidence, Frederick's tailor, Nathaniel Bilser (Leslie Allen), becomes creditor for both people. Bilser is very persistent in collecting Mrs. Stuart-Dodge's debt. Mrs. Stuart-Dodge, in anger, insults the Ossians, both mother and son, which does not prevent Frederick from paying Bilser, because of his love for Miriam.

Miriam breaks her engagement with Barrington; Frederick, in need of money, goes to work in Mr. Green's office; Mr. Green marries Mrs. Ossian; Suzanne makes Mr. Strong marry her. Miriam accepts Frederick, whose virtues even the snooty Mrs. Stuart-Dodge now condescends to recognize.

Maude's most memorable scene came in the final act, when Drew makes his declaration of love to her and when, after a long sequence of comedic misunderstanding, they both come to appreciate one another, and seal their mutual appreciation with a long kiss.

The fashionable and critical audience gave hearty approval to the play which promised "a long and prosperous life," according to one reviewer. Drew's success in the title role "was complete." Even in his drollest moment, Drew is always a man and a gentleman." In a ready-made role for the actor, his presentation of the character was an artistic triumph. Maude was said to have "a most congenial role."

The Act III scene contained Maude's first stage kiss, and it took some time for Drew to teach her the proper stage positioning and action to make it appear authentic. At first, Maude seemed self-conscious; but she was quickly able to incorporate the action into the totality of her role. Only Drew's large, bushy moustache seemed to bother her.

Frohman believed "The Butterflies" needed more seasoning before bringing the play to New York, so he sent the company to Chicago for a three-week engagement at the Columbia Theater. Box-office results during the second week confirmed Frohman's concern about the lasting value of the play. With falling receipts, he had the company switch to "The Masked Ball" for the third week. Still, "The Butterflies," and Drew especially, received good reviews.

> Mr. John Drew had a generous welcome to the Columbia last night, the theater in which he formally began his career as a star. The audience lost no occasion to express its kindness.[12]
>
> The play is entertaining, being admirably brisk and in action spirited, and the people all are clever.

Maude's role was correctly identified by reviewers—well done for what there was of it.

> Miss Maude Adams does not have as good chance for success as she had in "The Masked Ball," yet she is charming, sweetly attractive in a light sentimental vein that approaches the dramatic and is followed by a joyous mood of laughter.[13]

> The beauty, delicacy, sweetness and artistic intelligence of Miss Maude Adams are placed so much in perspective by the circumstances of the character she assumes as almost to be effaced.[14]

Although Drew had tried heroically, there was no question in Frohman's mind that the play was not of the highest caliber and would likely last but a short time in New York. "The Butterflies" opened at Palmer's Theater, on February 5, 1894, with "The Masked Ball" in the wings, ready to replace it.

According to the *Clipper* reviewer, the play was slight but witty. "The play is but a trifle, meager in plot and incidents, but its wit is very bright and sparkling, and is sure to win favor."[15]

Of John Drew:

> Mr. Drew was easy, graceful, and entertaining as ever. The wit and humor of his lines shown with added brilliancy because of his keen appreciation of their value and the deftness of his handling.

Comments about Maude were brief, although complimentary.

> Maude Adams was, as usual, charmingly natural, and in every way thoroughly pleasing, but she is not afforded in this work opportunities equal to her abilities.

Much to Frohman's surprise, New York audiences enjoyed the play and generated full houses for several weeks. It was so profitable that "The Masked Ball" was shelved. Frohman decided to run "The Butterflies" in New York for the remainder of the season, if he could.

The fifth week's review of the engagement reported that Drew continued to "meet with great success." It was also stated that fashionable audiences were filling the theater. The phrase "fashionable audiences" meant the play was especially attractive to the upper classes of theatergoers.

Drew received substantial recognition for his good work each week. By the seventh week, Maude began to catch the attention of reviewers. "Maude Adams is rendering excellent support and is sharing the honors with the star."[16]

The ninth week's report declared that Maude "was winning new admirers, and the scenes which she shares with Mr. Drew are thoroughly enjoyed and rapturously applauded."[17]

"The Butterflies" played in New York for thirteen weeks to crowded houses and excellent box-office receipts. The play closed May 5. Frohman put the company on a brief tour of Brooklyn and several weeks in Philadelphia — Drew had to appear in his hometown with a new play — before introducing his next production. While the company was playing in Philadelphia, they would rehearse the replacement for "The Butterflies."

Philadelphia audiences welcomed Drew even before he uttered his first line, applauding him for a full three minutes. He acknowledged them with bows and expressions of thanks. The entire three-week engagement elicited similar results, along with S.R.O. performances. Audiences seemed to show little interest in the play itself or its supporting cast; they were present to cheer Drew every moment he was on stage. Add numerous curtain calls and a speech after the final curtain, and delighted patrons left the theater well after midnight. The late hours made it even more difficult for the company to rehearse the new play the following morning. The new play was scheduled to be presented only two days after they finished in Philadelphia.

"Christopher, Jr." was slated to have its initial performance at the Grand Opera House in Wilkes-Barre, Pennsylvania, on June 4. According to reports, after the play was tested there, the company would take a month's rest — that meant rehearsals in New York to smooth out the production — before beginning a tour of the West.

"Christopher, Jr." was a four-act play written by Madeline Lucette. Christopher, Jr. (John Drew), a young man, is on a voyage to Trinidad. He unwittingly loses his way to his stateroom and, late at night, stumbles into another. Climbing into the upper berth, he quickly discovers that a lady occupies the lower. He makes a hurried exit, only to be confronted by Col. Dwyer, father of the lady, Dora Dwyer (Maude). A big fuss ensues, and it is finally agreed the young people must marry. Miss Dwyer and her father visit Junior's lodging, and Miss Dwyer is taken ill. All arrangements for the marriage have been made, and, in the dark, Junior, by mistake, has presented the card of his friend, Bert Bellaby (Lewis Baker). They are married in separate rooms, neither ever having seen the other. And so they separate, Dora believing she has married Bellaby.

Some years have passed. Miss Dwyer is now Miss Hedway. Her father is dead, and she has taken her uncle's name. Family members want Junior to marry Miss Hedway, although, in fact, they are already married. Christopher, Sr., (Harry Harwood), learns of the marriage and sends Junior to Bombay as clerk in the house of Cobb & Hedway. Junior discovers that Mr. Simpson, junior partner of the firm, has embezzled large sums of money. Revealing that he is Christopher, Jr., he discharges Simpson. Miss Hedway, entering the room, overhears this interchange. She is strongly attracted to Junior; but Junior is married to Miss Dwyer, and Miss Dwyer (Hedway) is supposedly married to Mr. Bellaby.

The discovery of the embezzlement brings Christopher, Sr., from London, along with his wife, daughter Nellie, and the real Mr. Bellaby, who is engaged to marry Nellie. Nellie introduces her fiancé to Miss Hedway, who believes she has found her husband. She quickly discovers she is, in reality, married to Christopher, Jr., whom she loves, but she resolves to keep up the deception. Bellaby tells his friends his wife is dead. Junior proposes to Miss Hedway. In a humorous final scene, the facts are revealed; and all ends happily.

Neither Frohman nor the company was enthused by the script. It seemed difficult to grasp the meaning of the play, let alone attempt to follow its plot; and the characterizations seemed unreal. Nevertheless, Frohman decided to keep it in the company's repertoire. Maude's role as Dora contained some humorous passages; but she, too, felt uncomfortable with the part.

Thus, when the company reached Denver for a week's engagement, their first stop on the Western tour, they played only "The Masked Ball" and "The Butterflies." A three-week appearance at the Baldwin Theater in San Francisco would offer another opportunity to perform "Christopher, Jr." and determine if the play had any real future. Frohman had so little confidence in the play that he directed the author of a successful English play to ready it for American audiences as quickly as possible.

For two weeks, the Baldwin Theater was "filled to the doors" with patrons anxious to see the Drew company perform "The Butterflies" (week one) and "The Masked Ball" (week two). Drew received his share of praise from the 'Frisco audience, just as he had when he was with Augustin Daly. His droll comedy and manly presence only solidified admirers to his cause.

Maude's work was almost equally lauded, the *Chronicle* reviewer calling her "a versatile actress."

> She plays with delicacy, grace, and, at the same time, with point and effect. She is equally good in light and serious work, and she has a sympathetic quality which tells all.[18]

When "Christopher, Jr." was presented the third week, attendance gradually dropped. Drew and Maude gained their share of attention, but the play was considered entirely too convoluted and improbable. Again, the play had failed to interest audiences and critics picked it apart unmercifully. Frohman decided to put "Christopher, Jr." to rest temporarily; he never liked to dismiss a play outright. Instead, he would wait for the proper time to use it again. The company was happy to be relieved of the burden.

Salt Lake City theatergoers anxiously awaited the arrival of the Drew company. Met at the train by a crowd of admirers, the company was escorted to the hotel. The engagement at the Salt Lake Theater was for four performances, two each for "The Butterflies" and "The Masked Ball." To no one's surprise, both plays were well received; Drew was complimented "in his starring expedition"; but most of the hometown attention was focused on Maude. "The Butterflies," said the *Deseret News*, "does not give Miss Adams the opportunities of the other play." Commentary about Maude's role in "The Masked Ball," however, overflowed with optimism.

> It is indeed not too much to say that at the present moment, should Charles Frohman provide her with suitable material and mount it as he is accustomed to mount his plays, Maud Adams would sustain herself as one of the leading lady stars of the country.[19]

The newspaper specifically mentioned the "tipsy" scene as Maude's ascension to stardom.

> There is a strong desire to see "our Maud" in the tipsy scene of "The Masked Ball," which she made famous, or which, to be more accurate, has made her famous.

Many of her admirers were upset to discover that Maude had not received her share of flowers at any of the performances. To answer these people, the Frohman office declared that Mr. Frohman forbade the delivery of flowers across the footlights because "it does not add to the harmony or continuity of a performance." Such tokens of regard, said Frohman, were private or personal and should go to the actress in her dressing room. Nonetheless, to acknowledge having received flowers, Maude had the bouquets placed on the stage in the drawing room scenes of both plays.

Salt Lake City was the final stop on the Western tour. At the conclusion of the last performance, the company boarded the train for New York. Upon arrival, they would begin rehearsals for their new offering, "The Bauble Shop," scheduled to open at the Empire Theater on September 10. The company had less than three weeks to rehearse the play and no rest after an arduous tour, but returning home seemed to spur them to the challenge.

Several critics questioned Drew's role in the new play. Could he play the role of a sober, serious, and staid man of forty, a leader in the House of Commons? Who could imagine it? Others believed that Drew could make anything "go" in New York, as long as he was in the cast. Similar questions were raised about Maude, who was to assume the role of a poor toymaker's daughter with whom Drew fell in love. Maude tackled the part as she did any new role, with a seriousness and motivation that affirmed her commitment to acting.

Frohman was the least concerned. He was confident that both of his stars would fill their roles to perfection. Giving his stars the opportunity to expand their artistic abilities was one of Frohman's goals, a very enlightened view among producers, who otherwise tended to cater to mainstream audiences. As usual, he was correct, both in his assessments and his motives.

"The Bauble Shop" played for one week in Brooklyn, opening September 3, to finalize the script and settings. It appeared to be well received by audiences, although no reviewers showed up to appraise it. Instead, they were waiting for the play's introduction in New York. Frohman encouraged their attendance by giving all the critics complimentary tickets for opening night, scheduled for September 10. Everyone was momentarily disappointed when the opening was delayed one day to accommodate a full-dress rehearsal by the company under Frohman's critical eye.

"The Bauble Shop" was a drama in four acts by Henry Arthur Jones, the English author whom Frohman had contacted after "Christopher, Jr." had failed to move audiences. The play had originally been produced at the Criterion Theater, London, in January 1893. Frohman had seen the play, bought the rights, hired Jones to modify it for American audiences, and put it at the top of his list of the new season's productions.

The play takes its title not only from the toy shop, in which a portion of the action occurs, but also from significant references to the morally stern House of Commons, of which several of the characters are members. Lord Clivebrooke (John Drew), leader of the House of Commons, has been attacked by some ruffians and seeks refuge in the toy shop. He is admitted by Jesse Keber (Maude), a young girl who lives above the shop with her old father (J.E. Dobson), who is an inventor of toys and also a drunkard. His lordship is smitten with the girl. Since he is unable to forget her, he conceives plans concerning her and puts them into operation. He visits the girl at late hours on the pretense of consulting her father about the design of some toys. Even after many visits, the girl's ingenuousness and innocence baffle him. He is preparing a new home for Jesse and her father and refers to the happier life they will lead in the new surroundings. Showered with the girl's gratitude, he obtains a promise that she will do anything he may ask of her. Nonetheless, he is so taken with the goodness of the girl that his mind is changed; and he asks her never to see him again because it would be injurious to his public career. Mr. Stoach, M.P. (Harry Harwood), sees Clivebrooke leave the toy shop, having been spying on his Parliamentary rival and collecting much incriminating evidence. Stoach taunts Clivebrooke and the girl concerning their relationship. Clivebrooke claims all of his visits have been in her father's presence and that the old man is in the house at that moment. Stoach, knowing that the old man had gone out for a drink, challenges them to produce him. At that moment, old Keber totters in from the street. Clivebrooke is compromised and at the mercy of his foe.

The next day, in the House of Commons, members consider the Public Morals Act. Stoach demands that the Lord change his position, but Clivebrooke refuses. A division of opinion occurs, and with it the downfall of the government and Clivebrooke's political ruin. Clivebrooke announces his resignation but declares he will return to confront his foes. Stoach is informed that Clivebrooke intends to marry Jesse, but the cynical moralist sneers at the news. In fact, Clivebrooke has already proposed but has been blocked by his father, the Earl of Sarum (Leslie Allen). When the father recognizes the work of Stoach, he relents, withdraws his opposition to the marriage, and warmly welcomes Jesse into the family.

"The Bauble Shop" opened at the Empire Theater, September 11, 1894, to an S.R.O. audience who received the play with "uncommon warmth." According to the *New York Times* reviewer, rarely had first-night audiences responded as favorably as they did to this new play. The reviewer believed that the work was superior to any the author had previously written and dealt with the love theme "in cleanly fashion."

Supposedly influenced by a rash of recent plays, producers had been roundly criticized for employing questionable devices to portray love and illicit sex. Critics and audiences condemned them for going beyond the usual rules of propriety. Frohman would allow no semblance of sexual innuendo in his plays, and he made public statements to that effect. The reviewer's reference to the play's purism only increased its appeal.

"There is no taint, past or present upon the heroine," declared the reviewer, "nor is there a shadow of offense in the method of Clivebrooke's pursuit of her." For this, the reviewer complimented the author's "wonderful deftness and charming delicacy." Jones was praised for having characterized the heroine "with grace, and shown us a creation of girlish innocence and loveliness of which no recent play can boast."[20]

Maude was now being identified as playing innocent, clean roles, an image she would carry throughout her career. Theater reviewers connected these stage roles with Maude's personal life, and these convictions would continue throughout her life.

In "The Bauble Shop," Maude was praised for her "innocent and clean" performance, a stage persona that continued throughout her career. Maude captured the minds and hearts of women in the audience. (San Francisco History Center, San Francisco Public Library)

The reviewer spoke of Maude's having essayed the role "with fidelity to life." Maude's impersonation of the innocent Jesse Keber was described to be in thorough accord with the author's belief. In speech, action, and changing facial expression, Maude gave the character a vital, almost spiritual spark.

The poetical lines accorded her, wherein she describes to her father the charms of their new home, were spoken by her in a manner that could not be surpassed, and as one gazed upon the speaker, and listened to the mellifluous flow of her words, she afforded a perfect study of ecstatic delight, and the workings of an unsullied soul were admirably portrayed.[21]

The *Times* critic was equally complimentary of Maude's acting.

> To the expression of the traits and moods of his heroine, Miss Maud Adams had lent a variety of tone, pose, and gesture, which made it all the more interesting.[22]

It was Maude's greatest stage triumph to date and raised both critical and public admiration of her to a level equal to that of Drew. In successive weeks of reporting, newspapers spoke both of John Drew and Maude as sharing honors and called the play "a triumphant success." "The Bauble Shop's" engagement was extended once to the end of October and again to December, as houses were filled at every performance.

Whether the Frohman office announcement that "The Bauble Shop" would go to London was true or not, its (intended?) effect was to increase advance sales for the play during its final weeks at the Empire. Yet nothing more was said about London as the company prepared to take the play on tour. In fact, over the years, although Frohman frequently mentioned that Maude would appear in London, she never did.

First stop for "The Bauble Shop" was Philadelphia, where Drew's hometown admirers filled the Broad Street Theater at every performance. Audiences cheered, whistled, stamped their feet, and vigorously applauded everything that Drew did on stage. He was forced to make curtain calls at the end of each act and a speech at the conclusion of every performance — for three straight weeks.

There were two changes made to the cast when the road trip began. Annie took the place of Kate Meek in the small role of Lady Bellender. A pretty niece of Drew, eighteen-year-old Ethel Barrymore, in her first stage appearance under Frohman's direction, took the part of Lady Kate Fennel.

Ethel's first impressions of Maude are interesting. She described Maude as gay and friendly, noting that they spent some time together outside the theater. In one city they were visiting, Maude had noticed a photography shop and persuaded Ethel to have their picture taken. The photograph displayed two happy young women. Ethel also claimed that Maude often enjoyed attending Drew's after-theater parties.[23]

According to Ethel, Maude's new fame was closely managed by Frohman. "He was married to the theater," she reported. "He expected his actresses to take the same vow." Ethel recalled coming home after an evening out to find the door to the Adamses' room firmly shut. According to Ethel, Annie was serving as her daughter's supervisor. The gossip columns of the press jokingly nicknamed the boardinghouse "Maude Adams' Adamless Eden." Frohman was not at all pleased with such suggestive references to his budding star.

In contrast to Maude, Ethel was a socialite who was often seen at dinners and parties. Possibly, Frohman tolerated Ethel's socializing because it offered a dramatic contrast to Maude's reclusiveness.

After leaving Philadelphia, Frohman had the company set aside "The Bauble Shop" and perform "The Butterflies" instead. It was his belief that less sophisticated audiences would not respond favorably to "The Bauble Shop" but would prefer a more traditional farce comedy. As a result, Maude's appearances were greatly diminished, and she received scant attention. The company played one-night stands in Pennsylvania towns, on their way to Pittsburgh for a New Year's week engagement. On New Year's Eve, Drew held one of his familiar after-theater parties. Just back from a trip to Europe was Drew's close friend, Richard Harding Davis.

Davis was born in 1864, in Philadelphia, to a literary family.[24] After attending Johns Hopkins University, Davis began his career as a reporter in Philadelphia and then moved to the *New York Evening Sun*. Soon his articles and short stories attracted considerable attention, and his reputation as a writer of both fiction and current events was established. In 1890, he became managing editor of *Harper's Weekly* and initiated a series of foreign trips, reporting on current events, usually on regional wars. In 1894, Davis was splitting his time between jobs as foreign correspondent, reporting from the world's hot spots, and writing theater reviews for *Harper's*. To observers, Davis was a handsome, larger-than-life, outspoken personality, sometimes referred to as "journalist-of-fortune," who liked people and liked a good time. When Davis was in town, he enjoyed attending his friend Drew's parties and gave many of his own. It was at one of these events that he met Maude.

From Pittsburgh, the company jumped to St. Louis for a week, where they did good business at advanced prices. Then to Chicago, at Hooley's Theater, where they performed "The Bauble Shop." Results of the engagement were similar to those in New York and Philadelphia, where the theater "was filled completely by the fashionable set, and the star and play were equally well received."[25]

In Detroit, Cincinnati, and Baltimore, the company again performed "The Butterflies," to good crowds. Cincinnati experienced a snowstorm and business suffered. The blizzard also affected Baltimore; but, by week's end, the play was attracting excellent houses. When the company appeared in Brooklyn, "The Bauble Shop" was reintroduced. The same good business held true in Boston, where demand for tickets was so great, the company stayed for four weeks. Frohman visited the company in Boston. It was his desire to try "Christopher, Jr." again for a week, to determine its viability with Boston audiences, then finish the week with "The Masked Ball," as it had never been performed there. A cheerless company hastily went into long rehearsals to prepare the plays.

"The Bauble Shop" drew large crowds and good reviews; "Christopher, Jr." continued to attract large crowds but mediocre reviews; "The Masked Ball" attracted fine business. Boston's theater manager claimed that this was the most successful engagement ever for any company at the theater.

Still facing an already tired and disgruntled company were six more weeks of touring, made up primarily of one- and two-night stands through New England and New York, forty-eight performances in eighteen towns. They did "big business" at all of these stops but were nevertheless happy to reach Binghamton, New York, where the season ended on May 8. The relentless Frohman sent a message to the company telling them they were to report early in August to rehearse a new play.

Maude and Annie returned to their boardinghouse on Thirty-Sixth Street in New York City. While Maude was reported to be enjoying the sights of the city and attending the theater, Frohman was made aware of rumors that appeared in a local gossip column regarding Maude's supposed liaisons with other actresses. While he was unable either to verify or disprove them, he was disquieted by the implications such reports could have regarding his new star. Whether or not he confronted Maude with the information is unknown. Nonetheless, on June 28, the Frohman office released an announcement to the *New York Clipper* and the *Dramatic Mirror*, quickly picked up by the local newspapers. "It is reported that Richard Harding Davis, the author, and Maude Adams are engaged."[26]

It must have come as quite a surprise to Davis, who, although he knew Maude and had gone to parties that she also attended, had no romantic interest in her whatsoever. Still, the announcement conveyed to the general public that Maude was nothing less than a brilliant young actress involved in a close relationship with a well-known young man, with matrimony on the horizon.

At the time the announcement was made, Davis was on his way to another foreign country and never publicly alluded to the supposed engagement. Nor did the Frohman office ever mention the subject again. Maude retired from public view until rehearsals were called for Frohman's new production.

8

The Making of a Star

No sooner had John Drew arrived from his summer vacation in Europe than he began rehearsals for the season's new play, "That Imprudent Young Couple." Maude was seen waiting for him at the theater. Even though critics had not yet seen the play, they were already proclaiming it a success. With both John Drew and Maude Adams starring in a Frohman production, how could the play be anything but a winner?

Near the end of rehearsals, a confident C.F. invited reviewers to attend, so that they might prepare preview statements about the new play. The reviews were all quite positive, especially so for Drew and Maude. Now labeled a "most promising leading lady," Maude found her artistic endeavors lauded for their naturalness and irresistible sweetness. The play itself, however, was considered secondary to its co-stars; and because of that, Frohman thought it could easily end up being another short-lived production.

To gain some needed publicity and to sharpen the play itself, Frohman decided to send the company West, to San Francisco, for a four-week engagement. During the run, the company would introduce the new play and also include a repertory of all previous plays featuring Drew and Maude. San Francisco audiences had seen none of these plays, so full houses were almost guaranteed. The author of the new play also joined the company, to rework his script in anticipation of its New York debut. Rehearsals for the revised "That Imprudent Young Couple" would take place while the other plays were being performed.

The Drew Company opened at the Baldwin Theater on August 19, 1895, in "The Bauble Shop." The production was well received. "The house was crowded, the elite sitting in the front rows, and all were cordially friendly to the cast."[1]

Drew was recalled four times at the end of the second act. This act, featuring Drew and Maude, "was an artistic performance on both sides." "The Bauble Shop" was played to full houses for the entire first week.

"That Imprudent Young Couple" was introduced at the beginning of the second week. Claiming that the play seemed to have been written especially for Drew and Maude, which it was, one reviewer noted "it fit thoroughly." Nonetheless, although nicely received, the play itself was considered crude and ragged; "only being got into shape," declared the *Chronicle*.

Drew presented himself as a thoroughly attractive and agreeable figure and offered refined comedy business of which he had become a master. Yet, as witnessed by 'Frisco audiences, Maude seemed to upstage Drew because of her freshness.

> Nor do we recall other actresses who could make so light and dainty the part of the young wife as Maud Adams. She can do the ingenuous and girlish without being namby-pamby.[2]

Ethel Barrymore had a larger part in this play and was seen to be "amusing and attractive." Annie performed "as might be expected from such an experienced person."

Nevertheless, further work had to be done with the play. Its author was diligently adding and subtracting new dialogue as quickly as he could write it, much to the consternation of the actors, who were required to memorize new lines at each rehearsal.

The third week of the engagement consisted of "The Masked Ball," which made quite a success. The fourth week included a repertory of plays, beginning with "The Butterflies," then "Christopher, Jr.," ending with "The Bauble Shop." It had been an exhausting run, considering that five plays were presented and one of them continued in rehearsals. The final night of performance featured an S.R.O. house that gave extended ovations to both Drew and Maude.

The long train ride back East included further rehearsals for "That Imprudent Young Couple," which the cast was now calling "That Imprudent Script" because it had yet to be finalized. Frohman had the company stop in Syracuse for several days to perform the play before heading for New York. Everyone hoped that the play would be ready to face New York audiences and critics. Frohman, however, had his doubts.

"That Imprudent Young Couple" opened September 23, at the Empire Theater, to an audience full of anticipation and optimism.

The plot: John Annesley (John Drew) has met Marion Dunbow (Maude) at a resort. After a ten day's acquaintance, they marry without notifying their families. Annesley is financially dependent upon an uncle, Daniel Tobin (Harry Harwood), who is a foe of women and matrimony, yet to whose home Annesley takes his bride. Marion, under her mother's influence, had previously engaged herself to Langdon Endicott (Herbert Ayling). To Endicott and her mother she has now written letters announcing her marriage. Annesley has neglected to post these letters; and when the main characters meet, serious complications ensue.

Prior to meeting Marion, at the resort, Annesley had flirted with Katherine Kingsland (Ethel Barrymore). Katherine presumed upon their friendship to announce their engagement, which Annesley has quite forgotten, as he never considered the matter more serious than a summer flirtation. Annesley now discovers Endicott taking liberties with Marion and confronts him, declaring that he and Marion had exchanged vows the previous day. Meanwhile, Annesley's uncle discovers that Marion's mother (Virginia Buchanan) is his former wife, who has remarried. In anger, he cuts his nephew's allowance from $15,000 to $1,800. The mother-in-law, learning that her new son-in-law is now a poor man, becomes indignant and urges her daughter to break off the marriage. The complications are straightened out, and happiness and prosperity finally favor the "imprudent young couple."

While the author of the play was complimented for "furnishing entertainment to his audience," he was castigated for careless workmanship. "It is somewhat surprising," said the *Clipper* reviewer, "that with the trials already given it ... [such problems] should have been allowed to remain."[3] Again, a mediocre play had been made a success by its stars, although they too received indifferent reviews.

Regarding John Drew: "His performance lacked the polish which has made him a favorite."

Of Maude: "Maude Adams has a role that is far beneath her powers."

By the second week, reviews damned the production with faint praise. In spite of the adverse criticism, audiences accepted the play. Frohman, however, was not at all pleased with the result. For the third week of the engagement, the Drew company played "Christopher, Jr.," which made a hit, at least better than the previous play.

"Christopher, Jr." was now justifying Frohman's retention of it in the company's repertoire. For seven weeks, the play drew crowded houses and profitable box-office receipts.

During "Christopher Jr.'s" run, Maude celebrated her twenty-third birthday. After the November 11th performance, she was given a party and flowers by the cast. When asked to sing a song, Maude complied with the request, rendering, in a pleasant voice, a current number. The cast applauded in appreciation, and Annie beamed with pride at her daughter's popularity.

The Drew company's winter tour began December 2 at the Harlem Opera House. Frohman had ordered that only "Christopher, Jr." be performed on the tour, which included visits to seven cities, mostly in New England. The cast was not very enthusiastic with Frohman's edict; nor was Maude pleased, since her role in that play did not offer the opportunities she enjoyed in other plays in the repertory. Frohman, however, needed the potential profit from the play to pay off all its expenses, which were considerable. At the same time, he selected the work of another author to be performed by the Drew company when they returned from their brief tour. Quietly, "That Imprudent Young Couple" was unceremoniously buried.

On January 6, 1896, the company reappeared in New York, at Palmer's Theater (the Empire Theater was booked) in "The Bauble Shop." Simultaneously, the cast was put into rehearsals for "The Squire of Dames," a play Frohman wished to introduce in three weeks. The company was again thrust into a now familiar situation: one play was being intensively rehearsed while another play was being performed. To meet these increased demands, Maude's normal routine became almost a ritual. Early each morning, Maude practiced her part for the new play, the theme of this one leaning more toward fatefulness and pathos. On Sundays, she and her mother (Annie was not appearing in the new play) acted out the script, Maude her own part, Annie reciting all of the other parts, so Maude learned her cues and correct inflections of emotion. Generally, the cast itself was having difficulty integrating the new play because of its convoluted plot.

Frohman promised that "The Squire of Dames" would open after "Christopher, Jr." had played for two weeks. Advance sales for the new play were good; but Frohman, and the company, remained uneasy about managing the script.

"The Squire of Dames" opened at Palmer's Theater on January 20, enjoying what seemed to be immediate success, particularly for Drew. "His performance left nothing to be desired," reported the *Clipper* reviewer, "and it is likely that his Mr. Kilroy will win for him increased regard, and will be esteemed as one of his finest creations."[4]

The play was adapted from the French script of Alexander Dumas by R.C. Carton. It had been first produced in Paris thirty years earlier. At the time, the play was not a success, but it had won favor the previous year in a London revival. Carton was cited as having done an excellent job of adaptation, in which he retained the spirit and form of the original while, at the same time, eliminating the portions offensive to American audiences, that is, those related to sex and infidelity.

Mr. Kilroy (John Drew), the Squire of Dames, is a gentleman of wealth and leisure who has made the study of women his specialty. He is a close observer, a quick thinker, and a cogent reasoner. He retains a genuine desire to help those of his feminine acquaintances who desire the services of a sincere and discreet friend. Kilroy meets Adeline Dennent (Maude), a recently married woman, who has left her husband shortly after their marriage because of her revulsion upon learning of a prior indiscretion by the man she married. Kilroy meets her at a critical time, when she is yearning for sympathy and love. Indeed, she is even now being tempted and in danger of falling victim to a specious lover, one by whose attentions she would be compromised. The lover, Sir Douglas Thornburn (Arthur Byron), lacks both honor and discretion. Kilroy discovers the situation and, in spite of Mrs. Dennent's irritation at his meddling, declares himself her friend and guardian. He wins her confidence, saves her from error, and restores her to the arms of her husband. While engaged in this noble endeavor, he meets his own happy fate in the form of a wealthy American woman of spirit and worth.

The play was hailed as an immediate success by the *New York Times* critic. "After a single hearing here we have no hesitancy in saying that its success in this city is already assured."[5]

For her part, Maude received good notices for a touching portrayal.

> Maud Adams gave admirable shading to the role of Mrs. Dennant, and made us wait with sympathetic anxiety for the arbitrament of her fate. Her smiles, her sincerity and her innocence were all equally convincing, and altogether she suggested that she was worthy of the service of her faithful squire.[6]

What pleased Frohman was not only the unexpected success of the play, but also Maude's sophisticated and professional portrayal of Mrs. Dennant. She had proven that she could play pathos equally as well as comedy. He also noted the "electricity" between Maude and Robert Edeson, a young actor of excellent talent, another of Frohman's "finds." Together, Frohman mused, they could make a winning combination.

Prior commitments for the theater interrupted the five-week engagement for "The Squire of Dames." Frohman quickly booked the company into Philadelphia for two weeks and rented the Garrick Theater for another five-week run back in New York. He hoped that the play's initial success would not be dissipated. Of course, in Drew's hometown, the play generated crowded houses at every performance.

Heavy advance sales at the Garrick Theater persuaded Frohman to extend the engagement of "The Squire of Dames" for another four weeks, until the middle of April. There were no problems with audiences; they greeted the Drew company with approval. Wednesday matinees were added to accommodate the demand. Both Drew and Maude continued to receive rave reviews for their performances. Primarily due to Maude's outstanding triumph, Frohman initiated planning for her to become a future headliner of her own company, in her own play. It might take some time to find the right vehicle for Maude, but he was convinced she was ready and able to control her own destiny.

The company's next engagement was a four-week run in Chicago at Hooley's Theater. Since Frohman believed "The Squire of Dames" might be too sophisticated for Chicago audiences, he had the company play "Christopher, Jr." the first two weeks, before the new play was introduced. In spite of the impending end of the theatrical season, when audience attendance normally declined, reviewers called "The Squire of Dames" an excellent success, with the ability to continue playing several more weeks.

However, ticket sales for the third and fourth weeks declined, primarily because Sarah Bernhardt had come to town with a repertory of well-known scenes from her best plays. It was the first but would not be the last time that Bernhardt and Maude competed for patrons. In fact, one of Chicago's critics drew a direct and highly flattering comparison between the two actresses, calling Maude "a young Bernhardt." Reviews of her performances in Chicago tended to support his assessment.

One reviewer compared Maude's progress from the ingenue days up to her current sympathetic role.

> When one remembers Maude Adams in "The Midnight Bell," only six years ago, and studies the beauty, charm, sincerity, and correctness of her work in a role that unites comedy with emotions of that type that is gentle, and of which no woman need be ashamed, the conviction is forced upon one that Miss Adams has used her time well, that she must have studied with truth for a model and art as a guide. She plays the characters from within; and, whether she weeps or smiles, the spirit of the character is so well defined as to give the semblance of effortless endeavor in which the heart dominates the mind.[7]

The reviewer continued his analysis of Maude's acting by reporting her role as Mrs. Dennant in detail.

As Mrs. Dennant, Miss Adams is a young married woman separated from her husband and standing on the brink to which so many men delight to lead a woman in doubt. It is a blending of comedy and of serious thought. Miss Adams represents her with as great finesse as one finds in every phase of the art that has built this play. It was the most ambitious bit of work in which this gifted, young, and promising artiste-actress has ever been seen here. It was no easy task to assume a role so trying, so versatile in its moods, and so full of dangers to a girl who has played only the comedy heroines, but Miss Adams passed through the ordeals with success.[8]

The tour continued. When one-night stands were scheduled, the company performed "Christopher, Jr." When the company played a city for several days, both "Christopher, Jr." and "A Squire of Dames" were performed. In each city, they were greeted by enthusiastic audiences. Advanced prices did not seem to deter attendance.

In the middle of June, while working their way west, the Drew company visited Salt Lake City for three performances (two of which offered "Christopher, Jr."). As had occurred in the past, Maude and Annie were met at the train and given a loud and colorful welcome. The theater was filled nightly; and Maude received excellent reviews, leading the casual reader to believe that she was the real attraction and Drew only a convenient figurehead. In fact, in response to these chauvinistic comments, Maude was quoted as saying she had no sympathy for such "outlandish" statements, or their authors, since Mr. Drew was the headliner. That did not prevent local reviewers from calling the company "the best in the country" and Maude "the best in her line."

While in Salt Lake City, at a luncheon, Annie met Harvey Glidden, a prominent attorney and rancher from Jackson Hole, Wyoming. They were introduced by Joshua Adams, a cousin from Jackson Hole, who was in Salt Lake City visiting relatives. Joshua had persuaded Harvey, a widower at age thirty-five, to accompany him on the trip.

For the company's brief time in the Mormon city, Annie and Harvey became inseparable. When the company traveled to San Francisco, Harvey followed.

The tour ended in 'Frisco the following week, at the Baldwin Theater, where it had begun the season the previous August. The week's engagement was equally split between the two plays. But it was "The Squire of Dames" that audiences came for. Reviewers declared the play a "very decided success," particularly the acting of its principal characters. Drew received a large share of the accolades for his "manly and virile role, for no man else has the ease and refinement distinctly of high society and as a man of the world."[9] Maude was again lauded for her finely detailed, interpretive, and emotional acting. "A very notable figure among our actresses," wrote the *Chronicle* reviewer. He went on to discuss the specific features of her performance.

> If we are to go wild over natural acting, we should not find much better to gush about than that of this little Western girl who has a wider range of art than any but the rare geniuses. There is in Maud Adams the vibrant, spirituelle force that is found in great artists. Her figure is fragile, her voice is not strong, but the purely feminine music is in her laugh.[10]

Of Harvey and Annie, observers believed the two were in love, even though they had only recently met and Annie was thirteen years older. But bizarre things often occurred in the theatrical profession.

On the long train ride back to New York, a Frohman telegram informed the company that rehearsals for a new play, "Rosemary," would begin August 6. He sent along scripts for each member of the company to study.

Frohman had recently returned from a trip to England where, among other transactions, he had purchased the rights to a play written by James Barrie, "The Little Minister," from his book of the same name. It was Barrie's first full-length stage play, although he had already written a number of successful one-act dramas produced in England. Frohman had in mind to restructure the play to accommodate Maude's introduction to stardom. Barrie, however, believed it was almost impossible to change the play by making the play's original hero secondary to his wife.

Frohman invited Barrie to visit the U.S. in September for several months. The plan was for Barrie to obtain a better understanding of American audiences' tastes and the quality of American actors. While here, Barrie was also to rework his play as Frohman desired. Upon Frohman's announcement that he had secured the rights to the Barrie play, A.M. Palmer (owner of Palmer's Theater and also a producer) disputed the claim, revealing that he had purchased the book rights from the London publisher. After a series of mutual accusations of theft between the parties, Frohman went to court to clarify his ownership of the play. Since the British publisher did not own the play, and Frohman had purchased its rights directly from the author, the court confirmed that the play was his property. At the time, it was a common occurrence among producers to argue over the rights to a play because there were no effective copyright laws to determine ownership. Usually, it was the person with the most money who won court battles; and it was no different in this case. Yet, no one involved could have realized how significant this decision would be.

When Barrie eventually arrived in the U.S., Frohman immediately put him to work rewriting the play to feature a female star. Again, Barrie expressed considerable reluctance and doubt that it could be done.

Prior to Barrie's arrival, Frohman announced that "Rosemary" would open at the Empire Theater at the end of August. No out-of-town performances were planned to "finish" the play. Instead, Frohman had the scripts of two other plays available in case "Rosemary" faltered. To assist in "Rosemary's" success, Frohman used all of the promotional devices at his disposal to presell the play. He badly wanted to showcase Maude, to bolster his future plans for her. "Rosemary" was heavily reworked by its authors, Louis Parker and Murray Carson, to ensure that Maude would be compelling. And indeed she was.

Meanwhile, when the company returned to New York, Harvey Glidden followed several days later to continue his courting of Annie. On July 29, just over six weeks after they had met, the couple crossed the Hudson River into New Jersey and were quietly married. Whether she disapproved of her mother's decision or had not been told, Maude did not attend the ceremony. The newlyweds immediately left for Glidden's ranch in Wyoming.

Maude offered no explanation for her mother's behavior, or any opinion regarding the hasty marriage. Yet, Annie's actions must have surprised Maude as well as made her consider the implications of living alone for the first time, apart from her mother's supervision. Her confusion and concern were short-lived.

Less than two weeks after traveling to Wyoming with her new husband, Annie suddenly returned to New York, coincidentally in time for the beginning of rehearsals for "Rosemary." Apparently, Annie did not care for the isolation of living in Wyoming, or for being so far away from the theater and, very likely, her daughter. What Harvey might have done to cause the separation is unknown. Nor could Maude understand her mother's quixotic decision-making. Still, the episode had to have had some effect on her views toward close relationships with males in general and marriage in particular. Glidden did not follow Annie back to New York. Several years later, he filed for divorce, claiming desertion. Annie's actions were a disturbing episode in Maude's life; but, on the surface, they did not seem to distract her from preparations for the new play.

"Rosemary" opened at the Empire Theater on August 31, 1896. With the opening of the theater's doors, the S.R.O. sign was displayed. An attentive, fashionable audience was liberal with their applause, "most of which was fittingly bestowed."

The play was first produced by Charles Wyndham at the Criterion Theater in London on May 16, 1896. Its action begins in England at the time of the Queen's coronation. A chaise (coach) containing an eloping couple breaks down near the country residence of Sir Jasper Thorndyke (John Drew), a wealthy bachelor of forty. He gives the couple shelter in his home; and, when the parents of the girl arrive in pursuit, he receives them kindly as well. With persuasive words, he gains their consent for the marriage of Dorothy Cruickshank (Maude) and a young ensign, William Westwood (Arthur Byron). In the meantime, the young girl amuses herself by flirting with her host, which arouses the jealousy of her lover. In order to put everyone in better humor, Sir Jasper suggests a trip to London to view the coronation.

While in London, the group visits an old coffee shop in the Strand. Sir Jasper has lost his heart to Dorothy and, as she reads from her diary, he discovers that she regards him with much favor. He is tempted to win her for himself. His friend, Professor Jogram (Daniel Harkins), dissuades Sir Jasper, suggesting he conceal his love; and thus, he gives the young couple his blessing. Nonetheless, he buys the coffee shop, the scene of his abortive romance, and once a year returns to the room where his unrequited love first bloomed.

Fifty years pass. Sir Jasper again makes his annual pilgrimage to the old coffee shop. The occasion is Queen Victoria's Jubilee Day. As the ninety-year-old man sits bowed, he babbles on about the old days and his departed friends. A heavy pull at a bell causes a panel to crumble from the wall and discloses a hand-written note. It is a leaf from Dorothy's diary, which he had pushed into a crevice in the wall. Slowly, the memory of her suffuses him. She has been dead for many years, but he takes from his wallet a sprig of rosemary she had given him fifty years before. Sir Jasper ponders all that might have been had fate been more kind.

The *New York Clipper* reviewer called the play "charmingly idyllic."

> The atmosphere is perfect and the literary quality of the word is of the highest. Its dialogue is sprightly, humor and and pathos are judiciously blended, and the character drawing is true, varied, and sharply defined.[11]

The *Times critic* was equally affirmative. "There's fun in it and nice sentiment and pretty pictures, all painstaking and credible."[12]

Drew received his usual share of compliments, particularly his portrayal in the last act of the distracted old gentleman, his emotional passages rendered so tactfully and brilliantly.

Interestingly, the feminine reaction to Maude's role as Dorothy Cruickshank caused a decided difference of opinion. One side claimed that no such girl as Dorothy ever lived, none so naive and ingenuous. The other side believed that Dorothy was simple and silly, but good and real. In any case, Maude's role was lauded, her "shading exquisite with a delicate and delicious charm."

Ethel Barrymore's part as an impressionable sewing maid showed promise, but it did not justify the loud applause her friends in the audience gave her. Annie's role, as Mrs. Cruickshank, Dorothy's mother, was mentioned in the program only. It would be the last play that Annie shared with Maude. Frohman believed that Maude no longer needed Annie for support, a position with which, he felt, she sincerely agreed. Instead, he promised Annie that she would appear in other Frohman productions.

Upon his outstanding success in "Rosemary," Drew agreed to another three years as Frohman's leading man. Instead of introducing another play, Frohman announced that Drew would appear in "Rosemary" for the entire season. By the fourth week of the engagement, the house was filled to capacity at each performance, and a Wednesday matinee had been added. Fifth week reports said Drew's role "was the best he has ever played here." Seventh week results indicated that the house remained full and Frohman announced that the play would likely continue through the remainder of the season.

In dramatic fashion, Frohman also acknowledged that the rumor circulating in newspapers was true: that Maude would be leaving the Drew company at the end of the season to star in a new play, as yet not decided upon. Several weeks later, in a premeditated public relations ploy, Frohman announced his willingness to guarantee American dramatists $10,000 in royalties for a proper play in which he could star Maude Adams. This was reported at the same time that James Barrie, now in the U.S., was already laboring over his script for Maude.

During "Rosemary's" tenth week at the Empire — still high in "popular esteem" — Frohman told the press that Ethel Barrymore had been selected as Maude's understudy, a significant move coming after his affirmation of Maude's future plans. Interestingly, this would be the only time in Maude's entire acting career that she had an understudy for her role. Without an understudy, if Maude were forced to miss a performance — by illness, for example — the show would be closed.

Crowds continued to fill the Empire at the seventeenth week of "Rosemary," while advance sales guaranteed several more weeks of performances. As part of Frohman's campaign to promote Maude's new enterprise, he reported that her "starring tour" would begin in early September, 1897, and that she would arrive in New York in October. "She will open in a new play," Frohman stated, "which is yet to be written." Meanwhile, Barrie's struggle to revise "The Little Minister" continued with little success.

On December 1, the 100th performance of "Rosemary" was a gala evening, the stage filled with floral bouquets (delivered after the performance), speeches by the primary performers (all but Maude), and souvenirs for patrons. The *Clipper* noted: "The play has won enduring regard by absolute merit, and its success should prove gratifying to all who hope for the reign of cleanly and wholesome drama."[13]

"Rosemary" played in New York until December 26. Frohman expressed delight with the financial results from the play but even more with the acclaim his two stars, John Drew and Maude Adams, had received from both critics and audiences. It certainly assured him of their future success, although new plays had not yet been decided upon for either of them, let alone found. It was an unaccustomed dilemma for a producer who normally planned productions a year in advance. He did announce that Robert Edeson, the young and handsome actor who had recently played opposite Maude, would be her leading man the following season. Of even greater significance was his reference to the new production as to be performed by the Maude Adams Company.

After leaving New York, the Drew company visited Baltimore during New Year's week, to great success, then moved to Boston for a three-week engagement. Reports

from first-nighter critics at a theater filled to capacity hailed the show. "Enthusiastic plaudits prevailed throughout the evening expressing appreciation of the excellence of the play and the artistic manner of its presentation."[14]

Again, the wholesomeness of the play resonated with critics.

> "Rosemary" is dainty, wholesome and refined, and will be welcomed as a refreshing contrast to the sensational melodramas, the morbid problem plays and the unhealthy sociological studies which crowd the modern stage.

When Robert Edeson, another of Frohman's discoveries, was selected to play opposite Maude in her debut as a starring actress, the *Clipper* gave him front page coverage. He was a handsome, earnest actor, and he and Maude made an attractive couple.

Maude could not have found a better role to play. "Much of the applause," wrote the *Globe* critic, "was intended for Miss Maud Adams, a dainty, winsome little woman in a role so thoroughly congenial."

There was no question that Maude was being identified with clean and refined plays, a likely Frohman objective. This kind of careful play selection would continue during coming years, thereby further enhancing Maude's piquant, innocent, ingenuous, and natural stage persona. It was what she did best, and audiences loved her all the more for it.

Providence offered "the largest and most fashionable houses of the season," as did Washington, D.C. In February, the company played Philadelphia for three weeks, where Drew not only attracted capacity houses, but also spent his days as a guest at numerous luncheons to honor "the local hero." To maintain full houses, "The Squire of Dames" was performed the final week.

During the Philadelphia run, Drew and Maude appeared at a benefit in aid of the children's ward of the Medico-Surgical Hospital, where they put on a program of a one-act play, "Too Happy by Half," and the second acts of "The Geisha" and "A Contented Woman."

The company returned to New York in late March for a week at the Harlem Opera House, which became a record-breaking week for the theater. On the road again to Pittsburgh, where they had a "brilliant engagement," then Columbus, Ohio, at "S.R.O.," and on to St. Louis, attracting "excellent business." Audiences were anxiously awaiting "Rosemary" when the company arrived in Chicago for a two-week run.

The play achieved immediate success. Drew was cited for his grace and finish, his stardom continuing "in the ascendant." Yet, it was Maude who received the greater acclaim from reviewers.

> Miss Maude Adams achieved a triumph as the fascinating, ingenuous Dorothy Cruickshank. Her naivete is delightfully winsome, while her sincerity is charming in its convincing power. She was a dainty stage figure in her quaint, old-fashioned gowns, and she revealed the heart of a girl with the graces of nature and art that was at once dainty, delightful, and satisfying in all its varied phases. She captured the audience, heart and hand.[15]

The two-week engagement at Hooley's Theater in Chicago created a financial record. Frohman could only smile at the reviews Maude received for her performances. "As fresh as a rosebud," said the *Daily News*. "Like out of a Charles Dickens novel," wrote another. "Thoroughly permeated with the manner of the time," reported the *Chicago Tribune*. No question in anyone's mind that Maude was ready for stardom. Now all Frohman needed was a play that would give Maude the opportunity to display the fill range of her talent.

The close of "Rosemary" in Chicago was also the end of the company's season and the end of Maude's affiliation with the cast. After nothing more than a few warm good-byes and good-lucks—Maude would have it no other way—she and her mother returned to their boardinghouse in New York. Maude now had only to await Frohman's call to discuss the beginning of her new career.

Meanwhile, James Barrie continued his labors attempting to reshape "The Little Minister." As he had expressed the problem to Frohman, he did not see anyone who could play the part of Babbie, the minister's wife and now the leading lady of the play. One afternoon, Barrie was waiting in Frohman's office for C.F. to return. "Why don't you stop in downstairs and see 'Rosemary?'" suggested Frohman's secretary.[16]

"All right," said Barrie, no doubt eager for any break from his fruitless labors.

He went down into the Empire Theater and took a seat in the last row. An hour later he came rushing back to Frohman's office, found him in, and exclaimed, "Frohman, I have found the woman to play Babbie in 'The Little Minister!"

"Who is it?" asked Frohman, though he knew without asking.

"It's that little Miss Adams who plays Dorothy."

"Fine," said Frohman. "I hope you'll go ahead now and finish the play."

Between 1892 and 1897, Maude co-starred with John Drew in five plays. Praise for her acting increased with each. At twenty-five, she was ready to star on her own, even if she did not realize it. Frohman was confident that she was ready to dominate the dramatic stage. (California Historical Society, FN-23016)

9

The Little Minister

The fall of 1897 was a pivotal point in Maude's career. Her five-year association with Charles Frohman, who served as her mentor, had now prepared her for stardom. J.M. Barrie's play, "The Little Minister," was to become the vehicle for her astounding "overnight" success. This was the moment when three remarkable personalities—Charles Frohman, J.M. Barrie, and Maude Adams—began a friendship and professional association that would profoundly influence American theater for the next twenty years.

James M. Barrie was born in Lily Bank, Scotland, on May 9, 1860, the ninth of ten children.[1] As a child, he was of average height, with a slight frame and fine features. Little James was a sensitive child who quickly demonstrated an impish liveliness. He enjoyed childhood pastimes like any other boy of his age, particularly fishing, a hobby he carried into adulthood.

His parents came from educated backgrounds and believed all of their children should, likewise, be educated. From an early age, James liked to listen to stories and invent them himself. His interest in settings, characters, and situations had a strong influence on his later writing career, especially when dealing with the lives of the common people living in Scotland. At school, during these early academic years, he was a better than average student, particularly in composition, for which he gained honors.

In 1872, he was enrolled at Dumfries Academy, similar to American middle and high school, and was quickly identified by the faculty for his writing skills. James was soon submitting stories for the school magazine and preparing sports reports. He joined the dramatic club as an actor but found writing plays more to his liking. Several of his plays were performed by students of the academy.

In 1878, James entered Edinburgh University, with a special interest in journalism. His academic work was exemplary and won him high honors. Enlisted as a member of the debating society, he became known for his humorous monologues. Yet, public debating was a trial for him because of shyness. The fact that he seemed indifferent to friendships and was quite reserved tended to isolate him from his fellow students. Instead, James became a writer for his college literary magazine and had many stories published. He received his degree in 1882, with the sole desire to begin his career as a journalist. His first job was as drama critic for a local newspaper, *The Daily Courant.*

A year later, young James Barrie obtained a job at a small Nottingham newspaper as lead writer. He was paid three pounds a week, barely enough to cover his food and housing. Although he worked long hours at the newspaper, he still found enough time to write short stories, many of which he submitted to London periodicals. In late 1884, his first article appeared in a London publication. That success was followed by articles published in the *St. James Gazette* and *Home Chimes*, a weekly. Nine short stories were published in 1885, all of them humorous, all laid in the rural society of Scotland. His stories offered a light-hearted view of life, while giving common experiences a comic twist.

Encouraged by his short-story successes, Barrie decided to move to London to seek his career as a free-lance writer. While gaining a reputation as a

Already renowned in England as an exceptional novelist and playwright, James M. Barrie prepared "The Little Minister" to highlight Maude's acting skills. He wrote seven other plays for Maude. They had a longstanding professional association although it may have been more than that for Barrie.

humorist, he began experimenting with book-length fiction. Late in 1889, Barrie joined the staff of the *British Weekly* and became its most frequent contributor. His first book, "Better Dead," was called a "shilling shocker" (for the price of one shilling a reader could purchase a horror story). Barrie's second book, "Auld Licht Idylls," received good reviews; and he gained recognition as a respected author of Scottish themes.

Barrie's third book, "When a Man's Single," showed he was also a master of pathos and an acute observer of the larger and more obvious aspects of life. By 1890, he was included with Robert Louis Stevenson and Rudyard Kipling as the best among young British writers. His next book, "A Window in Thrums," used the Scottish dialect heavily; it was a mixture of realism and romanticism, coupled with humor and sentiment that seemed to attract readers. The book was introduced in the U.S. and received a good reception. Another book, "My Lady Nicotine," on the pleasures of smoking (Barrie switched from cigarettes to a pipe while writing the book), became a good seller in both England and the U.S.

In 1891, Barrie wrote "The Little Minister" in serial form; it was later published as a full-length novel. Reviewers noted his talent for giving sympathetic characterizations and descriptions of personal emotions. About this time, Barrie became interested in writing plays and turned a number of his short stories into short plays, some of which were accepted for the stage. In 1893, he wrote a comic opera that appeared at the Savoy Theater, but was considered a failure by critics. Unfortunately, during this period Barrie suffered from a series of respiratory illnesses. In early 1894, he became very ill. Doctors diagnosed pneumonia, a disease that could easily have been fatal. His nurse of several months ultimately became his wife; they were married in July 1894.

Barrie's fateful visit to the U.S. came in late 1896 when he wished to clarify a number of copyright problems with American publishers, particularly with Scribner's, the firm that sought to publish a collection of his books. His most recent play, "The Professor's Love Story," had done poorly in London but proved quite successful in the U.S. It was during this time that Barrie met Charles Frohman.

Frohman encouraged Barrie to rewrite his novels as plays, starting with "The Little Minister"; but Barrie expressed reluctance at the project, believing that U.S. audiences would not be interested in rural Scottish people speaking local dialects. Frohman's insistence, however, persuaded Barrie to "give it a try."

When Barrie discovered Maude, he believed he had found the actress to play Lady Babbie, the heroine of "The Little Minister." Shortly after submitting the script to Frohman, Barrie returned to England. He never saw Maude rehearse the play or perform it, but the letters and copies of the play's reviews he received from Frohman spurred him to initiate other projects specifically for Maude. The outstanding success of "The Little Minister" would splendidly compensate the Frohman-Barrie-Adams combination.

Rehearsals for the new play began early in August. Although Barrie was not in New York, he and Maude communicated about various aspects of the play. Maude made dialogue suggestions to enhance her role. She also involved herself in production values, particularly lighting, which Maude believed needed modification to feature the leading performers more clearly. Actually, Maude was almost as involved in the production of the play as she was in the acting of it.

For example, several scenes took place in wooded areas, where normal lighting could not adequately penetrate the dark scenery. Maude had the stage and fly lights realigned from the sides and rear of the stage, so performers would be highlighted. She found that costumes of certain colors did not display the leading actors well enough, so she changed their texture to improve the lights' reflection.

Maude's greatest challenge, however, was to learn to speak her lines with the appropriate Scottish dialect, neither so decided that audiences would be unable to understand her, nor so weak as to make it seem she was uncomfortable with the language. Few American plays featured the use of foreign dialects, and both Barrie and Frohman were seriously concerned about how audiences would respond. From the opening curtain, they would be required to interpret what was being said. Maude worked daily on the dialect she planned to use, to make sure it did not in any way interfere with the dialogue's emotional impact.

Following what had now become her working method, Maude attempted to insert herself into the mind of the audience. She devoted many weeks to the study of the Scottish dialect. She even introduced Scottish domestic activities into her daily life. One member of the cast humorously suggested that Maude, while rehearsing to gain increased realism, had put herself on a diet of Scotch broth.[2]

By the final rehearsals of the play, the cast had been so well trained by Maude to render their Scottish characterizations perfectly, that even they were amazed at the end result. After he witnessed the rehearsal, an impressed Frohman told Maude that whatever she needed to improve the play, if she believed such improvement was necessary, she had his authority to do as she wished. It was a license rarely given by a producer, even to a director, let alone to an actor. Yet it was obvious to Frohman that Maude had mounted an excellent production. And she was only twenty-five years old!

"The Little Minister" opened at the Lafayette Square Theater in Washington, D.C., on September 13, 1897. Maude had two weeks of performances to sharpen the play prior to opening in New York. Frohman attended opening night to observe how the audience responded to Maude and this unique play. From the very first scene, he was convinced the play would be a hit.

Since the play was reported to be a sizable departure from the usual drama of the day, a *New York Clipper* reporter covered the opening. Afterwards, he dispatched a glowing report to his editors. The article appeared in the *Clipper's* next edition, alerting New York readers that a theatrical triumph was coming their way.

> Maude Adams commenced her starring tour, under the management of Charles Frohman, last night under the most auspicious circumstances, making her first appearance in J.M. Barrie's own dramatization of his well read novel, "The Little Minister." Miss Adams success was instantaneous and complete, and the large, fashionable and representative audience repeatedly gave expressions of approval of both the star and play. Curtain calls for Miss Adams were frequent. Manager Charles Frohman, who is here attending the performance, has staged the play in a manner that evokes loud words of praise.[3]

Not all critics agreed with the *Clipper* reviewer. One believed the story was pretty but quite weak. Another suggested the "superabundance" of Scottish dialect mitigated against the play's thorough enjoyment because the audience was "not well up in the peculiarities of the language." Attendance during the latter part of the week's engagement declined.

The following week, at Baltimore's Nixon and Zimmerman Academy, the opening again garnered good reviews—"Miss Adams was warmly welcomed to the stellar ranks"—but critics again identified the dialect as a detriment to the play. One reviewer recommended that it be eliminated altogether.

Nonetheless, while Maude made some minor changes in the dialogue, she refused to disturb the use of the dialect in any way. Frohman concurred, although he now seemed a bit unsure how New York audiences would respond.

When a number of New York newspapers reported that Maude Adams was about to make her debut as a star actress at Frohman's Empire Theater, they suggested that it was going to be a somewhat risky venture, due to the uncertain conditions of theatrical affairs, a phrase the precise meaning of which was left unexplained. Judging from the comments, it seemed that critics were dubious about the combination of a new leading actress and an almost unintelligible dialogue. Yes, they admitted, Maude had personal charm and sensibility. Yes, she possessed a style all her own. But, they wondered, would her talent be up to the standard demanded by the role?

On opening night, September 27, a standing-room-only crowd filled the theater to witness Maude's stellar debut. The *Clipper* reported that the production had been introduced two weeks earlier in Washington, D.C., where it had received favorable reviews, yet the "measure of success then achieved gave no cause for anticipating the ovation which awaited Miss Adams in this city."[4]

Frohman had warned Maude that she should not be taken by opening applause. He offered her an anecdote about a lion tamer who, when he walked up Broadway, was disconcerted by the noise and crowds. He quickly retreated to the circus to sit in the cage with the lions, where it was safe and quiet.

Frohman pointed out to Maude that, previously, she had felt safe with John Drew next to her, to save her if needed. Maude admitted that it would be hard facing a New York audience on her own and felt a "fright creeping over me." In fact, she was so nervous that on opening night she arrived at the theater two hours early. Frohman was already there, ready to calm her nerves. He stood by her in the wings before she went on stage. Once she spoke her first lines, she was in command.

Upon entering the stage, Maude received a standing ovation for two minutes, as Frohman had predicted. At the close of Act I, she was recalled four times. Enthusiasm for Maude blazed even more strongly as the play progressed. At the end of Act II, she was recalled ten times. At the conclusion of the play, Maude broke down crying when she left the stage, all but swooning into Frohman's arms. He helped her recover enough to make her first curtain call. In fact, there were so many curtain calls that Robert Edeson, Maude's costar, complained his arm grew tired from leading Maude to the footlights. Finally, she was urged to go on stage alone; but Maude hesitated. The stagehands had to shove her on stage. All in all, Maude made twelve curtain calls and a short speech before the audience was sufficiently satisfied to leave the theater.

> Miss Adams possesses, as did Babbie, the heroine of the play, that witching power of beguilement that captivates the heart and makes impulse usurp the place of dethroned and banished judgment.[5]

In other words, Maude had magnetized the audience and captured them as few other actresses could have done. The *Clipper* critic went on.

> Miss Adams has been endowed with two gifts invaluable to an actress, brains and temperament, and by means of these she legitimately won her triumph.

Audiences quickly realized that the play bore little resemblance to Barrie's book, which many of them had read several years earlier. As in the book, Gavin and Babbie

Maude became an overnight success with the role of Lady Babbie in "The Little Minister."
One reviewer supposed that she might become "a popular idol." She was a dramatic star
for more than twenty years. (San Francisco History Center, San Francisco Public Library)

were hero and heroine. In the play, however, Babbie dominated the plot. Many per-
sonages and incidents from the book had disappeared. Babbie was now the daughter of the local lord, not his ward and affianced wife. Somber and dark moments had
been omitted altogether, replaced by Barrie's characteristic "sunshine" and humor.
Nonetheless, the new play seemed more cohesive than the book.

The first scene takes place in Caddam Wood, where Lady Babbie (Maude), disguised as a gypsy, surprises Gavin Dishart (Robert Edeson), the little minister, on the road. There has been trouble between the weavers of the town and the soldiers. A warning signal would alert the weavers to the approach of the redcoats. Babbie persuades the minister to give the signal. Thus, a confrontation ensues, Gavin on one side, Babbie on the other. Babbie, hooded and cloaked, passes through the soldiers' lines, announcing herself as the little minister's wife. Protecting his beloved, he offers no words of denial. She easily makes her escape.

When Gavin goes on a mission of charity, he meets Babbie at an old nannie's cottage. At the cottage, their conversation reveals to Babbie that Gavin is in love with her. Gavin is later found following the gypsy girl, and they share a love scene. Yet, Gavin's parishioners disapprove of Babbie and express sorrow that the minister is paying attention to a gypsy, thus, making a fool of himself.

The action carries the lovers to the castle of Lord Rintoul (Eugene Jepson). There, Lady Babbie is revealed in her true character as the daughter of Rintoul. The minister is completely taken aback, since he thought she was a gypsy. The pair declare their love and ask her father's consent to their marriage. Lord Rintoul, however, has other plans for his daughter, wanting her to wed someone of higher standing. In defiance, Lady Babbie insists that Gavin shall acknowledge her as his wife, just as he did the night in Caddam Wood. Based on this previous commitment, by Scottish custom, Gavin is already wedded to Babbie. They are later officially married; but only after Babbie has coaxed her father out of his rage, into good-humored consent to her marriage.

Yet, had Maude really won the hearts and minds of critics and the audience? Beyond the changes between book and play, duly noted by critics, and the overwhelming response Maude had received on opening night, some critics censured the audience for its apparently insincere applause, enthusiasm almost to the point of hysteria. Critics believed that the audiences' approval had been clouded by Frohman's aggressive promotion. Only future performances, they insisted, could reveal the truth of the viability of the play and its star. "As for Miss Adams, she must wait to know how she is going to be received by the public."[6]

Even given the initial reactions to Maude and the play, Frohman was convinced it had gone well. Intensely nervous about seeing the reviews in the morning papers, Maude was up all night. The following morning, when she and Frohman met, he said warmly, "I'm very proud of you." As Maude wept in relief, Frohman read the reviews to her. Her anxieties relieved, Maude went home and slept. Surprisingly, the use of dialect was not even mentioned by the critics.

By the second week, even the most obdurate critics had changed their views, having nightly seen Maude repeat her triumph to packed houses. "She is now firmly entrenched in her new stellar position," said the *Clipper* reviewer, "and is likely to become a popular idol."

The *New York Times* critic now elucidated his belief that Maude had, with each performance, entranced and captivated audiences.

> Very charming was this Babbie, with her swiftly changing moods, her rippling laughter, her demure sarcasm, her spontaneous humor and her gentle womanhood. No man of one and twenty could resist such beguiling, nor would many older heads and hearts be less in jeopardy.[7]

Now that the production had been favorably reviewed and Maude was being acknowledged as his new "find," Frohman's convictions were confirmed. With two weeks of performances behind her, Maude now seemed remarkably calm and self-assured. Yet, in spite of her obvious success, there was no question of her commitment to improve her artistic efforts. Each day followed a specific ritual: arise by 10:00 A.M.; a light breakfast; practice of the lines she believed needed strengthening; a full lunch, followed by rehearsals with the cast; a light dinner; a walk through the empty theater before retiring to her dressing room, where she reclined, almost in meditation, before applying her makeup and putting on her costume. As she waited in the wings for her cue to enter, Maude appeared solemn, as if in a trance. Upon entering the stage, the carefree, flirtatious gypsy girl emerged.

At the end of the show, Maude would leave the theater unnoticed, enter a waiting taxi, and return to her Thirty-Sixth Street residence. Rarely was this routine disturbed, except when Maude believed a certain scene or part needed improvement. She also continued to work on the stage lighting to obtain better effects.

During the fifth week of "The Little Minister," Frohman was forced to move the play to the Garrick Theater, due to prior commitments for the introduction of John Drew's new production in New York. The move did nothing to diminish the play's popularity. Maude's brief engagement at the Empire Theater was reported to have been the most profitable ever played at that house.

Robert Edeson and Maude found their pictures on the front cover of successive issues of the *New York Clipper*. Edeson's background was discussed, and his choice as Maude's leading man "furnished abundant proof of his fitness for this responsible position." Maude's entire performance history was clearly embellished, and her affiliation with Frohman considered the catalyst for her current success. As an odd addition to her biography — a likely attempt by Frohman to shape Maude's public persona — it was stated that her success had "in no way spoiled her. She delights in study, and gives much attention to the harp and banjo and to the acquisition of the French language."[8] An astute reviewer mused about where the "stage" Maude ended and the "real" Maude began.

On December 3, Maude and John Drew agreed to perform a one-act play for an Actor's Fund benefit staged at the Knickerbocker Theater. Before an audience made up almost entirely of stage performers, the two former partners received particular recognition. As Drew pointed out to Maude, when "your own kind" give their blessings, you know you have joined the ranks of headliners.

Advance sales at the Garrick were so promising that Frohman announced "The Little Minister" would play the entire winter and that another play fashioned for her (there was none) was to be delayed indefinitely. As the play continued to attract capacity audiences through December, Frohman canceled Maude's upcoming tour (none was planned) and lengthened her stay in New York until spring. The 100th performance of "The Little Minister" occurred on December 22, and souvenirs were given to the audience.

In December, upon hearing of the continued success of his play, Barrie wrote a letter to Maude wishing her a happy Christmas and thanking her for doing "so much for me."[9]

> I only wish I could come in person to tell you how I delight in your success and to see the delicious things you do with Babbie of which many tell me with enthusiasm.

Barrie closed his letter with an adoring comment.

> Please give our kindest regards to Mr. Frohman and accept our assurances that you are the nicest girl in America, with our warmest good wishes.

Maude cherished this letter and retained it as an important keepsake among her personal possessions. It was a fitting tribute to conclude an auspicious year.

In the middle of January 1898, Frohman cheerfully announced that Maude would remain at the Garrick for the remainder of the season, likely playing to June. He also pointed out, for all newspapers and critics to remember, that " 'The Little Minister,' which has been the most conspicuous success of the season, is perfectly clean in theme and treatment."[10] It was just a gentle reminder to the press and public of how Frohman ran his business. Not two weeks later, unfortunately, Frohman was stricken and hospitalized with what doctors reported to be a congestion of the spine. The illness would keep him off his feet for several months; but it did not curtail his daily activities, only his place of business. Maude visited him several times a week to keep him apprised of the production.

By the end of February, Maude was into the twentieth week of her engagement, playing nightly to the capacity of the house. Seats were being secured four weeks ahead; and when seats for March were put on sale, the first day's receipts amounted to more than $6,000. When critics returned to view Maude's performance, they came away with the sentiment that she was even better than she had previously been. The dialect used in the play was now considered an amusing touch to an overall enjoyable experience. Not even the Lenten season, notorious for diminishing theater attendance, reduced the house. The 200th performance of "The Little Minister" was given March 19, with the distribution of red roses to all women in attendance. (Maude used a red rose in one of the play's scenes.)

Advance sales for the month of May guaranteed almost S.R.O. at every performance as Maude began the thirtieth week of her engagement. At the 250th performance, Frohman announced that Maude would appear for 300 and then end the season in July. A week later, however, Frohman told the newspapers that, since Maude was in need of rest, her season would close June 14. Actually, Maude confided to Frohman that she was having problems sleeping, the rising tension of continuous performance now causing some distress. She reduced rehearsal time and rested several hours before each performance, but these slight changes in routine did not seem to lessen the incipient tension.

For the 300th performance of "The Little Minister," Frohman had the play moved back to the Empire Theater and prepared a gala ceremony for this milestone in theatrical longevity. Seats were sold at advanced prices; yet scalping was rampant, no matter how many police Frohman stationed outside the theater. Scalpers just moved down the block where they continued to accost theatergoers.

In typical Frohman fashion, the house was lavishly and handsomely decorated with plants, flowers, bunting (the colors of England, Scotland and America), and electric lights. Even backstage, the surroundings were festive; and Maude's dressing room had become a bower effusive with floral offerings. The house was filled "to the rafters," each seat commanding a high premium. In fact, there were more patrons than souvenirs; and many in the audience had to be content with cards entitling them to a souvenir upon later presentation. The gifts commemorating the occasion were small American flag pins of gold, set with red rubies, white rhinestones, and blue sapphires.

The enthused audience was exceptionally demonstrative throughout the performance. At the close of the show, they remained in their seats until Maude, after ten curtain calls, came forward and spoke a few words of thanks for their appreciation of her efforts, then quickly bade them good night.

Maude had played "The Little Minister" for thirty-seven weeks and two nights. The 300 performances in New York alone grossed more than $370,000, an unprecedented financial, as well as artistic, triumph. For James Barrie, the overwhelming success of his play provided him royalties of $2,000 a week, making him a very rich English author. Maude had been paid $500 a week, or more than $18,000 for the season. For her next season, Frohman promised a substantial raise; but Maude refused. Instead, she proposed that her salary remain the same but she be given a percentage of the gross profits. Unhesitatingly, Frohman agreed to her terms. Maude also requested that she be allowed to have more control over production features, to which Frohman also agreed.

For the summer, Maude found a cottage in the Catskills, where she could rest and enjoy the natural surroundings. During this time, her mother joined her.

Rehearsals for the second season of "The Little Minister" commenced in early August. With Barrie's agreement, Maude made some minor changes in the script and modified the Scottish dialect so that audiences outside of New York could comfortably understand the play's dialogue. Although Maude had asked Frohman to replace Robert Edeson — his amorous feelings toward Maude seemed to be extending beyond the stage — Frohman did not want to jeopardize the on-stage rapport they conveyed to audiences. He instructed her to avoid Edeson offstage, which advice she apparently carried out in diplomatic fashion. This season, "The Little Minister" would be on tour to all the major eastern and Midwestern cities, and a few smaller towns that happened to have large theaters. All tickets would be sold at advanced prices, with box seats at two dollars each.

Maude's company opened at the Wieting Opera House, Syracuse, New York, on September 7, to an S.R.O. house. What followed was a week of one- and two-night stands through the state of New York, all of them to large audiences and excellent reviews. Apparently, adjustments to the play's dialect had been sufficient to satisfy audiences, since no one complained of any difficulty in understanding the dialogue.

The company arrived in Boston for a planned two-week engagement that was extended twice to the middle of November because of the strong demand for seats. Reviewers remarked how Maude's acting had affected audiences. "The young actress has made a pronounced hit and has taken the audience by storm and, they, in turn, have taken her into the warmest corners of their hearts."[11]

Henry Austin Clapp of the *Boston Advertiser*, one of the country's most renowned and ill tempered critics, bestowed considerable praise on Maude.

> It is doubtful if Madam Bernhardt or Adelaide Neilsen ever encountered in this highly cultivated city an enthusiasm more demonstrative than that which was excited last evening by Miss Adams' impersonation of Babbie. It was hard to keep count of the number of her calls to the footlights, and at the close of the entertainment the curtain was lowered and raised some eight or ten times for her appearance.[12]

The *Boston Globe* was even more flattering, as it described the audience's reception for Maude throughout the performance. Similar to the show's opening in New York, the audience overflowed with exuberance and fervor.

> The enthusiasm of the brilliant gathering was really remarkable, perhaps unrivaled in the annals of this theater. The storm of applause which broke forth when the young actress made her appearance grew in intensity until it reached the proportions of a cyclone of approval, and the calm came only when sheer exhaustion compelled the audience to stop applauding. After every fall of the curtain there were demonstrative demonstrations of delight which caused the curtain to be raised again and again, and at the conclusion of the performance the charming actress was recalled to bow her acknowledgements times innumerable.[13]

Seated in the audience at one of the performances was fifteen-year-old Phyllis Robbins, who immediately fell in love with Maude's performance, so much so that she returned to see Maude a second time. Phyllis was born on January 27, 1883, the fourth and last child of Royal and Mary Robbins. Royal Robbins was a watch manufacturer and long-time resident of Boston who had amassed a sizable estate due to his successful business. The family lived on Commonwealth Avenue, in Boston's Back Bay neighborhood, known for its stately homes and elite society.

At the time, Phyllis could only admire Maude at a distance. It would be another two years before they met. That personal encounter would initiate a friendship that lasted until Maude's death and beyond. Three years after Maude died, Robbins wrote an adoring biography about their relationship. What little in ephemera Maude possessed at her death was given to Robbins, who, in turn, donated the material to the Harvard Theater Library. Whatever Maude did that captivated audiences captured Phyllis even more deeply, and her admiration for the actress was unbounded.

From Boston, the company traveled to Providence, which proved to be the biggest week of the season for the Providence Opera House. Their opening in Brooklyn was delayed several days because the company became snowbound in New Haven. Still, the almost three-week engagement was a sellout. "Maude has captured Brooklyn," reported the *Clipper*.

While in Brooklyn, Maude had the opportunity to visit with Frohman, still recuperating from his illness but now doing so from behind his desk at the Empire Theater. Maude sought to convince Frohman to allow her to produce and act in a Shakespearean play, namely, "Romeo and Juliet." Maude firmly believed she had the ability to undertake Shakespeare, and the role of Juliet was her choice. While Frohman was not against the proposal, he pointed out to Maude that the role she aspired to would be quite controversial. Several famous actresses, including Mrs. Sarah Siddons, Ada Rehan, and Sarah Bernhardt, had already interpreted the role. Frohman warned that critics would compare Maude to these actresses and assess her every move and phrasing. He questioned whether she could handle the criticism that was bound to occur, let alone the controversy that might ensue. Of course, she also had to consider her growing reputation; it could very well be compromised by playing a role critics believed was beyond her at this point of her career.

Nevertheless, Maude persisted. Every actress brought her own interpretation to the role of Juliet, she noted, and she was no different. Indeed, Maude believed she held an advantage, being younger than her precursors, much closer to Juliet's actual age and, therefore, better able to interpret young love and pathos. Maude also believed that her acting experiences during the previous years had prepared her for a part that demanded a combination of piquancy, innocence, femininity, and compassion. Frohman could not argue these points, although he remained concerned about the critics' reactions toward her bold endeavor. He agreed to star her in the play and promote it heavily, with one proviso. "The Little Minister" was still in great demand. The play could tour successfully for at least another year. A run of "Romeo and Juliet" would have to be brief, so that Maude could soon return to her role of Babbie. Maude readily agreed, knowing that no matter how well Shakespeare might be performed, its audiences were limited. She was aware that her desire to play Juliet would be controversial, but she expressed a strong determination to accept the challenge. It would entail matching her interpretive efforts against critics, audiences, and comparisons with other actresses that could very well transform the euphoria of playing Shakespeare into an acting nightmare.

When Frohman announced that Maude was to appear as Juliet, critics and theatergoers alike were first taken by surprise. Almost immediately, opinions about her ability, experience, and her possible interpretation of the role filled the newspapers. The controversy surely helped the enterprise by creating interest in the project; but it also revealed the barriers that Maude would have to overcome to win the minds of doubters.

Maude would open "Romeo and Juliet" at the Empire Theater on May 8, only a short while after the conclusion of her second season with "The Little Minister."

The logistics meant she would be required to rehearse Shakespeare at the same time she was touring the Barrie play. How, critics wondered, was a young and relatively inexperienced actress going to handle that situation?

"The Little Minister" opened in Philadelphia for the Christmas and New Year's holidays. Advance ticket sales were so vigorous that the three-week engagement was extended to six. Knowing the length of her stay in Philadelphia and seeking the quiet needed to rehearse Juliet, she rented a home on Delancy Place, thereby avoiding crowded and noisy hotels and restaurants. Her retirement from the public eye did nothing to diminish the demand for Babbie.

> The success with which this offering has been credited in other cities has been duplicated here, houses overflowing in size and enthusiasm. The production is all that could be desired — a strong cast and effective scenery, and at the head of it all, the bewitching personality of the star.[14]

At the end of the six-week run, the *Clipper* reported that Maude "finished her engagement in a blaze of glory." Not missing a promotional opportunity, Frohman then announced in the Philadelphia newspapers that Maude would be returning soon in her new production of "Romeo and Juliet."

The next month included visits to Washington, D.C., Baltimore, Pittsburgh, Cleveland, and Chicago, the latter for a six-week stay at advanced prices. Judging from the newspaper coverage, Maude's appearance was highly anticipated.

> The advance sale is breaking all precedents, so far as Chicago is concerned, and it will be surprising indeed if Miss Adams does not duplicate in every way the great prosperity which she enjoyed in New York last winter.[15]

The omnipresent Amy Leslie, veteran theater critic of the *Chicago Daily News*, wrote about Maude's opening in terms that extolled her acting ability, seemingly beyond that of any current actress. Leslie predicted that Maude "will be popular probably as long as she lives."

> Miss Adams is a frail, spiritual girl of delicate perceptions and exquisite intelligence; she knows so well her own resources and the nightly demands of her ambitions that her modest, girlish understanding lends the most winning touch of sincerity and simple truth to herself and her hopes. Her talent is exquisite and her temperament flawless in its magnetism, her eyes lustrous and face alight with expression.[16]

In her review, Leslie mentioned that, with salary and a portion of the box office receipts, Maude would be earning close to $50,000 for the season, a phenomenal income for any performer at the time. "She has the mental grace to completely know herself," Leslie went on, "and that is her most delightful quality as an actress." Patron response further demonstrated Maude's success by filling the theater at every performance during the entire engagement.

A newly mobile Frohman traveled to Chicago to watch Maude perform but primarily to discuss with her the plans for "Romeo and Juliet." He brought copies of paintings from the Luxembourg Museum, Paris, from which Maude could select the scenery, and drawings of costumes for Maude to choose from. Frohman told Maude he had engaged William Faversham to play Romeo (a risk, since he too had little experience with Shakespeare) and veteran James K. Hackett to play Mercutio (an excellent choice, if his voice could hold out). Others in the cast were to come from Frohman's stock of players.

Still, this was to be Maude's own production, with Frohman giving her full discretionary power. Interestingly, at the same time that "The Little Minister" was drawing full houses in Chicago, just down the street, Julia Arthur was reviving "Romeo

An accomplished rider, Maude admitted to being frightened by horses. In this photograph, the young actress displayed a confidence beyond her years. (Photo: Pach Bros. 1896. Museum of the City of New York. Gift of Mrs. Frederick R. Brown. 37.298.72)

and Juliet" with some success, although this was her first attempt at a Shakespearean play. Maude attended several of the matinees to study the production and Arthur's interpretation of Juliet. Arthur was a year younger than Maude but played the part of Juliet as a mature woman, similar in her choice to others who had played the role.

The last performance of "the Little Minister" at the Powers Theater was a gala occasion. Manager Powers filled the theater with flowers, garlands of evergreens festooning the galleries, the rails of boxes abloom with spring flowers, bouquets of hyacinths, azaleas, tulips, and daffodils suspended from the ceiling. Members of the audience wore their most elegant fashions. Even before the first curtain, Maude was called to the stage to receive a standing ovation. The *Inter Ocean* declared that "although it was her 549th performance in the heroine's role, her Lady Babbie never seemed more spontaneously humorous and charming."[17]

Following the show's closing, Frohman sent a cable to all local newspapers, thanking the theatergoers of Chicago for their enthusiastic acceptance of Maude and "The Little Minister." "I congratulate the citizens of Chicago and thank them sincerely for their courtesy to my star during the past six weeks," Frohman wrote.[18] A significant feature of Frohman's success as an impresario was that he never forgot who bought the tickets for his plays. Besides, Maude would be returning to the city in several weeks with her production of "Romeo and Juliet."

Trenton, New Jersey, was the season's last performance for "The Little Minister," a one-night presentation that generated, according to the local newspaper, the "largest business of the season." Maude then announced she would begin formal rehearsals for "Romeo and Juliet" upon her return to New York. She had two and a half weeks to "finish" the play.

About the time Maude arrived in New York, newspapers were featuring articles with headlines such as "Maude Adams In Gold." The story was told that Maude had inspired her "gold mining admirers" in Salt Lake City to undertake a project to sculpt a life-size statue of her in pure gold and present it at the 1900 International Exposition in Paris. It was estimated that the design and casting in gold bullion of the statue would be valued at $346,000. At the close of the exposition, the statue would be returned, melted down, and turned into coins. The proposal got as far as the U.S. Congress, which supported the idea. However, the French governing body for the exposition refused the offer, saying that the statue of an actual individual (an actress, no less) was not in keeping with the theme of the event.

A brief note in the press mentioned that Maude had just purchased a small farm on Long Island, near Lake Ronkonkoma. It was the first tangible manifestation of her exceptionally profitable season.

10

Testing Her Skills

Prior to Maude's return to New York, "Romeo and Juliet" was being rehearsed in two sections. One portion of the cast, including Faversham and Hackett, was working in New York under the supervision of William Seymour, Frohman's stage manager. The other section was rehearsing with Maude while on tour. Seymour visited both venues continuously but found it hard to integrate the material. Only when Maude arrived in town did the play begin to take shape. After Seymour had the opportunity to work with Maude, he came away quite impressed with her new ideas and work ethic. "Miss Adams has opened a new and wonderful field for me," he told Frohman. Frohman, however, was not entirely pleased by Seymour's recently acquired enthusiasm. It suggested to him that, while Maude might have been constructing an appealing play, she might also have been taking too many liberties in her interpretation of Juliet.

Visiting rehearsals, Frohman was reassured that the play was going well and that Maude's Juliet would be both appealing and romantic. His primary concern had to do with Maude's ability to perform tragedy, that particular Shakespearean form of tragedy that combined honor, love, and death.

Throughout all of Maude's stage experience to date, comedy had been her primary acting style. In several instances, she had shown that she could portray pathos. But pathos was not tragedy, and Frohman wondered whether Maude was able and seasoned enough to handle the difficult assignment. While Maude had long desired to play tragedy — actors believed it was their most momentous career impersonation — neither her mother nor Frohman had given her the opportunity. Now, given the chance, Maude found herself struggling with the complexities of Shakespearean drama. Frohman noticed it as well. No question in his mind that Maude had staged the play well. Yet, she did not seem to be displaying the same spontaneity, naturalness, and humanity that she had in her previous roles. The role was going to be an interesting challenge, Frohman believed, and, he hoped, not a personal setback. He liked "Romeo and Juliet" and intended to support Maude's venture. The play could prove quite profitable, although Frohman seemed to care little about any financial rewards it might bring. "Romeo and Juliet" was as much a personal venture for him as it was for Maude.

Maude herself was concerned about her acting. She admitted to Frohman that she was not entirely confident of being at her best in the role of Juliet; still, she promised to work hard to master it. Maybe it was the short rehearsal time; maybe it was the combination of hero (Faversham) and heroine (Maude), neither of whom had any real experience with Shakespeare; maybe it was Maude's own insecurity in pushing her acting skills beyond her experience. Despite all these possible dangers, Frohman nevertheless opened "Romeo and Juliet" at the Empire Theater, May 8, 1899. As Frohman had anticipated, the play produced its share of praise and criticism.

Comments made in anticipation of Maude's appearance demonstrated how interested both critics and audiences were in her Shakespearean debut. Critics acknowledged that Maude was "now the most popular actress in this country." Nor did they have any dispute regarding her artistic intelligence and personal charm. Yet, critics cautioned about praising Maude's portrayal of Juliet until she had actually performed the role. Could she really handle a role that demanded extraordinary skill and power? That doubts already existed about her formidable task would make it all the more difficult for Maude to win the critics' approval.

There were no com-

Performing Juliet was a risky choice for Maude, but she took the challenge despite having had little experience with Shakespearian tragedy. According to critics, the result was mixed. This did not prevent her from continuing to interpret Shakespeare during her career.

parisons afforded for "The Little Minister"; Maude had set the acting parameters herself. In contrast, comparisons abounded for "Romeo and Juliet." The play's familiarity, along with favorable interpretations by some of the theater's most distinguished actresses, left Maude open to critical evaluations and opinions. She was compared to Julia Marlowe and Helena Mojeska, the late Adelaide Neilson, Margaret Mather, and, of course, the great Sarah Bernhardt. Critics opined that Marlowe fell short in parts of the play, Mather had force without power, and Neilson only generated harsh criticism. On the other hand, Ellen Terry and Bernhardt set such high standards in the role of Juliet, who could possibly match them? Maude's challenge could be almost overwhelming. Yet, in contrast to this critical debate, all the seats for the sixteen performances at the Empire Theater had been quickly sold.

As reported by the *Times* reviewer, audiences seemed to be infatuated with Maude's interpretation of Juliet.

> Maude Adams acted Shakespeare's Juliet for the first time in her life at the Empire Theater last night. The immediate result was a prodigious triumph. At the hands of an audience of extraordinary quality, the young actress received a mighty tribute.[1]

The reviewer also praised Maude for her sincerity and simplicity, free from affectation and extravagance, fervent and affecting, sustained by "a natural eloquence of speech, gesture and facial play."

At the same time, however, he stated flatly that "the manner of classical tragedy is not in Miss Adams's equipment." The reviewer pointed out that Maude's strength in the early acts, particularly the love scenes, was touching and charming. It was the later scenes, the parting with Romeo, in life and death, where Maude faltered. "Dramatic genius has not yet reached her," he declared. Her acting in the latter scenes of the play was called unconventional, almost too realistic for the grotesque horror as conceived by Shakespeare.

Faversham was said to have done an admirable piece of acting as Romeo, from the discreet balcony scene to killing Tybalt with vehemence. Hackett was condemned for his lack of elocution and his portrayal of Mercutio as "a raw boy." The production itself was praised for being remarkably tasteful for its pictorial excellence.

The *Clipper* reviewer offered a different view of Maude's performance. The audience was seen as enthusiastic, perhaps overly enthusiastic, compared to what the performers accomplished. Yet again, the reviewer questioned the audience's response, saying its apparent lack of discrimination seemed to make it insincere. (The same reviewer, on the occasion of Maude's opening night for "The Little Minister," had chastised the audience for the same reason.)

Nevertheless, it was a night of triumph for Maude, "and her laurels were as fairly won as they were modestly worn."[2] This reviewer, as well, believed Maude's performance to be different; but he lauded her for it.

> Miss Adams gave us practically a new Juliet, and while she by no means made us desire to forget those who had previously charmed us in the role, she made an impression that we will always cherish.

Her Juliet was rich in those personal charms which have won for this winsome little woman our affectionate regard; simplicity, tenderness, modesty, sensitiveness and
unaffected grace of speech and manner.

Instead of suggesting that Maude's later scenes were flawed, the *Clipper* reviewer
acknowledged her lack of physical force but claimed that she had chosen her method
of acting and "her success must be measured by her fidelity to her ideal." If she did
not appeal as much to the mind—a reference to Shakespearean purists—she surely
reached the audience's heart.

Faversham's acting was considered conventional and not well-suited for the role.
Hackett was a capable Mercutio who met the requirements of his role, prevented from
being great due to his gravelly voice.

When the curtain fell on the first show, backstage was bedlam, the noise and
activity from all those involved in the production expressing their relief from the
strain of the play. Members of the cast were hugging, shaking hands, and thanking
one another for their efforts. Frohman was there to take congratulations and share
them with his stars. Bowers of flowers filled Maude's dressing room. The *Herald*
reporter somehow got in to obtain some comments from Maude.

"I was as nervous on the first night I played Babbie," Maude said. In answer to
the reporter's probing questions, Maude responded, "Yes, I really believe I was more
nervous. This is almost like another debut for me, you see, for Juliet is totally different
from any of the roles in which the public has been accustomed to see me."

"I was very nervous all day, so nervous I was at the theater and made up for my
role an hour before the performance began," she revealed. "It must have been a severe
hour for Mr. Frohman, who had to keep chatting with me to brace me up."

"Then the applause which the audience so generously bestowed on me when I
appeared first. It almost stunned me!" Maude said. "But with the first word I spoke,
I was all right. It was just that way with 'The Little Minister,' scared half to death
when in the wings waiting to go on, myself once more as soon as the cue came."[3]

John Drew, David Belasco, and William Gillette were the first people backstage
to congratulate Maude. Cablegrams were waiting from Sir Henry Irving and James
Barrie. In Mrs. Cornelius Vanderbilt's entourage was Mrs. Antonio de Navarro—for-
merly Mary Anderson—one of the most accomplished Juliets America had produced.
Upon entering her dressing room, Maude was met by Mrs. de Navarro, who took
her in her arms, kissed her several times, and showered her with compliments. Along
with Mrs. Vanderbilt were many of New York's social elite, who also rushed to congratulate Maude. When Frohman was asked his opinion of the backstage tumult, he
said amusingly, "We have been living on chicken sandwiches the last two weeks. We
now hope to be able to dine."

All in all, Maude had totally won her audiences. The critics, however, gave her
mixed messages. She received plaudits for her professional effort and unique interpretation, but they raised misgivings about her ability to present a tragic figure. Although
Maude took these comments seriously and spent the next two weeks working to better

express the heroine's misfortunes, the critics' judgments did not change. They had declared their opinions about Maude's performance and would not be convinced otherwise.

Nonetheless, the Empire continued to attract S.R.O. crowds at every performance; and patrons came away totally charmed by Maude's romantic rendition in her now familiar style. It became a common occurrence for Maude to have ten to twelve curtain calls at the end of each evening's performance; finally, she sent the audience home with a short speech of thanks.

During the entire time Maude appeared at the Empire, critics argued about her interpretation of Juliet. It was as if each critic attempted to outdo his or her colleagues by demonstrating knowledge of Shakespeare and how each wanted the role of Juliet to be performed, an intellectual debate that seemed to go far beyond the relevance of Maude's role. Generally, Frohman was satisfied with Maude's acting but agreed that she had not yet achieved the expertise required to perform tragedy. Maude herself believed she could have done better. But no one could argue with S.R.O. houses and excellent box-office receipts.

Maude embarked on a short tour, traveling on the special train Frohman had provided her, with visits to Boston, Philadelphia, Providence, Brooklyn, Pittsburgh, Buffalo, Cleveland, and Chicago for week-long engagements; one-night stops in Rochester, Syracuse, Albany, Springfield, Hartford, and New Haven. "Romeo and Juliet" would be performed in fifteen cities in six weeks, forty performances in all. Production for the play was reported to cost $30,000, an exorbitant sum for any play at the time and especially so considering its short run. Yet, Frohman grossed more than $137,000. Because of the special arrangements for the presentation, Maude received almost $3,500 a week salary, plus a percentage of the receipts. Still, it was a strenuous tour for her.

First stop of the tour was Boston, at the Hollis Street Theater. Prior to the opening, the *Boston Globe* gave its readers a first-hand account of Maude's New York performances. Audiences gave her "a great wave of popular approval," the *Globe* reported, "but critics had engaged in a lively war" over Maude's rendition of Juliet. Advance sale of seats was said to be "phenomenal."

No matter how much audiences adored her, Boston critics did not care for Maude's interpretation. Yes, the young actress won a great triumph "if success is to be gauged by tumult of applause," they said. Nonetheless,

> [the play] was a new and wholly unconventional creation, one that defied all tradition of the stage and absolutely ignored the cherished ideals of the Shakespearean student.[4]

The *Globe* critic attributed Maude's success to her reputation with audiences rather than her "inherent greatness." Sarcasm about Maude's Juliet abounded. A characterization more for the general public than for those knowledgeable about Shakespeare, said one reviewer. An innovation that can do no possible harm to dramatic art, said another. Some reviewers pointed out that a few of the more difficult lines had been omitted so as not to tax Miss Adams beyond her resources.

Romeo (William Faversham) and Juliet in love. The critics believed Maude's love scenes were not delivered nearly as well as her scenes of girlish pathos.

No matter the debate and open criticism of her acting, Maude filled the theater to capacity each evening, leaving audiences enthralled with her Juliet. It continued in all other cities on the tour. Audiences cheered Maude from the moment she entered the stage until her final curtain calls. Critics, however, argued the merits of her interpretation, the majority agreeing that she failed to adequately give expression to the character.

In Chicago, it was Maude's personal popularity that overshadowed the play.

> The house was packed to the doors with a sweltering crowd, which was so demonstrative, despite physical discomforts, that the star was brought before the curtain a score of times.[5]

One reviewer gave Maude a rare compliment, stating that "a modern age demands a modern production," and that "Maude should be praised for her efforts." Several others, however, insisted that "the woman who excels in comedy should not attempt a tragic part."

When Maude left Chicago—and the end of the Shakespearean tour—local newspapers reported that her personal popularity was greater than ever, in spite of their differences as to the merits of her Juliet. Summing up "Romeo and Juliet," the *New York Clipper* told of the play's surprising financial success, but the consensus of the critics' opinions concerning the play resulted in a verdict where "the weight of numbers and of authority were unfavorable to the new creation." Nevertheless, Maude should be pleased, they said, for the high esteem in which she was held.

> The outpouring of the people everywhere was a tribute tendered to her gentle womanhood and blameless life, an ovation to a woman within whose frail frame reigns indomitable will and dauntless courage, a woman who has shown the best traits of sturdy Americanism and who is a type of all that we most admire and revere in womanhood.[6]

The article sounded like a news release from the Frohman office. Nonetheless, it summarized audiences' views as to what made Maude so endearing. Still, the critics pleaded with Maude, saying, "Don't do Shakespeare again; please, for our sake."

Maude did agree that she "might have been better than I was."[7] The venture had been an experiment and a challenge. She might not have been ready for Shakespeare but, Maude promised herself, she would be soon.

Maude's summer consisted of purchasing two properties, a cottage in the Catskills, which she named Caddam Wood after the location in "The Little Minister," and a home on Forty-First Street in Manhattan. Rest and relaxation meant furnishing these homes to her desires. Frohman had informed Maude that Barrie was writing another play for her. For the coming season, however, she would return to the now familiar and popular "The Little Minister." Maude was slated to start the season on the road, then return to New York at Christmas to introduce Barrie's new play.

Maude's season was scheduled to open in early October. It had to be delayed two weeks due to a case of the grippe, a respiratory infection that forced her to bed during rehearsals. Actually, little had to be done in preparation for the play. No changes in the script, scenery or costumes; the cast remained the same; and travel would again be undertaken in the comfort of a private train.

"The Little Minister" opened the 1899-1900 season in Syracuse on October 18, at the Weiting Opera House. Maude delighted "a large and enthusiastic audience."

Maude's cottage at Onteora Park, in the Catskill Mountains, was her retreat where she studied and planned plays. One large room was configured as a stage to practice her roles. A
few years before she died, Maude donated the cottage to the Cenacle religious order. (The
Harvard Theatre Collection, The Houghton Library)

A series of one-night stands culminated in Wilkes-Barre, Pennsylvania, where the
audience nearly rioted in their attempt to see Maude.

> For this show it was announced that checks would be given out at 8 A.M. and tick-
> ets sold on the checks, in regular numerical order, at 9 A.M. At 3:30 A.M. there were
> boys in line in front of the theater waiting for the box office to open. When the doors
> were thrown open fully 300 were in line. The rush was so great the giving out of tick-
> ets was discontinued. A cordon of police were unable to control the people. At 11 A.M.
> every seat was sold, the prices the highest of the season; and not half of the people who
> desired to go had tickets. Manager Burgunder at once telegraphed Mr. Frohman ask-
> ing him to play a matinee in addition to the night performance. A favorable reply came
> speedily and at 3:30 P.M. every seat of the house had been sold for the matinee. Throngs
> were turned away.[8]

In Brooklyn, audiences' response to Maude was no different. "The house was
packed to the doors," declared the reviewer. "She is a prime favorite here, which was
evident by the spontaneous outburst of applause and the many curtain calls she
received." In Newark, advance sales ensured S.R.O. for the entire week. Much to
Maude's surprise and embarrassment, the Newark Theater management presented
her with a silver service on the evening of November 11, to celebrate her birthday.
"How old are you?" the audience shouted. "I'm twenty-seven years old," Maude
shouted back; and the audience cheered her for several minutes.

As observed by reviewers in all the cities, there was no question in anyone's mind that Maude remained a star, in spite of the controversy inspired by "Romeo and Juliet." In fact, it seemed that Juliet had been completely forgotten when Babbie took her place. Yet, Frohman showed no hesitancy to publish a volume entitled "Maude Adams Acting Edition of Romeo and Juliet." Ornately bound and illustrated, it was filled with photographs of Maude and lines from the play. "Equally worthy of a place in a collector's library or upon a young lady's table," declared a promotional piece for the book. The book sold out in a matter of days.

Although "The Little Minister" had played in Philadelphia the previous season, the two-week engagement again filled the theater to capacity, "duplicating last seasons' success." A first visit to Cincinnati became an unqualified triumph. "'The Little Minister' was presented to audiences of magnificent proportions, and at every performance curtain calls ran closely to the dozen mark."[9]

Detroit generated crowded houses for the week. Christmas week was made up of one-night stops, Toledo on Christmas night "to very large and enthusiastic audiences" and Indianapolis on New Year's Day "to the largest in history of the house."

Frohman had originally planned to have Maude return to New York for the holidays to open a new play, but her continued success with "The Little Minister" changed his mind. Maude would now play for the remainder of the season on tour. The canny producer could not ignore the financial rewards being reaped by this play and its bewitching star.

At the beginning of 1900, Milwaukee was visited, with advance sale of tickets already over $4,000, an extraordinary amount for any city. In spite of tickets' costing two dollars, the Davidson Theater was filled at every performance. Maude was tendered high praise from reviewers and many curtain calls from audiences each night.

Much to her surprise, Maude was abruptly called back to New York by Frohman to play "The Little Minister" at the Criterion Theater for an indefinite stay. Not only did Frohman want to take advantage of the play's significant popularity, but also a New York run offered him the opportunity to make several cast changes. Due to Maude's prodding, Robert Edeson was replaced by Orrin Johnson, a veteran Frohman stock company actor. Maude had been feeling more and more uncomfortable in her love scenes with the ardent Gavin (Edeson). Frohman also introduced new scenery. The original scenery had become shopworn due to its continued use on tour, and cast members had been joking about the shabbiness of Lord Rintoul's Castle. "He (Rintoul or Frohman) should be able to afford new furniture and rugs," they suggested. "Maybe we should take a collection from the audience." Obviously, Frohman received the message. No play of his would ever appear shabby.

New York's opening night for "The Little Minister" was no different than it had been originally. Audiences were vigorously enthusiastic. This time, however, critics did not comment on the audience's behavior, except to say that patrons greeted Maude as a welcomed star. "The charm of Miss Adams' acting in this role is, indeed, irresistible. And in no other role has she exerted so strong a spell upon the public."[10]

In a subsequent article, the *Times* critic wrote about the features that he thought made Maude's acting in "The Little Minister" so successful. His insights revealed important aspects of her emerging talent at this point in her career.

> Miss Adams is an artist of really uncommon gifts.... Her most striking artistic trait is her absolute simplicity and naturalness of utterance.... Her greatest charm lay in the effect of sincerity she secured.... Her facial expression is often admirable and never excessive.... She has a keen sense of artistic proportion.... Her voice has a quality of its own.... There is never a hint of the conventionally theatrical in her poses and gestures.... She can express the sentiment that hovers on the borderland between laughter and tears with irresistible effect.[11]

In summary, the critic believed that Maude was a surer actress than she had been two years ago; and he predicted even greater improvement.

During the fourth week of the engagement, Frohman announced that Maude's stay would be limited to eight weeks, since she had been committed to visit a number of other cities before the end of the season. Managers in these cities had petitioned Frohman because of the revenue potential such a visit offered. A new play, of course, was unnecessary, since no new play had even been considered by Frohman and Maude. Local newspapers repeatedly informed readers that the amount of time remaining to see Maude was rapidly dwindling. In mid-March, when Maude began her eighth and last week at the Criterion, she had passed the 800 performance mark, a New York record for any legitimate play. To date, "The Little Minister" had been presented to over a million and a half people, earning gross receipts of over $1,500,000.

Prior to leaving the city to complete her tour, Maude discussed with Frohman the play in which she should next appear. Frohman suggested a new Barrie play. "After all," he noted, "he is writing the play just for you." Maude, however, had recently been studying the work of Edmond Rostand — he had gained major playwright status with his stirring and imaginative "Cyrano de Bergerac" — and she wished to try his new play, a story of the sickly child of Napoleon who attempts to learn statesmanship from Metternich at the same time he is dying. Frohman was dubious. He pointed out that Maude had just returned to stardom after having stumbled with tragedy. Worse, Bernhardt had originated the role in Paris just the previous season. It would surely mean the undertaking of another venturesome role. And, besides, Maude would be playing the part of a boy!

In spite of Frohman's arguments against the play, Maude convinced him she was able to accept the challenge and unafraid to deal with critical debate. She truly believed that audiences would understand and applaud her work. Compared to Bernhardt, Maude would give the ill-fated hero the youthfulness he deserved. Maude also believed she could lend the role the necessary pathos and tragedy it required, thanks to her experiences as Juliet.

Frohman finally acquiesced, albeit reluctantly. He would feature Maude in Rostand's "L'Aiglon" (The Eaglet); but if the play failed, Maude would perform in the Barrie piece Frohman had already bought from the Scottish author. Frohman quickly purchased the American rights from Rostand and commissioned Louis N. Parker to adapt the play in English. In early April, he publicly announced that Maude would appear in "L'Aiglon" next season. Her appearance as a boy would demonstrate her artistic versatility, he said. She would study the part for many weeks.

Almost immediately, critics questioned what Maude and Frohman were attempting to do by presenting another risky production. They still believed that Maude was not yet ready to take on such a demanding role. And they predicted shock among audiences, who, after enjoying the carefree, innocent, yet womanly Babbie, would now be faced with a masculine youth entangled in the complexities of French politics, carrying the name of Napoleon to a premature death.

No one thought or cared to mention that, given the more than 800 times Maude had played Babbie, she might have become bored with the role. Surely, the longer she performed it, the more laborious and difficult the role became. Again and again, she had raised the curtain, although her interest in the play had doubtless diminished: speaking the same lines, experiencing the same feelings, eliciting the same laughter, the same applause, bowing to the same curtain calls, and endeavoring to show the pleasure of it all. It was more a wonder that she had played the role so long while remaining the perfect Babbie to the end. Lewis Strang, a theatrical historian and biographer of the stage's best performers, claimed to have noticed a decline in Maude's recent performances of "The Little Minister." Such lapses were not easily noticeable, he said, but they were, nevertheless, a loss due to boredom.[12] No question in his mind, Maude needed a fresh challenge; and she would likely have agreed with his observations, given the opportunity.

Now presenting what were billed as "farewell performances" by the Frohman office, Maude began a two-week engagement at the Hollis Street Theater in Boston. Although she had appeared there in the same play for eight weeks the previous year, advance sales guaranteed full houses for the brief run.

> Lady Babbie received a welcome so cordial that there need be no fears about the regard in which she is held by Bostonians. The theater was filled and the audience was as demonstrative as any star could reasonably wish.
> Lady Babbie, as depicted by Miss Adams is singularly attractive, and will live long in the memory of the playgoer who has witnessed the beautiful stage creation.[13]

It was during this engagement that Maude met Phyllis Robbins for the first time. Thanks to Phyllis's aunt, she was brought backstage after a matinee, her first view "behind the scenes." At the time, as Phyllis later described herself, she was shy, in awe of Maude, rather plump, and with a stammer. She was further taken aback to see firsthand that Maude did not actually resemble Lady Babbie. Over tea, Maude talked about Scottish pronunciation, giving examples of what the authentic dialect sounded like, compared to how Americans used it. Maude was cordial to the almost speechless Robbins. Indeed, their meeting began an increasingly close friendship between the teenage girl and the already famous young actress.

HOLLIS
ST. THEATRE.
ISAAC B. RICH......Proprietor and Manager

BEGINNING TOMORROW. MONDAY EVE'G,
FOR
12 EVENINGS,
4 MATINEES.

"A TRIUMPH FOR PURITY IN THEATRICALS."—New York Herald.

CHARLES FROHMAN
- Presents-

Maude Adams

In Positively Her
FAREWELL APPEARANCES
As "LADY BABBIE" In J. M. Barrie's
THE
Little Minister

"MISS ADAMS' ART IS UNIMPEACHABLE."—New York Herald.

EDITORIAL IN N. Y. EVENING JOURNAL.
"Miss Adams' Theatre is packed. Men and women are glad that they took their daughters there. They go again and again."

When Miss Adams next appears in Boston it will be in a new play.

EVENINGS at 8.
WEDNESDAY and SATURDAY MATINEES at 2.

SEATS ON SALE FOR BOTH WEEKS.

Why had Maude befriended Phyllis? In her book, Robbins offered some possible reasons: she may have appealed to Maude's mothering instinct; she did not appear to be stage-struck; her New England upbringing may have struck a sympathetic cord.[14] Or could it have been Maude's particular interest in seeking friendships with young women? Possibly, Maude saw in Robbins her own lost youth.

From Boston, the company traveled to Chicago, another city that had seen "The Little Minister" before. Nevertheless, the return engagement represented substantial financial gain. As in Boston, Maude's appearances were promoted as farewell performances: "she will never again be seen in Chicago as the heart-winning, fascinating, elfish Babbie."

Suffering from a bad cold, Maude made a brave attempt to rise above her illness and entertain an audience sympathetic to her condition. Her voice was dry, sometimes breaking; and her eyes were obviously affected by the stage lights. But it mattered not.

> This amiable young woman is a sure box-office attraction and her following seemed not at all vanquished by her affliction. She is charming and immensely attractive and she is more beloved of refined women and youth than any actress on the American stage.[15]

Although Maude played her role with verve, a reviewer felt that she was "wearying a bit of Babbie" and her illness seemed to make her more nervous. Actually, Maude had been ill twice during this tour and was having increasing difficulty sleeping, possibly a factor

The Hollis Street Theater, in Boston, was one of Maude's favorite places in which to perform. Admirers jammed the theater during her engagements and demanded dozens of curtain calls at every performance.

contributing to her nervousness. It was becoming obvious to Maude that fatigue and stress were likely responsible for these ailments and they signaled the urgent need for rest.

On May 4, after brief visits to Kansas City and St. Louis, then a long jump to Buffalo for a three-day engagement, "The Little Minister" ended its long run in Bridgeport, Connecticut. A very tired company packed their bags and went home with a minimum of goodbyes and the usual tearful separations associated with the close of a season. The run of 841 performances had been a magnificent achievement; and the success of the play, both financially and critically, would not be overshadowed for years.

Six days later, Maude boarded a ship bound for the continent. Her itinerary was to include London, Paris, and Vienna. Maude's first stop was Vienna. She wished to see for herself the places where the young Duke of Reichstadt had lived and obtain a better understanding about this mysterious character she was about to impersonate in "L'Aiglon." She visited his home in Schoenbrunn. While it exhibited beautiful surroundings, Maude felt it had been, nevertheless, an exile for the sickly boy. She stopped at the Capuchin Church in Vienna to see where the royal family of Austria was buried and the Eaglet interred.

The next stop was Paris where Maude met with Rostand to discuss his play. Bernhardt was performing the play while Maude was in Paris, but she avoided seeing a performance because she was afraid of how it might influence her. "It was bad enough to have to play the part," Maude recalled, "without being completely terrified by seeing Madame Bernhardt in it."[16]

Then to England to meet Barrie for the first time, although they had been corresponding for several years. There, Maude found "the great man," courteous, friendly, and inviting. He showed her where he worked; and they discussed his current projects in depth, one of which was likely to be the next play for her. Barrie accompanied Maude to the train for Southampton. In her view, "it seemed there had never been a time when I had not known him."[17]

The trip was reported to have been Maude's first vacation since 1897, if such a schedule could be considered rest and relaxation. She returned to the U.S. in the middle of June and finally retired to her Catskills cottage to prepare for "L'Aiglon."

Before going to the Catskills retreat, Maude spent several weeks at her farm in Ronkonkoma. The fact that the young actress had chosen to satisfy her leisure time on a farm was enough to inspire newspaper reporters to visit Sandygarth, Maude's name for the property. Rarely was anybody able to interview Maude, but they were given the opportunity to tour the house and grounds. The outcome of such tours were articles describing the house and farm, complete with drawings.

An earnest reporter from the *Herald* went into great detail about his trip to visit Sandygarth. After a ride of two hours from the city, the train stopped at the tiny shelter called Ronkonkoma. It was said that, after purchasing the property, Maude had persuaded the railroad to stop at Ronkonkoma so she could more easily commute to the city. Waiting at the station for the reporter was a surrey, driven by Mr. Kessler, the farm manager. After a fifteen-minute ride over a rough, dirt road, Maude's home came into view, perched on top of a hill, overlooking a calm lake. To the reporter, it was a structure "the portals of which are jealously guarded as the inner temple of ancient mystics."

The house was two stories high, painted dark green, with a mansard roof of dull red. From the low porch, one entered via a large door featuring an old fashioned knocker. Once inside, the visitor found a large room that was subdivided into self-contained nooks and corners. Facing the door was an enormous fireplace built of large stones. Stained rafters formed the ceiling, on one of which the date 1803 was roughly carved. This was believed to be the year in which the house was originally built. (Current owners believe that the house was built in the 1700s and owned by the Stuart family until Maude purchased it.)

Along the front of the room, which faced south, there was a window seat piled with cushions, from which one could admire the lake. To the left stood an old fashioned piano, crowned with antique candelabra and backed by towering palms. To

Maude's home at Lake Ronkonkoma, New York. She gave the property to the Cenacle in 1921 in gratitude for their tender care of her while she recovered from a nervous breakdown. As the Cenacle benefactress, Maude was buried in the cemetery at Ronkonkoma, although she was not Catholic. (Courtesy of the Cenacle of St. Regis)

the right was an old, narrow staircase screening the dining room. Maude's "own chair" was kept reverently untouched during her absence. It was of dark, carved wood and upholstered in tapestry, similar to the chairs used in "The Little Minister." Near the chair was an ebony glass closet filled with cups and dinner service. An adjacent cupboard held several tea urns of silver and copper.

In a corner near the staircase was a table holding a large assortment of brass candlesticks. "We use them constantly," said Mr. Kessler, "because we have no gas out here." A nearby bookcase revealed editions of Shakespeare, Victor Hugo, Robert Lewis Stevenson, Marion Crawford, and J.M. Barrie. The library opened onto a guest chamber with bedroom furniture and a small bookcase.

According to Kessler, Maude wished to rehabilitate the house to preserve its characteristics and natural beauty. For her own personal comfort, there was a completely equipped modern bathroom, next to a sleeping apartment with colonial furniture and a gabled roof, the slanting ceiling comprising one wall. Two sides of the room were covered with windows. Tall palms and bookcases adorned Maude's bedroom.

Maude had five dogs: three shepherds, a greyhound, and a mastiff. The fields outside, said Kessler, were used to raise all the vegetables eaten by residents of Ronkonkoma. Pigs were raised to be killed and cured. A chicken house produced enough eggs for Maude's home in the city. Two cows and four calves were in the barn, along with twelve horses. Most of the horses were for work, but a few served for riding. Maude used a little pony cart when she drove across the property. As Kessler explained, "It is because this house of hers lies very near to Babbie's heart that she refuses to allow inquisitive people on the grounds."

"My private life is my own," Maude had once declared quietly but emphatically.

The reporter left Sandygarth with a new admiration for Maude —few other performers had ever chosen this way to live — and remarked on the "perfect hospitality" of everyone at the farm.

Maude had recently purchased additional acreage and renewed her interest in raising Shetland ponies and collie dogs. The 1900 census described that, besides Maude, thirteen other people were living at the farm. Eight were laborers, one of whom had his wife and three children living with him. There were two boarders, both of them actresses, either off for the season or without current stage assignments. According to Ada Peterson, a writer and critic for *Harper's Weekly,* Maude often housed needy actresses in her Forty-First Street home as well, a commendable act of charity, in Patterson's view.

For a month prior to the beginning of rehearsals Maude worked on her role as the Duke of Reichstadt, L'Aiglon (the Eaglet), son of Napoleon. She focused on sharpening the emotional dialogue needed to convey the frustration, pathos, and tragedy that imbued the young man. When she arrived in New York to begin full rehearsals, she spent additional time with the scenery and costumes. These had to represent European fashions of the post–Napoleonic era in Vienna. One other scene, the Wagram battlefield, had been carefully researched by Maude. Frohman saw to it that the production would be mounted in his usual elegant manner. Frohman and Maude together had selected the cast, drawing heavily on Frohman's stable of stock performers. Hired were J.H. Gilmour, Sara Perry, Margaret Gordon, Oswald Yorke (from England), Peyton Carter, and Edwin Arden as the cunning, manipulative minister, Metternich.

For a month, the cast worked hard, attempting to achieve the proper exposition of character and action. The Eaglet was a symbol of a most complex spirit. He was a sympathetic and pathetic young man who struggled against overwhelming odds. Interestingly, instead of questioning Maude on her ability to interpret such a potentially difficult role, critics seemed to be more interested in her ability to play the part of a teenage boy. Again, it represented a dramatic change, from the piquant Babbie to the ill-fated Eaglet, that critics found hard to comprehend. Why would Maude ever attempt such a role? Because she wanted to, Maude had responded. No one could argue with her motivation, only the way in which she wished to enhance her stardom.

Another challenge to Maude, and likely to American audiences, was the fact that the entire dialogue would be in verse. Could Parker's translation from French be true to the meaning of the original language of the play? Could Maude interpret the life of the troubled Eaglet in such a way that the verse sounded like "normal" conversation? Would audiences be able to follow the cadence of the script? These questions remained at the top of Maude's mind as she fashioned the play. When Frohman viewed the full-dress rehearsals, he was deeply moved by the pathos of the play and, at the same time, elated by its potential audience appeal. It was definitely a different role for Maude — unconventional, in the view of critics— but Frohman believed that her acting versatility and audience appeal should make the play a success.

When "L'Aiglon" had been presented by Sarah Bernhardt to French audiences, the play had been heralded as a triumph for both Bernhardt and Rostand, maybe even better than his "Cyrano." The drama (called a romantic drama by the French) embraced a series of magnificent scenes. The plot carried the touching story of the mind of the Duke of Reichstadt, haunted by the memories of paternal glory (his father, Napoleon), yet hesitant in action (like Shakespeare's Hamlet), fearing himself inferior to the tasks his heritage had thrust upon him, and further dismayed at his personal weaknesses in comparison to his father's greatness. So entangled was she with the intricacies of the role, Maude's nervousness caused a brief illness, sufficient to delay the opening for two weeks. When she recovered, however, she was ready.

"L'Aiglon" was introduced to the public on October 15, at Baltimore's Academy of Music. Frohman felt that one week of performances would be sufficient to prepare the company for New York. The *Clipper* reviewer traveled to Baltimore to see Maude inaugurate a new and decidedly different role.

> Miss Adams' impersonation of the weakling son of Napoleon was marked by sympathic feeling and evidence of careful study, apart from the nervousness incident to a first performance, was distinctly successful. The house was filled and there were several calls before the curtain.[18]

By the end of the week's engagement, Maude and the cast had settled down and were reported to have made "a decided success." Frohman was present at the opening to observe and offer suggestions. He left Baltimore believing that the play, and Maude, would be victorious, though possibly not with the critics.

On October 22, 1900, "L'Aiglon" opened at the Knickerbocker Theater in New York.

> The play was followed with close interest and respect by the audience and was frequently interrupted by applause that truthfully indicated the feeling of the spectators toward the play and the acting of it.[19]

For the most part, Maude was lauded for acting a difficult, complex role and praised for being "in the front rank of the younger English-speaking actresses." Nor did critics have any problem with Maude's portraying the part of a boy.

> She looks the scion of the Bonaparte-Hapsburg union to the life. One never thinks of her as a woman from the beginning of the play to its sad last scene. In every pictorial and superficial attribute her portrayal is flawless. Not a gesture or a pose is out of place or awkward.

The critic went on to describe Maude's performing style.

> The young artist's integrity of purpose, her dramatic aptitude, and sympathy shine through all the performance, and her own uncommon personal charm is continuously exerted. She has shown an unexpected command of declamatory force and elocutionary skill.[20]

In the opinion of the critic, the play was a "splendid triumph" for Maude, having won "the admiration of the whole audience."

The same critic, however, felt compelled to point out that Maude had not yet reached the experience necessary to portray tragedy. Certain episodes in the last two scenes, he identified, "required technical skill far beyond her command."

And so it was with other reviewers, as well. Maude was a great crowd pleaser who did a fine job of acting, except she could not yet interpret tragedy. Not surprisingly, her portrayal of L'Aiglon was compared to her efforts in "Romeo and Juliet." Nonetheless, audiences were in awe of her presentation; and S.R.O. signs appeared at every performance.

Likely persuaded by Frohman, reviewers visited the theater several days later to again evaluate Maude's performance. "Easier and more enjoyable than the clamor of a first night," they said. Nonetheless, reactions to Maude's acting had not changed. "A good piece of acting," they all agreed. Still, they all seemed to be in concert that Maude was "sometimes over-weighted" and that she did not "reach every height of her role or sound all its tragic depths."

As was inevitable, Maude was compared to Sarah Bernhardt. Bernhardt particularly excelled in those latter scenes, "an artist who can exactly interpret the poet, whose Gallic sentiment and power are exerted in every passage." Still, Maude was able to convey the pathos of a young man, something Bernhardt did not, or could not, do. Maude was acknowledged as an outstanding young actress but one who, so far, lacked Bernhardt's élan.

Reports of the second week's attendance surpassed the first, which, itself, had broken a record for the house. By the fifth week, all performances were not only S.R.O. sellouts, but advance sales were also very heavy. Then, during Maude's seventh week, Bernhardt arrived in New York to open an engagement at the Garden Theater. Her first play: "L'Aiglon" in French. The *Clipper* could not refrain from comparing the results of their competing performances.

> Maude Adams is still playing to phenomenal success. She is now in the seventh week of her engagement, and it is claimed that the presentation of the same play in the original tongue at another house has in no way injured the receipts. French is sparingly spoken in American cities and doubtless many avail themselves of the opportunity to hear the English version before hearing the French.[21]

In the spring of 1901, Frohman had planned to feature Maude as Rosalind in a lighter Shakespearean play, "As You Like It"; but the success of "L'Aiglon" persuaded him to postpone the production. Frohman then announced that Maude would appear as the Eaglet for the remainder of the season, until June. She would, however, begin a tour of the larger cities beginning in early 1901. Down the street, after a less than successful week, Bernhardt changed the bill to "Cyrano" and did not perform "L'Aiglon" for the remainder of her stay in the U.S.

After ten highly successful weeks at the Knickerbocker Theater, Maude was ready to launch her tour. No question, however, the past four months had been very strenuous; and Maude was feeling, although not yet showing, fatigue and stress. The very demanding role, combined with her own drive toward perfection, had physically drained her; and she was not entirely enthused about embarking on a tour at this time. Maude knew she would have to conserve her energy and, at the same time, give audiences what they now expected from her.

The tour began with a two-week engagement in Boston, at the Hollis Street Theater. With Maude already beloved in this city, the response to "L'Aiglon" was one of public adoration. Her scheduled appearance had met with excited anticipation. Although the play had previously been associated with the world-famous Bernhardt, known for her "histrionic resources," the *Boston Globe* believed that Maude had shown great courage in offering the play and, from the accounts of her New York engagement, audiences were in for a special artistic delight.

Maude did not fail her admirers; but several Boston critics complained about the same shortcomings as had their New York counterparts. As usual, the criticism did nothing to diminish audience attendance and enthusiasm for her interpretation, her popularity being so pronounced "that she would be sure of kindly acceptance in any character she chose to portray." Critics made the inevitable comparison with Maude's Juliet, who had likewise been deemed "beyond the limits of her powers."

> Miss Adams gave a performance last evening that was very gratifying to her admirers, surprisingly so, in fact, for her acting was far better than could reasonably have been

Another adventurous and complex role for Maude was her interpretation of the ill-fated son of Napoleon I in "L'Aiglon" (the Eaglet). The part established her as a versatile performer who could play male or female roles with equal artistry and popular acclaim.

expected from anything she has done here in the past. There was no moment when she did not hold the rapt attention and sincere sympathy of her audience. She displayed powers of sustained force not heretofore suggested and there was good reason for the thunderous applause which rewarded her when the curtain fell.[22]

"Few actresses," the *Globe* reviewer observed, "could physically present the character so satisfactorily."

The reviewer also noted that the mental and physical strain of playing the ill-fated son of Napoleon was "tremendous," and he marveled how "this frail young actress" could accomplish the task. When Phyllis Robbins visited, she also observed that the role was putting heavy pressure on Maude. Robbins had seen the play once in New York and was about to see it again. As they parted, Maude said to Robbins, "Take care of yourself," as if she were ignoring her own precarious condition.

Providence attracted full houses; and, when the company returned to Harlem for a week's stay, not only were the seats sold out, but police had to be called to keep ticket buyers in line. Similar reactions to "L'Aiglon" were experienced in Pittsburgh and Cincinnati.

Even before the company reached Chicago, local newspapers were heralding Maude's appearance.

> Miss Adams's triumph has been all the more complete because the role is essentially different from any she has heretofore played. In her impersonation of the Eaglet she has dwarfed all her previous efforts and triumphed to a degree exceeding any of her previous accomplishments in high comedy.[23]

With that kind of publicity, it was not surprising that tickets were quickly sold out for the two-week engagement at the Illinois Theater. As had now become characteristic of the advertising for Maude's plays, her name was featured in print three times larger than the name of the play in which she was appearing.

Critics immediately compared Maude to Bernhardt, who, just weeks previously, had performed in Chicago and given "memorable performances." They acknowledged that Maude would likely do well in the play, primarily because she had a large following of admirers, not necessarily because her interpretation of the Eaglet could rank with Bernhardt's. The public would crowd to see her perform; but "what this player will develop, as yet is not decided."

Chicago reviewers were not as kind to Maude as their colleagues had been in other cities. They agreed "the young woman was unhappily over-weighted," particularly in those scenes that demanded the acting of tragedy.

> The impression in the strong, highly keyed scenes, the scenes that palpitate life, and even call for strength from an utterly weak character, was that she was struggling against great odds.[24]

In turn, Frohman was blamed for presenting Maude in this role, either because he was exploiting his star or because he overestimated her abilities. Frohman defended his decision vigorously and suggested that these veteran critics seemed to be against all new and experimental ideas in theater. And for whom does one produce plays? asked Frohman. Not for the critics, surely; but for audiences to enjoy.

Maude admitted to being bothered by the negative comments regarding her interpretations of pathos and tragedy. Complaints from Chicago critics troubled her even more, which only added to her tension and stress while performing. It seemed that nothing she did in those later scenes could please the critics. Nor were they to be moved in their comparisons between Maude and Bernhardt. Indeed, critics grew even more opinionated when audiences ignored their interpretations of Maude's acting, filling the theater and cheering her most enthusiastically at the end of each performance. Yet, Maude had internalized the critics' comments; and she now found herself ailing, not enough to cancel performances, but enough to make her work more difficult to interpret. And she still had seven weeks remaining on the tour.

In Detroit, Maude did banner business. In Cleveland, she took the audience "by storm," although she missed a day due to an unexplained illness. So packed was the Cleveland theater, the orchestra was forced to give up its place and perform from the side of the stage. By the time she reached Philadelphia, critics' negative comments had become so pronounced that audiences were now all the more curious to see Maude as the Eaglet, so they could form their own opinions about her interpretation. The *Clipper* reported: "The star, in her interpretation of the stellar role, surprised even her admirers."[25]

Maude had won the audience once again. The critics, however, refused to change their opinions.

The last two weeks of the tour were difficult for the entire cast. Everyone was tired and glad to see the end of the season near at hand. As for Maude, she was not sleeping well. She had become discernibly nervous. She shut herself off even more than usual from the rest of the cast. She was undoubtedly depressed from the onslaught of criticism she had received these past several months. Notwithstanding Frohman's warnings, Maude had never before experienced such negative reactions to her work. Unfortunately, Frohman, in England at the time, was not around to give her reassurance.

In Hartford, Maude missed another performance and was forced to present a matinee to satisfy all the ticket purchasers. The season closed in Rochester on May 9, to an immense house, cheering throngs, and floral tributes. She had portrayed the Eaglet in 196 arduous performances.

The cast knew that Maude had immediately returned to New York. Yet, when the Frohman office attempted to contact her, she did not respond. When an announcement was made about Maude's coming season, she could not be found to discuss her new play. Checking on the three possible places where she might be resting, reporters were unable to locate her. Maude had seemingly disappeared.

A rumor suggested that Maude had undergone an operation for appendicitis, but it was proven to be false. Another rumor arose, claiming that she and Frohman were going to be married. The rumor had surfaced several times before; and the parties involved denied it, as Frohman did again.

What had happened to Maude?

11

Overwrought and Overworked

Under the name of M.A. Kiskadden, her face hidden behind a dark veil and bundled up in a fur coat, Maude boarded a German liner bound for Calais. Rarely seen outside her stateroom except at mealtimes, Maude had begun her quest for a place to rest and escape from the stress that had so affected her ability to act these last several months.

Besides Maude's onboard reclusiveness, her mealtime behavior was perceived to be odd, if not extremely idiosyncratic. Much to the chagrin of waiters, whatever the meal or menu, she ordered only a drink and a chop. Although they brought her other foods to tempt her, she rejected their every offering. After several days, the chef approached Maude and remonstrated about the peculiar order that he received three times a day.

Spreading out his arms dramatically, he declared: "I can give you anything you want to eat." He followed this theatrical gesticulation by reeling off a long list of dishes that he was prepared to serve her.[1]

"But I like only chops," replied the unknown lady simply. Shaking his head in complete frustration, the chef disappeared from the dining room without another word.

Upon reaching Calais, Maude went to Paris to meet friends. Newspapers had been alerted to her arrival and reporters rushed to question her about how she would spend her days and evenings "on the town." Instead, after no more than a day in Paris, Maude secretly left her lodgings and was driven away in a carriage. No one knew where.

Maude's destination was a Catholic convent located outside of Tours. Called "La Maison de Retraite," it was run by the Sisters of St. Augustine, a service-oriented rather than a contemplative order. Ever since the revolution, Catholic orders had been banned in France; but, in recent years, individual convents had been allowed to operate by the French government, as long as they devoted themselves to social service, like teaching or running an orphanage. Maude's friends had recommended this retreat as the perfect place for her to regain her health.

With the St. Augustine sisters' usual graciousness, Maude was welcomed into the convent. Fearing that they would not accept an actress, she did not reveal her true occupation. The sisters likely assumed that this frail American woman had chosen the convent as a place to recover from a personal crisis, seeking solitude in order to mend a broken heart.

Since, during the summer, the convent was not crowded, Maude was able to select her own room. From the many available to her, she chose a small cell on the third floor of the building, overlooking plowed fields, thick clusters of trees, and, in the distance, the church steeples of Tours. The tiny room contained a narrow, steel-framed bed with a thin mattress, a stand with a basin and water jug, a chair, and a small oratory. One wall was covered with tiles upon which were floral designs. Nothing adorned the other smooth, plastered walls except a crucifix which hung over the bed.

From the very beginning of her stay, each morning, Maude attended the 6 o'clock chapel service. Since she had rarely risen this early, the event was a unique experience for her. Breakfast was served in the refectory, located in the basement of the main building. For Maude, breakfast consisted of a chop and a piece of fruit. Again, she had difficulty persuading the cook that these items were all she desired. After breakfast, Maude took long walks. She soon became friendly with the peasant children, several of who became her daily walking companions. After dinner, served at

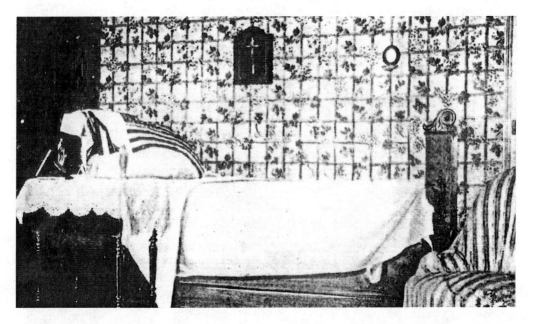

When Maude entered the convent in Tours, she chose this room. Her first experience with spirituality was extremely influential.

midday, another prayer service was held, which Maude attended. Later, to study French, Maude went into the flower garden, where she copied pages and pages of conjugations to memorize; all were recorded in a notebook that she kept for several years. (They were later discovered among the papers donated to Harvard). Supper was served at 6:00 P.M., followed by prayers and a mandatory quiet period before retiring. At 12:00 P.M., the chapel bell rang for midnight services. During the entire time of her stay at the convent, Maude faithfully followed the sisters' prescribed schedule. She even tried wearing a nun's garb but found it did not suit her.

After several weeks, Maude had been fully accepted by the sisters. She revealed to them that she was an American actress, having chosen the convent to recover from a severe illness and to study French. For most of the sisters, including the mother superior, her true identity did not seem to matter. "But you were a woman before you were an actress," one sister remarked on Maude's behalf. While there was no thought of expulsion, some sisters deprecated the fact that such a sweet creature should be addicted to such awful work; and they attempted to convert Maude, an offer that she courteously rejected. After a short time, however, the sisters were begging Maude to recite Shakespearean passages to them.

Rest, the slow pace of living, and the absence of anything theatrical definitely contributed to Maude's recovery. The forced seclusion also helped in clarifying feelings she had formulated about herself and her profession. Unencumbered by deadlines, production demands, and the rituals of performance, Maude had regained much of her self-confidence. Not only did she come to realize that she did not need to be surrounded by people, she found that she felt more unburdened when alone.

Yet, while resisting attempts by the sisters at her religious conversion, Maude nevertheless assimilated their sense of spirituality. These feelings gave her a clearer insight into the nature of her performance, especially those times when reviewers spoke of the audience's response to her "spiritual qualities." According to reviewers, Maude's spirituality was defined as being airy, animated, sparkling, brave, bold, and representing the best traits of womanhood. (Of course, all of these traits had been represented in the roles she played on stage and comprised the patrons' sole view of her.) Thanks to the sisters, Maude also discovered a spirituality of the ethereal and soulful. Incorporating these characteristics, she promised herself to follow them as best she could, for example by attempting to lead a more simple life. A separation between her theater life and private life also had to be nurtured. She was surely aware that these resolutions would not be easy to accomplish, given the demands and distractions of a starring actress's life; but Maude was convinced they would be in her best interests.

Near the end of her stay at the convent, Maude received a large package from the Frohman office. (Her mother had revealed to them where she was staying.) Contained in the package was the script for the next production in which she was to appear, a Barrie play called "Quality Street." She now directed her free time toward learning the new role.

There had been keen competition among London producers to obtain the rights to Barrie's new play, but Frohman prevailed. Barrie himself was responsible for the arrangement, since it was his wish that Maude should be the first to present his play.

After having lived at the convent for close to three months, Maude returned to New York. The rest and seclusion had undoubtedly helped her regain her health, but the residual effects of the nervous condition remained. Moreover, it was not helped when she plunged into learning the new script. Yet, the retreat had been a happy and refreshing experience; and she would not forget the care, kindness, and spiritual exhilaration she had received from the sisters. Their parting was tearful.

On August 20, Maude arrived in Hoboken on the *Kaiser Wilhelm der Grosse*. During her return, she made no effort to hide herself, nor did she exasperate the chef with her culinary demands. On the same ship, sharing the spotlight, was Madame Mojeska. One actress was on the threshold of new stage successes, while the other was in the twilight of her career. When Maude stepped down the gangplank, to the enthusiastic welcome of the people awaiting her arrival, she looked almost robust. Frohman was among that group, with much news to impart.

First of all, he told Maude that everything was ready for her to begin rehearsals for "Quality Street." Second, her real estate agents had been successful in acquiring another 130 acres adjoining the Ronkonkoma farm, from the estate of Adeline Nichols, for the absurdly small sum of $1,500.

Third, Frohman revealed to Maude that he had been aggressively pursuing Sarah Bernhardt to perform "Romeo and Juliet" with her. It would be a theatrical coup if Bernhardt agreed to the arrangement, which, from all reports, she was seriously considering. Maude's immediate reaction was one of trepidation.

Finally, the unpleasant news. Maude was informed by Frohman that her mother had been made the defendant in divorce proceedings instituted by Harvey Glidden, who had remained in Wyoming after her hasty defection several years before. The *Chicago American* mentioned that the marriage had been a source of much unhappiness to Maude.[2] Whether that was true or not, she was now faced with helping dissolve her mother's marriage as quietly and peacefully as possible. Frohman lawyers would help, but the public had already been made aware of the situation. One way to deflect news coverage about Annie was to put her on the road with one of Frohman's touring companies, ensuring that the lawyers themselves would come to a quick resolution. Still, Maude would have to appear in court to monitor the proceedings. Although extensively questioned about the situation, Maude refused to offer any indication regarding her feelings toward her mother's divorce.

As part of her resolution to lead a more simple life, one of the first things Maude did upon returning to her Forty-First Street home was to convert her bedroom, redecorating it to resemble her convent cell. The revamped room included a narrow bed, a washstand holding a basin and water jug, and a chair. The walls of the bedroom were left uncovered. It was a hallowed reminder of her stay at the convent.

Bernhardt then dramatically announced that she had agreed "to play Romeo for one hundred nights in America to Maude Adams's Juliet."[3] The arrangements had supposedly been made at a supper given by Madame Bernhardt for Mr. Frohman and her manager, Maurice Grau. The tentative plan indicated that she and Maude would appear in America and then play in London and on the Continent. But there was one stipulation. "If I can learn the part of Romeo in English, I will play with Miss Adams," Bernhardt was reported to have said. Several critics, both in England and America, doubted the production would ever be presented, not because of Bernhardt's inability to speak English, but rather because the two actresses would not be able to share the same stage. The target date for opening the play was scheduled to be the fall of 1902. With all of the commentary emanating from various theatrical sources describing the proposed illustrious event, Maude's views on the subject were never revealed.

A further announcement from the Frohman office, which described Maude's new season, surely must have troubled her. Along with the planned performances of "Quality Street," Maude was scheduled to offer special matinees of "As You Like It." (She had not been studying the part, nor had any production elements been prepared.) In addition, her stay in New York would last only ten weeks. She would then embark on a short tour. In the spring, the Frohman announcement continued, Maude would appear in London to give a repertory of her plays.[4] All of this information had been distributed prior to Maude's return from Europe. A week after her return, Maude was quoted in the *Clipper* as saying:

> In London, I met Mr. Barrie, who was working at his new play, "Quality Street," in which I am to play. Mr. Frohman stated that he had made arrangements with Mr. Grau and Sarah Bernhardt by which we were to play "Romeo and Juliet" together. Of course I shall consider it a great privilege to play with so great an artist as Madame Bernhardt. I have had a very good rest, and am eager to begin my season's work.[5]

No mention of "As You Like It"; no mention of any trip to France. Maude went to her Catskills retreat to practice her part for Barrie's play. Actual rehearsals would begin in the middle of September, with the production opening on the road in October.

"Quality Street" opened on October 11 at the Valentine Theater in Toledo, Ohio. As was his usual routine, Frohman spent several days in Toledo supervising the final dress rehearsals. Maude and the play were greeted "by a large and enthusiastic audience." The company then moved to Detroit and Baltimore for a week's performance each, followed by one-night stands in Wilmington, Harrisburg, Buffalo, and Rochester, before arriving in New York. It was an odd initial tour for an Adams play, but Frohman wanted to collect as many good reviews in these cities as he could and use them to promote the play in New York City, thereby ensuring large audiences. The effect on the company, however, was already one of fatigue.

Why did Frohman have any doubts regarding Maude's drawing power at this point in her career? For one thing, he had had portions of the play rewritten because they "dragged," in his estimation. For another, Frohman was concerned that a new role, totally different from those she had recently played, might again confuse the audience's perception of Maude.

In each of the tour cities, however, reactions from the audiences quickly resolved

Frohman's concerns. "'Quality Street' was another of what came to be known as a typical 'Adams success.'"[6]

The story is set in a village in England during the time of the Napoleonic Wars. Dr. Valentine Brown (Sydney Brough, an English actor brought over by Frohman expressly to play opposite Maude) is on very friendly terms with two sisters who reside on Quality Street. He is trusted by the elder, Susan Throssell (Helen Lowell), and loved by the younger, Phoebe Throssell (Maude); and he has invested some of their inheritance for them. One day, he tells Phoebe that he has something important to tell her. Convinced that there can be but one story he would now reveal to her, she is jubilant in expectation. Thus, she is hurled into despair when he announces his intention of going to fight in the war.

He leaves and, after nine years, returns. He is not aware that the investment he had managed for the sisters has turned out badly and that they are now compelled to teach in order to live. Upon his return, he remarks about Phoebe's altered looks; and she, grief stricken, tries on a dress that had been prepared for her nine years before, then lets her hair down in girlish ringlets. Valentine enters unexpectedly, does not recognize her, and is led to believe that it is Phoebe's niece, Libby, whom he sees in the girlish attire. They go to several balls together, Phoebe just escaping recognition by some friends and being led to believe that Brown is in love with her, in the guise of her niece. One evening he talks to her and, believing her to be Libby, tells her of his great love for Phoebe. She, not sure she believes him, receives Brown at her home as her own self. He then discovers the deception. Thus, the lovers are brought happily together.

On November 11, 1901, "Quality Street" opened at the Knickerbocker Theater, New York City. The house was crowded to the limit, and the new play was "voted a success."

> The play was written for Miss Adams, and it was admitted by all that her role of Phoebe Throssell fitted her admirably and afforded opportunities for the display of her most pleasing powers.[7]

The *Herald* reviewer was effusive about Maude's return to roles she could express without strain.

> Miss Adams as Phoebe Throssell is once more her seemingly ingenuous self, an innocent and lovely girl, artless, buoyant, piquant, brisk, sometimes demure, sometimes mischievous, now pensive in response, now tantalizing in pretty coquetry, now impulsive with pouting resentment, now sweetly wayward and pert, and now arch and reckless in the perversity of a rebellious heart. And this volubility carried her audience to wild enthusiasm.[8]

Nor could the reviewer, Dorothy Dix, forget about Maude's attempt at tragedy before praising her for her charming role as "Phoebe of the Ringlets."

> Maude Adams, no longer the unhappy L'Aiglon, but once more a dear and dainty flower of girlhood is back with a charming new Barrie comedy, and last night a big audience that packed the Knickerbocker Theater gave her a glorious welcome home.[9]

That Maude's innocent and piquant roles appealed to women was beyond doubt, said Dix. "The piece is as feminine as a cup of tea. Mere man has nothing to do with it. Maude's part fits her like a glove." And in closing her review, Dix wrote: "Somehow nobody else can quite portray the innocence, the poetry and the grace of girlhood like she can."

The *Times* declared Phoebe Throssell "charming," and acknowledged that Maude had "repeated her former successes." When Maude entered the stage in the first act, she received "the friendliest of greetings." Applause after the second and third acts was "tremendous." In fact, at the end of the third act, she received so many curtains that, finally, she came forward and made an eleven-word speech: "I cannot thank you. You have been too good to us." Then she stepped back and vanished behind the curtain.

> The quaint little actress, as full of mannerisms as an Irving, seems a magnet for theater-going folk and a hypnotist as well, for she can bewitch any audience into an evening of fancied enjoyment.[10]

Maude played to S.R.O. houses for the first six weeks of the engagement. With three more weeks to go, advance tickets had all been sold out. Coming into the holiday season, Frohman added additional matinees to Maude's schedule.

Then, to everyone's surprise, came a message from Bernhardt that she could not do "Romeo and Juliet" in English, causing Frohman and Grau to scramble to keep the play alive. When Frohman cabled Maude of Bernhardt's decision, she promptly telegraphed a return message:

> Charles Frohman, Empire Theater, New York.
> I'll do it in French. Who's afraid?
> Maude Adams

Maude's response was so dramatic, Bernhardt could do nothing but accept the new arrangement. Plans for the tour were operative again. The opening date was left undecided because both parties had long-term engagements to fulfill.

Would the play be staged in London or Paris? What sort of Romeo would Bernhardt "spring" upon audiences? How would the two leading ladies set each other off? How would the genius of Maude contrast with that of the temperamental Bernhardt? Newspapers peppered the public with various scenarios while contemplating the alliance of these very different actresses. Still, a number of astute theater observers doubted any of this would ever come to pass. Meanwhile, it made for great press.

Maude's tour in "Quality Street" began 1903 in Brooklyn, where she attracted a week of S.R.O. audiences. Next stop was two weeks in Philadelphia, where theatergoers turned out "in such large numbers as to leave no doubt of the success of Maude Adams in this new comedy." Advance sales were so large in Boston that additional matinees were added to the schedule.

"No actress occupies a warmer place in the affection, esteem, and admiration

Maude's role as "Phoebe of the Ringlets" in Barrie's "Quality Street" was considered the essence of womanhood. Women in the audience identified with Maude's characterization and wished they could emulate her.

of local theatergoers than does this gifted little American woman," declared the *Boston Globe.* Not surprisingly, seats for the entire two-week engagement, even at advanced prices, were sold out days before Maude arrived in the city. "Miss Adams plays the part of Miss Phoebe Throssell—'Phoebe of the Ringlets,' as she is familiarly called," continued the *Globe* article. "She is of the type of the wholesome womanly character in which Miss Adams has so strongly endeared herself to theatergoers."[11]

Maude did not disappoint her devotees.

> Miss Maude Adams returned to the Hollis Street Theater last evening and was warmly welcomed by a houseful of admirers, who were glad that she returned to the style of play in which she first won fame and for which she is so admirably equipped by physical and mental endowments.[12]

Reviewers reported that Maude had given a captivating performance on opening night. Further thanks were given to James Barrie for writing a play with Maude's capabilities in mind. "No one could have created a character and devised a story more admirably adapted to her personality and methods than he has in this instance," said the *Globe* reviewer. When the final curtain fell, Maude was repeatedly recalled to tremendous applause. Though the audience hoped for a speech, the actress did not heed their wish.

Phyllis Robbins had traveled to New York to see "Quality Street" on opening night. When the play reached Boston, she called on Maude. They took a carriage ride, and Maude invited Phyllis up to her hotel room for tea. This time, their conversation consisted of sharing family stories. Phyllis observed that although Maude's tour was in its early stages, she was already showing signs of the nervousness that had plagued her the previous spring.

In spite of the fact that Frohman had scheduled a hectic tour for Maude — twenty-six cities in a little over four months— she believed it was her responsibility to honor these engagements and never to disappoint an audience. Other actors called Frohman's demanding program "overwork," but Maude did not appear to have that word in her vocabulary. Though critics had observed a healthy Maude the previous October, they now questioned whether she would be able to finish the season. Indeed, critics now openly wondered if Frohman was pushing his box-office sensation too far.

Annie's divorce proceedings added to the stress of the moment, since Maude had to monitor the lawyers and attend court several times. This exposure to public scrutiny had made Maude quite uncomfortable; and, unfortunately, there was no way that she could limit or cancel her appearances. Annie had been accused of desertion — there was no dispute about it, since she had left Glidden only a few weeks after they were married — and her husband was now demanding the return of a ring and other articles. The outcome of this dispute was being argued.

In addition, the situation involving Maude, Bernhardt, and "Romeo and Juliet" remained unresolved: no agreed date; no determination where the play would be presented or, for that matter, rehearsed. Moreover, Bernhardt's notorious volatility seemed to keep all those involved on edge.

Boston was followed by two weeks of one-night stands through New England, then one-week engagements in Washington, D.C., and Pittsburgh. While all tickets were at advanced prices, the theaters were filled to capacity. While Maude was playing in Pittsburgh, another announcement made by Frohman suggested that plans for the Adams-Bernhardt play were still in flux. He had once again left for Paris to complete arrangements with Bernhardt.

Chicago newspapers predicted that "Quality Street" would be "one of the most brilliant theatrical events of the present season." No matinees had been planned; but the demand for seats was so strong, three of them were inserted in the schedule. On opening night at Powers Theater, Maude was afforded an ovation when she entered the stage and curtain calls at the end of each act. At the final curtain, she was recalled ten times before a tired but satisfied crowd was willing to depart the theater. Said the *Tribune:* "Miss Adams's acting is a brilliant example of artistic characterization, a perfect study of harmoniously blending effects."[13]

Amy Leslie of the *Daily News* considered "Quality Street" another financial success for Frohman and another display of artistic talent by Maude.

> It is the age of specialists, and Miss Adams specialty is a bewitching set of nerves always alive and tingling. She is a delicate, plain, small person, with a choky, sweetly babified tiny voice of singular carrying power and sympathetic penetration.[14]

At the beginning of the second and last week of the engagement, Leslie again commended Maude upon her unique acting talent.

> Tears lie very close to smiles in the art of Miss Adams, and few actresses upon the American stage can carry roles of the order she has created better, through sheer force of personality.[15]

Yet Leslie also noted a touch of fatigue in Maude's acting, particularly near the end of the evening's presentation. Her sprightliness and vivacity seemed a bit strained. And Maude was again having trouble sleeping.

Another week of one-night stops through the Midwest, a week-long visit to St. Louis (to capacity houses), then a week of single performances in cities from Omaha to Milwaukee further fatigued Maude. She missed an evening in Kansas City and a matinee in Milwaukee, no reasons given. In Columbus, Ohio, Maude had trouble going on but forced herself to perform the entire play. The audience did not notice her shortcomings, but the cast did. The next night, in Youngstown, Ohio, Maude faltered in the third act. Two days of engagements had to be cancelled because she could not perform. Nervousness caused her to remain in seclusion on her train. The next stop was May 12, Elmira, New York, where she did appear. At the end of the evening, however, Maude telegraphed Frohman. She could not go on!

She was returning to New York. Then, she told Frohman she was going to Europe. According to her doctor, she was suffering from a nervous breakdown, an inability to function due to mental distress. No one knew when, or if, Maude would return to the stage.

12

Return to Popularity

When rumors of Maude's ill health swept theatrical circles, she confirmed them by declaring she would not appear on the stage for several months. She admitted to having taxed her vitality by performing almost incessantly for seventeen years. Her vacations had been short and, with the exception of three months at the Tours convent, filled with preparations for the coming season.

In a confiding and apologetic letter to Phyllis Robbins, Maude admitted her need for recuperation.

> The long seasons of "The Little Minister," "L'Aiglon" and "Quality Street" had taken a rather heavy toll. Even at the beginning of the third year of the "Minister" I had wanted a holiday. It had not seemed possible to give the play another year and endure the fatigue of traveling. And then insomnia set in. No sleep at night, and cat-naps in the day. But it was plain that to stop would be unfair to the managers who had been waiting two years for the play. They could not be expected to have confidence in me if I did not keep my engagements. So more of each day was given to rest. I had never bothered much about strength, because I was not supposed to have any. But whatever it was, it gave out.[1]

No mention of the constant pressure put on her by Charles Frohman, whose desire to showcase Maude seemed to supersede his concern for the physical and emotional health of his popular heroine. No mention of the tribulations with her mother. Only considered was her devotion to her profession.

A paragraph about her illness in Maude's 1926 autobiography in *The Ladies Home Journal* further revealed her worries.[2] "There was no freshness, no spontaneity; her mannerisms were becoming more and more marked and objectionable. She began to realize she was 'through.'" (In the entire series of articles, entitled "The One I Knew Least of All," Maude referred to herself in the third person.) She also wrote that Frohman had given his approval for her to take a year off, although reports at the time suggested that Maude alone had made the decision.

Reactions from the press upon hearing the news of Maude's retirement "for an unspecified period of time" made her life seem even more mysterious. At the close of her season in "Quality Street," the *Clipper* briefly noted that Maude was leaving the country in four days and would "spend a long vacation in France."[3] The *Herald* headlined: "Where, Oh, Where Has Maude Adams Gone?" They reported she had been seen in four different places at one time. The one fact that all the newspapers agreed upon was that Maude would not appear on the stage during the coming season.

The Frohman office released a simple statement saying that Maude planned to visit friends in Paris. The press, however, raised questions about her supposed illness. Was she really ill, or not? They cross-examined Frohman, but he remained noncommittal. Rumors from Paris suggested that Maude's health was quite poor and that a long rest was essential for her ultimate recovery. Yet, when the press sought to verify the rumors, Maude was no longer in Paris. When Frohman was again dogged by reporters to respond to the various reports of Maude's condition, he laughed at the reports and stated that "Miss Adams was enjoying excellent health in Paris."[4]

In reality, Maude had suffered a nervous breakdown brought on by a demanding schedule and her own need to excel at every performance. There was no question that it would take some time for her to recover sufficiently to assume the responsibilities of a new stage production. The mystery surrounding her illness, recovery, and the date of her return to the stage continued throughout the period when she purposely secluded herself from public scrutiny.

Traveling under her family name of Kiskadden, Maude had departed New York on the *Kronprinz Wilhelm* less than a week after the completion of the season. After a brief stop in Paris, she continued to St. Moritz, Switzerland. Her doctor had given her strict orders for a complete rest.

At about the same time Maude reached St. Moritz, Sarah Bernhardt, then in London, released a statement announcing that she had finally decided to produce "Romeo and Juliet" in England during her next season's tour. She would play Romeo to Maude Adams's Juliet. She and Maude would recite the play in French, Bernhardt stated, while the supporting cast would use the English language. Critics found her announcement strange, since Maude seemed to be in no condition to take on the assignment. Or, they wondered, was that why Bernhardt had announced it at this time? Frohman was in London at the time and had himself been surprised by the press release. To counter Bernhardt's announcement, he said that he had planned to have Maude appear in London in "Quality Street"; but her illness "barred the way." It was his first public admission that Maude had been ill. In spite of that, he followed up by declaring that a "refreshed" Maude would play in "As You Like It" and a revival of "The Little Minister" when she returned to New York. As for Bernhardt's proposed "Romeo and Juliet," Frohman had no comment.

At the end of August, although Frohman had received a cable from Maude that she was "not equal to the task of opening the season on scheduled time," he repeated for the press his earlier announcement regarding Maude's upcoming engagements. It appears that he refused to recognize that Maude's nervous condition remained serious and that her recovery would be much slower than either she or her manager had envisioned. Maude was now on a regimen of complete rest, long drives over country roads, a strict diet, and recreational reading—"no classics," the doctor strongly advised. Although psychiatrists were available, Maude decided to consult none of them.

Frohman was then caught by surprise when Maude cabled him to say that she was feeling much better and planned to sail for the U.S. on September 25. Yet his elation proved brief. A week later, Maude cabled to tell him she was remaining in Switzerland "because of her nervous condition." Moreover, she was unable to assure him when she might return. With reluctance, Frohman was forced to release a statement to the press regarding Maude's uncertain schedule. It caused a flurry of speculation, with implications that Maude might never again appear on the stage.

> I regret to hear that Maude Adams's state of health makes it inadvisable for her to leave Switzerland for America just now, or to resume work for at least another year. The whole of her projected tour has accordingly been cancelled.[5]

Another reversal of opinion occurred a week later when Frohman received a cable saying that Maude was sailing for New York in a week. On the date of her supposed arrival, reporters followed Annie from Ronkonkoma, where she had been spending the summer months, to an incoming transatlantic liner. However, Annie returned to Ronkonkoma alone. A few days later, Annie suddenly left the summer home for the city, carrying several valises with her to Maude's Forty-First Street home. Reporters learned that a special train would bear Maude to Ronkonkoma after she arrived in the city, that is, if she really were arriving. Frohman admitted he had no idea when Maude would arrive in New York or where she planned to go. He did not even know the berth where her ship would dock.

Maude finally did return to New York, on November 2, aboard the *Nordam*, with her friend and *nurse de voyage,* Miss S. A. Kedney. (She had acquired Nurse Kedney in Switzerland.) Maude had traveled under the name of Miss I. A. Kedney and kept to her compartment for the entire journey. At customs, she claimed $700 worth of tapestries and books and fourteen trunks. Maude had been veiled when she boarded the liner. When she disembarked in New York, she wrapped herself in a heavy cloak. Maude went immediately to her Forty-First Street home. After consultation with her, the Frohman office released a statement that Maude "had not entirely recovered from the illness that caused her to cancel her engagements for the theatrical season now open, although," the report added, "she looked cheerful when she landed in New York."[6]

With Frohman's consent, Maude gave a written interview to the *New York Herald,* designed to answer the questions and rumors regarding her health and her future in the theater.[7] In the interview, she stated that she had left the country in the best of health (not true); had visited London to see Barrie (not true); moved on to Paris and Amsterdam (not true); and suddenly discovered that she suffered from nerves, "as most women have," deciding then to go to St. Moritz for a short stay. (In fact, her respite had lasted more than four months.) When it seemed she was better, Maude claimed, she had returned to Paris for morning walks along the Champs Elysées, afternoon drives to various parts of the city, and evenings at the theater (not true). "The aggravating part of it was that I looked exceedingly well in every way, except for nervous depression whenever I began stage study." She returned to St. Moritz, she said, to continue her rest cure. Upon her return home, Maude claimed, at a meeting with Frohman, he had told her to "continue your holiday" (not true), which she intended to do. Maude concluded this rare interview by declaring that "I am myself again, but hoping to be a discreet young woman who once unknowingly went a little beyond present limits of endurance, and who perhaps errs now in the other direction. I have decided that it shall be all play and no work for a while yet."

The letter to the *Herald* seems to have been carefully manufactured by the Frohman office to preserve, if not enhance, Maude's image. In fact, Frohman followed up with an interview of his own in the *Herald*, stating that Maude had not revealed the entire story. "She is not only a constant student," he related, "forever reading and studying and perfecting herself for the play in which she is to appear. She has had an active part in selecting, designing, and planning the scenes, costumes, and even the stage business of her plays."

"Though slight and seemingly not over-strong," he continued, "her physical and mental strength is marvelous. We have to almost drive her out of the theater."

From Frohman's description, it sounded as if Maude were going to return to the stage momentarily. Instead, she quietly moved to her farm at Ronkonkoma to continue her recuperation for an indefinite time. She stayed on the farm the entire winter, not once venturing into the city. Nothing was reported about her during this time, in large measure because she refused all attempts to interview her.

In early March 1903, the *Clipper* scooped other newspapers when they reported that Maude had recently sailed for Liverpool to confer with Frohman (in England since February) and Barrie regarding a new play for herself for the following season. She stayed with the Barries for several weeks, sightseeing, attending the theater, even watching the changing of the guard at Buckingham Palace. The Barries treated her like royalty, watched over her activities, protected her from the press, and made arrangements so that she was often the sole visitor at many sites. Frohman was surprised when Maude announced that she was soon leaving for an extended tour of Egypt, traveling for her health. When the press questioned Frohman about this latest of Maude's adventures, he admitted that nothing had been settled with regard to Maude's theatrical plans. Privately, he was concerned about his mercurial star.

In April, Maude left for Cairo with two other women, a maid, Mary Gorman, and a companion, Miss Ray Rockman. They traveled by train to Dover, ferry to Calais, and train to Paris. From there, the three women took the train to Brindisi, Italy, then the Pacific & Orient ship to Port Said, Egypt.

No sooner had they left Paris than the French conductor, in great excitement, informed the women that they had no sleeping-car tickets and, thus, had no choice but to return to Paris. Maude had no intention of returning. When she found a fellow traveler from California, he kindly offered his compartment to them; and the remainder of the trip produced no more surprises.

The women arrived in Cairo at sundown and were advised by the hotel clerk to watch the sunset from the Alabaster Mosque, several miles away. Racing the decline of the sun through the crowded streets of Cairo in a carriage conducted by a driver determined to please his foreign passengers, the pressing throngs warned away by his constant shouting, they finally galloped up the ramp leading to the mosque. Upon reaching the mosque's summit, they found they had won the race with the sun, which was just now caressing the horizon. From this height, they had a breathtaking view of the pyramids, the Nile, and the desert beyond. So began their tour of Egypt.

The noise and bustle of Cairo persuaded the women to reside out of the city and closer to the Sphinx and pyramids. Maude believed their visit to the Sphinx demanded ceremony. Waiting for night and a full moon, the women hired a guide with camel transportation and made their way across the desert to their destination. Maude wrote that "the great creature seemed to draw the breath of eternity."[8] The experience impressed her with its intense beauty and grandeur. Although Maude and her companions viewed the Sphinx many times during their visit, this first majestic impression of the monument remained in their minds. The fact that the women had ridden camels for the first time to and from the site astonished their guide and all those natives to whom he related the episode.

Further amazing the hotel staff, the women decided to travel via camel to visit desert villages and encampments. Gathering together tents, food, camels, donkeys, and their keepers, the women began their trek early one morning. Whenever they pitched camp, the chief of the neighboring village sent guards to protect them. At some villages, they were invited to the chief's house, a rare honor, if not a serious break with cultural tradition. They were even invited to visit a harem. There, they were entertained by dancing girls and men giving burlesque imitations of the girls. By the time they returned to Cairo, the women had become the talk of the town.

Though the heat had reached almost unbearable levels, Maude decided she wished to visit the temples of Karnak and Luxor up river. A boat trip got them to the site just as the Queen of Austria was ending her own visit with an illuminated feast on the temple grounds. To their surprise, the Queen sent them an invitation to attend.

A slow train returned the women to Cairo. Waiting at their hotel was a note from Frohman outlining the play he had chosen for Maude upon her return to New York. Maude expressed displeasure with the play — she believed she would not be good in it — but said nothing to Frohman about her concern.

A cablegram from Maude, received by Frohman in London, told of her arrival in Jerusalem, where she intended to spend some weeks visiting sites in the Holy Land. Most important to Frohman was a report that Maude was "without a trace of illness" that might prevent her from playing next season. Frohman announced that he and Maude would meet in London on her way back to the U.S. to discuss the new play.

On June 25, 1903, Maude arrived in New York on the *Deutschland*. Again, she had traveled under an assumed name, rarely left her cabin, and informed no one except her mother of her homecoming date. Only Annie was at the dock to meet her. They immediately retired to Ronkonkoma. Several days later, the press and Frohman were notified that Maude had returned home. Two weeks later, Maude left for her cottage in the Catskills to await the arrival of the script for the new play. While Maude offered no press interviews, Annie was more than willing to share her own views, telling reporters she had never seen her daughter in such excellent health.

"Maude is constitutionally vigorous," Annie assured enthusiastically. "Her tour through the Holy Land, France and Egypt seems to have given her new life, and she is stronger than she ever has been since her stage debut."[9]

Instead of sending the script to Maude, Frohman insisted on a meeting at his office on August 3. Apparently, he believed he would have to convince Maude to perform the new play because it had not come from Barrie's hand. In addition, there were elements in the play that Maude had not performed before. When she arrived at Frohman's office, she was greeted by a round of applause from stage managers, scenic artists, and supporting players, all awaiting her entrance.

Within minutes, the issues of the play were settled. This meeting was very important for Frohman since it represented Maude's return to the dramatic stage after an absence of almost two years. He admitted to being concerned whether audiences would respond to Maude in the same way they had done in the past. Had Maude lost her following? Had other young actresses usurped her appeal? How well would she be accepted in a role that did not entirely repeat the characterizations with which she had become identified? In contrast, Maude seemed totally unconcerned by the challenge.

Maude would make her reappearance in a play by Mrs. Frances Hodgson Burnett, entitled "The Pretty Sister of José." Frohman had received a part of the script while Maude was in Egypt and believed the play would prove a proper vehicle for her. He received the final script just days before the meeting and was even more convinced of its qualities, both for Maude and the attending public. Remodeling of the Empire Theater, however, would force Maude to begin the season on the road and return to New York in December, not an especially advantageous way to reintroduce one's star actress in a new and possibly unconventional play.

"The entire story of the play is laid in old Spain," Frohman outlined for the press, "revolving around the mutual and intense love of a man and a woman." He hastened to assure critics that "the piece furnishes ample opportunities for the expression of Miss Adams's gifts in both comedy and sympathetic acting." Still, he was not personally confident that Maude felt the same way about the play.

In fact, Maude was uncertain about playing the same character-type she had so often played previously. The trials related to the restoration of her health, coupled with the long tours' wondrous experiences, had led her to an intense evaluation of her future career.

Yes, Maude was pleased with her artistic progress. Nonetheless, she had no desire to repeatedly play the same character-type. Her adventures while performing "Romeo and Juliet" and "L'Aiglon" had given her the opportunity to deviate from familiar roles and expand her talents. In spite of the caustic reviews these plays had engendered, Maude had found that playing these roles gave her an exhilaration not otherwise felt. These feelings appeared to provide the impetus to push the parameters of her acting even further. Only in this manner, she believed, would her unique theatrical abilities be fully realized.

Governing her own actions for almost two years had given Maude a sense of empowerment not consciously felt before. Men were amazed by her daring and boldness while confronting and conquering cultural differences and physical discomfort. Maude believed that she was now in control of her life and could direct this energy to advancing her career. She now felt that maintaining a private life apart from the stage had its professional advantages and allowed her to pursue personal goals. She had once viewed solitude as a luxury; she now believed it to be a necessity.

The long layoff from the theater had also given Maude additional insight to better understand her strengths and weaknesses. Typical of her drive toward perfection, Maude now consciously strove to pattern her life to accentuate the former while attempting to minimize the latter. Taking complete charge of the new production was the first obvious example of her new attitude. Renegotiating her arrangement with Frohman was another. Instead of agreeing to an increase in salary, Maude proposed that she receive a larger percentage of the gross profits, with which Frohman concurred. The decision would soon make Maude the richest actress on Broadway. By the end of 1904, she would earn more than $100,000, equivalent to $3 million in today's currency.

Maude expanded her property on Forty-First Street with the acquisition of the adjacent building, bringing the assessed valuation of both buildings to more than $64,000 ($1.9 million today). She filled her home with tapestries, furniture, travel ephemera, and all the books that she had wished to read and own. When she changed her bedroom decor from its convent-style simplicity to one of Edwardian comfort, those around her sensed a serious rearrangement in her personal approach to life. Frohman noticed these alterations as well, and he was delighted. They augmented his star's professionalism, he believed, even more than he could have hoped to accomplish himself.

At one time, Frohman had advised Maude to "please the women; for without them, the theater would have to close. If the women do not like a play," he declared, "it is doomed. If they do not like a player, he or she may as well take to another profession."[10]

Maude had obviously heeded his advice. There was no question that she pleased women and had become the idol of many. Her unique ability to touch women's hearts had been continually reaffirmed in reviews of her performances. Cognizant of this ability, Maude now strove to capture women's minds as well. She wished to become their ultimate favorite among all actresses. The new production would be her first challenge.

Rehearsals for "The Pretty Sister of José" began in early September. Maude had selected the cast, supervised the scenery design and costumes, and consulted on the lighting, a vital aspect in which she was increasingly recognized as an authority. The scenery and lighting were saturated with earth tones, which evoked the visual sense of Spain. She not only performed her role, but also led rehearsals with a friendly but firm command. When Frohman witnessed the production's first dress rehearsal, he was so impressed with the result that he had little to suggest. When he had originally told Maude that she would be singing and dancing in the play, stage managers had harbored doubts that she would be able to perform adequately. After viewing the rehearsal, Frohman was convinced he had another box-office success. Yes, it was likely the critics might question Maude's interpretation; but crowds—especially women—would pack the theaters. In the advertising broadsides, Maude was pictured dancing, with her dress flowing around her.

On October 14, 1903, "The Pretty Sister of José" opened at the Weiting Opera House in Syracuse, New York. Since the event was Maude's return to the stage after a prolonged absence, the occasion made her entrance all the more appealing. The audience rose from their seats and applauded her for several minutes, stopping the play before it had really begun. A *Clipper* reporter, sent to witness Maude's return, cabled a brief resume of opening night.

> Maude Adams in "The Pretty Sister of José" drew an immense audience. The new play is interesting, and Miss Adams's portrayal of the title role adds another to her long list of successes. The supporting company played their roles to perfection, and the mounting and costuming were elaborate.[11]

Rochester, Detroit, Toledo, Fort Wayne, and Grand Rapids followed, all to S.R.O. performances. Yet the next stop, Chicago, would test the critics' sensibilities. As described in the program, the story of the play reveals the romance of Pepita (Maude), a beautiful Spanish girl, who scoffs at love. At a bullfight, she sees a matador, Sebastiano (Henry Ainley, a young English actor appearing for the first time in the U.S., brought over by Frohman especially for this part). Pepita is impressed by his skill and daring. He falls in love with her at first sight. The bullfighter meets with her brother José (Edgar Selwyn), in an attempt to gain Pepita's love; but she, not admitting the true state of her feelings, scorns him. He leaves Madrid, but returns; and at his next fight, catches sight of Pepita just as he is being charged by the bull.

The knowledge that she is near unnerves him; and before he can recover, he is seriously injured. The girl, believing him to be dying, reveals her love. Sebastiano recovers, and the play ends with the union of the lovers.

"The coming to the Illinois Theater tomorrow night of Miss Maude Adams," declared the *Sunday Tribune*, "will by the majority of theatergoers be regarded as the most interesting event in the present week." The *Tribune* went on to point out that not only was Maude held in high esteem by local audiences, but she had also been absent from the stage for two years because of ill health. Reviews from the East, the

Tribune reported, had been unanimous in their praise, not only for her characterization as a comedienne, but also for her display of emotional range. Full houses were predicted.

As much as Frohman would have liked to minimize concern about Maude's health, critics brought it up constantly. Actually, the issue turned to Maude's advantage. When it was found that she was healthy and strong, critics waxed ecstatic about her return to the stage almost as much as they praised her actual performance.

> She gave of her best abilities and of her sincerest endeavor last evening, and her audience were similarly generous in their expression of appreciation and approval. Hearty applause greeted her when she first entered, and after every act the recalls were numerous.[12]

Amy Leslie, of the *Daily News,* lauded Maude and panned the author of the play for her stilted, priggish plot. Maude had turned a less than liked, rakish, physical character, Leslie reported, into a charming and appealing young beauty, because "the actress herself has a certain gentle and beguiling personality."

Leslie was pleased when Maude sang and accompanied herself on the guitar. Her dancing, however, was done "frigidly and in ungainly clumsiness." Still, noted Leslie, she did it with so much confidence and spirit that it satisfied the audience.

The *New York Clipper* simply reported that Maude brought excellent financial rewards to the Illinois Theater (and, by extension, to herself and Frohman).

The second week of "The Pretty Sister of José" brought equally excellent reviews, full houses, and "a warm welcome after her absence from Chicago of over a year." The New York opening was Maude's next engagement, and Frohman was making sure it would be a gala event.

The play opened at the Empire Theater on November 10, 1903, to an enthusiastic crowd "perhaps the largest and most representative audience assembled at any premiere this season." The *New York American* began their review with a paragraph on Maude's health. "It is a pleasure to record," they said, "that she is now the picture of health, full of vitality; and she impresses one with the sense of physical strength." And her acting?

> As charmingly, as dainty as ever. She threw herself into the role of the pretty, enthusiastic gypsy in the first two acts, with a rare understanding of and sympathy of the past. In the last two acts, when the girl has come to love the matador whom she had spurned before, she showed the woman's soul awakened with a truth of touch, a depth of feeling, a wildness of despair and delirium of joy with her lover snatched from death that left few dry eyes in the audience.[13]

And the reviewer thoroughly enjoyed Maude's singing and dancing, calling her dancing an "embodiment of grace" and her singing "sweet," with guitar accompaniment no less.

The *Herald* critic believed the play to be inferior to Maude's talents. Still, since the audience had come solely to see her act, she "captivated the town, and a more enthusiastic audience was never seen in New York."[14] With heroine worship, curtain calls, shouts of bravo, and speeches, "it was one of those nights that are not soon forgotten." By actual count, Maude made forty-eight curtain calls. At the last, she shyly said to the audience, almost in a whisper: "It would be simply impossible for me to express what I feel toward you, or to describe my happiness in being back here with you again." There were tears in her voice.

The *Times,* speaking with joy of Maude's return to the stage, also observed the actress's enhanced talents. "She has gained freshness and color, and her art has ripened, rounded out, and mellowed."[15]

That the effusive accolades from critics and the overwhelming response from the audience came on her thirty-first birthday could not have been more gratifying to Maude. In her dressing room, after the final curtain calls, Frohman embraced Maude warmly and smiled in triumph.

By the third week of the play's sustained prosperity, newspapers broke out in a rash of feature articles lauding Maude's return to the stage and her reawakened ability to capture women's hearts. "Actress Worship Reaches Its Highest Point in the Mad Way Women Worship Maude Adams," head-

Maude's commitment to her profession made her a dramatic star and attracted thousands of admirers. Photos like this were given out as special souvenirs when each one of her plays had reached its 100th or 200th performance.

lined one newspaper. "Maude Adams Returns to Stage and All Feminine New York Goes Crazy Over Her," proclaimed another. "Why do women rave over and adore Maude Adams?" asked a third.

On opening night, an hour before the curtain went up, Broadway had been packed with carriages and pedestrians. Indeed, it had been necessary to employ a special force of police to keep them all moving. Standing-room seats were almost impossible to obtain — ticket scalpers were enjoying a financial bonanza — yet theatergoers were willing to stand five deep back of the orchestra and balcony.

After the show, women rushed from their seats into Fortieth Street and waited at the stage entrance nearly an hour to see Maude come out. When she emerged, she calmly walked from the stage door to her carriage, nodding her head in acknowledgment through the narrow lane of admiring women. "And all this because Maude Adams is shrined in the very heart of her own sex," commented critic Charles Darnton. As much as the authors of these articles tried to explain her appeal, no one seemed to be able to define it. It was as if her acting were as mysterious as the actress herself.

Maude played to nine weeks of S.R.O. audiences at the Empire. During the holiday season, extra matinees were scheduled at her request to satisfy the overwhelming demand for tickets.

Phyllis Robbins traveled from Boston to New York to attend Maude's opening night. A few days later, she and Maude enjoyed a carriage ride through Central Park. A week later, Maude invited Phyllis to have lunch with her at the Forty-First Street home. Revealed to Phyllis for the first time would be Maude's inner sanctum. Previous to this, several people had visited Maude at home and reported on their observations.

Robbins would later recall the quiet atmosphere, the darkened rooms, and the myriad books lining the walls of several rooms. She observed a glass cabinet that contained items belonging to Maude's father. She admitted having noticed little else in the house as she sat down to lunch in what Maude called her conservatory.

Other visitors had noted the narrowness of the four-story English-style house, its thick walls and doors blocking the sounds of the city outside. Servants spoke in hushed tones. The furniture was elegant and simple, manifesting Maude's interest in antiques and art obtained during her various travels. Dark green was Maude's favorite color, the hues of which were carried through several rooms. In the central hall, a French sedan chair served as a telephone booth. The library walls were lined with rare books from floor to ceiling, complete sets of English classics, English and French plays, and the works of English philosophers, of whom the positivist Herbert Spencer was her acknowledged favorite. At the end of a long, dark hallway was Maude's private suite. A fernery graced the entrance. Previous visitors' descriptions of her bedroom had emphasized its convent-like furnishings. No one had yet reported on the recent redecorations accomplished since Maude's return to the U.S. As Ada Patterson, writer and sometime visitor, reported in her 1903 article on Maude's home in *The Theater* magazine: "Here Maude Adams finds the silence and the peace she loves. Here she can indulge to the full her fondness for introspection."[16]

Patterson mentioned two additional features discovered in Maude's home. First, there were no items in the house that suggested religiosity of any kind. "The actress is not a devotee," Patterson wrote. "She belongs to no sect, has adopted no creed." Second, Maude was said to give to many charities and to house young women who were temporarily destitute. Who they were or how they came to appeal to Maude is unknown. What is known is that Maude often helped out novice actresses with housing and money as they attempted to pursue their careers in the harsh arena of New York's theatrical world.

In January 1904, Maude began an extended tour of "The Pretty Sister of José." Frohman had announced that she would be appearing in eastern cities and that, later in the season, she would travel to the West Coast, not having appeared there for several years. Critics questioned Frohman about this proposed tour, suggesting that the grueling schedule might possibly be detrimental to Maude's health.

Their concern was reinforced when, in late January, Maude canceled an appearance in Waterbury, Connecticut, because of illness, said to be a cold and sore throat. When Maude was reported to have left the company and gone to Ronkonkoma, critics were sure her tour was in jeopardy. In fact, Frohman cancelled visits to Hartford, Northampton, and New Haven — a week of disappointment to many theatergoers — with no indication when Maude would return.

Nonetheless, Maude told the press the setback was only temporary and she would soon reappear. The following week, she opened at the National Theater in Washington, D.C., seemingly in good health. The only noticeable difference was that she had eliminated her singing. It made no difference to D.C. audiences; they provided full houses the entire week.

Still, the tour had not started out well, and Frohman, especially, was concerned about his star's health, reported by newspapers to be quite fragile. The press noted that "she became exhausted after even ordinary exertion." While Frohman knew the description was not true, Maude's high-strung temperament and perfectionism might likely create a situation where a cold or sore throat might serve to interrupt the schedule. To anticipate any such episode, Frohman had the stage manager report daily on Maude's well being.

"The Pretty Sister of José" arrived in Boston for a two-week engagement at the Hollis Street Theater in the middle of February. The city's theatergoers anxiously awaited the appearance of their great favorite. The *Boston Globe's* review reassured everyone that Maude was better than ever.

> Miss Maude Adams was greeted with tumultuous cordiality by a house full of devoted admirers last evening. She had been absent from the stage for more than a year and during that time there had been all sorts of direful rumors circulated regarding her ill health. It was, therefore, with genuine delight that she was seen to trip gayly and joyously on the stage — the same fascinatingly winsome and deliciously vivacious little creature whom everybody had held in such affectionate remembrance.[17]

"Rarely has an actress received such a reception in Boston," the newspaper went on to report. Maude made a dozen curtain calls after the first act and an equal number after each act and the final curtain. Women in the audience were seen to cry and laugh with Maude throughout the play, again raising the question of Maude's exceptional hold over females. The *Globe* critic answered his own question with an insightful description.

> Miss Adams has a charm that is entirely her own, a bewitchingly dainty girlishness that is captivating, a tender sense of feminine weakness that is irresistibly appealing; and her personality is so alluring that the pleasure she affords an audience is not to be measured by the limits of her artistic attainments.[18]

In other words, Maude epitomized the ideal of what young womanhood in America dreamed to emulate. Identifying with those features of femininity that she exemplified, how could they not wish that they too might be like Maude Adams?

In order to preserve her strength, Maude instituted a tightly scheduled daily regimen. After a busy morning of rehearsals at the theater, she rested for the entire afternoon, coming to the theater an hour before the opening curtain. After the play, she immediately returned to her hotel room. While traveling, she was not to be disturbed between stations. While Maude was in Boston, Phyllis Robbins saw her only once, briefly, to Phyllis' disappointment. Still, she saw the play twice more.

The next few weeks saw the "José" company play one-night stands through Massachusetts and Connecticut, where they visited the cities that had been cancelled earlier in the tour. A two-week engagement in Philadelphia attracted crowded houses and warm welcomes. Critics and audiences together rejoiced at Maude's return to the theater and her apparent good health.

At this time, Frohman announced that Maude would shortly conclude her season appearing in "The Pretty Sister of José" although her tour would extend to the Pacific coast. "While on this special tour," Frohman stated, "it has been decided that she will appear in "The Little Minister."

In spite of her success in the current play, Maude had never been entirely happy with it, believing the script to be inferior. No amount of rewriting seemed to improve it, so Maude requested that the play be shelved. In its place, she and Frohman chose to revive "The Little Minister," last performed nearly five years before. Few audiences in the West had seen the play; and it was believed that it remained an excellent moneymaker. While the company performed "The Pretty Sister of José" in Pittsburgh, St. Louis, and Cincinnati, the cast rehearsed their parts for "The Little Minister," to open in St. Paul the end of April. Frohman merely shipped the scenery and costumes and had advance men paper the scheduled cities with broadsides announcing Maude's impending arrival.

Three performances each in St. Paul and Minneapolis proved that "The Little Minister" was as popular as ever. For three weeks in May, the company played in thirteen cities, gradually moving west. At all of these stops, the *Clipper* reported "big business," "large audiences," and "excellent box-office receipts." Most of all, Maude was reported to be in good spirits, seemingly energized by playing the Lady Babbie role.

A week before Maude's appearance in Salt Lake City, local newspapers ran photos and feature articles about her career, from youth to current stardom. Annie was already in town, visiting an old friend, Mrs. Isabel Pitts. This afforded newspaper reporters the opportunity to interview her and print numerous stories about her old performances at Brigham Young's theater, as well as the oft-told tale of Maude's first appearance on stage. Annie said she was awaiting her daughter, whom she would accompany to San Francisco. She was also hoping to be able to escort Maude throughout her western tour.

This was Maude's first appearance in Salt Lake City as a star. The box-office rush for tickets was so great, the three evening performances and one matinee were sold out in a matter of hours. Receipts were expected to exceed $2,000 at each performance.

What was considered easy travel from Denver to Salt Lake City turned into a race to have Maude arrive in time for the first show. A washout on the Denver-Pacific line prevented the train from reaching Cheyenne. Normal rail travel from Denver to Salt Lake City demanded a train change in Cheyenne. Railroad management ran a special train out of Julesburg to intercept Maude's train. Unfortunately, the locomotive broke down; and, although a stiff run was made, Maude's train was missed. Another train was dispatched to catch up with Maude at Green River, where the theatrical cars were attached and brought into Salt Lake City. Instead of going to a hotel, where she would be subject to innumerable visitors, Maude joined her mother at Mrs. Pitts's home, where she rested.

When Maude entered the theater's dressing room, she was surprised to find it transformed into "a dainty boudoir." Crepe tissue in pink and blue had been hung from the walls and ceiling. Hundreds of flowers were attached to the crepe hangings. A sign — "My Lady's Bower" — was affixed to the mirror.

As Maude made her entrance at the first performance, the audience rose in unison, applauding and cheering the actress who, this night, returned to her native ground. In the audience were friends and relatives, many of whom remembered her as a child beginning her stage career. Not surprisingly, Maude was perceived as the embodiment of fine acting. Yet, the audience saw two Maudes: one, the sweet young girl under the guidance of her actress mother; another, the mature,

When Maude visited Salt Lake City on a tour, she and her mother were given acclaim, Annie for her years as one of the city's leading actresses and Maude for being Annie's highly successful daughter. (The Harvard Theatre Collection, The Houghton Library)

charming woman who had, in six short years, become the most renowned actress in America.

> Throughout "The Little Minister" she captivates. With glance and tone and movement, coquettishness and mock demureness, and a touch or two of woe, she holds us all.[19]

Curtains were so numerous, people lost count. The dressing room was filled with well wishers; and Maude, uncharacteristically, received them all. At each performance, the scenario repeated itself—a grand welcome at her entrance and endless recalls following each curtain.

After one performance, Annie gathered her old theatrical friends together to go backstage and greet Maude. At another, she led the governor of Utah and his friends to wish Maude well. The governor brought a large loving cup to present to Maude. It was filled with champagne and handed around for each person to sip from the contents. No one seemed to notice that the theater's strict fire regulations had been completely ignored.

Accompanying the presentation of the loving cup was a brief, but moving, speech by the governor. Maude seemed visibly affected, her stage presence momentarily forgotten. "I cannot make a speech," she began, when the governor came to her rescue. "Don't say a word," he said as he grasped her hand. "But I must," she continued, seemingly assured by the governor's manner. "I must say how much I thank you for all this handsome remembrance, and so much more for the motive which prompted it; for I know that deep down in the bottom of this cup is the affection you hold for my dear mother."[20] There were tears in Maude's eyes. Nearby, Annie was radiant with delight and pride.

For those friends and relatives who could not afford the price of admission, Maude sent tickets that she had purchased. To each of the stagehands, Maude gave liberal tips. On the way to San Francisco, Maude sent a note to the governor, thanking him for his kindness toward her and her mother. Yet, Maude was not pleased with having her mother as a companion, less so with the likelihood of her presence during the entire Western tour.

As had been the case in Salt Lake City, Maude was appearing in 'Frisco for the first time as a star; and Frohman saw to it that advertising for "The Little Minister" blanketed the city. She was to appear at the Columbia Theater for two weeks. Additional matinees were added when the demand for tickets exceeded the number of seats available.

Maude received an enthusiastic greeting and was deemed a great success.

> There is radium in Maude Adams. At least there comes from her a current as distinct as electricity, and the more excited she grew the more irresistibly it seemed to bombard us. She puts more acting into one scene than the ordinary actress knows how to use during the entire play.[21]

Reviewers had anticipated that Maude, after playing Babbie for so many performances, would have become complacent about the role. They again underestimated her professionalism. Maude played Babbie with vivacity, the kind one usually sees at the beginning of shows, not a thousand performances later. "The effect is simply startling," said the reviewer, "for she carries the audience into her new mood as fast as she changes into it herself."

In San Francisco, Annie visited friends and old colleagues while Maude remained in her hotel room, adhering to her daily regimen of rest and seclusion. Just about the time that Maude was ready to begin the remainder of the West Coast tour, Annie received a cable from Frohman asking her to join a company for an upcoming road production. Coincidence?

From San Francisco, the company visited Los Angeles (S.R.O. for the three-day stop); Portland (advance sellout); Tacoma (full house); and Seattle (turn-away business). They then began the return east with one-night stops in Helena and Butte, Montana, and Duluth, Minnesota, where the house was sold out before the doors opened. On July 9, five days later, in Kalamazoo, Michigan, Maude's season ended. For the 1903-04 season, Maude played thirty-seven weeks, appeared in sixty-three cities, and played 296 performances. As the cast prepared to return to their respective homes for the summer, Maude gave each member a token of her appreciation for their efforts on her behalf — brooches for the women and stickpins for the men, all set with diamonds.

Maude had no sooner arrived at her Ronkonkoma farm than Frohman announced that she would begin her new season in October, making a brief tour outside New York, and then returning to the Empire Theater for the holiday season. She would continue with "The Little Minister" — Frohman could not bring himself to set aside such a moneymaker — and a new play by Israel Zangwill, called "Jenny." He also stated that he had secured for Maude a fifty-minute character play, called "Op O' Me Thumb." Frohman had been reluctant to agree to this play because Maude's role would be as demanding as she had ever played. Yet, Maude insisted. The challenges, she believed, would offer another opportunity to expand her acting abilities.

Frohman also alluded to having Maude play "L'Aiglon" in London, if her schedule permitted; but she expressed no desire to perform there. Added to his flurry of announcements was a brief statement that he had secured a new play by Barrie, which would first be produced in London and then brought to the U.S. Barrie's play was called "Peter Pan."

Moving from Ronkonkoma to the Catskills cottage, which Maude used each year to prepare her roles, she reviewed Lady Babbie once again. Frohman was planning to send her on a southern tour (new territory) before returning to New York. In spite of the long season just finished, Maude reported herself to be in excellent health.

Maude opened the new season in Norfolk, Virginia, on October 13, 1904, at the Academy of Music. Norfolk had six theaters, two for legitimate drama and four for variety, characteristic of the expansion of theater in the South in recent years. Here, Maude first experienced southern hospitality — polite applause and few curtain calls, although newspaper reviews were as enthusiastic as ever.

One- and two-night stands in seven cities brought Maude to New Orleans at the end of October. There she was greeted with the kind of audience enthusiasm for Lady Babbie that she had found in the North. Another two weeks of one-night stops, in ten cities in the South, netted excellent box office receipts and well-behaved audiences. Southern women were rarely found haunting the stage door after performances.

A return to Pittsburgh for a week in November brought enthusiastic S.R.O.

business again and a present from the theater manager on Maude's thirty-second birthday. While in Pittsburgh, Maude received a draft of Barrie's "Peter Pan" to study. She found that the hero of the play would be performed by a woman.

Two more weeks of one-night stands ended in Chicago with a week's repeat of "The Little Minister." Response to the play was as if audiences had never before seen it, although Maude had staged it in Chicago twice before. Frohman apologized to theatergoers that Maude would appear for only one week, giving as his excuse that she needed rehearsal time for a new play that would soon be opening in New York. The statement, as most of his public announcements were designed to do, helped to sell out every performance, even two added matinees.

Amy Leslie, of the *Chicago Daily News*, wrote that Maude had delighted the crowd "in her old success," which Leslie believed to be her best work.

> At the Illinois a fashionable audience in a sympathetic and amenable temper last night took the piece as avidly as if it were brand new and hanging in the balance with favor written on its untried edges. Miss Adams has lost none of her magnetism, girlish sweetness or fitful little flames of power.[22]

Like critics before her, Leslie attempted to define why women so loved Maude, why they were continually drawn to her theater.

> Her talent is undeniable though pale and ethereal, her personality unavoidably endowed with a kind of perpetual youth which lies feverishly on the surface of fragile constitutions and her temperament glows and throbs and scintillates in a spring-like attractiveness.

Her assessment did little to explain women's attraction to Maude, obscured as it was within Leslie's baroque use of breathless superlatives and dependent clauses.

The *Tribune* remarked about Maude's spirit while performing Babbie, features that she had not lost since first appearing in the role several years previous.

> Miss Adams was as blithe and as fascinating as she ever has been as Babbie. She is evidently in good physical condition this season, and enters into her performance with as much zest and spirits as if it was her first season in the role.[23]

The audience's unqualified commendations included more than thirty curtain calls and such a jammed stage-door crowd that police had to escort Maude to her carriage.

Maude opened with "The Little Minister" at New York's Empire Theater on December 26. The plan was for her to play Lady Babbie for four weeks and then introduce another play. Overwhelming demand for tickets forced Frohman to extend "The Little Minister" indefinitely.

The *Times* gave Maude a brief but eloquent review.

> The memory of her characterization is still fresh in the minds of theatergoers, and her interpretation of Babbie is already too familiar to need more praises. Miss Adams

is the same slender, winsome, witching Babbie, and her appeal is as strong as it used to be.[24]

The *Clipper* suggested that first-nighters all knew the play, so they obviously attended the theater solely as "a demonstration of welcome."

> When she first appeared, the house rang with applause, and it was some minutes before she could proceed with her lines. At the end of each act the curtain had to be raised from four to eight times and so great were the calls for a speech at the end of act three that the little lady very feelingly said: "I thank you. I thank you." It is only necessary to note that she has never given a finer impersonation.[25]

Seated in the first row was Phyllis Robbins. She would attend "The Little Minister" several times before returning to Boston to await Maude's arrival on her spring tour.

After two weeks of full houses, Frohman announced that he had canceled the greater part of Maude's tour for the remainder of the season and extended her engagement at the Empire until March 11. Along with a slightly shortened "Minister," Maude would introduce an entirely new character in the short play "Op O' Me Thumb" on February 6. The character was indeed the antithesis of Babbie, and Maude embraced it with ardor.

The plot: A poor laundry drudge, Amanda Afflick (Maude), the butt of taunts and jibes by her associates, a workhouse child with a romantic imagination, lives in a fantasy realm that raises her above the ridicule of her fellow workers. It is her dream that she is the child of millionaires, who will someday claim her and place her amid the rich surroundings to which her soul aspires. Her hero is a coster, a fruit and vegetable seller, Horace Greensmith (Arthur Byron), who, more than a year before, had left a shirt to be laundered. She has cherished this personal item of his; and when he returns, he is impressed by her devotion. A bank holiday is approaching, but Amanda has never known the delights of a trip to Hampstead. The coster, amused at her ingenuousness, invites her on an outing. Yet, afraid of provoking derision, he suggests they should proceed in secrecy; and the implication of his suggestion shatters Amanda's dream. She tearfully concludes, "It is not to be."

At the same show that Maude performed "The Little Minister" for the 1,000th time, she introduced "Op O' Me Thumb." Audiences were shocked to see her in almost unrecognizable costume, taken aback by her Cockney accent, and enthralled by a performance that brought them to tears. This, indeed, was a different Maude; but a tremendous success nevertheless. Her transformation from Babbie to Amanda astonished audiences. When they recovered, their response was one of supreme respect and enthusiasm. The *New York Sun* reported that "in all her career of victories she has never scored a more heartfelt and tender success."[26]

The Theater magazine, usually quite reserved in its praise, stated unequivocally that "no one, after witnessing her artistic rendering of the leading role in this very human little one-act play, can other than admit that her histrionic art is of the very highest quality."[27]

Critics suggested to Frohman that the short play should be the curtain raiser instead of the after-piece. Frohman, instead, chose the opportunity to discuss the contrasts between Maude's two parts. "Maude plays," he hesitated, "or rather, actually lives the two characters in one and the same evening."[28]

"It is a veritable *tour de force*," he continued, "with the element of the uncanny in it, such as dwells in all the work of this frail, ethereal, yet indomitable-spirited actress." No one disagreed.

The combination of "The Little Minister" and "Op O' Me Thumb" played to capacity houses throughout the ten weeks of Maude's engagement. She could have stayed at the Empire for the entire season, but Frohman had promises to fulfill with theater managers in other cities. Unfortunately, Maude found herself ailing.

She had been experiencing sharp pains on her right side for several days. Only Frohman and her doctor were aware of the problem. The doctor diagnosed it as an irritated appendix, to be carefully monitored. Under Maude's pressure, he reluctantly agreed to allow her to finish the season. Frohman decided to keep the tour close to home, no farther south than Philadelphia, no farther north than Boston. During one-night stands, only "The Little Minister" was performed. In Philadelphia and Boston, "Op O' Me Thumb" was included in the program. Between the middle of March and her last performance in Lawrence, Massachusetts, on May 18, Maude performed in pain. The last week of her tour was particularly uncomfortable. Yet no one in the cast was aware of her difficulties.

Maude's pain had now become so unbearable, she found it difficult to walk. At the same time that she was meeting with her doctor, Frohman announced that she would appear in Barrie's new play, "Peter Pan," next season. He indicated that Maude would visit the Barries that summer in England.

On May 23, Maude had an emergency appendectomy. Delaying the operation for so long had placed her life in danger. The public was not informed until three weeks later, once she was considered "out of danger."

On May 21, Maude had been seized with severe pain while resting at Ronkonkoma. Brought to the city by special train, she was operated on by Dr. Robert Abbe at his private sanitarium on West Fiftieth Street. Only Annie was in attendance. Frohman was in England, but he was kept informed of her condition by cable. Maude had given her property manager a sealed envelope to keep until the operation was over. If it were successful, he would return the envelope; if not, he was to give it to her lawyer.

The doctor later reported that the operation was a complete success but that, during its progress, Maude had "hovered very near death's door." For several hours after the operation, Maude remained unconscious, breathing shallowly. At this point, the doctor instituted unspecified procedures to "retain the spark of life." Several hours later, she returned to consciousness. Within a week, Maude had sufficiently improved to be moved to Ronkonkoma. Only later was the public informed how close they had come to losing their esteemed and beloved actress.

The summer trip to England had to be cancelled. Reporters questioned whether Maude would be healthy enough to appear in Barrie's play. At the time, the prognosis was uncertain.

13

Peter Pan

James Barrie took bits and pieces from his children's stories and put them together to create his famous fairy tale, "Peter Pan."

In 1896, Barrie had written a tale about a boy who enjoyed being a child and never wished to grow up. The character's marriage failed because his emotions had not matured. Barrie's biographers believe the story was an allegory of his own marriage. Barrie had originally harbored doubts about his marriage with Mary Ansell because of his insecurity about physical intimacy. The couple remained childless, which was difficult for Barrie because he liked children and for his wife because of her desire to be a mother. Although biographers viewed their union as unhappy, it was during their marriage that Barrie wrote his most successful plays.

Another important woman in Barrie's literary life was Sylvia Llewelyn Davis, daughter of George de Maurier, the celebrated actor. She had two young boys whom Barrie enjoyed entertaining in Kensington Gardens. The Davises became the prototype for the Darling family, later featured in Peter Pan. Barrie wrote short stories for the boys; often, the entire family acted them out. Barrie embellished the stories to include talking birds and fairies. Somewhere in the process, he introduced the character of Peter Pan. In 1902, Barrie incorporated these short stories into a fantasy called "The Little White Bird."

Barrie produced another manuscript, entitled "The Boy Castaways of Black Lake Island," in a limited edition of two copies. This told of the make-believe adventures of the boys and their dog. The Davis children (now numbering three) and their dog were included in the story.

During 1902 and 1903, Barrie continued to write children's stories. Certain characters reappeared: Mrs. Darling, the picture of motherhood; Mr. Darling, a father who had little time for his children; one daughter, named Wendy; sons George and Michael. All of the children were named after their counterparts in the Davis family. Peter Pan's name was given to the hero of the story. "I made Peter by rubbing the three children violently together," Barrie wrote in the dedication to the published version of "Peter Pan." "That is all he is, the spark I got from you."[1] Captain Hook, the villain, was an offshoot of Captain Swarthy, from "The Boy Castaways." Other pirate names were taken from literary figures or actual pirates. Tinker Bell had been Tippy in earlier stories.

When Barrie completed the initial draft of the fairy tale, he titled it simply "Anon — A Play." He was convinced that the play would be rejected by producers due to its many scenery changes and special effects, for example, children flying. Barrie showed the play to Sir Beerbohm Tree, one of London's most successful producers. Tree categorically rejected the play and told Charles Frohman, who had already purchased several of Barrie's plays, that Barrie "had gone mad with his latest writing."[2]

Characteristically, Frohman was not in the least bothered by Tree's assertion. Barrie had already proved himself an able and theatrically successful author. And Frohman himself had a reputation for taking risky plays and turning them into box-office triumphs.

Barrie submitted two plays for Frohman's consideration: "Alice Sit-by-the-Fire," which Barrie believed to be his best play, and "Peter Pan." ("Alice Sit-by-the-Fire" was produced in London, starring Ellen Terry, and in the U.S., starring Ethel Barrymore; the play barely lasted two seasons.) When Frohman read the "Peter Pan" script, he believed it to be "the most thrilling pleasure of my life." So enthusiastic was Frohman that he immediately set in motion plans to have the play open in London in December 1904. The London engagement was also seen as a trial run for an American version, starring Frohman's favorite, Maude Adams.

Gerald du Maurier, having already appeared in several Barrie plays, was asked to play Captain Hook. His costume was designed by the artist and famed printmaker, William Nicholson. Dion Boucicault, Jr., the director of the play, chose his sister, Nina, to play Peter. He selected the young woman to perform the role of Peter Pan because he felt there were no men who could authoritatively play the role of an adolescent boy. A popular Barrie character actress, Helen Trevelyn, was chosen to play Wendy, whose role was considered equal to that of Peter. Dorothy Baird, another alumna of Barrie's plays, was to play Mrs. Darling. George Sheldon took the role of Smee, the pirate, a part that would become his most famous.

Rehearsals began in the fall of 1904. An observer would have considered them chaotic by American theater standards. Actors were given scripts that represented only their parts, and then only a few pages at a time. "Wendy" was unaware she would be flying until the moment she had to don the mechanical apparatus. Miss Boucicault received no help from Barrie regarding her interpretation of Peter, likely an order from her director brother.

"Peter Pan" was to open December 22, 1904, but had to be delayed five days because of mechanical problems with the flying mechanism. At the opening, two scenes were omitted because the complex gadgetry was not yet reliable.

The managers and cast worried about audience reaction to Barrie's dramatic fantasy. Since the press had been banned from rehearsals— another of Dion Boucicault's decisions— there was little promotional material to satisfy theatergoers' curiosity.

Boucicault himself was so nervous about the audience's response to the play that he instructed the orchestra to initiate applause if the audience seemed hesitant to respond on their own. Once the curtain rose, however, the audience of adults and critics needed no prompting. They applauded "Peter Pan" with enthusiastic fervor.

Next day, reviews for the play were universally excellent; and headlines extended accolades for outstanding acting. Four nights after opening, mechanical problems finally solved, the omitted scenes were included.

Miss Boucicault soon found Peter to be a stressful and exhausting role. A month after opening, she missed the first of what would prove to be several performances. By the end of the play's run, her understudy was appearing regularly. On April 1, 1905, the play closed after a run of fourteen weeks, a long engagement by London standards, with a promise to return for the holiday season. In December the entire cast, minus Miss Boucicault, returned to the stage.

In April 1904, Maude had received a letter from Barrie introducing her to "Peter Pan." In the letter, Barrie implored her to consider playing Peter.

> My dear Maudie,
> I have written a play for children, which I don't suppose would be much use in America. She is rather a dear of a girl with ever so many children long before her hair is up, and the boy is Peter Pan in a new world. I should like you to be the boy and the girl and most of the children and the pirate captain. I hope you are coming here before the summer is ended, and I also hope I may have something to read you and tell you about. I can't get along without an idea that really holds me, but if I can get it how glad I shall be to be at work for little Maudie again."[3]

Several months later, Frohman gave Maude the script of the play to read and decide if it fit her talents and desires.

> I read the play after going home, and was so completely won by the character of Peter and so thoroughly interested and thrilled by his numerous adventures that I fell in love with him at once. In the evening, when I saw Mr. Frohman at the theater, I said: I would like to act "Peter Pan."
> Each line of it thrilled me, and as I passed from scene to scene an affection for Peter grew and took hold of me, until I was perfectly wrapped in a spell of desire to be Peter Pan himself.

Only days before Maude's emergency operation, Frohman had announced to the newspapers that Maude would introduce "Peter Pan" to American audiences in the fall. Barrie admitted that he wished Maude would play Peter, not only because of the artistic relationship that had developed between them, but also because of his fondness for her, albeit at a distance.

Because of Maude's operation and long recuperation, Frohman was again faced with the possibility that she might not be able to appear in the play. Nina Boucicault's short stint as Peter also raised questions about Maude's physical strength and emotional endurance performing such a uniquely demanding role.

Frohman returned from Europe in early August. His first order of business was

Charles Frohman at first spent heavily to promote "Peter Pan." By its third year, all Frohman needed to attract capacity crowds was a small ad in the newspapers. (1905. Museum of the City of New York. The Strowbridge Collection)

to meet with Maude, to evaluate her recovery. To his pleasant surprise, he found her well and eager to begin rehearsals for "Peter Pan." She had already been studying the role while resting at her Catskills cottage. Barrie was making alterations in the play to give more importance to Maude's role. Frohman's stage managers were busily working to perfect the flying mechanisms. Frohman told the press that "Peter Pan" would be introduced on the road, probably in the middle of October. He happily reported that Maude's health was excellent and that she was eager to assume the title role with her usual vigor.

Showing her usual work ethic while preparing a new role, Maude isolated herself at the cottage. Few visitors were allowed. While she studied the character of Peter, she walked, rode, and observed nature to gain inspiration for her interpretation of the magical boy. When rehearsals began in New York, cast members were taken with the almost ethereal manner Maude had assumed. This aura carried beyond the stage, as if Maude had herself become the embodiment of Peter. Once more she had become a boy; but, this time, unlike the doomed Aiglon, she was now the unconquerable Peter Pan.

While in the Catskills, Maude had befriended John and Elizabeth Alexander. John Alexander was a well-known painter and designer; his wife often brought her husband's designs to fruition. At Maude's suggestion, the Alexanders created costume designs and scenery for Peter Pan, many of which were ultimately used in the play. John Alexander was credited with designing Maude's costume, including the Peter Pan collar; Elizabeth prepared it for wearing. Their friendship joined, Maude would call on the Alexanders often to help design her plays. After John died in 1915, Maude and Elizabeth corresponded and visited occasionally for many years.

Frohman chose the National Theater, in Washington, D.C., to introduce "Peter Pan" to American audiences. On October 16, 1905, to a crowded and fashionable house, the play was presented with a minimum of fanfare, because Frohman was not yet convinced of its American appeal. So frenzied were the final full-dress rehearsals that the play was delayed a day to ensure everything would work as it should. Five run-throughs of the play, with Maude directing the action, lasted into the late evening.

A five-page brochure relating the story of "Peter Pan" was handed out to patrons. Frohman claimed the brochure was produced for those people arriving late at the theater. Actually, the synopsis had been prepared and distributed because of Frohman's concern that audiences would not understand the play.

Initial audience reaction in Washington, D.C., seemed to bear out Frohman's worry. Applause at the end of each act was polite, and reactions to humorous scenes were slight. The first-night audience seemed somewhat mystified, not sure what to say or do. The *Washington Star's* reviewer panned Frohman for producing the play, called it a "nightmare," and questioned why Maude was considered a great actress.[5] Other reviewers were more kind, but they too seemed perplexed by the play's action. One reviewer did admit that the fantasy elements had "gotten to me."

When the play moved to Baltimore for a week's engagement, nothing in the presentation was changed; yet critical and audience response proved favorable. The play was lauded as a beautiful excursion into fantasy; and no one could do it better than Maude, even at advanced prices.

Maude admitted to nervousness about the critical scene dealing with the near death of Tinker Bell. The audience knows that the invisible Tinker Bell does all the mending in Never-Never-Land. She loves Peter. The audience never sees Tinker, although they see the little bed she sleeps in. They can tell when she is on stage because she makes a sound like a sleigh-bell jingling and shows herself as a spot of light that follows Peter everywhere.

Tinker is poisoned by a drink that was meant for Peter. As the little sound fades and the spot of light grows dim, Peter rushes to her aid. Maude boldly moved to the front of the stage, disarming patrons because her action created a completely new, intimate dynamic between actor and audience. "Tinker is dying," she pleaded to the audience. "The only thing that can save her life is for you to believe in fairies." Pointing directly at the audience, Maude asked: "Do you believe in fairies?" Invariably, as if on cue, the entire house would rise and cry: "Yes! Yes! We believe in fairies!" Tinker was saved, and the audience's spontaneous and heartfelt action lifted the play to a success all its own.

Maude had been concerned that the audience would be so surprised by her question, few would respond. She was wrong. The audience had grown so involved in the action of the play and its fantasy characters, that their burst of support served as a welcome opportunity to unite with the play itself. The episode soon took on a life of its own. It became a symbolic moment that represented the delights of fantasy and imagination to an audience already imbued with these elements. Adults, as well as children, when asked the enchanting question, answered with conviction in the affirmative. Critics wondered: Have we outgrown fairy tales? To which they themselves answered: No, we have not.

Capitalizing on the audience's spontaneous response to Maude's question, Frohman had signs strategically located in the theater lobby. The placards read simply: "Do you believe in fairies?"

"Peter Pan" opened at the Empire Theater, New York City, on November 6, 1905, to an audience of first-nighters that represented the elite of the metropolis. They obviously believed in fairy tales, for they greeted the new production with unbounded applause and demands for countless curtain calls. The play and Maude had captivated audiences. Her performance launched the play on its way to becoming a nationwide vogue and made James Barrie's play one of the most beloved of children's stories.

The plot and its background: Peter Pan is the boy who refuses to grow up. He ran away the day he was born, because he heard his father and mother talking about what he was to be when he became a man. So, rather than grow up and become president, as they had planned, he ran away and lived a long, long time among the fairies in Never-Never-Land, which is "second to the right and then straight on till morning" from anywhere. There, Peter became captain of all the lost boys, who had fallen out of their carriages when their nurses were looking the other way and had been wafted away to Never-Never-Land to live. As the lost boys have no mothers, they are rather lonely at times; and, to make matters worse, none of them know any stories, so Peter tries to hear some by flying far away to nursery windows to hear the bed-time stories that mothers tell their children.

On one of Peter's journeys he visits the house of the Darlings, where he becomes so interested in the story of the prince who couldn't find the lady who wore the crystal slipper that he steals into the room. Nana, the faithful dog, who has always been the nurse and guardian of the Darling children, spies him and rushes to close the window so he cannot get out; but Peter escapes. So quickly, however, does Nana close the window that Peter's shadow hasn't time to get out with him. Mrs. Darling rolls the shadow up carefully and puts it away in a drawer in the nursery. The disconsolate Peter returns from time to time to search for it. At last, one night, with the aid of his personal fairy, Tinker Bell, he finds it. When Peter tries to fasten his shadow to his heel with soap, he finds it will not stick. His struggles awaken Wendy, the Darlings' eldest child. Wendy comforts him in his distress and sews his shadow to his heel. In return, Peter tells her of the delights of Never-Never-Land. He persuades her to go with him to be a mother to all the lost boys. Peter wakes all the children and, after blowing fairy dust on their shoulders, teaches them to fly. They all fly out into the night, bound for Never-Never-Land.

The home of the lost boys is in a land infested by a band of pirates whose cunning and bloodthirsty leader, Captain Hook, is Peter's sworn enemy. It is a country full of ferocious animals, which are kept at bay by the lost boys' looking at the beasts through their legs. Nervous while Peter is gone, the boys discover a great white bird flying toward them. They shoot an arrow that brings the bird to the ground. Then they discover the bird is Wendy. Fortunately, the arrow encountered a charm that Peter had given to Wendy, so her life is spared. When Peter returns, they all build her a beautiful little house. Wendy then assumes her duties as a mother to the lost boys and puts them to bed. Meanwhile, guarding the house, Peter cuts off the tail of a predatory lion that is prowling about.

Graver dangers await them. Hook, with his lawless band of cutthroats, attacks a friendly tribe of Indians who have been guardians of the children's home. The Indians are defeated, and the children are carried away to the pirate ship. Only Peter escapes. Hook attempts to poison Peter, laughing spitefully as he imagines Peter's dying moments.

Tinker Bell saves Peter by drinking the poison. Tinker's life is saved only by the cheering message from the audience that they all believe in fairies. She and Peter set out to rescue the lost children from the pirates.

Hook believes he has at last disposed of Peter. Now, Hook has only one other fear in the world — a terror of the man-eating crocodile that has pursued him ever since Peter cut off Hook's hand and threw it to the voracious saurian. The crocodile, liking the taste of Hook's hand, pursues him constantly. Luckily for Hook, the crocodile has also swallowed a clock, the loud ticking of which always warns Hook of impending danger.

Hook has the captured children brought on deck. He is about to make them all walk the plank when he hears a loud ticking. Suddenly, Hook and his crew are overcome with fear. Peter, who has been doing the ticking, scrambles aboard and provides the children with arms. Under his brave leadership, they attack the pirates and drive them into the sea. Peter himself thrusts Hook into the sea, where the eager crocodile waits to snap him up.

Then, the victorious Peter flies with Wendy and the children back to the Darlings' home. Sadly, he will miss them all; but he knows that the one thing children want after an adventure is their mother's love and sympathy. He returns them to their mother's arms; and he and Tinker Bell go to live in a little house in the treetops. There, they can always be young. There, the fairies come at night to light up their house; and nightingales sing them to sleep.

The *New York Times* headlined their review: "J.M. Barrie in His Most Fantastic Mood — Maude Adams in Perfect Sympathy With Its Gladsome Text." Few other plays had ever received such coverage from the *Times*.

> It will be many a long day before the memory of J.M. Barrie's "Peter Pan" fades from mind. Its gentle humor, its tender pathos, will linger like the far-away echoes of some childhood song. "Peter Pan" is boyhood's dreams dreamed all over again.
> Of all the gladsome Barrie fantasies, none has seemed so truly satisfying, so fully wholesome, so tenderly appealing as "Peter Pan." He knows the heart of mankind, he understands its workings, and burrows deep in the mentalities of his subjects. No man could write a "Peter Pan" who in himself was lacking in the qualities which make the heart of a child such a wondrously beautiful thing.[6]

And, of Maude:

> The little people of Never-Never land are children, and yet they are something more than children, and Peter Pan himself is a rare breed of the real and the supernatural. It would be impossible to name any one who could meet the requirements as Maude Adams has done. Her frail, delicate personality has taken on, the last two or three years, just enough of the more material substance to make her Peter Pan in appearance exactly the being that Mr. Barrie had conceived. There is the lightness of Ariel in her movements, and the grace of Puck: half spirit and half human, she has the gossamer, fairylike freedom of one and the human heart-throb of the other. Her earnestness in the role is a testimony at once to the quality of her art, an evidence of her capacity for expressing the most tender feeling, and a vindication that she shares the author's enthusiastic love for the subject of his story.

The Theater magazine, the theatrical profession's arbiter of good and bad plays, believed "Peter Pan" to be "an epic of childish joy and fancy; it is the apotheosis of youth and all its high colored fictions."[7]

> Judging by the rapt attention with which the play is followed, New York audiences, sophisticated as they may be, still have a corner in their hearts for the time when the sun was always smiling and the birds were always singing.

Maude's acting qualities were seen as the "secret of her success."

She has a sweet, lovable personality which fascinates and endears her to her audiences. There was not a flaw in her performance of the title role. She was, in turn, elfish, wistful, tender, joyous, sad. She danced and tripped, whistled and sang as gayly as the rest of the children, and invested the part with so much charm, poetry and atmosphere that it would be difficult to conceive of the part being better played.

Yet, not all the critics liked the play. One critic called Barrie "a madman" for writing it. Another called the play simple, too simple to benefit Maude's true acting abilities. A third bemoaned the fact that no boy could be found to play Peter and that, among "the lost boys," most were girls.

None of this prevented audiences from jamming the Empire every night during the first several weeks. When the holiday season began, matinees were scheduled, which allowed children to attend. The play took on an added dimension as children dominated the audiences and outdid their parents participating in the play's action: cheers, clapping, hisses, foot stamping, singing along with Maude, and responding with loud enthusiasm when Maude asked them if they believed in fairies. At several performances, children shouted "I love fairies" before Maude even asked the now famous question. Others jumped from their seats during every action sequence.

These experiences also raised Maude's consciousness about the power of children in the theater. She now added them to her list of particular admirers, alongside women.

The production itself became a vehicle around which other social activities flourished. Various dance and dramatic groups bought large blocks of tickets, saw

the play, and then went to Delmonico's for a late supper. Children's groups attended the play as part of a day's outing in the city. Maude contributed to this vogue by donating tickets to children's hospitals and orphanages.

The fashion industry, always in search of the next fad, designed and sold thousands of Peter Pan hats, and the Peter Pan collar quickly found its way to children's and women's clothing.

Maude had her Peter Pan costume designed by artist John Alexander and made by his wife. The Peter Pan collar was quickly introduced into women's and children's clothing and became a popular fashion. (Photo: Otto Sarony Co. Circa 1905. Museum of the City of New York)

Even more significant were the hundreds of letters Maude received from children. How could they learn to fly? Could she send them some fairy dust? Could they join her in Never-Never-Land? Such correspondence continued the entire time Maude appeared in New York and it followed her wherever she appeared. Unfortunately, the vast majority of these letters went unanswered; no one had been prepared to handle the overwhelming volume.

For the Christmas season, Maude did not forget her cast and stagehands, putting on a holiday party after one matinee. The women received bunches of violets delivered to their dressing rooms. The children in the cast received toys. Everyone in the cast was given a bonus of fifteen dollars, the envelope signed "Tinker Bell."

In honor of Maude's friendship and her success in "Peter Pan," John Alexander painted a full-length portrait of her, dressed in her costume. He captured Maude's ethereal qualities, showing her with arms outstretched, soaring high about the earth. Frohman hung the portrait in the Empire lobby.

However, during her run at the Empire, Maude was involved in several episodes that gained public attention, some of it negative. She had recently purchased a high-powered automobile, which she used for tours of the suburbs. One afternoon, at Broadway and 195th Street, a bicycle policeman stopped the auto. "I've been timing you," he said, "and you've been reeling 'em off at a twenty-five mile clip. You're under arrest." After Maude's explanation, the policeman consented to accept her chauffeur and the auto as hostages. Maude returned home by trolley, in time for the evening's performance. The episode cost her a $200 fine.

During a matinee, as the curtain fell on the third act, Maude was called out to take her bows. Someone in one of the front rows tossed a large bouquet of roses toward her. Maude moved to pick up the flowers. Just then, a sudden draft caused the heavy drop curtain to bulge out, and it pitched her forward over the footlights into the orchestra pit. The alert conductor caught her as she toppled over the lights. With the aid of orchestra members, he pushed her to an upright position and stood her back on stage. Maude was trembling and visibly shaken by the incident.

Morris Gottlieb, the man who supplied the sounds and light for Tinker Bell, secretly fancied that Maude had grown fond of him. In his fantasy, when Maude smiled at the audience, she was really looking at him. His belief in her love for him increased at every performance. He wrote several letters to her, professing his love and begging her to reciprocate. Maude discarded his letters. When he claimed actually to hear her voice complimenting him, he was quietly dismissed. No one at the theater had known of his obsession.

Gottlieb decided to go to California but stopped in Chicago, where, he claimed he had a dream that Maude really loved him. When he returned to New York, he sent her a note saying how glad he was that she cared for him. Maude immediately called the superintendent of Bellevue Hospital. Orderlies arrived to pick up Gottlieb. He was asked, as a favor to Maude, to accompany them to the hospital. "I will go anywhere to oblige Miss Adams," he faithfully replied. Gottlieb quickly became a patient in the Bellevue psychopathic ward and later was transferred to an asylum. Maude had encountered many odd people; but none as frightening as Morris Gottlieb, the voice of the invisible Tinker Bell.

Mercedes de Acosta was the beautiful, impetuous daughter of a rich Cuban family that lived in a fashionable area of New York and claimed as best friends members of the city's social elite. As a teen-ager, she became known for her extravagances, which included wild parties, smoking, and dressing as a boy. To inculcate femininity, she was sent to a boarding school outside Paris. The cure, however, did not change her inclinations. Into young adulthood, she remained sexually ambivalent. De Acosta loved the theater and found "Peter Pan" an especially attractive play. She was often seen backstage at the Empire.

A notorious gossip newspaper, *The Tattler*, printed an article in which Maude was implicitly connected with de Acosta's scandalous activities. Frohman moved quickly to prevent the story from spreading. Reports indicated that he had held several meetings with Maude, but the information is unverified. In any event, less than a week after the sensational news came to public attention, Frohman hired a secretary for Maude. The secretary was supposedly to replace her previous employee, who had actually died three years earlier.

Mary Louise Boynton joined Maude in December, 1905. She became Maude's friend, secretary, companion, and protector for forty-six years. Newspapers suggested that Frohman hired Boynton to serve as Maude's "outside contact," to oversee Maude's life beyond the theater. In Robbins's book, she declared that Boynton "dedicated herself to Maude and won her lifelong love."[8]

Mary Louise Boynton was born in 1868 in Massachusetts, the first of eight children. The family dated back to the early 1700s, working farms in the New Hampshire colony. Boynton's great-grandfather had fought in the Revolutionary War, rising to the rank of captain. He had been present at the surrenders of Burgoyne and Cornwallis. The family later moved to Bangor, Maine, where Mary Louise's father became a rich lumber merchant. Upon his retirement, the family moved to Sewaren, New Jersey. Mary Louise was sent to school and wished to become a journalist. She and her younger sister started and ran a local newspaper for several years. She was particularly interested in the theater and often wrote reviews of New York plays. She never married. Louise — the Mary was dropped — was thirty-seven years old when she joined Maude.

On January 17, 1906, during Maude's eleventh week at the Empire, the 100th performance of "Peter Pan" was presented. The customary floral decorations and buntings gladdened the theater; each member of the audience was given a sterling silver thimble as a souvenir. Frohman took the occasion to announce that he had canceled all of Maude's touring engagements and that she would remain at the Empire indefinitely. In addition, Maude had agreed to continue her appearance in "Peter Pan" for next season, primarily on tour. An illustrated souvenir book, filled with photographs of "Peter Pan" scenes and complete with the play in narrative form, would soon be published. The limited edition sold for one dollar.

Maude's 150th performance was given on February 28. In her seventeenth week,

S.R.O. prevailed and tickets were sold out a month in advance. On April 20, during the twenty-fourth week of "Peter Pan," Maude appeared in the play's 200th performance, to the now usual S.R.O. house. On that day, Easterners first heard about the devastation caused by a tremendous earthquake in San Francisco. (A week later, moving pictures of the quake's aftermath filled New York theaters.) Several days later, Maude held an auction at the Empire in support of the San Francisco Relief Fund. Her autographed photos netted hundreds of dollars, and the evening's entire receipts were donated. Aiding in the program were Frohman, David Belasco, and Lew Fields, who ran the aisles collecting money from patrons. Other theaters on Broadway followed Maude's lead. The next week, Maude attended a benefit at the opening of Luna Park, on Coney Island. More than $2,000 was collected at this event. Maude treated the crowd by initiating several rides—shooting the chutes, exploring the Devil's Gorge, and sliding down the Helter Skelter—to the amazement and delight of all in attendance.

Frohman announced that Maude would continue at the Empire through June 9, a predicted thirty-one week run, the longest in New York theater history. He also spoke of her tour the following season. A Pullman car was being specially outfitted to accommodate Maude on her future travels across the country. The car would combine living space and a completely equipped theater for rehearsals. When finished, the car would cost nearly $30,000.

According to plans, the car was to be divided into three parts: a stage, outfitted with the necessary equipment; a section designed for rehearsals; and Maude's private quarters, which included a kitchen and dining room, two toilets, a complete bathroom, sleeping accommodations for three (Maude, a maid and Boynton), and a section for costumes. Pullman claimed this theater car was unique in the world and "would relieve transcontinental traveling and one-night stands of much of their traditional horror."[9]

Large crowds at the Empire's stage door had become commonplace. Often, several hundred people waited to see Maude emerge and walk to her waiting automobile. Police were always in attendance to make way for her. Most of the crowd wished only to say "good night." Some, however, strained to touch her and ask for an autograph, which she never gave. In contrast, at matinees, Maude often appeared in her Peter Pan hat, waved to the children, clasping the hands of many of them. At every departure, children were surprised to see that Peter was actually a woman.

As late as April 23, reviews of "Peter Pan" continued to border on the incredulous. Fashionable people and adults, acting like children, cheered and clapped when Peter asked the crowd to save Tinker Bell from dying, and gasped in delight when Peter and the children flew.

> The Empire Theater was filled last evening by an audience which was almost wholly adult, and many of those present were of the fashionable and obviously world-wise type. And yet not half of the first act of "Peter Pan" had been played before that whole audience was smiling, chuckling, laughing, and fairly glowing with enthusiasm and delight. And the enthusiasm and delight were those of a child—emotions which the majority of us had not felt in kind for many and many a year.[10]

As the heat of June began taking its toll on the cast and stagehands, Maude ordered in lemonade for all of them to enjoy during performances. When the newspapers heard of her gesture, they suggested that lemonade be provided to audiences as well. Several years later, when theaters remained open during the summer, drinks of all kinds were made available to patrons.

As the final performances of the season approached, newspapers noted its impending end with disappointment. "Broadway has seen nothing comparable in many, many seasons," they declared. Actors affirmed their pleasure at having performed in the play. Audiences spoke glowingly of having attended. Critics believed the play to be one of the most entertaining they had ever seen.

At the close of the final act of the season, after bowing to torrents of applause, Maude came down to the footlights with her arms around John and Michael. To the surprise of all her admirers, she made one of the longest speeches of her career. "You have made me very, very happy for many months; and I thank you very, very much." The crowd cheered for many minutes before leaving the theater.

A few days later, Maude left for her Catskills retreat to spend the summer. Onteora Park was an exclusive settlement, a gated community, guarded by a watchman. No one was permitted to enter the grounds unless approved by the occupants. Also living in the community were the Alexanders and Hamlin Garland, a well-known author who recalled seeing Maude at least once each summer.

The first floor of her cottage was arranged so that it could be made into one large room, where Maude could rehearse. A photographer somehow got into the enclave and took a picture of the cottage, which was printed in a New York newspaper. When Maude heard of the photograph, she bought up all existing copies and compelled the photographer to destroy the plates. Her actions were duly reported by the newspaper, thereby adding another fascinating element to Maude's idiosyncratic persona.

Maude and "Peter Pan" opened on October 8, 1906, in Rochester, New York, for a three-day engagement at the Lyceum Theater. A total of $7,700 was taken in, breaking all records for the theater. Similar results occurred in Syracuse, Hartford, and New Haven, on the way to a scheduled two-month engagement in Boston. There were no changes in the cast, a rare occurrence in the theater, although all of the children were now a year older and looked it. The *Syracuse Post* reported that "Peter Pan" was charming "from beginning to end." Maude was called before the curtain at the end of each act, "as the audience expressed its approval of her artistic work."

"Peter Pan" opened at the Hollis Street Theater in Boston, October 22, for an indefinite run. Performances were already sold out for weeks.

> Like a panorama Easter egg, the mind of childhood was held up last night to the delighted eyes of a great throng at the Hollis Street Theater. They saw there the dear, delicious dreams they had imagined when they were children; playing house, and being carried off by pirates, and vanquishing them gloriously in the end, and fairies and magic, and being able to fly![11]

For Maude, the acclaim continued. "Maude took the part of Peter herself as she has taken no other in her whole career." A second-week review declared that "Miss

Adams vanishes in Peter and is so much more the better actress than she even was before." A third-week review spoke approvingly of her singing "Sally in My Alley," to the children. A fourth-week report remarked about Maude's emotional investment in the Pan character.

> It is her positive belief in the realism and actuality of everything that goes on about her directly. Her way of thinking is that when she steps into the scene called Never-Never-Land she actually is in the land of Make-Believe.[12]

During the fourth week of the Boston engagement, a new act was added. Barrie had written the act in the spring, and it had been introduced in the English production. With slight modifications for American audiences, the act, "The Terrible Encounter With the Mermaids," appended new dimensions to the play's fantasy. Audience acceptance was immediate; critics questioned its inclusion.

In the new act, Peter saves everybody from the mermaids and from the sea; but in rescuing Wendy, he nearly loses his own life. Wendy escapes on the back of a bird; but Peter is left on a tiny rock, with the sea rising about him. "To die," he cries, "that would be a pretty adventure!" When Peter's "cock-a-doodle-doo" is finally heard, he floats safely away in a bird's nest.

Phyllis Robbins attended Maude's opening and three other performances. Maude visited Forty-Four Commonwealth Avenue, where Phyllis was presently living with her aunt. They took carriage rides together on occasion. It was reported that, on Maude's birthday, she visited the Robbins farm in New Hampshire and was nearly marooned by a snowstorm. Maude found the afternoon teas relaxing and enjoyable, an opportunity to briefly distance herself from the rigors of the stage.

After eight weeks in Boston, the company embarked on two-day engagements in Portland, Maine, and Worcester and Springfield, Massachusetts, in all of which they drew record business. On December 24, Maude returned to the Empire Theater. "It is sufficient to say," remarked the *Clipper*, "that the high favor she won last season in the same work will doubtless be equaled, if not exceeded, during her present stay."[13]

The *New York Herald* welcomed Maude back, yet seemed more concerned with the increased length of the play. The addition of the new act meant the evening now ended close to midnight.

> Peter Pan, on the wings of Miss Maude Adams, flew back to the Empire Theater last night and delighted a large holiday audience, composed of some who haven't "grown up," and many others who wished they hadn't. There was a new third act. Instead of displacing the former one, it merely moved it up a bit, making the production as a whole, six, instead of five, acts, and, as a consequence, bringing the curtain down not much before midnight.[14]

The *Herald* reviewer believed that the added act was superfluous. Other critics were in accord, and Frohman considered dropping the act altogether. Maude preferred the new act to continue, although, depending on audience response, it might

As Peter Pan, Maude saved the lost boys from the clutches of Captain Hook. In a battle with the pirates, Peter tossed Hook into the sea where he was eaten by a crocodile. Peter then returned the children to the Darlings' home since all children need their mother's love. (Photo: Hall. 1907. Museum of the City of New York. Gift of Walter Alford)

be dropped when she went back on the road. Actually, audiences did not seem to mind the late hour.

When Maude arrived in New York, however, it was not "Peter Pan" that occupied her complete attention. It was her mother who briefly took the limelight, although for unpleasant business.

On December 16, 1906, Arthur Brown, ex-senator from Utah, died in a hospital in Washington, D.C., of complications from a gunshot wound. Anne Maddison Bradley, his mistress for many years, had shot him. It was the violent culmination of a turbulent love affair.

While Brown was in the hospital, Mrs. Bradley believed that he would recover, not prosecute her, and a reconciliation was possible. After his death, however, a case was opened against her by Brown's son, who declared he would press charges against Bradley "to the end, as it was his dad's wish." Mrs. Bradley believed she had ample defense.

After Brown had fathered two of her four children, postponed several wedding dates, and evaded all opportunities to fulfill his promise of marriage, Mrs. Bradley had traveled to Washington, D.C., to confront her feckless paramour. She registered at the hotel as Mrs. Brown and gained access to his room. There she found letters to him from Annie Adams. Enraged by the letters and certain that Brown and Adams planned to marry, Mrs. Bradley shot Brown as soon as he entered his room.

The *Washington Post* learned that, when Brown's death was near, a message had been sent to Annie and that she planned to come to the city and attend his funeral. Efforts were made by Brown's children to remove their father's body prior to her arrival for fear she would accompany it to Salt Lake City. When Annie arrived, she refused to be interviewed and was immediately secluded by her lawyer. She would, however, be required to meet with the district attorney. Prior to leaving New York, Annie did give an interview, which her lawyer tried to prevent. "If Mrs. Bradley had come here to me, the tragedy would have been averted. Senator Brown and I were to have married. When the news of the tragedy came, I was expecting him to join me in New York."[15] Maude was made aware of the events by the Frohman office. Frohman immediately canceled Annie's appearance in a local play.

It was discovered that seven letters from Mrs. Bradley and five from Annie had been in Senator Brown's room. Mrs. Bradley's letters were full of ardor and included threats about his seeing "that actress." Annie's letters, in contrast, were cautious and almost businesslike. They all began: "Ex-Senator Brown"; three were signed "Annie." Annie was informed that she would be summoned as a witness for the defense.

The prosecution planned to use the letters to show that the shots were fired deliberately. When Annie's name was mentioned, she refused to say whether she would testify at the trial. Since she was no longer employed, Annie declared her retirement from the stage and left for Salt Lake City.

The actual trial opened November 14, 1907, in Washington, D.C., almost a year after the shooting. Mrs. Bradley claimed temporary insanity. The jury deliberated for a day and returned a verdict of not guilty. Annie never testified at the trial, but the event ended her theatrical career.

Annie left New York before Maude returned to open at the Empire Theater, December 24. What, if anything, had passed between Annie and Maude is unknown. Nonetheless, when Maude visited Salt Lake City in June with "Peter Pan," no mention of Annie was made in any of the newspapers. Frohman was hard at work attempting to keep the story out of the local press, especially any reference to Maude. Displeased with Annie, he fired her and made sure that she would never again appear in New York. Moreover, he was very concerned about Maude's state of mind and its possible effect on her work.

He worried needlessly. Maude played her best to full houses during the five-week engagement. Extra matinees attracted hundreds of children, including those Maude had specially invited from orphanages. Within a few weeks, the Brown-Bradley affair had disappeared from newspapers.

> Good little Peter Pan is back again, bless his heart, and there is a new and undisguised joy among playgoers of all ages. For Peter Pan is unlike all other play heroes, as all other play heroes are similar to each other. He is absolutely the only unique person in the dramatics of Broadway today. That may be one of the reasons why so many people are head over heels in love with him.[16]

Billed as Maude's only engagement in New York that season, "Peter Pan" sold out quickly for the remaining performances. During the final week, Maude gave matinees on Wednesday, Thursday, and Saturday to accommodate demand from the large number of women who wished to see her before she departed.

The first stop on the tour was a short one, in Brooklyn, at the Montauk Theater. Maude traveled to and from Ronkonkoma each day while playing in Brooklyn. In early February, "Peter Pan" began a three-week engagement at the Broad Street Theater in Philadelphia. Noticeably missing from the play was the added Act Three that had been considered superfluous by New York reviewers. Apparently, Maude and the cast agreed. Maude's new private theater car seemed to be working well, although it had yet to be used extensively. For longer stays in a city, Maude preferred the conveniences of hotel suites.

Unique for the Philadelphia production was the introduction of new lighting techniques that Maude had devised to "brighten the stage." Bands of lights were specially built and hung to shine from the wings so as to minimize stage shadows, illuminate performers, and reduce the use of footlights, all to make the scenes more realistic. This proved particularly effective for full-stage scenes, like the pirate ship, sharpening audience visibility of all parts of the stage. The new lighting system in no way interfered with the thirty-two men required to carry out all the other stage mechanisms, like that which produced the effect of flying.

The *Clipper* reported that ticket sales in Philadelphia were "immense"; that Maude had carried the town "by storm"; and that, though the cast was playing to capacity, "the engagement was too short." A four-week engagement in Chicago was extended to six weeks, as ticket lines extended from the theater lobby into the street each day. The *Tribune* claimed "Peter Pan" was Maude's best.

> As Peter, Miss Adams is said to do the most imaginative acting of her career and her success has been even greater than in her first Barrie play, "The Little Minister."
> Peter has come to town, and that means that fairyland again is opened to us. Some of us chanced months ago to find its portals ajar and, slipping through, found the years had dropped away from us and that we were children again. And what is it all? The daintiest, finest, purest fantasy that has been placed before the public in the history of the stage. Miss Adams is Peter Pan himself — the most perfect art creation of her career, so perfect that it seems no longer art but nature itself.[17]

Along with the usual matinees for children, the company gave benefits for children's hospitals, the proceeds of the evening going to supply them with linens. Twenty-one hospitals shared in the collected funds. After each of these performances, Maude held a backstage reception at which children were introduced to members of the company.

Two weeks before closing, a typical Frohman announcement declared that this would be the final opportunity to see Maude as "the boy who would not grow up." "Les Bouffons" (The Jesters), a comedy then being presented in Paris by Bernhardt, had been secured for Maude's use the following season. Of course, the rush for tickets meant a complete sellout for the final fortnight of "Peter Pan" at the Illinois Theater.

Children and adults shouted they believed in fairies, cheered the demise of Hook, and cried when Peter left the Darlings. During the final performance of the play, a child's voice shouted out from the balcony, "Don't go, Peter, don't go!" Soon the audience joined in a pleading chorus. Maude struggled to contain her amusement. Fumbling with her cap, she finally was able to put Peter's pipe to her lips and skip away offstage.

In early April, the Frohman office released an updated version of Maude's schedule, which included the long-awaited trip to London. Maude would play "Peter Pan" until the end of May, return to New York for farewell performances of the play, then prepare for a new Barrie offering to be performed in London in early July. It seemed a typical Frohman smoke screen to increase attention for Maude. The critics debated the truth of this supposed schedule, for Maude had already committed to performing "L'Aiglon" at the University of California in late July. Critics asked if Maude would ever go to England, as the Frohman office had announced several times. As for Maude, she had no intention of performing before London audiences. Why her aversion? When asked the question by a reporter several years later, Maude frankly stated she was apprehensive of appearing on the London stage for fear of what critics and audiences might think of her acting. No matter how hard Frohman tried to persuade her, she never did appear in London.

Chicago maintained a child labor law that forbade children under sixteen from appearing on the stage. Frohman was aware of the ordinance but decided to perform "Peter Pan" in spite of the threat of having the play closed. To no one's surprise, inspectors descended on the Illinois Theater to prevent underage children from appearing. They found, to their amazement, that all of the children employed in "Peter Pan" claimed to be sixteen or older (they were not), even though they played much younger characters.

The "raid" on the Illinois Theater prompted theater managers to file a suit against the city to allow younger children to appear on stage. Hearings were held, but the results were inconclusive. Other items the managers included in their suit dealt with speculating in theater tickets, Sunday closings, and the caricaturing of nationalities, a very contentious issue. Had the proposed ban been put into law, it would have proved a serious blow to vaudeville and musical comedy, since many of the most famous comedians used dialect, costumes, and ethnic routines on the comic stage.

The extensive tour included week-long visits to St. Louis ("tremendously successful"); Cincinnati ("sales were largest of the season"); and Cleveland ("delighted large audiences"); with intermediate short stops of two and three days in Dayton, Columbus, Indianapolis, Louisville, and Kansas City. The company then began their move west, beginning with sold-out engagements in Omaha and Denver. Salt Lake City was next.

Arriving in her native city from Denver at 5:00 A.M., Maude went to the residence of Mrs. Isabel Pitts to rest; there she planned to remain during her visit. Her eighty-eight year old grandmother, now living with Mrs. Pitts, was there to greet her. No guests or visitors were invited while Maude stayed at the house, to "conserve her strength." It had been three years since she last appeared in the city, in "The Little Minister." The *Deseret News* instructed all theatergoers to empathize with their children before seeing "Peter Pan."

> We advise every man, woman and child who expects to see "Peter Pan" to begin at once digging into childhood memories and resurrecting everything they ever believed, heard, or know about fairies.[18]

Audiences treated Maude's five performances as if they were attending the coronation of a queen. Maude was viewed as extraordinary because she had begun her career in this city. She was honored for her appearances before achieving fame. She was crowned with tributes now that she was a star.

> The audience that filled the old theater was most beautiful to behold. The fashion, wealth, culture and brilliancy of the city were out in heavy numbers, every seat being occupied and much standing room besides. The series of ovations accorded Miss Adams has not been equaled by anything seen in the theater since she herself was the central figure three years ago. After every curtain she was called out for tempestuous applause. She was showered with floral offerings, her form hardly visible behind the small forest of American beauties.
>
> Miss Adams's ability to secure an audience, to pick up the entire house and carry off its imagination wherever she listed, was never better evidenced than last night. The whole gathering followed Peter Pan's heroic adventures with a breathlessness that must have been most flattering to the artist.[19]

In Pittsburgh, box-office receipts of $20,000 had broken records; in St. Louis, they reached $30,000. For the short stay in Salt Lake City, receipts were close to $10,000. In turn, San Francisco newspapers, abetted by Frohman, were working up a "furor" for Maude, owing to the time she had lived and performed there as a child. They predicted she would top all of the previous box-office records.

Shortly after Maude departed Salt Lake City, the Collegiate Institute held its graduation ceremonies. In recognition of her stay at the institute as a teen-ager, Maude sent a floral display of American Beauty roses. She apologized for being unable to attend.

The engagement in San Francisco presented especially complicated logistics and additional burdens for the company since, besides performing "Peter Pan," they were also going to play "L'Aiglon" and "Quality Street." Rehearsals for the latter two plays had been under way for several weeks; and, although the cast was slowly mastering their added roles, fatigue had affected their evening renditions of "Peter Pan." Yet, the Van Ness Theater (one of the few sufficiently rebuilt after the earthquake to be open for performances) was filled at every performance, and reviews of the play were outstanding.

> Probably never in the life of Maude Adams will she ever again appear with such consummate charm or appeal to the heart and imagination. Barrie has written a stageable fairy story and Maude Adams has given it life and plausible semblance, and she has played with the emotions, blending pathos and humor with a subtle charm.[20]

The biggest fascination of the play to adults, according to the *Dramatic Review*, was how "Peter Pan knocks at the doors of their hearts and recalls a time when they too were children and cherished dreams and illusions."

During the second week of the engagement, the company put on "L'Aiglon," to admiration, if not wonderment. That Maude, and the cast, could shed their roles in the fantasy of "Peter Pan" and take on the serious, pathetic story of the Eaglet with equal perfection, awed theatergoers. How could Maude transfer her talents so readily and with such panache?

> The powers of Maude Adams are wonderful, one cannot but imagine her exhausted after a role as the Duke of Reichstadt. The spirit of the frail actress flames up, the performance is not merely one of the mind, the body; genius transcends the physical; the actress is in a rhapsody, a frenzy, never for a moment Maude Adams, Peter Pan, or Maude Adams in Quality Street, but the Duke of Reichstadt.[21]

Not one reviewer raised the question of Maude's immaturity relative to playing tragedy. Apparently, the barrier had been surmounted. "She need fear no comparison with Bernhardt," one reviewer asserted.

To complete her tour of the West, Maude had agreed to perform "L'Aiglon" at the Greek Theater of the University of California. The play would be performed in an open-air venue devoid of wings and flies, in front of a crowd of thousands sitting on benches, a challenge Maude had never taken on before. She had built a maquette of the stage and laid out every scene, every moment for the players. Frohman supplied all the necessary materials and manpower, as well as the funds to promote the venture.

After a brief excursion to Los Angeles—where critics were proud that their city was considered large enough to support "a star of the first magnitude"—and three evenings in Oakland, the remaining days were spent on outdoor, full-dress rehearsals for "L'Aiglon." "The grand performance," the cast called it. When they were not rehearsing, Maude was working with stagehands on the sets and lighting.

On August 3, "L'Aiglon" was performed at the Greek Theater in Berkeley. The night was perfect, the audience ardent, the settings lavish, and Maude spellbinding.

> Maude Adams, most delightful of all American actresses. appeared at the Greek Theater last night in a sumptuous production of Edmond Rostand's "L'Aiglon" as the ill-fated son of Napoleon I and received an enthusiastic ovation from an audience which numbered several thousand.[22]

Maude's efforts in stage managing were viewed as a significant reason for the play's success, the stage illusions she prepared an "effective presentation" of the tragedy. Maude received assistance from a full moon, the effect of the natural lighting being "weird and startling," according to the *Chronicle*. "Miss Adams was repeatedly called upon to bow her acknowledgments to the applause," reported the newspaper, "and the occasion will be long remembered by all who witnessed it."

The classic portrait of Maude as Peter Pan, the model for the many Peter Pans of the next 100 years. Critics predicted that Peter Pan would never die. "Do you believe in fairies?" Peter asked the audience. "Yes! Yes! We believe in fairies!" the audience answered with fervor. (1906. Museum of the City of New York)

Maude would not forget her outdoor stage success. Others would be forthcoming, bigger and better. Her increasing abilities as a stage designer demonstrated knowledge and creativity, and she intended to use them even more in future productions.

Secluded in her private theater car, Maude quietly returned to New York. In a brief meeting with Frohman, she agreed to open the season on the road with "Peter

Pan." Then she retired to the Catskills cottage to rest. The only significant episode during her respite was Phyllis Robbins's first visit to the cottage.

Amazingly, through a season that ran for nine months, twenty-seven cities, and 378 performances, Maude had maintained her health, although she admitted to being quite fatigued. Unlike the previous summer, when she had enjoyed at least three months of relaxation, this one would be all too brief. Her new season would begin in early September with rehearsals and, later in the month, an opening tour of "Peter Pan."

Two performances of "Peter Pan" in Utica, New York, at the Majestic Theater, initiated Maude's new season. Frohman's plan was to play "Peter Pan" until it reached New York during the holiday season, present it until January 4, then introduce Maude's new play, "The Jesters," on January 15. Her final New York appearances in "Peter Pan" would be gala occasions.

In the three months that Maude was on tour, she visited seventeen cities, nearly half of them in the South, and performed "Peter Pan" 104 more times. In every city where she appeared she attracted packed houses, even though many in the audience had seen the play before. And unlike her past experience performing in the South, audiences were now as loud and animated as they had been in northern cities.

Maude opened her final appearance as Peter at the Empire on December 24, 1907, to a crowd so full of fervor that it was difficult at times to hear the players' dialogue. This was the third consecutive Christmas that Maude had played Peter at the Empire.

On Christmas Day, Maude set up a tree in her dressing room to celebrate the holiday with the cast and stagehands. The tree was festooned with evergreens and hung with red bells. Maude's "children" each received gifts from her, signed "Peter Pan." Carols were sung until food was laid out on the stage. Beneath the joyousness of the moment lurked the realization that the company's association for several years was now coming to an end, that the wondrous play would soon be history, and that the unique actress with whom they had been so intimately associated would be moving on. Such farewell events occurred often in the theater at the end of a show or a season; but, in this case, even more emotion than usual surrounded the occasion. The company knew that Maude would not tolerate sobbing and hugs; but when one of the actors raised a toast to Peter Pan, tears were observed in Maude's eyes.

At the final performance of "Peter Pan," on January 4, 1908, the Empire was lavishly decorated. Champagne was served in the lobby; autographed programs were given out to patrons; and no one wanted the play to finish. At the final curtain, instead of taking bows herself, Maude brought out the entire company to share the stage with her. Applause continued for many minutes. Although the crowd shouted for speeches, none were given. In a final gesture, Peter simply blew on his pipes and skipped merrily off the stage.

14

Jesters to Joan

After nearly three years as Peter, Maude opened in her new play, "The Jesters," in which she continued to assume male attire. It was her third boy's part under Frohman. The play had been written in verse by Miguel Zamaceis and adapted from the French by John Raphael, who retained the verse form for American audiences.

For almost two months, Maude and the company selected for "The Jesters" devoted mornings rehearsing the play, while performing "Peter Pan" at night. That Maude was able to juggle effectively two productions at one time struck critics as awe-inspiring, if not outright idiotic. Maude had again called on her friend John Alexander to design the costumes. In addition, he invented a new backdrop, made of gauze, which did not require extensive wood construction.

A sky was painted on plain gauze. Trees were sketched in lightly so that the gauze remained transparent. Black velvet was hung behind the gauze, and lights were thrown on the surface. The sky lit up blue; and the brown tree trunks melted into the black velvet, with only their highlights showing. Using various thicknesses of gauze caused the lighting to change its character, lending it a sense of distance. The entire piece of scenery was stretched on a frame and stood perfectly still. When the scenery had to be changed, the gauze was removed from the frame and rolled up, ready to be moved. This not only simplified scenery construction, but it made the materials easy to transport. Within weeks, other stage managers were copying the innovation.

Up to this time, actors and scenery had been equally visible on stage. The use of gauze and black velvet, which gave no reflection, created a softness which increased the amount of light on the actors. This solved a problem Maude had been working on for several years. She believed that a stage setting should exist primarily to form a suitable background for the players. Alexander's approach, coupled with Maude's lighting techniques, helped achieve that welcome result.

"The Jesters" opened on January 15, 1908, at the Empire Theater. The action of the play takes place in France in 1557. Baron de Moutpre (Fred Tyler), an impoverished son of nobility, lives in his dilapidated castle with his beautiful daughter, Solange (Consuelo Bailey). In the Baron's service is Oliver (Edwin Holt), devoted to the interests of Solange and her father. Also in residence are a few retainers, with a drunken Italian, Vulcano (Gustav von Seyfferitz), as their leader. The Baron's poverty has forced him to keep Solange in seclusion, while she, in the throes of young womanhood, pines for romance. Rene de Chancenac (Maude) and Robert de Belfonte (William Lewers), two rich young nobles, have heard of Solange and wager that they will penetrate the castle and captivate her. To this end, they engage the services of Oliver, who suggests that the Baron engage a jester to cheer up his daughter. The Baron agrees; and a notice is sent out to all jesters to come to the castle and compete for the position, the final choice to rest with Solange. Rene and Robert dress in jester attire under the assumed names of Chicot and Narcissus, and they arrive at the castle to take part in the competition.

The jesters are called upon in turn, and the quips and jests of Chicot place him in the lead. The Baron, however, decides that Chicot and Narcissus should stay for a month, at which time Solange shall choose. During this time, Chicot falls in love with Solange and, in fact, wins her love by his eloquence. He is the chosen one; but when the Baron discovers Chicot's true identity, the young man is ordered from the castle. Yet, Rene has prepared for this eventuality, burying near the castle gold and jewels which, at the proper time, would be brought forth. The hidden treasure softens the Baron's heart, and he consents to the union of Rene and Solange.

Declared the *Clipper* reviewer, "She was Maude Adams at her best."

> The role of Rene and Chicot offered Miss Adams much opportunity for good work, and she took full advantage of it. She dominated the performance by her personality and clever acting, as well as her excellent recitations of verse.[1]

Other New York critics offered a different perspective on Maude's accomplishments. Some believed the play to be "fragile and without compelling interest." Some questioned Maude's decision to play a male's role; "something to be regretted," they opined. Yet, in spite of these concerns, they all acknowledged that Maude played the role beautifully. "She was captivating to the eye and electrical in the manner in which she projected her elfin personality across the footlights."[2]

The *New York Daily Tribune* noted the "spirit of make-believe" in the play and Maude's new role, in keeping with her desire to do "novel" productions. She made a mediocre play interesting and exciting, they reported.

> Miss Adams herself playing with a fine sense of delicate values, gave to the figure of Chicot the charm of youth, his spirits, and sympathetic sensibility. She was a picture to look upon in a costume of cloth and gold, her trim and graceful little figure moving lithely and gracefully through the play, her richly pliant voice now gently soothing in the tender love passages, now manfully defiant when the deed of daring must be done.[3]

On opening night, Maude was called before the curtain a dozen times after each of the first two acts. After a dozen more curtain calls at the conclusion of the play,

Maude yielded to the demand for a speech, stating simply: "Thank you. I can't say any more."

For the first time, Charles Frohman made a stage appearance. Maude had caught him unprepared and pushed him onto the stage to share with her the plaudits of the house. He offered a few uncomfortable bows and hastily retreated to the wings.

"What made Maude Adams's plays so special?" asked critic Charles Darnton. To find out, he followed Maude for several months, especially observing her preparations for "The Jesters." "Lovely, charming and sweet" may describe her personality, he reported, but they do not reveal the "flexible art" this actress has created. "As a matter of fact, the success won by Maude Adams on the stage is the result of sheer hard work."

Between acts, Darnton commented, Maude was not in her dressing room but on the stage, directing the placement of scenery and giving hints to actors on the importance of the next scene. Six months before, she had been working on the costumes with John Alexander. For several months, she had been experimenting with lighting effects to obtain just the right visual outcome to suggest a sixteenth-century milieu. Darnton noted that she knew every part in the play and made suggestions to improve the other actors' delivery, continually awing the stage managers. Yet, instead of saying, "Do it this way," Maude would suggest, "How does this strike you?" Her skill often elicited wonder and admiration from the cast, as it seemed invariably to enliven the part. Stagehands told Darnton that "all hours are working hours with Maude Adams." Even after the curtain went down and the theater lights were extinguished, Maude's day had not ended. Items had to be reviewed to make the next day's presentation that much better, Darnton concluded.

Frohman was bothered by the critics' preoccupation with Maude's appearance in three consecutive boys' roles. It did not seem to occur to the critics that L'Aiglon, Peter Pan, and Chicot were distinctly different roles. A few of them insisted that Maude's unique characteristics of womanhood, which had first gained her recognition, were not being used to advantage. In other words, she was much more charming, delicate, and piquant as a woman than as a man. "Bring back Babbie," they cried.

Frohman got the message, but Maude was not pleased by the criticism. She chose roles to express her professional and dramatic art. She insisted that critics would neither dictate her choices, nor influence her interpretations. When Frohman spoke to her of his concerns, Maude was only willing to discuss expanding and challenging her abilities, whatever the role. Besides, she told Frohman, "I play youth, not men. No travesty is ever suggested."[4]

Frohman easily deflected the critics by announcing that Maude would be appearing at Harvard in June, as Viola in "Twelfth Night." The play would be taken on a brief tour of colleges through the end of the season.

Frohman also again alluded to Maude's playing in London in several new plays he had selected. But the London press indicated that Maude's current schedule would prevent her from appearing in London that season, and they believed that future appearances were doubtful.

Maude played her third male role, as Chicot in "The Jesters." While the play was not considered worthy of Maude's talent, the scenic elements and lighting techniques she introduced were quickly copied by rival producers. (Undated. Museum of the City of New York)

After seven weeks of appearances at the Empire, Maude began her tour with a weeklong engagement in Philadelphia. Rumors in New York newspapers suggested that "The Jesters" did not generate the kind of box-office receipts previously gained by an Adams play, and that Frohman had rushed to get it out on the road. The fact that only one week was scheduled in Philadelphia suggested that Frohman was unsure of the results. Only Maude's personal popularity filled the theater. The *Philadelphia Telegraph* reported, "The piece itself has no dramatic fibre. Its actionless scenes and the sing-song monotony of its rhymed couplets are not altogether exhilarating."

Two weeks in Boston satisfied Frohman's doubts. While Maude received excellent reviews, the end result was that she closed "with a good fortnight," not the usual S.R.O. houses afforded her plays. Some Boston critics attributed the less-than-capacity houses to a mediocre play; some suggested that presenting the play in verse placed it above the heads of many theatergoers. Some believed that Maude's role as a young man disappointed the women in the audience. It is likely that all three reasons convinced Frohman to schedule the play for an abbreviated tour.

In late April, when Maude arrived in Chicago, newspapers had already mentioned the less-than-stupendous success of "The Jesters." Again, Maude's popularity made the play and drew the crowds. Frohman's announcement that this appearance would be Maude's last in the city for two years undoubtedly boosted box-office receipts.

The *Chicago Tribune* wasted no time in criticizing the play.

> A pretty play for pretty children is "The Jesters," which is Maude Adams's contribution to the current dramatic season. The outside world, we opine, will not care for it. But offered as "a new play in four acts," it seems out of key with the atmosphere, and you fall to wondering at its choice by perhaps the best loved actress in America.
>
> She had many fine moments, but the character of the play does not permit a sustained interest of any kind, and she was not, therefore, at her Maude Adams best.[5]

Amy Leslie was even less kind to Maude, in contrast to her past comments on the actress's work.

> Miss Maude Adams's limpidly cooing verse in "The Jesters" means a great deal to hosts of worshipping admirers. She has encouraged herself in fanciful ideas of poetic life. In a little while Maudie will convince herself that she is the fairy child of the theater and insist upon wax wings of halos with musical atmospheres. She has been playing to fine houses and is admired strenuously by the crowd willing to accept "The Jesters" for the sake of applauding Miss Adams.[6]

From Chicago, the company embarked on several weeks of one-night stands through Illinois, Iowa, Missouri, Nebraska, and Minnesota. Many of the towns she played were first appearances for her. Her reputation "drew large houses" and proved to guarantee good box-office receipts. On May 30, in Toledo, "The Jesters" ended its season with the usual final-performance festivities. The same evening, Maude boarded her theater car for an overnight trip to Cambridge, where she prepared for "Twelfth Night" at Harvard.

Actually, rehearsals for "Twelfth Night" had been in process for several weeks. Maude had the orchestra and cast brought to Milwaukee to begin full-dress rehearsals. They all returned to New York to continue rehearsing while Maude made her way to Cambridge. Two days before the play opened, the entire orchestra and cast arrived in Cambridge and immediately began final rehearsals that lasted well into the evening. This was another attempt by Maude to perform Shakespeare, and she wanted to make good on the effort.

Maude had been invited to perform by Harvard's English department. This was the first time that an American actress would appear before faculty and students at the school. The Sanders Theater, usually used for commencements, was converted into a likeness of the Swan Theater where, in February 1601, "Twelfth Night" had first been performed. The outdoor platform featured a roof over the stage, with a painted-canvas sky above and circling the hall. Ornamental pillars masked the plain posts supporting the galleries, and tiers of boxes were erected at the side of the stage, in which were seated members of the audience appropriately attired in period costume.

"Twelfth Night" was presented on June 3 and 4, 1908, to full houses. The five acts were divided into a dozen changes of scene, a version arranged by Maude, with "bluecoat boys" rearranging the simple props to suggest different settings. Music was furnished by a small orchestra at the rear of the stage, invisible to the audience. This was Shakespeare as Maude interpreted it, and Viola was her own unique creation.

The *Boston Morning Telegraph* headlined their review "Maude Adams a Hit at Harvard."

> Miss Maude Adams and her company delighted a notable audience tonight in Sanders Theater, Harvard University, with a distinctive and pleasing rendition of "Twelfth Night," and met with decided success in her first appearance in the role of Viola. She portrayed the character in her own captivating style and was liberally applauded by her collegiate audience.[7]

While introducing Viola, all did not go as Maude had so meticulously planned. She quickly discovered that collegiate audiences were much less inhibited than traditional theater patrons. First, the students were restless before the curtain went up, prompting faculty members to try quiet them, without result. Then, when Maude appeared on the stage, she was greeted with a loud combination of applause, cheers, and stamping feet. The deafening demonstration momentarily threw Maude off balance, and it took some minutes for her to regain control. Many students were carrying copies of the play; and, at certain critical passages, they would repeat the dialogue out loud with Maude.

Because of these breaks in decorum, one critic believed that it might take Maude several performances to "round out her conception of Shakespeare's heroine. There is simplicity and girlishness in Viola, which the actress portrayed so charmingly."[8] Even when she seemed not to grasp the character, he went on, "one could forget it on account of the grace and sweetness of her impersonalization."

Though Maude dropped lines from the play — they added nothing to the narrative, she claimed — and, in some instances, her stage business was considered original, her departures were considered "always in good taste and usually warranted by the text." Her adventures in boy's attire were seen as the height of humor; and the audience responded accordingly, enjoying her amusement as much as she herself seemed to.

Maude received many curtain calls at the conclusion of the play. The Harvard cheer was given for her, and she was presented with a huge laurel wreath while all the players appeared on stage and bowed their thanks. Prior to the second performance, Maude drilled herself and the cast to disregard the unorthodox behavior of the collegians. A report on this performance showed how Maude could quickly meet the demands of her audience.

> Last night Miss Adams's Viola left little to be desired, for she imbued the character with a personal charm and infinite variety of humor and tender emotion thoroughly in the spirit of the role.[9]

The following night, Maude appeared in front of the professors and graduates of Yale on the grounds of the New Haven Tennis Club. This time, however, she did not have the benefit of theater or stage. Under stars and a silver crescent moon, cooled by gentle evening breezes, and surrounded by pine trees on three sides, Maude's presentation was lit solely by temporary footlights. There were no changes of scenery; darkening the performing area was the only indication a new scene was about to begin. All patrons sat in movable seats set up on the lawn especially for the event. Maude and the cast dressed in the clubhouse, and her one change of costume was accomplished in a small tent set back of a juniper hedge.

The Yale attendees behaved like traditional theater audiences. They politely applauded Maude throughout the play and, at its conclusion, bade her return to the front of the performance area many times as they displayed their approval.

Initially, Frohman and Maude had also planned to visit colleges and universities in Ohio, in an effort to bring live Shakespeare to their campuses. However, the episodes and arrangements encountered at both Harvard and Yale convinced them that the final nine performances of "Twelfth Night" should be played in regular theaters. The experience, however, had proved rewarding for Maude. First, she had performed Shakespeare to the approval of very discerning audiences. Second, her efforts in staging the play had met notable success. Frohman had spent more than $10,000 to put on the play at the two universities. All of the proceeds were donated to their respective English departments.

The events further convinced Maude that outdoor pageants offered new opportunities to expand the theater experience beyond its usual restrictions as to audience size, cast size, scenery, and plot. She told Frohman of her determination to produce another play the following year. Maude chose to portray her personal ideal, Joan of Arc. Frohman agreed to pay for the costs of the production. It would require almost a year of planning and construction and many months of rehearsals for a cast numbering more than two thousand. According to the Frohman office, the immense undertaking would be the "greatest outdoor theater event in American theater history."

Maude spent the next two weeks performing "Twelfth Night" in five Ohio cities, ending the season in Columbus. Reviews of her rendition of Viola ranged from "a

Shakespearean triumph" to a success based more on her appeal to women. From Columbus, Maude retired to her cottage in the Catskills, but only for a short time. This summer, she planned to travel to Ireland, with a brief stop in London.

On July 22, using the name Maude Kiscadden on the passenger list, Maude quietly boarded the *Mauritania*, steaming for Liverpool with London as its ultimate destination. She was accompanied by Louise Boynton and by a maid. As had become her usual custom on board ship, Maude rarely left her cabin.

While Frohman spoken frequently about Maude's playing a repertory of past productions during the coming season, she was primarily interested in Edmond Rostand's new play, "Chantecler," currently opening in Paris. A meeting with Barrie, however, changed her plans.

While she stopped in London, Barrie gave Maude the unfinished script for one of his plays, "What Every Woman Knows." Maude then went to stay in a small cottage in Milltown, outside of Dublin, where she planned to take courses at Trinity College. After reading Barrie's manuscript, she asked him to join her so they could review the play. With pleasure, Barrie hastened to see Maude.

Barrie's personal life was in disarray. He was currently in the process of obtaining a divorce from his wife. At the same time, the beloved mother of his Peter Pan children, Sylvia du Maurier, was slowly dying.

Being with Maude seemed to exhilarate Barrie, to inspire his creativity. It may also have been possible that Barrie had fallen in love with Maude, although he could not openly express it. When asked about his new play, Barrie admitted that he had written it because "there was a Maude Adams in the world. I could see her dancing through every page of my manuscript."[10] Indeed, "What Every Woman Knows" was written around Maude and her unique artistic gifts.

The authors of Frohman's biography noticed this affinity between Maude and Barrie, declaring that "they formed a unique and lovable combination."[11] Barrie himself agreed, noting that "Miss Adams knows my characters and understands them. She really needs no direction. I love to write for her and see her in my work." For Barrie, the relationship appeared to have moved beyond artistic adoration.

There was now no question in Maude's mind; she would introduce "What Every Woman Knows" to U.S. audiences next season. Frohman was informed of her decision and quickly announced Maude's fall plans to the press: she would play on the road until late December, then open in New York. The remainder of Maude's stay in Ireland was divided between learning Barrie's script and working on details for the special performance of Joan of Arc. It had been agreed that she would perform "Joan" at the Harvard Stadium the following June.

On September 25, Maude returned to New York aboard the *Carmania* to begin preparations for the new season. Critics quickly reviewed the play and deemed it worthy of Maude's talents, possibly even as good as "The Little Minister," and likely the best thing that Barrie had written to date.

"What Every Woman Knows" is the story of a very serious, young Scottish mechanic, John Shand (Richard Bennett), anxious for education, who is caught by two brothers, Alec Wylie (R. Peyton Carter) and David Wylie (David Torrance), breaking into their family library to get at their books for study. Being caught, he is in the brother's power; and they persuade him, by sharp business proposals, to marry their as yet unsought sister, Maggie (Maude), a studious young woman of twenty-six, with a sly and unsuspected sense of humor. They marry, and she immediately works to help him carve out a career for himself.

Urged on and directed by her, he grows rapidly and finds himself in Parliament. He is exposed to society and is struck with admiration for a young society belle of rank and fortune. Maggie, aware of the situation, encourages her husband to accept an invitation for him to visit the country home of the lady, foreseeing the outcome. The society belle and her friends are bored by the serious man, and he discovers the shallowness of the lady and the society about her.

When Maggie removes herself from supervision of her husband, John's speeches fall flat. He returns more dour than ever, and she sets to work to make him laugh. In the end, she makes him realize how much he depends on her for success; and she smiles in the knowledge of what every woman knows, that she actually rules her husband, without his being conscious of the fact. At the end of the play, Maggie finally makes her husband laugh when she states: "I tell you what every woman knows: that Eve wasn't made from the rib of Adam, but from his funny-bone." That short speech became symbolic of the play, enjoyed a wide vogue, and was quoted frequently.

Another speech in the play was often cited because it aided critics in defining Maude's particular stage persona, what made her so attractive to audiences, especially women. In the play, she is supposed to be a studious woman who possesses little charm. Yet, in fact, she is all charm. While discussing this gift with her brother, she explains: "Charm is the bloom upon a woman. If you have it you don't have to have anything else. If you haven't it, all else won't do you any good."[12]

"What Every Woman Knows" opened the season at the Apollo Theater in Atlantic City on October 16, 1908. The local critic simply reported: "Miss Adams has fallen heir to another 'Little Minister' and will go on playing Maggie Wylie for two years."[13] The Pittsburgh critic was even more enthralled with her acting.

> The most distinguished audience of the season greeted her last evening and the applause was really one long-drawn-out ovation. After every act there were curtain calls innumerable. Maude Adams, as Maggie Wylie, with her Scottish brogue, is the most delightfully humorous and quaint character one could imagine, more charming than ever.[14]

Of the Barrie play, the critic declared, "the appeal of 'What Every Woman Knows' is the quaintness of the dramatic proposition and the admirable humor and accuracy of character drawing that envelops it."

When Maude arrived in Chicago for a two-week engagement, seats for all the performances had already been sold out. A *Daily News* reviewer jokingly suggested that wives could get useful tips in the art of managing a husband, "so go see the play," he recommended.

"Never in their congenial association have Maude Adams and J.M. Barrie so completely touched the ringing melodies of humor and tasteful sentiment," reported the omnipresent Amy Leslie. "Miss Adams glows with tender lights and genuine charm, like a bewitching halo."[15]

Burns Mantle of the *Chicago Tribune* began his review by rhapsodizing about the artistic relationship between Maude and Barrie. No other actress could truthfully embody the whimsical Barrie, he wrote. It was like the doting father writing plays for a favorite child; and it was as if the child acted the plays in her own home, before her friends, so sympathetic was the bond between Barrie, Maude, and her audience. In conclusion:

> Miss Adams' own performance was filled with many graces and impressive with that beautiful and peculiarly personal expression of emotion that grips the heart of the audiences.[16]

So great was the demand for seats, the engagement had to be extended to four weeks; capacity houses continued. On Maude's birthday — her thirty-sixth — both Fritzi Scheff and William Collier, appearing in the city at the same time, brought gifts from themselves and Charles Frohman. In return, Maude gave a box party to see Scheff's play and, afterwards, attended a party given by Collier. Reporters, attending the party, were surprised by Maude's appearance.

Mantle attended the party and had an opportunity to talk to her. The next day, his article in the *Tribune* extolled Maude's acting abilities. "Though she is known to many as a star whose personality alone has made her the most popular of America's actresses, she drives to the heart of a vast majority in her audiences the fact that she is what she pretends to be. And no player can do more than that."[17] Mantle had quite obviously understood Maude's sincere commitment to her audiences.

For the remainder of November and December, Maude toured cities in Ohio and New York in anticipation of her grand opening in New York City. Frohman advertised her recent triumphs through broadsides and newspaper articles, resulting in a rush for seats. Frohman had originally declared that Maude would appear at the Empire for only a month. She actually played there to the end of the season.

Maude and "What Every Woman Knows" opened on December 21 to a gala first-night audience that applauded her every entrance and departure. She received more than a dozen curtain calls after the final curtain. Yet, while audiences cheered her every move, some critics believed the play was not up to Barrie's standards— too much Scottish brogue (the same critics who complained about it when "The Little Minister" opened), too much English politics, nor did it possess the charm of his previous plays. From their descriptions, it appeared the reviewers seemed to be more uncomfortable with Maude's role in "mothering her little boy" than any other aspect of the play.

Other critics praised her role, that of the "real" woman in our society, as being appropriate for Barrie's lines. "The part gave her full scope for the quaint witchery of her laughter and tear-compelling art with lines that caught the house again and again."[18]

One reporter told of taking his life in hand by approaching Maude backstage while Frohman was guarding her. "What is your Christmas like since the success of your new play?" he shouted. Although Frohman frowned and blocked the reporter's way, Maude spontaneously sang out an answer to his question. "My Christmas gift is a long stay at the Empire," she responded. Frohman could not have been more pleased with her answer — that, above all else, the theater was her life. And so the reporter published it.

One of the city's more enlightened critics, Ashton Stevens, called the play an eye-opener for men, especially at matinees when the theater was filled with women. "A thousand ladies will cheerfully fill in any little detail of your pride's undoing that Mr. Barrie may have left undone," he stated. "A performance of this play shows the dull sex you are, a heart-rending experience for the male ego." The satirical story enticed women to smartly champion the play and men to stoutly denounce it. Such articles only made the play seem more provocative.

The Lamb's Club announced that they were going to perform a travesty of Maude's play, calling it "What Every Woman Thinks She Knows." They chose only the best Broadway plays for their satires. Maude demanded a copy of the script. In response to her expressed desire — no one had ever presumed to make such a request before — the Club let it be known that their manuscripts, if actually written, were not suited to general distribution or to a course in home reading. Maude explained that since she was interested in anything that concerned Barrie, and since women could not attend the showing, she should be given a copy of the script, which had been written by George Hobart and William Collier.

The Club refused but did not in any way wish to offend Maude. They told her that their usual performances were of the happy-go-lucky, haphazard sort in which actors improvised lines. In other words, sorry Maude, you never will know.

In the Lamb's version, three Scottish brothers, named after three brands of scotch whiskey, have made a vow that their sister shall marry a burglar; and they have been waiting up nights for years in an effort to ensnare a candidate. Frank McIntyre, a burly man who weighed more than 200 pounds, had Maude's role. Shand is a millionaire who wants to be a waiter. The brothers pounce on him and demand that he marry their sister. "How old are you?" demands Shand, dubiously eyeing McIntyre's bulk. "I'm eighteen," insists Maggie. "Liar!" shout the brothers in unison. A conversation follows relative to Maggie's dowry and "quaint charm," all of it replete with funny business. Frohman, one of the guests of the Club, thoroughly enjoyed the festivities. Asked how Maude might have reacted to the travesty, he opined that she might not have felt the same way.

Shortly after the New York opening, after Barrie had received copies of the reviews from Frohman, he sent an almost passionate note of congratulation to Maude.

> My dear Maudie:
> How splendid you are. I feel I have exhausted all my superlatives upon you, and that none of them is superlative enough. It must be a bewitching performance, and I must manage to see it and you this time. In the meantime my great glory (and only

boast) is that it was I who first said "Behold my Babbie!"... Warm love to you, you amazing little Maudie.[19]

Maude played "What Every Woman Knows" for twenty-four weeks at the Empire Theater, a total of 204 performances. Every performance was filled to capacity. People who saw the play several times over the length of the engagement believed that Maude's acting improved with each showing. Full houses became so commonplace, newspaper ads merely mentioned the name of the play and the theater; schedules and ticket prices were omitted.

Since Maude's visit to Yale the previous summer, a group known as the Yale Dramatic Association had been formed to raise funds to build a theater. They appealed to Frohman to assist them in their endeavors. The result was a promise from him to have Maude visit the campus and put on "What Every Woman Knows," the entire proceeds to benefit their fund. Monday, April 19, at noon, was the day and time set for this unique performance.

On April 18, Sunday, the entire company left on a special train to New Haven, along with a baggage car containing the costumes and properties for the play. The performance was presented at noon, to a full house of 1,400 students and faculty paying five dollars each for tickets. Immediately after the performance, the company returned to New York, in time for their regular evening appearance. Close to $7,000 was collected for the dramatic association's building fund.

Several days later, Maude took the company, plus scenery and accessories, to the Thalia Theater in the Bowery to give an exclusive performance for children of the East Side settlement house. Maude paid for the rental of the theater and all additional expenses. In the past, Maude had given donations to the settlement house and distributed tickets to attend her plays. This time, she decided to visit them herself. "What Every Woman Knows" was presented before a houseful of children, delighted to be seeing Maude but possibly confused by the play's plot. Maude donated the money the tickets would have cost, to further settlement work.

During the entire time Maude was appearing at the Empire, she was also working on the upcoming presentation at Harvard. She held meetings each day with stage managers and construction people. She had maquettes built for each act so she could determine actor placement, action sequences, and lighting. When construction of the scenery began in the spring, Maude traveled to Cambridge each Sunday to inspect the progress. She enlisted John Alexander to assist in designing the costumes and scenery. Frohman had ordered that armor be manufactured in Europe for the more than two thousand supernumeraries appearing in the play. Frohman was fearful about Maude's appearing on horseback, and he begged her to use a double. Instead, Maude attended a riding school to acquaint her horse with the noises of sword and armor through the novel technique of tying pots and pans on the saddle while they galloped around a ring. She also improved her own riding abilities while working on the broad back of her white horse.

It was estimated that at least 10,000 people would be packed into Harvard

Planning for Maude's outdoor production of "Joan of Arc" at Harvard Stadium took close to a year. She used maquettes to delineate each scene and plot the movements of the more than 2,000 performers used in the pageant. The play was described as "the most wonderful out-of-door spectacle that has been presented in America." (Photo: Sarony. 1909. Museum of the City of New York)

stadium to see "Joan of Arc," scheduled for the evening of June 22, 1909. Portions of the field and one end of the stadium were to be used for the stage. The sets, currently under construction, were designed to be easily moved by the more than 200 stage-hands. Fifty captains were in charge of the supernumeraries; to dress them, there would be dozens of armorers and wardrobe masters. One chief stage manager and ten stage managers were employed to direct the performance. Over all of them was a stage director, Frohman's personal manager from the Empire Theater. Actors would receive their cues by means of signals on varicolored incandescent lamps (Maude's idea); and the movements of the mass of extras would be governed the same way. Under Maude's supervision, the master electrician constructed a complete electrical plant in the stadium, sufficient to brighten any modern theater, only on a scale vastly larger than had ever before been done in America.

The script was to be an English version of Schiller's "Jungfrau von Orleans"— likely because the university's German department and Germanic Museum were sponsoring the event and would be the recipients of the proceeds. Schiller's version of "Joan" was one of many dramas written on the theme. A review of the New York stage indicated that many versions of the story had been presented since 1834, but none had attained a great deal of success. Sarah Bernhardt, Charlotte Cushman, Margaret Mather, and Julia Marlowe, to name a few prominent actresses, had previously interpreted the role, all of the productions staged in a theater.

Schiller himself had gone through many versions of Joan, at first following the standard recitation of her life — the innocent maid set against the background of the vice and weakness of the times, ending with her being burned at the stake — but decided on a more original direction. Instead, he felt justified in writing an idealization of the young woman, changing the accepted tale to suit his own plot.

Schiller has Joan fall in love with an English army officer. Nor is Joan burned at the stake. Instead, after being captured by the English, she breaks her chains to go to her last conflict, in which she is slain. She dies in the sight of her French king, clasping his banner in her arms. No wonder Maude seemed to be pleased to interpret the Schiller version.

Phyllis Robbins had an opportunity to see preparations for the play on an almost weekly basis. She had not seen Maude for more than a year, because of Maude's road commitments. Boynton had written Robbins several letters explaining Maude's hectic schedule while working on "Joan." According to Boynton, a typical Sunday trip involved interviews on the train with stage managers, electricians, scene painters, and other artisans. At the site, Maude went over each scene in detail, checking on the position of scenery, the lighting, actors' entrances and exits, and the background music. An orchestra was to be stationed at the rear of the "stage," playing excerpts from Beethoven's "Eroica" Symphony.

Maude arrived in Boston a week ahead of the performance to begin full-dress rehearsals. Phyllis and her aunt were invited to observe them. One evening rehearsal ran for five hours, with Maude directing all the action. She seemed everywhere at once, making sure that every person knew his or her job and cues. On the night of the performance, Robbins noted, as she and her aunt left for the stadium, the temperature was ninety degrees.

Full-dress rehearsals made it evident that the play would run at least three hours, not the two-and-a-half Maude had hoped; but no changes were made in the script. Speculators were in evidence at the downtown hotels, asking for and getting $20 for a good pair of seats. The Cambridge police department assigned one hundred men and a large squad of Mounties to handle the traffic. Boston's elevated railroad added extra cars to their schedule, and other public transportation to the stadium was also increased.

Two days before the performance, Maude was feted at an afternoon reception given by the Harvard faculty and the city's leading literary people. They expressed their delight about her ambitious undertaking; and she, in turn, expressed her pleasure in presenting it. Afterwards, she was taken to her hotel. After dining, Maude returned to the stadium for the remainder of the evening, to deal with critical staging issues.

Fifteen thousand people attended the pageant. The Harvard football field had been transformed into the battlefields of France. One entire portion of the stadium comprised the stage. "It was more of a pageant than a play," reported the *Boston Transcript*, "more of a spectacle than a dramatic performance, headed by Miss Adams."

A *New York Times* review gave the details of the performance, with a large headline, "Miss Adams Thrills Throng in Stadium."

> When Maude Adams, clad in shining silver armor and mounted on a white horse, appeared on the top of a hill in the third act of "Joan of Arc," the vast audience, which filled every seat of the great structure, greeted her with a burst of hearty applause.[20]

Actually, from the moment in the prologue when Maude spoke her first words, "Give me the helmet," and received a resounding ovation, the audience lapsed into eerily rapt silence until her dramatic third act entrance.

The huge audience, the largest crowd ever to witness an outdoor drama in the U.S., sat on concrete seats in a semicircle surrounding the stage arena. The intricate lighting, which was set up to illuminate all angles of the stage, was so managed as to emphasize the scene being observed, while dissuading the eye from the rest. People were concerned whether it would be possible to hear the lines of the play; but when the first words were spoken, a sigh of relief came from the audience. Not only was it possible to hear clearly, but the voices carried well. No one in the audience had any difficulty understanding Maude. "Her voice sounded clear and pure as a bell," reported the *Times*, "and even when she was speaking in a low tone it carried."

Three great tableaux highlighted the pageant. First, there was the picture of Joan in silver armor on the hilltop, a thousand men with spears on the plain below following her to victory. Second was the entrance march into the Cathedral of Rheims before the crowning of King Henry VII, enlisting nearly 2,000 foot soldiers, monks with candles, altar boys, and seventy-five mounted soldiers. Third was the scene in the final act when Joan, breaking her chains to join the French troops, climbed the ramparts to shout "Men of France!" Later, mounted in armor on her white horse, she galloped across the field, leading the charge against the English. Behind her were seventy-five armored horsemen thrusting spears and 2,000 infantrymen. Spontaneously, the audience rose to shout their encouragement.

Then, deep silence again filled the stadium as the strains of the Funeral March from the "Eroica" symphony paid homage to the humble maid as she was carried off the battlefield after being killed. This dramatic, funereal picture ended the play.

> All that remained was the applause, which finally resulted in bringing Miss Adams and her horse forth, when the audience fairly thundered its pleasure. It was probably the most wonderful out-of-door spectacle that has been presented in America.[21]

Said the *Times* reviewer in conclusion: "Miss Adams's performance of Joan must have astonished even her warmest admirers."

No question, the play had been a magnificent success. For years, Maude had studied the character of Joan. To her, Joan was the very idealization of all womanhood.

With her usual hard work, planning, and commitment, Maude felt she had given the character an enduring interpretation.

"Joan of Arc" netted $15,000, which Frohman turned over to Harvard's German department. He also made a magnificent vellum album containing a complete photographic record of the play for the German Kaiser. Ironically, it was the Germans who would later be responsible for Frohman's death.

Joan is about to mount her white steed to lead her army to victory over the English. Maude had always dreamt about performing Joan. She fulfilled her wish in a highly dramatic fashion.

15

Hard Tasks, Long Seasons

Critics and theatergoers viewed Maude Adams to be at the apex of her career. Her name and plays had inspired innumerable articles, features, reports, and photo essays in the country's newspapers and magazines. Her unique stage persona had been questioned, explained, argued, dissected, and analyzed by hosts of writers, critics, and theater patrons. Yet her off-stage life was considered a mystery.

Critics used superlatives to describe Maude's acting skills. Even when reviewers deemed one of her plays mediocre, they recognized the effect of Maude's personality. "Charming" had become the catchall phrase that described her acting; and critics found additional descriptive words, like dainty, piquant, elfin, adoring, and captivating to denote her stage work. Critics frequently mentioned that Maude represented the ideal of womanhood, the ultimate compliment.

For some years, her mentor Charles Frohman, had carefully guided and promoted her career. Although he continued as her public protector, Maude was now her own boss. She selected the dramas and created the entire productions herself. Maude was unafraid of risk, and she embraced novelty. Her commitment to push the limits of conventional acting had assisted in expanding her own skills.

Maude was also the richest actress in America. Reports suggested she earned close to $200,000 a year, equivalent to four million dollars in today's currency. She had become an excellent businesswoman, using her earnings judiciously to invest in property, travel, antiquities, and making donations to a wide range of charities.

Everyone believed Maude loved children. "Peter Pan" could not have been such a success, they reasoned, without her innate understanding of children's emotions and interests.

In the matter of a few years, Maude had become the best-loved actress in America. She was the country's unequaled box-office attraction. Critics attributed her continuing success to a work ethic and commitment that seemed incredible.

Yet everyone was aware that Maude was not a woman of robust good health. That her slight, almost fragile figure was in direct contrast to the fashion of the day attested to the strength of her constitution. Driven to succeed, to seek perfection, Maude often did not safeguard her own well being, frequently giving in to the claims placed upon her. How she was able to meet the demands of strenuous tours, months of travel, and constant rehearsing, yet still entertain audiences as they expected her to do, remained another mystery. Such personal neglect occasionally led to temporary retirement; it would ultimately lead to an abrupt discontinuance of her career.

In the fall of 1909, Maude began an ambitious tour that, with minor pauses, would extend itself for the next several years. Columnists and critics were still talking about Maude's smashing success in "Joan of Arc" when she opened the new season with "What Every Woman Knows." Utica, New York, was not the usual city to begin a season, but it was on the way to Cleveland and Detroit, where she had week-long engagements. When he was able, Frohman liked to attend Maude's opening nights, partly as a way to observe how the production looked, partly in honor of Maude's elevated position in the theater. This opening night became a race by sleigh to arrive at the theater in time. Maude's train had been marooned just outside of Utica by a severe snowstorm. Sleighs were dispatched to rescue her, the cast, and Frohman and bring them directly to the waiting audience. The play was performed without costumes or scenery, and the audience's response to the actors' resourcefulness more than overcame the production difficulties.

Thus began a tour that covered cities in the Midwest and East until Maude returned to New York in December; she had visited fifteen cities in twelve weeks and performed more than one hundred times in all. Audience and critical reactions to "What Every Woman Knows" contributed to capacity houses and excellent box-office receipts, especially since they were all at advanced prices.

An interesting note appeared in the *Clipper*, reporting that James Barrie had obtained a divorce from his wife of sixteen years. The suit had been uncontested and the decree would be made absolute in six months. "They had lived happily together until about eighteen months ago," the *Clipper* article stated.

Maude's thirty-seventh birthday was celebrated in Philadelphia with a cast party following the evening's performance. Cast members gave her an elegant piece of jewelry, and her dressing room was filled with floral arrangements that Frohman personally delivered. He also wished to confer with her about the new spring production of "Chantecler." Maude's New York appearance would be short, playing "What Every Woman Knows" for only twenty-five performances before returning to the tour. In honor of Maude's birthday, Barrie sent her two one-act playlets written especially for her.

On December 25, Maude opened at the Empire Theater where, in spite of bad weather that reduced carriage and taxi traffic to a crawl, she received a royal welcome from a capacity house.

> Maggie Wylie is one of the most interesting of the Barrie characters that Miss Adams has created, and she was a source of pleasure throughout the play. The audience showed its appreciation of the star's efforts in many recalls after every act.[1]

As had become her norm, Maude filled the theater at every performance; and the reviews of her acting were written in superlatives.

The spring tour of "What Every Woman Knows" took Maude throughout the East and Midwest, with notable visits to Boston and Chicago. The Boston engagement had to be extended to a third week due to the demand for seats. Phyllis Robbins had a few short visits with Maude and saw the play three times.

Maude's arrival in Chicago was met with great enthusiasm by her legion of admirers. The two-week engagement was totally sold out, and additional matinees were added to the schedule. Amy Leslie of the *Daily News* believed that Maude had greatly improved in the Wylie role since she had appeared in the city the previous year. The combination of Barrie's play and Maude's acting were "splendid," according to the redoubtable Leslie. As for Maude herself: "She acts all comedy with subtle charm and elegance and her maidenly Miss Wylie is deliciously amusing and feminine."[2]

The ads for "What Every Woman Knows" indicated that Maude would be appearing in "Chantecler" next year, hence it would be the last Chicago performance of the current play. Frohman had been in constant negotiation with Rostand regarding his play's appearance in America, and they reached a final agreement on March 7. Frohman then hired Louis Parker, who had accomplished the translation for "L'Aiglon," to adapt "Chantecler" into English.

"Maude Adams will play the chief role on the American stage," Frohman stated. It had been her wish to perform "Chantecler," particularly after reading the script. It was reported that Maude was drawn to the play because of its theme, that man's glory lies in work, not the pursuit of thoughtless. In a significant departure from usual dramatic productions, all of the characters in the play would be dressed as barnyard animals. Maude was thrilled by the role.

About the time Maude's tour of "What Every Woman Knows" began its western route, Frohman announced that Maude would be appearing as Rosalind, in Shakespeare's "As You Like It," the play to be presented at the Greek Theater on the University of California campus. "Maude will personally produce the play on the order of her previous outdoor pageants," declared Frohman. Costumes were already in production, designed by John Alexander. Maude was designing the scenery and choosing the company, primarily from her current cast. According to Frohman, Maude would closely follow the original text but would add stage elements to give the play a beauty not available inside theaters. The Empire Theater's orchestra would be brought from New York to accompany a choral group. Maude also intended to bring the play "to the audience," that is, to enact some scenes among them to give the production a scale of immediacy and humanity. June 6 was the date selected for the performance.

The trip west included a three-day stop in Salt Lake City, and the usual civic festivities marked Maude's appearance. Theatergoers began lining up for tickets the night before the box office opened. When it did open, the line was a block long, with an estimated 500 people waiting. Some speculators were selling their places in line to the highest bidders. All of the tickets were sold out in two hours.

During a City Council meeting, Maude was given a special tribute, a resolution honoring her artistic accomplishments and contributions to the city. In return, Maude promised to give a special matinee to benefit the local orphan's home. Also attending the special matinee would be university students, complete with their pennants and streamers. Promoters of the annual Society Ball invited Maude to attend, which she agreed to do after her evening's performance.

To add to the festivities, Annie announced that she was arranging for a family reunion when Maude arrived to celebrate her grandmother's birthday. Included in the assembly would be aunts, uncles, and cousins from surrounding cities and towns. As the city prepared for her triumphant return, it was obvious that Maude would have little time for rest. According to the *Deseret News*, "our audiences reserve their praise for Maude Adams only."

> The house was packed from top to bottom with a brilliant and enthusiastic gathering, and the money count at the box office must have been superb. As Miss Adams stepped upon the stage, the house greeted her in a tumultuous fashion that plainly swept her off her feet. It was some time before she was allowed to proceed with the dialogue, and she could only stand still with tears in her eyes, bowing again and again to the demonstrative throng in front.[3]

John Alexander painted two portraits of Maude, the first as Peter Pan, the second a more idealized version as she had appeared in "What Every Woman Knows." Both portraits hung in the lobby of the Empire Theater. (Photo: De W.C. Ward. Undated. Museum of the City of New York)

Each performance was a repeat of the first. After the show, visitors streamed into her dressing room to congratulate her, hoping she would recognize them with a smile or a handshake. When Maude appeared at the Society Ball, the music and dancing stopped to honor her entrance. There were as many reporters attending the family reunion as there were relatives in attendance. The special matinee netted almost $2,000. After the final performance, the company left immediately for San Francisco. Along with performing "What Every Woman Knows," the company were also rehearsing "As You Like It," to be presented in three weeks.

The three-week engagement in San Francisco was marked with long hours of rehearsal to prepare for the Shakespearean play. Early each day, the company ferried to Oakland to hold their rehearsals on the actual site of the production. Maude also spent time finalizing the scenery and lighting, "on a scale quite unprecedented," said the *Chronicle*.

Since 1899, Maude had wished to play Rosalind. In 1905, Frohman had announced that Maude would appear in "As You Like It," but "Peter Pan" intervened. The previous fall, Maude began preparations for this one-time-only performance. Over the months, her needs and demands steadily grew until Frohman executives attempted to protest the high costs of production. Maude, however, was obdurate, responding to their exhortations: "For ten years I have been willing to play 'As You Like It,' and I haven't had the chance; now I am going to play it as I like it."[4]

Rumors of the impasse reached Frohman in London. Several weeks before the presentation, when the question of a very beautiful but expensive scheme of lighting was under discussion, Maude and the stage managers received a cable from Frohman with only two words on it, "*carte blanche*." The lighting scheme was put into effect, as were other production mechanics.

Eight thousand people filled the Greek Theater, which had been transformed into an Elizabethan arena. In fact, the entire arrangement was Elizabethan.

> What the audience saw was a consecutive series of graceful Quattrocento pictures, glowing in color, wonderfully framed by the purple night, and moving upon a canvas. Here, music, verbal, vocal and instrumental, was given in fullest measure, which served to reinforce an exquisite illusion already present in the beautiful panorama.[5]

Critics rated stage management of the spectacle excellent. Every actor's position was in a focus of light, finely calculated. A system of concealed lights gave the cues. For scene changes, the entire theater was darkened and stagehands worked rapidly and invisibly, so quickly, in fact, the audience was barely aware of what was going on. Regarding Maude's production, the *Chronicle* praised her brilliant execution.

> Maude Adams's production of the exuberant, yet delicate, forest fantasy, not only gave the poet's dream actual body and habiliment, but fixed and immortalized it in eight thousand memories.

Regarding Maude's acting, however, they were not as complimentary. "I would not say Miss Adams was the ideal Rosalind," opined the *Chronicle*.

There seemed to be something lacking in the buoyancy about her characterization. Her fun seemed to be rather quaint and roguish than effervescent, and her romance, while ardent, a little too repressed.

But, of course, all of this palled in comparison to the magnificence of the elaborate production. "It was big in conception and almost overpoweringly big in the labor of perfecting the multitudinous details that made the perfect whole," the *Chronicle* reported. "It produced, as if by magic, a series of unforgettable beautiful pictures blended into an enchanting evening."

Throughout the presentation, the audience was enthralled; and, when applause did occur, it seemed an afterthought. At the conclusion of the play, the audience sat in stunned silence for several moments, then broke out in an ovation that reverberated as if a thundering herd were galloping down the slopes of the outdoor theater. Critics compared the play favorably to "Joan of Arc."

Two days later, the company returned to their West Coast tour of "What Every Woman Knows," which finally closed the season in Spokane, Washington, on June 25. Maude immediately returned to New York to confer with Frohman regarding the details of "Chantecler." She then retired to a rented cottage outside Dublin for the remainder of the summer.

When Frohman had seen the production of "Chantecler" in Paris the previous spring, he was attracted to this unique drama. Although he knew from his experiences with American audiences that the play would either be a great success or a ponderous failure, he nevertheless purchased the American rights. In Paris, the title role of Chantecler had been taken by a man. But Frohman, aware of Maude's ability with such roles, chose her for the part. The choice of the play with Maude in the lead was a risky decision, yet one they both embraced.

In early September, Maude returned to the U.S. and left for her Catskills cottage to prepare for the new role. Within a few days, she realized that "Chantecler" would not be ready by October and informed Frohman that more extensive rehearsals would be necessary. They agreed that Maude would open the season with "What Every Woman Knows," play it on the road to the holiday season, and then introduce "Chantecler" to New York audiences. Already the play was presenting dramatic challenges; and Maude was not completely enthused with her role, at this point still in development. While she and the company performed "What Every Woman Knows" for three months, they were also rehearsing "Chantecler."

The new season opened in Waterbury, Connecticut, October 5, 1910. Two days later, Frohman announced that "Chantecler" would have to be postponed until the middle of January. A quick tour of southern cities and eastern Canada ended in Hamilton, December 13. Obviously, additional time was needed to make "Chantecler" an acceptable property.

Actually, "Chantecler" was tried in Newark the week of December 26. So many production problems were uncovered that Frohman was forced to postpone the play once again, to January 23. The delays caused critics to raise questions about the viability of the play and, particularly, Maude's role. Frohman and Maude now had to work against these doubts. Production elements were exceeding budget. The costumes being made in Paris were behind schedule. Casting was an enormous task. Many potential actors did not want to appear in costumes that disguised their identity; and some believed their outfits to be ridiculous. Through all of this turmoil, Frohman put additional money into promoting the play, more than he had for any previous production. His strategy would either excite patrons to see this extraordinary play or disappoint them after they had seen it. In the meantime, Maude was vigorously rehearsing the company to prepare them for the opening. At the last minute, the play had to be transferred to the Knickerbocker Theater because the Empire Theater stage was too small.

What factors made this play so distinctive? The entire play was set in a barnyard, and all actors appeared in the costumes of various animals and birds. They were all costumed life-size. All of the scenic elements, like a wheelbarrow or wooden shoe, were enlarged to equate to the size of the animals. Although Maude changed parts of the dialogue to communicate more clearly the main themes of the play, she remained unsure that audiences would understand the plot. And most important, the dialogue was to be presented in poetic verse. Maude already had experienced mixed responses to the form.

Maude played the role of Chantecler, the cock. She was completely covered in a feathered costume, from bird-shaped feet to a cockscomb and beak, which made her movements awkward and limited. The script called for her to leap onto a fence, which seemed impossible to achieve, but Maude accomplished it. To wrap poetic fancy, noble sentiment, and high ideals into the cock's role was Maude's difficult challenge.

"Chantecler" is the story of a plain barnyard cock who believes that his morning crowing actually causes the sun to rise. He feels an exalted sense of responsibility for this daily service to the world and guards it as the secret of his life, too sacred to be discussed. Moreover, he is truly humble, as all great idealists are humble; and he considers himself the unworthy instrument appointed by destiny for a glorious employment.

A pheasant hen appears, typifying a woman's love that is jealous of her lover's work because it compels her to share him with it. The hen sets her cap for Chantecler and, by her seductions, soon learns his secret.

Like all idealists, Chantecler has his enemies: those who, like the Blackbird, know that he does not bring the dawn and laugh cynically at his simple belief in himself; others, like the owl and night birds, who hate him because, whether he really brings the dawn or not, his song signals the end of night. He has become the triumphant hero, but with one vulnerable spot, his illusion about the importance of his work.

Led astray by the pheasant hen, Chantecler sleeps under her wing until morning has broken without his assistance. He then faces the great tragedy of the idealist, disillusioned and overwhelmed with despair. At length, however, out of his agony comes courage; and he is again able to believe in his mission, if in its figurative sense only.

Frohman's extraordinary promotions paid off. Two days prior to the box-office opening, people began standing in line. The day before the opening, the line stretched almost a block. Some purchasers engaged messenger boys to stand in line for them; that night, more than fifty messenger boys were observed. Shortly before the box office opened, Frohman employees examined the line and pulled out known speculators. Within three hours of opening, 3,000 tickets had been sold. For the eight-week period "Chantecler" was to appear in New York, sold tickets amounted to more than $125,000 worth of business.

"Chantecler" opened at the Knickerbocker Theater the evening of January 23, 1911. There was a jam of people and carriages on the street in front of the theater; and, in the lobby, crowds of theatergoers milled about; but police kept them all in order. Much to the audience's surprise, before the curtain rose, Maude came on stage in full evening dress to introduce the play and present its main themes. When she first appeared in the cock's costume, she received a standing ovation.

Audiences got what they were looking for, a colorful, barnyard extravaganza complete with beautiful settings, costumes, and flowing verse. The fact that the play achieved no real dramatic appeal was evidenced by the few curtain calls Maude received at the conclusion of the play and the speed with which the audience collected their hats and coats and left the theater.

Patrons liberally applauded Maude at the end of each act; yet their enthusiasm seemed mostly for the purpose of appreciating the actress rather than her work. She was almost universally criticized by reviewers.

"Compared to the other cocks impersonated by men," said the New York Star, "Maude appeared puny by comparison."

"Chantecler is essentially a masculine role," declared the World, "and Miss Adams is essentially a feminine actress." Again, arguments arose against her playing male roles.

"Her voice may be sweet, strong, and clear, but it does not reverberate with the resonance that one longs to hear," said the Times. The Tribune, while lauding Maude's attempts at playing the disillusioned cock, reported that:

> There is not the least likelihood that anyone thought Monday night, or will ever think, that in seeing her, he has seen Chantecler, the Chantecler of Rostand's wondrous fancy.[6]

With a degree of sarcasm, the Times reviewer stated that "all the same, all the world will run to see Maude Adams in Chantecler's plumage."

Frohman may have had some satisfaction in producing this spectacle for American audiences, but he was surely not pleased with the reviews. They signaled to him that "Chantecler" would likely have a short run, maybe not even travel beyond New York. For Maude, "Chantecler" was both a triumph and a disappointment. She enjoyed a personal success in acting a complex, unusual role; she suffered a disappointment

In "Chantecler," all of the performers were dressed in barnyard costumes and the scenery had been scaled to the size of the animals. Edmund Rostand's play, in verse, was difficult for American audiences to understand. Maude played the role of the cock who believed he caused the sun to rise.

because of her inability to capture audiences, as she had become so accustomed to doing. Maybe this was one male role too many, she reasoned.

Changes in dialogue were effected to make the poetry more conversation-like. Changes were also made in the cast. Maude may have attracted capacity houses for the twelve-week engagement; but critics did not change their opinions of the play, nor of Maude's acting. "Chantecler" closed April 17, the earliest end-of-season Maude had experienced since joining forces with Frohman.

Not surprisingly, Frohman wanted to shelve the play; but Maude categorically refused to give up on it. Rather, she planned to work on the production during the summer and reopen with the play in September. As was usual these days, Frohman acceded to her wishes. Ironically, reports from Paris indicated that "Chantecler" had not been doing well with audiences there either, even with a well-known male actor in the lead. Parisian critics suggested that Rostand's play might have been too intellectual even for French audiences.

In July, when Frohman returned from his annual trip to London, he outlined to the press his complete plans for the coming season. Included was a series of plays for Maude: besides playing "Chantecler" for the season, she would also appear in several one-act plays written for her by Barrie. Frohman also mentioned another planned trip to London for Maude, to appear in "Chantecler" and "L'Aiglon." It is not likely that Frohman conferred with Maude before making these statements. More likely, they may have been another of his promotion-oriented comments to satisfy hungry-for-news reporters.

Rehearsals for "Chantecler" began in early September, with changes in the script and scenic elements. Maude's appearance on stage to introduce the play was eliminated. The poetic verse was modified further to make it seem like normal dialogue. The messages of the play were highlighted in the program. Maude's own costume was modified to allow her more movement, as were those of the other actors to improve their identity. The total number in the cast had been reduced from 160 to 132. Because of the complexity of the sets, Frohman equipped the company with an Empire Theater crew.

A new, and lighter, "Chantecler" opened the tour in Buffalo, September 26, 1911, and seemed to be more favorably approved by audiences and critics. "The play wasn't great theater," a critic wrote, "but it was great Adams."

Eight weeks of engagements in the East and Midwest now established "Chantecler" as a seasoned production and Maude as its unqualified star. They attracted full houses of enthusiastic admirers, good reviews, and excellent box-office receipts. It appeared that Maude's summer efforts had transformed the play from an oddity into one with agreeable appeal. The result was quickly recognized by Frohman, who issued orders to his managers that, whatever Maude needed for the production, she should be given.

On November 11, in Bridgeport, Connecticut, no celebration for Maude's birthday took place. Nonetheless, when the company reached Boston the following week, her birthday celebration became two weeks of gala festivities at the Hollis Theater. Seats were already sold out a month in advance. Maude's dressing room became a flower garden each evening. At the end of each act and the conclusion of the play, Maude appeared for dozens of curtain calls (although no speeches). Tribute luncheons and afternoon teas kept her busy.

The *Boston Transcript* called the play, and Maude's performance, "better than New York." The *Globe* reviewer believed that Maude "had caught the spirit of the play." Nor were there any mentions about her role being more suited for a male actor. Phyllis Robbins had seen "Chantecler" twice in New York and twice more during this engagement. She had the opportunity to go backstage to view the inner workings of the production, marveling at its complexity yet simplicity of operation. She had but a few moments with Maude but noticed her fatigue due to the demanding role.

The company played in Baltimore at Christmas and in Pittsburgh at New Years (the first time in many years that Maude was not in New York during the holidays) with several matinees added. In fact, the tour had been going so successfully that Maude agreed with Frohman to extend it to the West Coast, to the middle of July. Would her stamina hold up? asked Frohman. Maude replied she was confident of remaining in good health.

The *Louisville Times* not only praised Maude for her acting but believed she was "a wizard for work and management." While the company was in Louisville, Maude held daily rehearsals for the play, as if they had never performed it before. "Why do you work the company so hard?" asked an inquisitive reporter. "They are close to total exhaustion." To which Maude answered, "I want them to be perfect as they can be, and it can only be achieved by hard work."[7]

In Philadelphia, Maude scored again, more so than the play.

> Maude Adams, in "Chantecler," was warmly welcomed by fine audiences. While the novelty of the story and the wearing of barnyard costumes has somewhat worn off, there was still much interest and pleasure in seeing Miss Adams.[8]

In March, when the company reached Chicago for a two-week engagement, theatergoers waited in anticipation of her play; "a barnyard fantasy filled with idealism, morality and the stern realities of life," declared the *Chicago Tribune*. As was usual for an Adams play in Chicago, all tickets were sold out for the run.

The ubiquitous Amy Leslie was enthralled with the entire production, calling it "a beautiful fantasy so abundantly poetic and so white with childlike humor and graybeard philosophy." Maude herself received superlative praise from the veteran critic. "Nothing Miss Adams has ever done can compare in power, tenderness, humor and beauty with this strangely vibrating romp in a barnyard."[9]

Other critics, however, were not nearly as complimentary. Percy Hammond of the *Tribune* called Maude's performance "a counterfeit of Chantecler." She is unable to produce heroes, he declared, only underdog parts. Another reviewer not only derided American audiences' inability to understand poetry and its romantic spirit, he questioned Maude's interpretation of a male role, an argument similar to that heard in New York. Still, the two-week engagement was a record-breaker for the Illinois Theater. Seemingly in defiance of criticism of the play and her role, Maude cabled Frohman requesting that she tour the South in "Chantecler" next season. This time, Frohman demurred and offered no definite answer.

April in Denver was the scene of snowstorms and cold, thus diminishing audiences at the Broadway Theater at the beginning of the engagement. To accommodate the number of people unable to attend performances, Maude gave several matinees. When the announcement of the *Titanic* sinking reached Denver, all commercial business except the theater closed.

The four-day Salt Lake City visit again became a theatergoers' love-feast. The *Deseret News* called it a "red-letter event. With Maude hailed as "the most popular actress this country has ever known," long lines and a quick ticket sellout assured capacity audiences. On this visit, Maude stayed with her mother and her grandmother, who was now visibly ailing. Luncheons, teas, and after-theater activities filled Maude's time, as they usually did when she appeared in her hometown. The play was deemed a "stunning piece of theater"; Maude was "phenomenal and breathtaking."

Stops in Los Angeles and San Francisco were equally successful. Ironically, at a moving picture theater in 'Frisco, Sarah Bernhardt was featured in "Camille," generating, according to the *Chronicle*, equal audiences to "Chantecler." The "Chantecler" season closed on June 22, in Billings, Montana. Maude had played "Chantecler" 320 times in eighty-nine cities, a personal record for any tour she had ever undertaken.

In a rare admission, Maude said she was fatigued from her travels and the demands of the role and was ready for a long rest at her Catskills cottage.

With one exception: a meeting with Frohman to decide on next season's plays and scheduling. The result was an announcement by Frohman, at the end of July, which surprised everyone.

> For Maude Adams, I have arranged an unusually long season entirely devoted to the plays of J.M. Barrie. We propose calling the year "Miss Adams's season with J.M. Barrie." First, Miss Adams will make a very considerable tour throughout the United States in "Peter Pan." Then, she will come to the Empire Theater and present for the first time an entirely new comedy by Mr. Barrie, his first long play since "What Every Woman Knows," and entitled "The Legend of Leonora." After the run of this comedy Miss Adams will appear in a special J.M. Barrie program, consisting of a fifty-minute play, called "Rosalind" and "The Ladies Shakespeare," being one woman's version of work edited by Barrie.[10]

Frohman also told the press that Barrie would be coming to America to assist Maude in preparing to perform his new works.

Critics expressed mixed feelings about the announcement. The duo of Maude and Barrie together! Maude reviving "Peter Pan!" Maude in a new Barrie comedy, written just for her! Why Frohman's and Maude's reliance on Barrie plays at this point in her career?

In recent years, Maude had achieved only limited success with plays other than those written by Barrie. Her forays into male roles had been met with resistance; audiences preferred the feminine roles generally written for her by Barrie. Her attempts at Shakespeare had received mixed reviews—praise for the production values, rather less for her acting. Further, critics argued that Maude's propensity for doing "novel" pieces sometimes extended her reach beyond her grasp. Better to apply one's efforts in roles one is more comfortable with, they recommended.

When Maude was questioned on why she had agreed to revive "Peter Pan," she responded by promising to carry the play to every city and town in America that contained a theater, a goal she had wanted to achieve for many years. Frohman pointed out that Maude had played "Peter Pan" in large cities only. "Maude's ambition," he declared, was "to visit nearly two hundred other places to spread Peter's story of fantasy." Critics lauded Maude's promise but questioned whether she could handle such a long tour. And what, they wondered, was Frohman's thinking in sending out his star on a tour no other actress had ever attempted?

In September, Maude left the Catskills cottage for New York to begin rehearsals for "Peter Pan." A new cast, a shortened production, simpler scenery, and new background music refreshed the play; and Maude too appeared refreshed when playing her favorite role. A new tune, "Won't You Have a Little Feather," was added to the production — composed by a young songwriter named Jerome Kern.

The extended tour began October 7, 1912, in Charlotte, North Carolina. From the moment the curtain rose to its final descent, audiences cheered, applauded, exclaimed that they believed in fairies, cried when Peter had to leave the children, hissed Hook's scurrilous threats, and delighted in his demise. The event was much the same as it had been five years earlier — an engrossing, winning play, starring America's best actress. What else could audiences ask for?

The moment it was announced that Maude was coming, performances quickly sold out. Theater managers cabled Frohman asking for additional matinees; after checking with Maude, he usually agreed. The

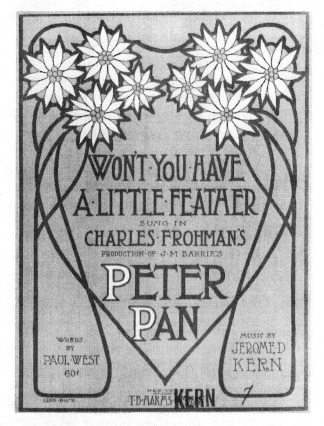

When "Peter Pan" was revived in 1912, several new songs were added to the play. One of them was written by young Jerome Kern, at the threshold of his composing career.

first part of the tour took Maude to Southern cities and towns that had never seen a New York production. Ten weeks and forty-seven cities later, the company laid off for two weeks before opening in New York for the holiday season. At every stop, the play enjoyed capacity business and Maude received so many superlatives, Louise Boynton could not fill her scrapbook fast enough. Maude's portion of the proceeds from the ten-week tour amounted to more than $180,000.

"Maude Adams Returns" headlined New York newspapers. Seats available, first come, first served. The entire three-week engagement of "Peter Pan" — even with additional matinees — was sold out in a day.

The opening of "Peter Pan" at the Empire Theater on December 23 was Maude's 904th performance of the Barrie play. The *Evening Post* reported that both play and Maude "were doing well."

She was greeted with uproarious welcome. Her Peter has been an especial favorite of the public ever since she first enacted it seven years ago. It is a part which adapts itself readily to her personality, temperament, and artistic methods, and her embodiment of it is full of grace, ingenuous humor, and wistful tenderness.[11]

The *Telegraph* called Peter "that well-known national hero." The first-night audience was so enthusiastic with applause and curtain calls that the theater's lights did not go out until well past midnight. The *Times* predicted that the play "will probably live forever." "Peter Pan," it seemed, had become an institution, to be crowned as one of the most popular plays ever produced in this country.

In a brief interview, Maude reiterated that the current "Peter Pan" tour reflected her sincere wish that all classes of people, and especially those remote from large metropolitan areas, would have an opportunity to see the play just as it had been given in New York. Critics again commended Maude on her aspirations; but they worried about her health.

The tour began again in Detroit, January 13, 1913. After seven weeks and twenty-six cities, "Peter Pan" arrived in Chicago for a two-week engagement. A.B. Walkley of the *Chicago Tribune* enthused about his personal experience seeing the play.

> The whole affair is delicious frolic touched with the lightest of hands, full of quaint wisdom and sweet charity, under its surface of wild fun, and here and there not without a place for a furtive tear.[12]

Amy Leslie talked of the crowds that surged inside and outside the theater at each performance. And, of course, Maude excelled in her most elegant role, said this critic. "Miss Adams beams with youth and mischief, dainty elegance of person and resplendent, poetic understanding of her delicious role just in filigree."[13]

Back on tour. Four weeks and seventeen cities later, the company arrived in Salt Lake City for four performances in two days. Theatergoers stormed the box office for seats to see the city's most famous actress in the greatest success of her career. One of the matinees was filled with children from the orphanage, tickets courtesy of Maude. At each performance, Maude received a "royal welcome," her initial appearance stopping the action for several minutes. After each act, she enjoyed many curtain calls. Given the demand of her pressing schedule, Maude had only a few moments to visit her mother and grandmother.

When Maude reached the West Coast, Frohman was there to meet her. What about Maude's other scheduled plays? he wanted to know. When would they be produced? Maude answered by persuading Frohman that "Peter Pan" should be performed through the next holiday season — another eight months — before any other play was considered. Frohman could only shake his head in agreement; he returned to New York to make the necessary arrangements.

Thirty-four more cities were visited on the West Coast and in western Canada before the company returned to the Midwest. On July 12, after playing in 133 cities and towns across the country, "Peter Pan" closed in Clinton, Iowa. Maude rushed to Ronkonkoma for a three-week rest before traveling with the company to La Crosse, Wisconsin, to reopen on August 11. When reporters questioned Maude's fall schedule,

The Frohman office told them that she would return to New York in "Peter Pan" during the holiday season and then begin her new play, "The Legend of Leonora." Of course, that meant the company would be rehearsing the new play during the last weeks of one-night stand performances of "Peter Pan."

One-night stands in the Midwest, Ohio, and eastern Canada preceded a two-week engagement in Boston, at which time the first rehearsals for "The Legend of Leonora" would begin. Maude had observed her forty-first birthday, but no one seemed to notice.

It was in Boston that Maude's health broke down. Although ailing, Maude gave "sparkling performances" with "the same vivacity which made her original appearance in the play," wrote the *Boston Transcript*. The *Globe* reported that "the play, and Maude, kept every quality that has made it one of the few modern classics of the English-speaking stage."[14] Only Phyllis Robbins and Louise Boynton knew that Maude's stamina had given out. They begged her to get some rest.

Maude's condition was finally revealed when the last few days of performance exposed her profound fatigue. Audiences appeared to applaud her more for performing while ill than for the actual quality of her performance. When Maude finally closed the show, Frohman announced that she was taking a month's rest, "the strain of playing one-night stands too much for her nerves and strength." Then why did you devise such a schedule for her in the first place? critics asked.

Frohman then disclosed that Maude would not play "Peter Pan" in New York during the holiday season, due to her condition; and she might not be able to begin her new play until sometime in January.

Not surprisingly, conflicting reports surfaced regarding Maude's retreat from the stage. Frohman claimed she was not ill, just tired from the long tour. Later, the Frohman office came out with another version, saying Frohman wished to avoid subjecting Maude to the strains of rehearsing one play while acting in another. Through Frohman, Maude herself apologized to the public for her inability to play "Peter Pan" during the holidays. At the same time, it was reported that she had asked to be relieved of any acting duties for several weeks. Rumors suggested that Maude had suffered a relapse of the profound fatigue she had experienced before, and that she might not return to the stage for some time. Actually, Maude was ill, suffering from a severe respiratory ailment, and her doctor had recommended a month's rest.

On December 27, Frohman cheerfully told the press that Maude had improved so quickly that she would be appearing at the Empire Theater on January 5, in "The Legend of Leonora." In fact, Maude had been rehearsing the play for the past two weeks. To perfect the new production, single performances were scheduled for Springfield, Massachusetts, on December 29 (the first time that "Leonora" was performed), followed by Hartford and Providence. The company then held two days of final dress rehearsals before officially opening in New York. According to the press and Frohman's office, Maude had made a "miraculous recovery" from whatever ailed her. Excellent reviews of the play in the three cities preceded the New York opening.

On January 5, 1914, "The Legend of Leonora" had its opening on familiar ground at the Empire Theater. Its first-night audience — replete with the city's social elite — cheered the embodiment of womanhood as portrayed by Maude Adams. Barrie's play had been produced in London under the title "The Adored One"; and London reviewers called it one of Barrie's most humorous, satirizing the English courts and burlesquing attorneys, witnesses, and the jury.

The legend concerns Leonora (Maude), a widow who, with Captain Rattray (Aubrey Smith), an explorer, is a guest at a dinner given by the Toveys (Fred Tyler and Leonora Chippindale). The captain arrives a little early, and his host tells him that seven types of women will be at the table for dinner: a "real" woman; a "suffragette"; a "flirt"; a "motherly woman"; a "woman with a sense of humor"; a "woman with too much sense of humor"; and a "murderess." When Leonora, who is a stranger to him, enters the room, he is anxious to discover what type of woman she is.

The Captain quickly learns that Leonora is the only woman guest and a combination of all the types described by the host. Without a moment's hesitation, she tells the captain how she pushed a man from a railroad carriage because he insisted on having the window open, despite the fact that her child was ill. Indeed, she is now out on bail, and her trial will begin in a few weeks. Despite her story, the Captain falls desperately in love with her.

At the trial, the Captain, who is a lawyer, defends her. The court scene is filled with humor as witnesses are made to lie and the solicitor for the crown tells the jury that he played golf with the dead man after his death. In fact, everything is done to save Leonora. The jury even wants her company while they decide on the verdict, which, of course, is not guilty. The play ends at Leonora's home with a love scene between her and the Captain.

It had been more than two years since Maude played in New York, and the fashionable audience gave her "a welcome to be remembered."

> While the play is admirable, much of its success is due to Maude Adams, whose performance is charming. Tender, sympathetic and delightful is her Leonora. Her thousands of admirers will love her in this new role, which is different from anything she has done in years.[15]

The *Telegraph* called the play an example of the power of the feminine mind, a comedy written for those who have a dear mother. "It is fantastic but convincing."

The *Sun* labeled "Leonora" a "burlesque" and "a beautiful travesty." Maude was "the epitome of the eternal feminine." "For it is as a type of the infallible and triumphant womanhood ruling the world that the dramatist has posed his heroine."[16]

Charles Darnton characterized the play as being "a good deal like Gilbert & Sullivan without music," another humorous success by Barrie in his quest to satirize English customs. Moreover, he noted, Maude had never looked so pretty as she did on this occasion.

"Maude Adams was just Maude Adams," declared Alan Dale. "She played as she has always played. She was the personification of charm and magnetism."

Within weeks, Maude found herself the center of a debate on feminism that had been inspired by her role in "Leonora." Yes, it was Barrie's intention to allow women to speak for themselves—and, at the same time, reveal the ridiculousness of men—but it was Maude who was the personification of his thoughts, as well as her own, according to reviewers.

> No doubt, many of the statements reflect Miss Adams's own sentiments, as it is known she is a student who is never content with the mere surface or emotional meanings of her roles but must dig down deep into the substructure of thought.[17]

"All simple men like clinging women," observed Captain Rattray in Act Two. "Do they?" Leonora answers. "What do they like them to cling to?"

Women in the audience loved such lines and applauded them heartily. With this play, Maude had once again captured her female admirers with such exemplary womanhood. The play's success was assured; it played for sixteen weeks to capacity houses.

Then, in early April, Maude added to her schedule by announcing that she would initiate matinee performances of "Peter Pan" four times a week until the end of her engagement. Her decision to perform "Peter Pan" was intended to make up for her inability to fulfill audience desires to see her during the Christmas holidays. Seats for the matinees were sold out in one day. While the Frohman office promised that Maude would continue in "Leonora" next season, her spring tour would be a continuation of "Peter Pan," stopping in those New England towns she had yet to visit. The brief tour began in Providence, Rhode Island, May 4, and ended in Portland, Maine, May 23; it included fifteen cities in nineteen days.

For her summer vacation, Maude went off to Ireland again. She met with Barrie to discuss performing his one-act plays next season. She also persuaded him to come to America to see her rehearse and act in his play. Louise Boynton was there to protect Maude from unwanted visitors and take care of her correspondence, a responsibility she assumed with skill.

In late July, upon her return to America, Frohman reaffirmed Maude's plan to continue with "Leonora." In addition, he told the press, she would introduce several of Barrie's one-act plays on the same program, in selected cities. He also spoke briefly about Maude's having been approached by the motion picture industry.

Moving picture studios had already made frequent advances to Frohman regarding the filming of Maude's plays, especially if they could be made with her as star. Charles's brother, Daniel, was now a part owner of the Famous Players Film Company; and he believed Maude could be persuaded to appear in their films. Maude in pictures? Charles Frohman believed it to be a good opportunity for her. He and his brother totally misjudged her feelings. Maude categorically refused to appear in her plays in moving pictures. Indeed, she took refusal a step further.

After discussing the issue with Frohman and Barrie, Maude got them to agree that none of Barrie's plays in which Maude had appeared would ever be produced as moving pictures. In addition, the statement also established that Maude would never appear in pictures, no matter what promises might be made to her. Neither Frohman nor Barrie was entirely convinced that the liabilities were greater than the benefits, especially the financial; but they willingly deferred to Maude's firm beliefs on the subject.

On September 18, James Barrie arrived in New York on the *Lusitania*. He was greeted at the dock by Frohman and immediately taken to the Empire Theater, where Maude and the cast were rehearsing "Leonora." In a statement to the press, Barrie spoke of the reasons for his trip.

> I am to be a month in America. I am making a long promised and frequently deferred visit to America, entirely for social reasons. I have always wanted to see Miss Adams play. I have to thank her entirely for the good luck I have had on your American stage.[18]

Asked about the war in Europe, Barrie believed that it was likely a necessity against militarism and that the U.S. felt likewise. "There can be no peace," he stated, "unless one side is thoroughly beaten." An observer of Broadway and American theater could find in Barrie's statement little concern about the war or its possible effects on the stage. Frohman, however, expressed worry because of the war's effects on his London theaters and productions. He would be required to visit London soon to assess the war's impact on his business.

Barrie's trip was extended to October 14. Not only was he present at Maude's rehearsals—"I have never seen rehearsals so thoroughly conducted"—he attended the opening of "The Legend of Leonora" in Atlantic City, October 6, and followed the company through a week of one-night stands. A week later, a completely exhausted Barrie boarded the *Lusitania* to return home. He was reported to be "a happy man" after having experienced "an inside view" of American theater.

Six weeks of one-night stands in the Midwest and East brought the company to Chicago during the middle of November. For the past three weeks, daily rehearsals of Barrie's one-act play "The Ladies Shakespeare" had dominated the cast's time and energy, for Chicago was to be the location where the new play would be introduced. Frohman came to Chicago to see the play and determine if it might ever reach New York.

"The Ladies Shakespeare" was Barrie's transcription of "The Taming of the Shrew," with the story line inverted. In Barrie's version, Petruchio takes on the characteristics that Shakespeare assigned Katherine; it is he who ultimately wears the collar of submission. She pretends to be a termagant, thereby inspiring his rough propensities. He wishes to be dominant; yet she, by feigning not to want supremacy, achieves it.

On the double bill, "Leonora" was considered delightful as it examined "the marvels of motherhood." "Miss Adams comedy was so deft and sure, her mannerisms so shrewdly applied to the impersonation. The performance was immaculate."[19]

"The Ladies Shakespeare," however, was viewed as "a Barrie prank" that did not quite come off. Women loved it; men found it discomfiting. One critic suggested that Frohman never mount the play in New York.

Amy Leslie found the playlet entertaining, and Maude "full of charm and mischief and melting prettiness." But she questioned whether the playlet was really worth the effort.

When the company visited Bloomington, Indiana, in addition to the regular performance, Maude agreed to put on a matinee for students and faculty of the University of Indiana, featuring both "Leonora" and "The Ladies Shakespeare." The matinee had a typical college gaiety about it, as the audience cheered, hissed, and laughed freely at the play's dialogue. When "The Ladies Shakespeare" was performed, the audience clearly divided its support — the women cheering Katherine and the men exhorting Petruchio.

The month of December found the company playing one-night stands in the South. In Nashville, Maude introduced another Barrie one-act play to complement "Leonora." Called "Rosalind," this story, too, dealt with womanhood. An actress who has reached the twilight of her career is compelled to stay young to please the public. The playlet ends in tragedy as the actress acknowledges her shortcomings and retires. "Rosalind" was met with enthusiastic applause from audiences. One reviewer, however, wondered whether the playlet was rather more biographical than fanciful. After all, he pointed out, Maude was forty-two years of age and had been appearing on the New York stage for twenty-two years.

After appraising audience reactions and critical comments regarding Barrie's one-act plays, Frohman decided on a significant shift in Maude's repertory. He planned to drop the playlets and reintroduce "Quality Street" to the schedule. Maude did not agree and wished to retain "The Ladies Shakespeare." They compromised. "The Ladies Shakespeare" would be included as an afterpiece to "Leonora" and "Quality Street."

The new program was introduced in Philadelphia on January 18, 1915, at the Broad Street Theater and was well received by audiences. Three weeks later Maude arrived in Boston to perform the same program for a week's engagement, a short run by Maude's standards in one of her best cities. As usual, she was welcomed by admirers who expressed enthusiasm for her every action. The critics, however, were hard on "The Ladies Shakespeare," chiding Barrie for his interpretation and Maude for accepting a weak role as Katherine. Still, capacity houses prevailed.

While in Boston, Maude had an opportunity to visit Phyllis Robbins. Phyllis and her aunt had been caught in Europe at the beginning of the war and had encountered difficulty in returning to the U.S. Thus, it was the first time Phyllis had seen Maude perform in her new plays. She attended the theater three times during the weeklong run.

In late February, Frohman announced that he planned to sail for England on March 13 to produce a new Barrie play and administer his London theater business, already hard hit by the war. At the last minute Frohman postponed the trip due to the premiere of a new, full-length moving picture called "The Birth of a Nation." The film was so popular that audience attendance at Frohman theaters had declined significantly. Frohman had to monitor the situation to determine why a moving picture had so dramatically siphoned off theater attendance. He never really obtained an answer to his question since he had to leave for England in early May. The success of "Birth of a Nation" signaled a change in audience interests and was to have a strong impact on the relationship between live theater and moving pictures.

Another reason for Frohman's delaying his trip was to prepare for an Empire Theater opening of a joint Frohman-Belasco production, a revival of "A Celebrated Case," starring Otis Skinner, Nat C. Goodwin, and Helen Ware. Critics were quick to point out that the "old war horse," rewritten by Belasco, had occasioned Maude's first stage appearance when she was four years old. Why was Belasco attempting to revive it now? they asked, unless it was for the money. A talented child actress, Ann Murdock, played Maude's part.

Maude's company spent the next eight weeks making one-night stands, with a weeklong interlude in both Cleveland and Baltimore, a grueling travel schedule that took them to thirty-one cities. Maude continued to draw full houses and excellent reviews, particularly in the smaller towns. Small-town audiences idolized "The Ladies Shakespeare" more than audiences in larger cities because of the larger proportion of women.

Charles Frohman sailed for London on May 1, on the *Lusitania*.

On May 8, while Maude was playing in Kansas City, prior to going on stage for the evening performance, she received a telegram sent to her from the Frohman office, a quite unusual occurrence. The *Lusitania* had been torpedoed and sunk by a German submarine. Charles Frohman was presumed dead.

16

Sadness and Disenchantment

Thousands wept over the unexpected death of Charles Frohman. Theater managers and stagehands mourned the passing of a man dearly beloved by his associates. The many performers in his employ expressed sadness but also wondered what would become of their jobs. The American and European public, although knowing the man only by his work, had greatly admired his contributions to theater. In their eulogy to Frohman, the *New York Clipper* called him one of America's most renowned producers.

> It is possible that no manager of any country or any time has been so identified with so many notable productions and stars here and abroad. In the death of Mr. Frohman the theater has lost one of its greatest producers.[1]

For Maude, the loss of Frohman was tragic. Her mentor, teacher, producer, protector, promoter, and close friend was gone. And with his untimely death, the man took with him the unique abilities that had so carefully molded Maude's life and career. At the moment, her grief overwhelmed any thoughts about her future career. Surely Maude believed that her life in the theater would never again be the same, but what might take place would only be speculation.

In Kansas City, when Maude had been informed of Frohman's death, she cried so hysterically that it was decided to cancel the evening performance. But when she was told that the banks had closed and it was impossible to refund the audience its money, she went on to perform. On stage, she appeared with puffed eyes and tear-stained cheeks and spoke many of her lines in a broken voice. The strain under which she was working was apparent, but it was not until after the show that the audience was made aware of Frohman's death. After the curtain dropped, Maude refused to see anyone and drove straight to her private car, the location of which was kept secret. Nonetheless, the next day she stated that she would continue the Western tour.

Almost immediately, the perennial rumor that Maude and Frohman had been secretly married appeared in newspaper headlines. Through the Frohman office, Maude denied the rumor. "Of course," said the spokesman, "a warm affection had sprung up between them during the years they had been associated with each other, and the fact that neither had ever married no doubt gave rise to the absurd reports."[2] Still, the rumor persisted until Frohman's estate was made public.

Details of Frohman's last moments filled the newspapers. They reported that an aura of romantic irony seemed to surround the man as he awaited death on the deck of the *Lusitania*. Standing with Frohman were Alfred Vanderbilt, G.L.P. Vernon, and Rita Jolivet, the latter being the only one of the four to survive. She reported hearing his last words: "Why fear death? It is the most beautiful adventure that life gives us." That exact phrase had been uttered by Peter Pan as he faced death by drowning. With that said, Frohman gave his life jacket to Mrs. Jolivet.

Several days later, Alf Hayman, Frohman's general manager, received a cablegram from London telling him that Frohman's body had been identified. Hayman sent instructions to have the body sent to New York on the first available steamer. Daniel Frohman began making funeral arrangements.

On May 25, Charles Frohman's funeral took place at Temple Emanuel, New York City. Thousands of people from the theatrical profession and allied arts attended to pay their respects to the man who had left "an indelible imprint" on the entertainment industry. Bowing to Frohman's deep aversion to the spectacular, the services were simple and brief. Attending the coffin were twenty-five pallbearers, among who were Augustus Thomas, George Ade, Richard Harding Davis, William Gillette, E.H. Southern, William Collier, Francis Wilson, and John Barrymore. Rabbi Silverman gave the eulogy, entitled "Why fear death?"

> Charles Frohman was not afraid to die because he was not afraid to live in the real sense, to live for the ideal, to struggle, to battle for a principle, to love the right, to do justice, practice mercy, and walk humbly before God and man.[3]

Augustus Thomas followed with a tribute to Frohman, speaking about his love for the theater, its players, and its audiences. "The history of dramatic enterprise," Thomas proclaimed, "holds no other name so potent, and his monument is the fact that for a generation he used his great power cleanly, wholesomely, optimistically, inspiringly. He was by character one of the strong, and just to be with him was to be decent."[4]

The coffin was then borne from the synagogue while the organist played Chopin's Funeral March. With a long entourage of carriages following, the coffin was removed to New Union Fields, Cypress Hills, for burial. After the burial, private services were held at Daniel Frohman's home.

Although the family had asked that no flowers be sent, several beautiful arrangements were displayed. The coffin was covered with orchids sent by Maude, and floral bouquets arrived from Frohman's other female stars.

On the same day as the New York funeral, Maude put together a tribute to Frohman at the Mason Opera House in Los Angeles, where she was appearing. Close to a thousand people came to pay their respects. A rabbi, a priest, and a minister each gave eulogies for Frohman. An orchestra played songs from several of his shows, as well as religious psalms, ending with the singing of "Nearer, My God, to Thee" by the audience. Maude's company was present; but Maude was not, prevented from attending by the depth of her bereavement. Indeed, West Coast audiences did not see the same actress they had known so well; only a deep commitment to her patrons made the haggard and depressed actress continue to appear on stage.

No sooner were Frohman's burial rites completed than the battle for his empire began. Charles Frohman left an estate valued at only $350,000, comprised mostly of stocks and bonds in various theatrical business enterprises. He did not leave a will. Daniel, Frohman's brother, applied to become the estate's executor and requested that Alf Hayman be associated with him. No written contracts were found between Frohman and any of his performers; all agreements had been made by handshakes.

This left Daniel Frohman and Alf Hayman with the best opportunity to assume operations of Frohman's company. Claims to portions of the business, however, also came from John Williams, Frohman's business manager; Klaw & Erlanger, who had several business deals with Frohman; and William Harris, a friend of the deceased. No written contracts supported their claims.

Since Frohman had no written contracts with his stars, they could now do as they pleased, moving to other producers if they so desired. These performers were quickly deluged with offers, some very lucrative. For the time being, none of the headliners gave any indication of leaving the Frohman organization, their loyalty to the man still strong.

Less than a month after Frohman's death, Alf Hayman announced that the Frohman name would remain on all properties and that his business would be continued "just as though he were making one of his annual European trips." Daniel Frohman took over working with the performers, all of whom stated their wish to stay with the organization. Alf Hayman was put in charge of the entire business. Still, his reputation as a salesman and treasurer suggested that he was more interested in the "bottom line" than the elements of theatrical production. Plans for next season's plays were already being examined for their profit potential.

In the middle of July, the Charles Frohman Company was officially formed, with Daniel Frohman as administrator and Alf Hayman as co-administrator in charge of operations. Soon Hayman announced that the Frohman business would be reorganized. The statement served as an ominous warning to people previously affiliated with Charles Frohman that the new company was about to "change the rules," particularly among its stable of headliners. Performers were presented annual contracts to sign. In addition, the new company planned to act as booking agents and play brokers, thus determining touring schedules and performer compensation.

During the several months that newspapers were preoccupied with the Frohman situation, Maude suffered two additional personal misfortunes. Allen Fawcett, who often aided Maude in the preparation of her productions, died while the company was playing in San Francisco. His death deprived Maude of a most efficient and loyal assistant. Of even greater sorrow was the sudden death of John Alexander, Maude's friend and chief designer for recent productions. Both deaths contributed to Maude's mourning through the end of her season, July 10, in Billings, Montana. The previous three months had been the worst Maude had ever endured. Only commitment to her deceased mentor and loyal audiences compelled her to perform.

Immediately after the close of the season, Maude and Louise Boynton retired to Lake Louise, in the Canadian Rockies, for a month of seclusion and rest. A brief note from Boynton to Phyllis Robbins on August 8 mentioned that Maude was returning to New York to begin work again. Boynton worried that Maude's rest had been too short.

Rather than assume the responsibilities for any new plays for Maude, the Frohman Company, in the person of Alf Hayman, decided she should make a tour of plays in which she had already appeared, making hers a repertory season filled with revivals. Although she tried, Maude found there was little she could do to change Hayman's plans. Her repertoire would include "What Every Woman Knows," "Quality Street," "The Little Minister," "The Legend of Leonora," and "The Ladies Shakespeare." While in New York, Maude would add "Peter Pan" to the repertory, plus "The Ladies Shakespeare," which had never been played in the city.

Hayman announced to the press that "an unusually large cast and entirely new sets of scenery" would enhance Maude's longest and most complex tour of the country. Critics were first to respond to this bold announcement, suggesting that the new Frohman organization seemed to be taking advantage of Maude's popularity "just to make money," at the expense of her durability. It was an accurate appraisal of the situation. Yet no word came from Maude regarding the potentially punishing schedule. Some hope for a change came in the form of a letter to Maude from Barrie, who told of a new script he was working on, his version of the Cinderella story. The play would be ready in a few months.

Meanwhile, rehearsals for the five plays began in early September. The various casts quickly saw a different Maude than the person they had become familiar with. Rehearsals went on many hours each day and on into the evening, particularly if Maude was not satisfied with the progress. Maude now seemed to be even more focused on perfection, and she worked the casts toward that goal to their fatigue. Instruction in acting by Maude increased in frequency, and scenes were repeated continuously. Maude seemed preoccupied with each play's production values, even to the point where she was personally changing light bulbs to improve lighting effects. Ruth Gordon, at the time only beginning her long stage and screen career, obtained a child's part in the revival of "Peter Pan." Her description of Maude's "different" behavior revealed how much she had changed.

> After the play opened, she never came on the stage until just before her entrance.
> Then she came out of her dressing room, preceded by one stage manager and followed

by another. Nobody ever thought of speaking to her on the way to the stage or between the scenes.[5]

What had happened to Maude's quiet friendliness and warmth toward her cast? For those company members who had been with Maude for years, her alterations in behavior made them uneasy and unsure of her confidence.

The new season opened on October 11, 1915, in Stamford, Connecticut, with the company performing "The Little Minister." Lady Babbie continued to entertain audiences. Three weeks of one-night stands were followed by stops in New York and Michigan towns, some of which had never seen Maude before. A week in Cleveland and another in Cincinnati gave the company an opportunity to perform their repertoire of plays, and they attracted capacity business. The only thing the cast did not care for was Maude's insistence on rehearsing almost to the opening curtain the play for that evening. Maude's forty-third birthday went by unnoticed; or, if people were aware of it, no one wished to mention the event.

During the engagement in St. Louis, Alf Hayman came out to confer with Maude regarding the holiday schedule in New York. Subsequently, he announced that "Peter Pan" would be performed during her brief stay in New York, after which she would resume her tour with the repertory. Visits to Pittsburgh and Washington, D.C., preceded Maude's opening at the Empire Theater, December 21, in "Peter Pan," scheduled for three weeks.

Three days into the New York engagement, Maude received another heartbreaking telegram, this one from Salt Lake City. Her beloved grandmother, Julia Adams, had died due to acute bronchitis; she was eighty-nine years old. Unfortunately, Maude could not attend the funeral, as to do so would shut down "Peter Pan" for a week, depriving the company of salaries and the theater of box-office receipts. Maude remained secluded at home and in her dressing room until she had to appear on stage. To avoid the usual crowds at the stage door, Maude had her maid, covered by a heavy coat and wearing a veil, walk out, climb into a taxi and drive away. After the crowd dispersed, Maude furtively left the theater. Among Maude's family, her grandmother had always been the most understanding and loving; and Maude grieved deeply for her loss.

"Peter Pan" remained a hit with New York theatergoers. One reviewer called Maude's acting "the most inspiring he had seen." The *Telegraph* simply reported: "The holiday season is really here. 'Peter Pan' is back again."[6] Capacity houses enthusiastically greeted Maude at every performance. The *Sun* declared that Maude Adams "seems to be Peter Pan in reality." Family audiences agreed and showered Maude with applause, along with floral arrangements and dozens of curtain calls. There was no mention that Maude was in mourning for her succession of personal losses.

New York theatergoers received another revival with delight when, on January 11, Maude reintroduced "The Little Minister" after an absence of ten years from the city. A handsome production and strong cast — which included two members from the original company, Wallace Jackson and R. Payton Carter — contributed to full houses.

In late January, E.H. Southern announced his retirement from the Frohman Company. Their separation was said to have been amicable. Southern was the first headliner to leave the reorganized company.

After five weeks of playing to capacity, Hayman announced that Maude would continue with "The Little Minister" indefinitely and no other plays would replace it. At about the same time, Barrie cabled Hayman that he had completed the manuscript of his new comedy and that it was ready for Maude to perform next fall.

Another wire from Salt Lake City informed her that Annie was near death. The news was not unexpected because Maude knew her mother was ill. This time Maude shut down the production and raced to her mother's bedside, hoping to arrive in time. Annie had been suffering from heart disease, which left her in a weakened condition. After the death of her own mother, Julia, in December, Annie had suffered a nervous breakdown. When Maude arrived at her mother's bedside, Annie seemed cheered. Nonetheless, she rapidly sank into unconsciousness and passed away painlessly. She died the evening of March 17, at age sixty-nine, the specific cause of her death being recorded as pernicious anemia. At Annie's bedside were Maude, Annie's brothers, a niece, several friends, and the attending doctor. Maude went into seclusion to await the funeral. Hayman wanted to know when she would return to New York; he received no answer.

On May 20, Annie was buried at Mount Olivet Cemetery in a plot of ground already covered with Adams gravestones, although she was placed beside the body of her husband. The funeral was private and brief. At the funeral, Maude was seen dressed in black, a diminutive figure bent over in grief. She was unavailable for any statements. At the conclusion of the funeral services, Maude left for New York on her private train.

Hayman cancelled the remainder of Maude's appearances in New York, returning the money to thousands of ticket holders. Instead, on May 27, Maude opened in Philadelphia in "Peter Pan" and "The Little Minister." A two-week engagement was extended another week to accommodate the crowds of people desiring tickets. Reviewers praised Maude for her charming acting. No one mentioned the recent death of her mother or even seemed aware of it. Apparently, Maude's acting dispelled any hint of grief or sadness she might have been suffering.

Two weeks of one-night stands through Pennsylvania, Massachusetts, and Connecticut continued to attract full houses for "The Little Minister." In late April, Maude arrived in Boston for two weeks of "Peter Pan" and "Minister." As usual, Boston theatergoers continued their adoration for Maude, applauding and shouting for curtain calls at the end of each act. During this visit, Maude stayed at Phyllis Robbins's home. Her stage manager picked her up after a light dinner to deliver her to the theater for the evening's performance. Upon Maude's return, Phyllis served her some food and the two of them sat by the fire and talked as Maude unwound from the tension of performance. For the first time in many months, Maude was able to unburden herself from the series of misfortunes that had befallen her.

Her demeanor was also brightened when she heard that Barrie's new comedy,

"A Kiss for Cinderella," had made its London debut successfully. Hayman agreed to have Maude introduce the play in America.

John Drew was the next actor to quit the Frohman Company, after being one of its leading stars for twenty-one years. This time, the departure was said to have been acrimonious. A rumor suggested that the Frohman Company name was going to be changed, but Hayman denied it.

At the newly opened Blackstone Theater in Chicago, Maude played Lady Babbie for two weeks to standing ovations. Percy Hammond of the *Chicago Tribune* called Maude's appearance "one of good cheer," even though the play itself was "aged and decrepit." Hammond wondered why Maude continued to appear in "elderly" plays.[7] Almost overlooked was the fact that Maude's innovative lighting techniques had eliminated the use of footlights or spots from the front, a technique not found in any other dramatic production at the time.

In contrast, Amy Leslie believed that "The Little Minister" could not grow old or stage-worn as long as Maude led the play.

> Miss Adams brings her exquisite Babbie of the rowan, berries and plaidie to the Blackstone and her welcome was like a sonorous roll of distant thunder, stirring and conclusive and genuine. Miss Adams has never been more delicately poetic and womanly. She has rounded out in her splendid art and holds the treasured place unchallenged in the hearts of her country's theater lovers.[8]

After a five-week series of one-night stands, Maude closed the season on July 1 with a final performance of "The Little Minister," in Springfield, Illinois. After playing Peter Pan more than 1,500 times, she would never again appear in the play. During the most recent tour, Maude had visited sixty-seven cities over a period of nine months, including her nine-week engagement in New York.

Before returning to the Catskills cottage for a summer's rest, Maude met with Alf Hayman to discuss the production of Barrie's new play. She found Hayman not as agreeable about her overseeing the production as Frohman had been. During their discussion, William Seymour, who, for more than a decade, had been Charles Frohman's general stage manager and a friend of Maude, severed his connection with the Frohman Company. Maude had lost another stage manager who had so ably assisted her in producing plays.

A week later, Maude was surprised to discover that Hayman had announced that she would begin the 1916-17 season with a brief tour of "The Little Minister," before returning to the Empire Theater to introduce Barrie's new play. Maude disputed the new schedule, to no avail.

"The Little Minister" opened the season in Montclair, New Jersey, October 2. What followed were six consecutive weeks of one-night stands through Pennsylvania, Ohio, and several Southern states. By the time Maude reached New Orleans in November, the company had visited twenty-eight cities and the players were already quite fatigued. While in Meridian, Mississippi, Maude found her forty-fourth birthday celebrated with a surprise party given by the cast. During the second act of "Minister," instead of a make-believe supper scene, the cast laid out an elegant feast, complete with a birthday cake, turning the play into a real party in which the audience participated. After the festivities, the play continued.

When the tour ended in Norfolk, Virginia, on November 25, Maude and the company rushed to New York to begin rehearsals of Barrie's new play. Although no one knew it at the time, the Norfolk presentation would be the last time Maude performed Lady Babbie.

Ironic in its timing — or carefully calculated by the Frohman Company — was the December 4 opening at the Empire Theater of Sarah Bernhardt, her first appearance at the theater. She performed three one-act plays to delighted audiences that showered the stage with floral tributes, an homage that Charles Frohman had always prohibited. Reviews of her performance were excellent. The scheduling of Bernhardt at the Empire just prior to Maude's opening gave critics the chance directly to compare these actresses, an opportunity they did not overlook. While Bernhardt was performing each evening, Maude and the cast were using the theater during the day for rehearsals. There was no mention in the press that the two actually met.

"A Kiss for Cinderella" was tried out in Baltimore on December 18. While several scenes still needed work, reviewers believed that Maude had another starring vehicle and that the Barrie-Adams combination would again please audiences.

Prior to the opening of the new play, an article in the *New York Clipper* surprised many people, particularly local theater managers. Maude had sold her properties on East Forty-first Street and was reported to have received $700,000 for them. That she had given up her New York residence suggested that she might be leaving the theater altogether, and rumors circulated as to the direction of her future career. It was no secret that she was not entirely happy with the new Frohman organization, nor with Alf Hayman, and that she was tired from the long tours that had been scheduled for her. Maude took up residence at the Colony Club and had most of her Manhattan furnishings moved to Ronkonkoma. Since she spent so little time in New York and there was no one else in the family to care for her home, Maude found her city quarters a burden rather than a place of rest.

Bernhardt having vacated the Empire Theater, "A Kiss for Cinderella" opened with a flourish on December 24. The play was another Barrie-Adams triumph.

The plot: A policeman enters the studio of Mr. Bodie, an artist, bearing a warning that there is an over-lit skylight. The artist fails to understand how this can be since he has carefully boarded up the window. The policeman and Bodie both watch and find that the artist's "slavey" takes away some of these boards each night.

This menial domestic servant is a queer little creature by the name of Miss Thing, although she persists in saying that she is really called Cinderella. The artist finds her a romantic and dreamy person, reveling in piquant fantasies and possessed of the idea that her godmother is about to grant her three wishes — an invitation to the royal ball, comfort, and love — but above all, the ball.

The policeman becomes suspicious and trails Miss Thing home. There he finds that she is "doing her bit" for those at the front by taking care of four little waifs whose fathers are in the trenches, one of the children a German, and that she uses the boards from Bodie's skylight to build bunks for the children.

Possessed by the idea of her fairy fortune, the little drudge, who supports the children by doing odd jobs for the neighbors, has converted the children to her beliefs. Every night they all expect the godmother to appear, bringing an invitation to the palace ball; and every night, Miss Thing goes out to meet the footman who is to take her to the dance.

On this particular night, she falls asleep and dreams that she is at the ball, such a glittering, grand, impossible ball as only a London slavey's fancy could conjure up.

In her dream, the policeman becomes the prince. Mrs. Maloney, the landlady, is the queen; and the court ladies emerge as the living copies of paintings in the artist's studio. Cinderella's slim foot is the only one that fits the lost slipper; and the lord mayor's heralds proclaim her marriage to the prince, while the four children shout "hooray!" and take up the princess's golden train.

Midnight sounds. The gorgeous scene melts away, leaving Miss Thing forlorn and shivering in a dark street, where the policeman finds her. She falls sick and is taken to the lovely home of the artist's doctor sister. There she finds other convalescents, soldiers from the war; and so she assists them. There, too, comes the policeman, who has grown sentimental over Miss Thing. Soon, he is not only Cinderella's dream, but also Miss Thing's waking reality. And they live happily ever after.

There were several strikingly new elements in this Barrie play: he placed it in contemporary times, tying it to the war; a dream sequence was used to dramatically separate reality from fantasy; Maude changed from the look and behavior of a slavey to that of a princess and back again; and she acted the entire play with a Cockney accent. Barrie used "Alexander's Ragtime Band" as the entrance music for the prince, proving his sense of the whimsical, while at the same time discovering a dramatic utility for distinctly American music.

The play was in three acts, the second act in four scenes, in which the magical transformation took place. Paul Tietjens, composer of the "Wizard of Oz" music, composed the background music and conducted the orchestra. Mrs. John Alexander was cited for her supervision of costumes and decorations. Homer Saint Gaudens, son of the famous American sculptor, was Maude's stage manager.

According to the *New York American*, "A Kiss for Cinderella" was "a fancy of J.M. Barrie" and Maude "Peter Pan's little sister." "Miss Adams, as Cinderella, was full of grace and daintiness, comforting, and good to look at, with her girlish slenderness and wistful earnest eyes."[9]

The *Bulletin* reported that Maude played Cinderella as she had played Peter Pan, "with a thorough understanding of a sympathy for Barrie's delightful writing and imagination."[10]

The reception given Maude was so gratifying that, although she tried to make a speech, the words refused to come, blocked by the tears in her eyes. Considering the past year of sorrows, the audience's recognition of her work impressed her deeply. Equally surprising, when Maude returned to her dressing room, she discovered a floral tribute and a note written on the mirror from Sarah Bernhardt. In translation, the note read: "Dear Maude Adams: Since I cannot be here to give Cinderella a kiss, I leave these flowers for her instead. May all your wishes like Cinderella's come true. Sarah Bernhardt."[11] Incidentally, critics placed both Maude and Bernhardt at the pinnacle of the actor's art, with no debate.

Critic Alan Dale gave special praise to Maude, pointing out that her acting style and appeal had not changed, even though she had been starring on the stage for years. Fine tribute from a well-known and well-respected critic, yet this was the first time that Maude's tenure and age had been openly discussed. Such comments often became telling milestones when an actress's stage longevity was revealed. They usually signaled that the best had been already secured from a performer, and it was only a question of time before his or her stardom began to fade. Surely, Maude was sensitive enough to understand Dale's implication, no matter how complimentary his review may have been.

"A Kiss for Cinderella" made more than $15,000 during its first week at the Empire Theater, a new one-week record. Successive weeks were no different. Maude's planned engagement of eight weeks was extended to twelve, and stops in other cities were postponed until the following season.

The Frohman Company made headlines again by announcing a new venture into films, not really surprising since Daniel Frohman already had ties with a Hollywood studio. Several of the Frohman Company players were placed under moving picture contracts. Maude refused.

The early spring of 1917 brought new concerns to the theater, particularly in New York. The White Rats, the actors' union, declared strikes in five cities, including New York. "A Kiss for Cinderella" was interrupted for a week until the strike fizzled, theater owners threatening the strikers with loss of their jobs. At the same time, the government announced a break of relations with Germany, thus setting the stage for the U.S. to enter the war. The announcement had a major impact on the theater. Some shows were cancelled; others saw sizable declines in attendance. "A Kiss for Cinderella" continued through this period of apprehension, but the play was unable to sustain full houses. Shortly after war was declared against Germany, the Frohman Company cancelled Maude's California tour, stating that she would stay at the Empire Theater through the end of the current season, which itself would be shortened due to falling attendance.

Maude's season ended in the middle of May, after twenty weeks. The press was told that, after Maude's summer rest, she would begin a tour of "A Kiss for Cinderella" that would take her to "every major city in the country."

Maude began the summer by attending a gala testimonial for a stalwart U.S. ally, French General Joffre, entitled "A Tribute to Maréchal Joffre from the Citizens of New York." A tableau "to a new democracy" featured Ethyl Barrymore, Antonio Scotti, and George Arliss. Classical music from the city orchestra, choruses, and piano solos highlighted the event. Maude, separate from the tableaux, represented Joan of Arc.

After the mammoth event, Maude traveled to Boston to spend the summer with

Phyllis Robbins. It would prove one of the most restful she had experienced in many years. She and Robbins explored the city and took trips to nearby historical sights. Robbins and her aunt rented a cottage in Harrison, Maine, and Maude was invited to spend time in the woods, playing at housekeeping. Often they took motor trips to various scenic locations in the state. The rest surely helped Maude face the arduous tour that was planned for the 1917-18 season.

The war had already affected producers' plans for the coming season. Many actors had joined the army, leaving few good substitutes available for new shows. A theater war tax of ten percent had been enacted by Congress, which forced theater managers either to raise ticket prices or reduce their profits. Railroads refused to carry touring companies in order to conserve coal, and many of these touring groups closed for the season. Many high-class theaters, those that normally featured the best in legitimate theater, had switched to showing motion pictures because fewer plays were available. Coal conservation changed theatergoers' habits: shows started earlier; and encores and curtain calls were restricted to shorten a show's playing time. Streetcar service stopped at 10:30 P.M., affecting theater schedules. When the government raised railroad rates, there was some question whether Maude would be able to tour. Somehow, the Frohman Company overcame the rail restrictions and confidently announced that Maude would begin her tour in October, embarking on one of the longest trips of her career. The grueling tour would take her to the West Coast and would not end until the following July. "A Kiss for Cinderella" would be presented during the entire tour.

Maude's season began in Plainfield, New Jersey, October 3, and moved to Philadelphia for a two-week engagement. Rehearsals for the play did not go well due to cast changes necessitated by the unavailability of actors and scenery cutbacks to reduce the costs for rail shipment. Even though Maude appeared to be well rested, she had trouble concentrating on her role, as familiar as it was, her usual motivation toward perfection seemingly absent. Observers noted that it was a bit more difficult for Maude to mobilize herself and, in turn, transfer that motivation to the cast. Even as she prepared for each night's performance, meeting the expectations of audiences became increasingly difficult. Yet, no one seemed to notice — surely, no one mentioned — these subtle changes in Maude's demeanor. She continued to work the company hard and used her dressing room as a sanctuary set apart from actual performance.

On November 12, the company arrived in Boston for a three-week visit. After the opening night performance, which filled the theater with hundreds of admirers, Maude celebrated her forty-fifth birthday with Phyllis Robbins. A review for "A Kiss for Cinderella" offered much praise for Barrie's fanciful story but questioned Maude's success in conveying to audiences "all that was in her mind, letting some lines go by not stressing their full value." Yet, she performed Miss Thing/Cinderella with her usual charm. The *Boston Transcript* called the Barrie-Adams combination "a rare and distinctive pleasure." The *Globe* declared that Barrie's play "proved delightful," and Maude's interpretation was "very congenial."

Since Maude had discarded footlights and border lights, she stationed the electrician in front of the pit, where he could see and control the effects he produced.

Using what Maude named "a dimmer box," the electrician operated the entire lighting sequence for the play. Batteries of nitrogen lamps, ranging in power from 100 to 1,000 candle power, illuminated the stage. They were particularly effective during the dazzling ballroom scene, during which lighting dimmed, brightened, and seemed to wash over the stage in shimmering waves.

Still, the play did not sell out every performance and, for several evenings, barely made enough to break even. Watching box-office results very carefully, the Frohman Company suggested that Maude reduce her lengthy stays in cities. Again, Maude refused, believing that she had an obligation to audiences to maintain the intended schedule. Nor did she intend to do anything that would jeopardize the cast's employment. Unfortunately, the problem would intensify as the tour progressed, putting additional pressure on Maude. To further complicate matters, the winter of 1917 was particularly harsh; and travel was especially difficult, with cold and snowy weather disrupting train schedules and arrival times.

From Boston, the company visited Montreal, Toronto, and Ottawa, to excellent reviews but only fair houses. In Toronto, the cast performed a special show for 1,500 convalescent soldiers. All of the women in the cast took to knitting army socks and one of them took charge of packing and mailing them.

It was fifteen degrees below zero when the company arrived in Chicago. Maude could not sleep in her private car because the train was unable to produce enough steam to heat her quarters. During the third week of the engagement, a severe snowstorm reduced attendance dramatically; still, every evening's performance was faithfully presented. No matter the inconveniences, the *Tribune* saluted Barrie as "the greatest and wisest of men who write for the theater" and Maude as "his ideal interpreter."[12]

Amy Leslie called the Barrie play both "baffling and bewitching," switching back and forth between humor, touching emotion, and imagery "that extends the minds of the audience." Regarding her evaluation of Maude's performance, Leslie questioned whether current audiences understood her as well as past audiences. "Those sweet, irresistible eyes and the Adams smile of truth," Leslie opined, "still win their ways, although the test of endurance is severe for those who sit before the Adams altar for the first time.[13]

Was it possible that Maude was losing her audiences? Leslie mused. Was a new generation of theatergoers viewing her charm in a different light? Chicago audiences gave Maude standing ovations and many curtain calls; but was it because, as Leslie had hinted, they were applauding her past rather than her present?

January and February 1918 saw week-long engagements in Pittsburgh, Cincinnati, St. Louis, and Detroit, with good box-office results but few sellouts. In a brief note to Mary Gorman, her maid during her travels abroad, Maude admitted to being somewhat frightened about her current traveling, particularly the night journeys.[14] Observers noted Maude's occasional bouts of nervousness. Boynton believed that the pressure of touring and Maude's need to make every performance "the best" added to her fatigue.

Two weeks of one-night stands through Michigan and upstate New York tormented the company because of snowstorms and irregular train service. The Frohman Company was particularly dismayed because the tour was not generating the kinds of revenue they had expected from Maude. Should they discontinue the remainder of the tour? Maude replied "No."

In Buffalo, however, performances had to be cancelled because Maude was reported to be ill. She was admitted to a hospital, suffering from a respiratory problem and insomnia. The layoff lasted almost two weeks, and there were questions whether Maude could continue the tour. Yet in early April, Maude was back performing "A Kiss for Cinderella" through eight more weeks of one-night stands, stretching from Wisconsin to the West Coast. On this tour, she would travel more than 18,000 miles.

In June, while in California, Maude cancelled several engagements due to illness. This time, however, it was solely the effects of insomnia that forced her off the stage. Her problems had become so manifest, the cast stayed away from her as much as they could. A week later, the company was playing in Southern California. Almost miraculously, Los Angeles reviewers lauded Maude's acting, calling it the finest they had seen in years.

There were two more stops before the end of the tour, one of them in Salt Lake City. The city again planned special events for Maude's homecoming, all crammed into the two-day engagement. But, instead of the usual crowd, only a few close friends met Maude at the train station. They escorted Maude and Louise Boynton to the Hotel Utah where, Boynton announced, Maude would rest while in the city. Several scheduled luncheons and teas had to be cancelled. Maude did give a brief interview, saying how happy she was to be back in the city of her birth. Yet she admitted that the season had been "most strenuous" and she was not sorry that it would end next Saturday in Denver. Maude received an "old-time welcome" from audiences who claimed again "the magic of her art."[15] It would be the last time her admirers would witness an Adams performance in Salt Lake City.

On June 29, in Denver, the long season ended, happily for the company and particularly so for Maude. They had been on tour for forty weeks, had performed 'A Kiss for Cinderella" 320 times, plus several special performances at army camps. Fatigued, suffering from a nervous condition and insomnia, Maude retired to her Catskills cottage.

In spite of her condition, Maude volunteered to work in the kitchen at Camp Upton for several weeks, serving the soldiers at mealtime. Phyllis Robbins joined her in the effort.

Maude fell ill when she began the autumn tour of "A Kiss for Cinderella." While playing in Nashville during the fall of 1918, she joined the many thousands who became sick during the great influenza epidemic. She was in a hospital when Robbins and her doctor came to take her back to Boston to recuperate. Because of her condition and the uncertainty of her return to the stage, the Frohman Company had to cancel all of Maude's future engagements. They told the press that they were not sure when Maude would perform again. Did that mean she had been fired? reporters asked. Or had she decided to retire from the stage? The Frohman Company denied both suggestions, pointing out that she had a contract to fulfill. Several newspapers reported that Maude had suffered a severe nervous breakdown. In this instance, they were correct.

Maude instructed Boynton to find a secluded place like the one she had found in Tours, France, seventeen years earlier, where she could regain both her physical and mental health. Boynton spent several weeks searching for such a sanctuary but found it no easy task. Some convents refused because of Maude's occupation; some because she was not of their religion; and some because they were fearful that she would attract the press and other unwanted visitors.

Boynton finally found a Catholic order in New York City that not only met Maude's needs but also welcomed her with warmth and affection. Secretly, Maude and Boynton withdrew into this cloistered retreat.

17

Dim Shadows and
Bright Lights

The Sisters of the Cenacle were first formed during the aftermath of the French Revolution. The sisters were part of a religious group of men and women united to overcome the years of turbulence that had created a shortage of priests and a paucity of religious instruction. In response to the French religious movement to revive Christianity in the land, the Cenacle was founded by Father Stephen Terme and Mother Therese Couderc. To their emphasis on religious education, they added a new concept in practicing their faith in God. "Retreats" represented a place people could congregate to "ponder on the mysteries of the faith, to seek the Lord in prayer and in the solitude of the heart."[1] Any person seeking such a haven was invited.

It was in 1824 that Father Terme founded a group of teaching sisters to assist in the task of religious instruction. He was also concerned about the lack of adequate housing for women pilgrims; so he rented a house and put two young women in charge. In three years, the group expanded to include a twenty-two-year-old nun, Sister Therese Couderc, who was assigned to run the house. A year later she was named superior. She initiated a plan to open the facilities as a hostel, particularly for women on pilgrimage. Father Terme expanded these services as a retreat where women visitors were taught how to pray and understand the Sacraments.

After Father Terme's death, the group was divided into two parts: the Religious of the Retreat (later the Religious of the Cenacle) would devote themselves to retreats; the Sisters of St. Regis (named after a famous Jesuit missionary of the seventeenth century) would continue as a teaching congregation. For a brief period, Sister Therese Couderc was superior general of the Religious of the Retreat. In her later years, she was active in the ministry of retreats and of religious education, until her death in 1885, at the age of eighty. Prior to her death, the sisters were officially named Religious of Our Lady of the Retreat in the Cenacle.

The Cenacle of St. Regis was a Catholic retreat for people in need of spiritual and physical restoration. Maude was cared for by the sisters after her nervous breakdown in 1918. Many religious groups would not accept actresses; the Cenacle had no such restrictions. In gratitude, Maude donated her Ronkonkoma property to the Cenacle in 1921. (Courtesy of the Cenacle of St. Regis)

The congregation spread outside France, the Cenacle sisters operating retreat houses and centers for spiritual renewal in many parts of the world. One such retreat was located at 140th Street and Riverside Drive in the Washington Heights district of New York City. Occupying almost a city block, the large, four-story Victorian mansion was situated on a rise, overlooking a large garden. A broad deck extending across the front of the house and a tower were the main building's distinguishing features. Directly behind the main structure was a more modern building comprising apartments to house the sisters, novices, and visitors.

One story suggested that Maude had asked a dress designer if she knew of a convent to which she could withdraw. Another story mentioned a visit by Louise Boynton to a hairdresser. When Boynton complained that several convents had refused Maude, primarily because she was an actress, the hairdresser suggested contacting the Cenacle. In any case, Boynton inquired of the mother superior if she and Maude could possibly be guests of the religious house on a two-week trial. They were immediately accepted and assigned rooms, and they quickly moved in.

Maude stayed at the Cenacle on and off for more than two years, whenever she was residing in the city. She would use it often in later years as a temporary escape from the stresses of life. The fact that Maude was not a Roman Catholic made no difference to the sisters. They cared for her during a period of great personal distress, and a loving relationship developed between Maude and the Cenacle.

For more than a year, Maude was under the care of her doctor, as well as benefiting from the attention she received from the sisters. Rarely did she leave the Cenacle; Louise Boynton handled all of her affairs and nearly all of her correspondence. During this time, Maude's mailing address was at the Colony Club, Manhattan. (Incidentally, Maude was the only performer who held a Colony Club membership.) No one — neither reporters, critics nor the Frohman Company — knew where Maude was living.

The Cenacle had no restrictions on length of stay, nor were boarders required to attend religious services. Almost nothing was expected from boarders. Although the sisters did not engage in any therapeutic rehabilitation, each boarder had a sister responsible for her well being and the boarder could speak with the sister once a week about herself. Boarders were required to pay according to their means. They could come and go as they pleased. According to the Cenacle archivist, Maude was seen praying occasionally and volunteered her services to teach elocution to the sisters. To what extent Maude received any additional emotional help from her doctor or the sisters is unknown.[2]

When Barrie was informed of Maude's illness and retirement from the stage, most likely by Boynton, he wrote Maude a letter filled with concern and affection.

> My dear Maudie,
>
> Is it this influenza scourge that has got hold of you, or have you been working too hard? My report is too vague to tell me and I had hoped to have a wire from you in answer to mine. I hope earnestly that you are well on the way to recovery by now, but whatever they call it I am sure that you have been overworking, and if I was on the spot I should simply compel you to take a long rest....
>
> I am not doing anything just now except working at the plays for publication which you don't want anymore. I don't tell you what a melancholy person I grow lest it should disturb your kind heart. I feel very much like driftwood flowing on the bank with one foot only in the water. But I have had a good time — long ago. And part of it I got from you, and am forever grateful. So my warm love to you at all times.
>
> Yours, J.M.B.[3]

There is no indication that Maude responded to Barrie for some time. Phyllis Robbins spoke of visiting Maude the summer of 1919 and of her stay at Pinehurst, North Carolina, the following winter, the only time she appears to have left the Cenacle during these years. In the few letters Maude did write, she admitted to being under doctor's orders and wishing to stay away from the theater "as long as I can."[4]

The issue of the Frohman Company stars' appearing in motion pictures arose again, initiated by the company's announcement that all of their headliners except Maude and Otis Skinner were appearing in films. Regarding Maude's refusal:

"Endeavors had been made in the past to obtain Miss Adams to appear in pictures, but all such proffers were declined by the late C.F.'s favorite."[5] Whether Maude was even aware of the announcement was doubtful, since she rarely read the theatrical papers and Louise Boynton was carefully screening her from such matters.

Although they attempted to reach Maude through the Colony Club for several months, the Frohman Company heard nothing from her. They then released a somewhat disparaging statement about Maude, revealing their increasing impatience with her.

> Maude Adams is the only one of the Frohman stars who does not seem to have a vehicle this season. She was to have opened with Barrie's "A Kiss for Cinderella," in which she toured last season, but her sudden nervous breakdown caused all plans to be called off and, as yet, no announcement of whether or not she will act this season has been made. Her friends in the profession are particularly anxious to know if she will appear.[6]

In December, the Frohman Company provided a statement to the press that appeared to be more wishful thinking than fact. Whether they had heard news of her recovery or made it up themselves only added to the mystery of her whereabouts and intentions.

> Maude Adams, it was learned last week, is well on the road to recovery from her recent breakdown. It is not expected, however, that she will be able to resume work this season.[7]

In early 1920, Maude came out of her self-imposed isolation. She was seen with Louise Boynton, shopping and walking along Riverside Drive. Yet no one dared to attempt an interview. When *Variety* reported that Maude might return to the stage, a *New York Times* article declared that her health was not improving and "reports of the artist's condition are not encouraging."[8]

It soon was reported that Maude had shown an interest in Barrie's new play, "Mary Rose." This signaled everyone that she would soon be returning to the stage.

Variety stated that Maude would return next season, either in a new play or a revival such as "Peter Pan." In the article, Alf Hayman made sure to point out that he and the Frohman Company still managed Maude and would select her new play. The Frohman Company quickly issued a statement of their own in an attempt to scoop *Variety* and disclose that they already had a play in mind for Maude.

> It is reported that Maude Adams will return to the stage next season in the new Barrie play, "Mary Rose," at present scoring such a success in London. Miss Adams has been ill for some time and has been living in seclusion. But, with her recovery now assured, it is expected that next Christmas will see her again at the Empire.[9]

According to Robbins, Maude was waiting for Barrie to send her the manuscript for "Mary Rose." She fully intended to play the title role, wrote Robbins. So sure was critic Alexander Woollcott that Maude would appear, he declared she would open at

Christmas. Supposedly, Alf Hayman returned from London in August with the "Mary Rose" script and proclaimed that Maude would open the new Barrie play at the Empire on Christmas night. When Maude turned down the role, the Frohman managers, as well as theatergoers, were shocked.

Reporters speculated as to why Maude had refused the play, citing everything from her fear of returning to the stage to her current state of health. Those more knowledgeable about stage affairs suggested that Maude had refused because the role called for an actress who was in her early twenties. The fact that the play dealt with youth and age, that Mary Rose must remain eternally young while all the people around her grow old, made the question of age an important one for Maude to consider. Moreover, the part of Mary Rose was not a dominant one. Rather, the roles of her husband and son were not only longer, but also more exacting. Such sages of the theater pointed out that Maude only appeared in plays where her roles were stellar.

The Frohman Company recovered from their initial surprise by giving the role to Ruth Chatterton and claiming they were not unduly distressed by the change in personnel. They reaffirmed that the new Barrie play would open as planned during the Christmas season.

Yet, there was more to Maude's refusal than speculated upon by the press and theater people. She had finally become completely disenchanted with the Frohman organization. Prior to signing a contract to appear in the play, Maude requested a change of managers. She did not care for Alf Hayman. Besides, Hayman was ill and could not meet his obligations. The Frohman Company refused her request. When the final contract was submitted to her, Maude found a clause that required her to give up all rights she owned to certain Barrie plays, "The Little Minister," "Quality Street," and "What Every Woman Knows," so the company would be free to sell them for use in motion pictures. She balked at this requirement, declining not only the film clause, but the entire contract. She then took her refusal one step further; she decided to quit the Frohman Company.

A week later, the management team of Erlanger and Dillingham claimed that Maude would return to the stage under their guidance; she might even appear in Shakespeare. Their announcement proved premature. Maude had not signed with the producers, and her future remained uncertain. Still, her improved health suggested that she would be seen again on stage before long.

At the same time that these negotiations were making newspaper headlines, theater managers around the country began reporting a business slump, although producers and touring company managers continued to prepare new shows, seemingly oblivious of the ominous signs. What managers were noticing was the beginning of an economic recession that would, in a few months, dramatically affect theater business. After the euphoria of a victorious war, the combined impact of unemployment, increasing debt, and higher taxes forced people to reconsider their personal priorities. The first area to be hit by a cutback in spending was the entertainment industry. The situation would grow progressively worse during 1921.

The obvious decline in audience attendance might very well have convinced

Maude to refrain from any stage activity. It did not, however, prevent her from planning for the future. It was reported that she was soliciting ideas from various playwrights, including Booth Tarkington, for her use during the next season. In a letter to Tarkington, February 25, 1921, Maude talked about the kind of roles she particularly enjoyed, comedic but with a serious intent. She expressed pleasure that Tarkington might prepare something for her.[10]

While the *Clipper* reported the possibility that Maude might return to the stage under the auspices of Erlanger and Dillingham, of even greater moment was the revelation that she was now beginning work at the General Electric Laboratories, in Schenectady, New York, on a moving picture project. In reality, she had begun work on new lighting techniques for both the stage and screen.

As far back as the opening of "The Little Minister," Maude had shown interest in stage lighting effects. In successive productions, she had experimented with various lighting systems to brighten the stage, do away with shadows, and focus spots on the interactive dialogue rather than on one specific player. Her achievements in "Peter Pan" and "Chantecler" demonstrated that incandescent lighting showed a marked improvement over arc lamps. By the time that "Leonora" and "A Kiss for Cinderella" were produced, Maude had eliminated footlights and border lights altogether. Her innovations were so revolutionary that many stage managers incorporated these changes into their own productions. As Maude became more familiar with moving pictures and the lighting systems they used, she believed that they, too, could be improved to eliminate flickering and, at the same time, brighten scenes to achieve increased clarity.

It was the problem of illumination that drew Maude to the General Electric Laboratories. They were currently experimenting with lighting, using tungsten filaments; and Maude believed these could be readily adapted for the stage and film. She approached Willis Whitney, head of the G.E. Laboratories, and offered her ideas and goals. So impressed was Whitney that he gave her a small office in the laboratory of Darcy Ryan, a research scientist.

The lab occupied Building Thirty-One, overlooking Dock Street and the Erie Canal, outside the main gate. Ryan was in charge of the group working on tungsten filaments. Working at the same lab were Irving Langmuir and William Coolidge, who likely shared their efforts with Maude. Also a part of this project was Barrett Jones, who had assisted her in several of her productions and championed her plan with the G.E. people. Maude and Louise Boynton first stayed briefly at the Hotel Mohawk. Once she had settled into her activities at G.E., they rented a house at Forty-Three Washington Avenue, within walking distance of the G.E. plant.

Maude, of course, had no scientific training. Yet her remarkable insight into mechanical and electrical problems for the stage gave her an intuitive accuracy that the engineers found pleasantly surprising. Even when they initially dismissed some of her suggestions, many turned out to their advantage. This enhanced their respect for her even more.

When it was discovered that Maude was working with G.E. engineers, reporters rushed to Schenectady to find out what she was working on. Thanks, no doubt, to her typically reclusive desires, little information was provided, except to say that experiments were ongoing and no one could predict how they would turn out. No details of the experiments were given.

Maude had already replaced arc lamps with incandescent lamps to project light for the stage, the first time they were ever used for that purpose. Her stage innovations coincided with G.E.'s development of tungsten lighting for motion pictures. Together, she and the G.E. scientists would seek the best way to use this method for both stage and film. Maude did not visit the lab every day, but she came often enough to observe progress and meet with the scientists to discuss procedures. She remained on call whenever they especially wanted her views and suggestions. Yet, the process moved very slowly.

After several months of experiments, Maude persuaded Dr. Whitney to look at the work already achieved. Not only was he surprised at the progress, he immediately recognized the potential. He called in Dr. P.G. Nutting, former research scientist at Westinghouse, to supervise further activities. It took almost fifteen months to produce the first operative, large, tungsten filament bulbs to test. One broke in transit; the other worked superbly. Dr. Whitney was immediately summoned to observe the lamp. Just as he arrived, the lamp blew up. Three months passed before three more lamps could be delivered; but they all functioned well. Now the work of refining them and applying them to the specific needs of the theater occupied Maude's time, as this would be her professional contribution to the invention.

At the same time that Maude worked on perfecting the lamps, she became very interested in the lighting mechanics for moving pictures. She now believed that her efforts could equally apply to film, and she devoted some time to understanding that medium, particularly its production for colored motion pictures. Since no one before had directed their efforts to the photo-chemistry of film, experimentation went along entirely new paths. George Eastman became involved in the exploration because his company was the biggest producer of film.

Rumors that Maude was engaged in the production of a colored film, "Aladdin," were entirely unfounded. She was particularly annoyed at the press, who lent the rumor credence, since she felt the public had a certain confidence in her and such vague news items would arouse a sense of expectation. If the research delivered nothing, people would be disappointed. However, that did not prevent motion picture studios from sending "visitors"—actually spies—to make a tour of G.E. and try to find any color motion picture machines that might be the product of Maude's experiments.

In May 1921, an announcement in the press again upset the theater industry. After almost eighteen months of illness, Alf Hayman died; and the Frohman organization appeared destined for another upheaval. Although Daniel Frohman headed the company, he had been devoting most of his energies to the motion picture business. Gradually, the once formidable Frohman empire would disintegrate and disappear, its best performers signing with other producers, its theater properties sold off. Only the statue of Charles Frohman in the Empire Theater lobby reminded people of the company's halcyon days.

At the time, however, theater managers and producers were more concerned about the state of their own business. Some of the highest-class Broadway theaters switched to showing moving pictures to offset their loss of business from stage productions. Even a reduction in theater prices did not tempt customers to attend more frequently. Many of the out-of-work actors went to Hollywood, only to find that the picture business was suffering from the same lack of attendance. Chicago theaters reported they were in the midst of their worst slump in years. Ethyl Barrymore went into vaudeville, as did other star entertainers. Those touring companies that were lucky enough to complete the season reported the worst box-office receipts for one-night stand shows. Many New York producers said they were not going to invest in new shows for next season until the economy improved.

Rumors about Maude's shooting a moving picture surfaced again when it was reported that she had asked several actors from a company in Albany to take part in a film. Actually, she planned to use them to test the new methods of lighting being developed and to determine their viability. So eagerly attuned were the motion picture studios, they again sent people to uncover any new ideas they could use.

In June, much to Maude's surprise, she received an invitation to attend Union College's 125th annual commencement. The reason: she was to be honored for her contributions to the theater, by being awarded the degree of Doctor of Laws. Maude was the first woman to receive an honorary degree from the prestigious college. She shared honors with Dr. James R. Angell, president-elect of Yale; Thomas W. Lamont, a J.P. Morgan banker; and New York Governor Nathan L. Miller.

John William Davis, former ambassador to Great Britain, delivered the graduation address. Dr. Charles Alexander Richmond, president of Union College, presented her degree to Maude.

> The subtle charm of your acting, the truth and delicacy of your interpretations, and the melody of your voice, the fresh young spirit that is in you — all these have captivated the children of all growths and made us all your friends.[11]

Amy Leslie, Charles Darnton, and Alan Dale could not have said it better.

The next day, Maude was back at the laboratory working on the problems of properly illuminating a movie set. A letter from Louise Boynton to Phyllis Robbins in November 1921 indicated that Maude's work was near the point when the lamps would be operative. Another letter a month later indicated that Maude would begin using the equipment in January. Yet Boynton wrote warily: "The burden continues, however, to be very heavy."[12] It appeared that Maude's health remained delicate.

After many months of experimentation, the influence of Maude's ideas and G.E.'s technological inventiveness resulted in the manufacture of the world's largest incandescent lamp. The lamp measured eighteen and a half inches high, and its bulb was twelve inches in diameter. The filament inside the bulb was made of tungsten wire one-tenth of an inch in diameter and ninety-three inches long, constructed in four coils. The lamp required 30,000 watts to operate and gave 60,000 candlepower of illumination. A G.E. unit in Cleveland produced the lamps, with thirteen of them made for possible sale to motion picture studios. The lamps were no longer just an experiment, and the studios vied to purchase them.

G.E. considered the work so valuable that a tripartite agreement was drafted, to include the General Electric Company, Eastman Kodak Company, and Maude Adams. The agreement committed the three parties to the building of a motion picture laboratory in Schenectady, the laboratory to be supported by the motion pictures produced under Maude's name and directed by her. Both G.E. and Eastman Kodak signed the agreement. G.E.'s president had taken the agreement before his board of directors and told them that Maude was the only person in the theatrical profession with whom G.E. could afford to have its name connected.

In spite of the potential financial benefits, Maude refused to sign the agreement. Dr. Ryan and old friend Bassett Jones took Maude to lunch to persuade her to sign "what was probably the most far-reaching and important agreement that either company had ever offered anyone." Still, Maude refused to sign. Jones was perplexed. "I gave her hell and walked out. What an opportunity! She would have been a rich woman in a few years."[13]

Maude gave as her excuse the fact that setting and lighting the stage was her joy, not "hopping about for a living." Besides, she already had plenty of money. Given the circumstances, G.E. and Eastman Kodak proceeded to manufacture this new lighting technique for the motion picture industry and reap the financial rewards. Because, in effect, Maude's job was finished, she returned to New York and the Cenacle. Maude's lawyer advised her that she could likely secure a settlement from G.E. for $500,000. But Maude refused to bring suit.

At the G.E. Hall of Electrical History, the company archive located in Schenectady, many articles relate the development of large incandescent lamps but offer only a few words about Maude's involvement in their production. Articles about Whitney describe experiments leading to the lamp; other articles speak of the advances in lighting technology, thanks to G.E. engineers. Strangely, the Schenectady archive holds no information about Dr. Nutting, scientists Ryan and Coolidge, or Maude. Archive officials reported that most likely these papers had been destroyed.

In January 1922, Maude made the headlines again, not for anything related to theater, but rather for her philanthropy. She gave her 300-acre estate at Ronkonkoma to the Cenacle. It was her way of showing "her gratitude for the comfort and peace she found in their convent on West 140th Street after a nervous breakdown, which caused her retirement from the stage." [14] In fact, Maude had offered the estate several months earlier. At the time, however, Bishop McDonnell of Brooklyn was in poor health; and Mother Marie Majoux could not accept the gift without his permission. Once Bishop McDonnell died, and the issue was brought to the attention of his successor, Bishop Molloy, the gift was heartily approved.

The property was valued at $130,000 when Maude first put it up for sale in 1910. She then withdrew it from the market and improved it considerably, building another house, adding a large hennery, and planting acres of locust trees. Maude had spent many summers at Ronkonkoma, either resting from the fatigue of touring or preparing for a new play.

When Maude learned that the Cenacle on 140th Street was overcrowded and the sisterhood desired to expand their work, she decided to offer the estate to them. Her gift was unconditional. A spokesperson for the Cenacle said that they would not take possession until the spring. They also indicated that they planned to add a large structure, one more suitable as a retreat for women in search of spiritual solace. While most of their work was among Catholics, it was not unusual for Protestants to seek refuge at the Cenacle. It was said at the convent that, so far as they were aware, Maude had never contemplated becoming a Catholic. Of course, the Cenacle sisters were elated about Maude's generosity, viewing her gift as divinely-inspired.

A month later, the producing team of Erlanger, Dillingham, and Ziegfeld announced that Maude would return to the stage next season under their management. A play had not yet been chosen, but the press believed it would be written by Barrie. It was also possible, they reported, that some of her old successes would be revived.

Soon, rumors flew that Maude would return to the stage in "Peter Pan." Several of the actors who were members of the original cast of 1915 said they had been approached and that rehearsal dates were part of the discussion. The offices of Charles Frohman, Inc., who still owned the U.S. rights for the play, denied all knowledge of any revival or that Maude would return to the stage. Erlanger, Dillingham, and Ziegfeld offered no explanations; and, as usual, no statements were forthcoming from Maude. The rumor soon passed like so many others.

Meanwhile, theater business in the U.S., both stage and motion picture, continued to feel the brunt of the economic recession. Road companies reported high failure rates. On Broadway, 184 plays had opened in the fall of 1922; eighty-eight were complete failures; only twenty-three lasted long enough to make a profit. Broadway producers indicated that they had lost more than $1.5 million. As they were contemplating the risks of investing in the new season, moving picture studios reported a gradual increase in attendance. By September, theater producers were encouraged by reports that the recession was ebbing and patrons were finding their way back to theatrical entertainment. The improvement was selective, however. Musical comedy seemed to be prospering, while legitimate theater remained static. The American public's tastes were obviously in transition.

Several reviewers noted in their feature columns that Maude was about to celebrate her fiftieth birthday on November 11, 1922. Paragraphs were devoted to her rise to fame, her starring roles, and her abrupt retirement from the stage. Nothing was mentioned about her work with G.E., nor was any indication given of her possible return to theater. Reviewers admitted that her current life and her future intentions were a mystery to them. What Maude actually did to celebrate this milestone birthday is unknown.

Maude's donation of the Ronkonkoma estate to the Cenacle now raised rumors that she was to become a nun. The arguments seemed plausible, and Maude did not

deny or confirm the rumors. That she had
sought seclusion with the Cenacle at the time
of her nervous breakdown suggested an affinity toward the Roman Catholic religion.

But like most of the rumors that had
surrounded Maude these past few years, they
disappeared from the newspapers as quickly
as they had appeared. What reporters and
critics were actually admitting was that they
had little inkling of what Maude planned to
do with her life or whether she would ever
return to resume an illustrious stage career.

**Maude was fifty-five years old when this formal
photograph was taken. She divided her time in
New York between her residence at the Colony
Club and the Cenacle on 140th Street. (1927.
Museum of the City of New York)**

18

The One I Knew Least of All

In November 1922, Maude sailed for England to speak with Barrie about obtaining the rights to his plays for use in motion pictures. Maude's plan was to produce them but not play in them. There was also some question about using Barrie's stage plays in America after the reorganization of the Frohman Company.

An American producer had claimed he had secured the rights from Barrie to produce a musical version of "The Little Minister." Barrie replied that he had no knowledge of any such arrangements. Nevertheless, a film version of the play appeared in theaters. Maude had her lawyer, Mr. Delafield, contact the Famous Players studio to stop distributing the film, which they did.

On her first London visit, Maude and Barrie discussed all of these topics, but they came to no conclusions because a variety of artistic and business considerations remained to be resolved. When Maude returned in March 1923, their discussions continued, the end result being that she would become Barrie's agent in the U.S. and Canada, either to produce or to license others to produce his plays. Later, Delafield heard from Mr. Gilmore, Barrie's lawyer, that Barrie had expressed reluctance to sever his connection with the Frohman Company, now managed by Famous Players (Daniel Frohman). Maude, of course, no longer had any association with Famous Players.

For several months, there was no contact between the negotiating parties until Delafield wrote Gilmore of Maude's concern about Barrie's reluctance to make a final judgment on the matter. "Whether rightly or wrongly," Delafield wrote, "Miss Adams construed your letter of June 19 as a practical refusal by Sir James of the propositions contained in the letter which I had written to you on her behalf on May 22, 1923."[1] A month later, Gilmore informed Delafield that Barrie was going to make other arrangements as he thought best.

What was Barrie thinking? Had his feelings about Maude changed? Due to Barrie's decision, a curious one, or so it seemed to Maude, she was obviously hurt and disappointed. Because of this disagreement, they did not communicate for several years; and newspapers were quick to report that the "warm relationship" between Maude and Barrie had broken down, likely for money reasons.

Maude's trips to London were similar to those she had previously taken. She still tried to remain anonymous by identifying herself as Miss Kiscadden, although, on the pier, she wore no veil. She had come to believe that, due to her not having been on the stage for several years, no one would recognize her, that the world had passed by Maude Adams. She was wrong. Indeed, she was confronted by a reporter's question regarding her identity. She offered him some unusual answers.

"Where are you going, Miss Adams?" she was asked.

"But Miss Adams is not here," she responded.

"But, Miss Adams, I have seen you too often from the gallery of the Empire Theater not to remember the voice, and the eyes, and the personality."

"No," she repeated, "Miss Adams isn't here."[2]

As Maude repeated the denial of the identity she had once so proudly owned, the reporter turned to Louise Boynton and said: "Please tell Miss Adams I wish her a most delightful voyage."

Turning to the reporter, Maude smiled softly. "Miss Adams thanks you," she said. "Goodbye."

In April 1923, upon Maude's return from England, rumors intimated that she was going to appear in several of Barrie's plays, including "Peter Pan." No one knew at the time of the Adams-Barrie impasse. That information was not divulged until months later.

Maude now began examining the potential for producing her own moving pictures, as Phyllis Robbins romantically described the action in her biography.

> But her mind had been turning not only to the use of her lamps for stage scenery but for the "real thing," the life of the people—human creatures in their native environment.[3]

A plan was already taking shape in Maude's mind to produce a color film of "Aladdin" and also filming Rudyard Kipling's "Kim" in India. It had become an ambitious adventure for Maude, and, although she put much money and energy into the project, it eventually failed. As numerous critics examined her aspirations, Maude's plans were deemed to be several years ahead of what could be accomplished mechanically with motion pictures.

Maude had spent some time working on the screenplay for "Kim." Typical of her obsession for completeness, Maude's scenario included costumes, scenic layouts, and picture management. It was almost as if she intended to handle each task herself. She even believed that "Kim" could be shot on location, although such a formidable project had never before been attempted.

While in London with Phyllis Robbins, Maude had obtained the rights to "Kim" from Rudyard Kipling for a sum of $50,000, with the unique proviso that the filming would take place only in India. (Kipling was later chastised for "stealing" Maude's money for a project deemed impossible by the press.) Even when Maude discovered that moving picture studios were experimenting with "talkies" and her financial backing had been withdrawn, she continued working on the screenplay. A quick trip to Paris to see "Saint Joan" extended itself into further work on the film script. Maude seemed unable to drop the project, or she simply failed to recognize its impracticability. When Robbins returned to the U.S., Maude spent a month at the Cenacle of St. Regis in Versailles working on the script.

When Maude returned to the U.S., she secluded herself to devote full energy to the movie project. When she did go out, she evaded recognition by wearing her usual disguise, a long coat with a fur collar and a veil covering her face.

Yet, all of Maude's efforts at producing "Kim" came to nothing. No financing was available for so risky a venture. Shooting on location in India? Filming in color? Using native actors? The studios examining her proposal regarded it as "out of the question," if not downright "insane." Sadly, Maude was finally persuaded to set the project aside.

Then, *Variety* picked up a rumor that B.C. Whitney, a theatrical manager and head of the Theater Guild's road production of "Saint Joan," had intimated that Maude would appear in the lead of George Bernard Shaw's play. The arrangement, however, contained one obstacle; it would be necessary for Maude to join Actors' Equity. This was a rule demanded by the actors' union for all independent producers. That Maude might be returning to the stage, and in a non–Barrie play, made headlines. Whether she would actually appear, posed the critics, was another question. (Ironically, Charles Dillingham was planning to revive "Peter Pan" this year, featuring former Ziegfeld Follies star Marilyn Miller.)

Plans for the play were still unsettled a month later, *Variety* reported. Equity had informed Whitney that Maude was required to join the union. Maude was said to have declared she was opposed to becoming a member of a labor union. Due to her unique standing in the theater, however, the Equity board expressed a willingness to give Maude an honorary membership, sensing that by not providing membership — thus preventing her from appearing on stage — they would be subject to substantial adverse publicity.

In September, a month before the play was to open, *Variety* stated that Maude had rejected the offer of life membership in Equity.

> In declining, the former star is reported stating that she appreciated the honor intended, but preferred remaining in retirement from the stage rather than sacrifice her principles.[4]

After hearing of Maude's final decision, Whitney engaged Julia Arthur for the lead in "Saint Joan."

Maude now turned again to her motion picture aspirations. She formed a corporation with a capitalization of $3,500,000 to "produce motion pictures." Incorporators of the new company included Frank Kewton, Thomas F. Compton, and

Leander Sniffer, all of them likely solicited for funds by Maude's lawyer. It was stipulated that all future announcements as to the plans for the corporation would come from Maude. One rumor suggested that "Kim," Maude's pet project, would be shot in India next year. *Variety* announced the formation of the Maude Adams Company, Inc., which would begin producing pictures with a color device and a new lighting system that created the equivalent of sunlight indoors. Her studio was reported to be located at 11 East Fourteenth Street, New York City.

Shortly after, Maude announced that she would be appearing in "Kim," her first production. She planned to sail for Europe in September to consult with Kipling on the making of "Kim," in an attempt to resurrect the project. On this voyage, Maude was joined by Phyllis Robbins.

After Maude's meeting with Kipling, however, the "Kim" project seemed to expire. The specific reasons for its demise were never revealed, but *Variety* believed that the costs of production and the problems of shooting a film on location finally conspired to kill Maude's project.

Maude also had devised an idea for Barrie to write a travelogue for her, to be produced on film. While in England, she contacted Barrie (their first communication in several years) to determine his interest. He expressed a desire to accommodate Maude — he would almost never turn down one of her requests — but was not sure what she specifically wanted.

> It is delightful to hear from you again, and as I said in my cable nothing could please me more than to do anything you want me to do, but what precisely it is I can't quite make out.[5]

Barrie went on to ask several questions in order to clarify his task. A few weeks later, he again wrote Maude, who had attempted to answer his questions, and enclosed several scenarios that she might consider. Still, he expressed some confusion regarding what Maude intended to do. Like "Kim," the project ended when Maude failed to follow through with her notion.

At about the same time, Scribner's, the book publisher, asked Maude to submit a manuscript about her life and career. In a letter to Maude, on May 18, 1925, Maxwell E. Perkins, chief editor of Scribner's, expressed their interest in publishing her story.

> We are extremely interested to hear last Friday that you are writing your reminiscences. Naturally, we should be delighted to cooperate with you as publishers in bringing them out in book form when the time comes.[6]

Scribner's hoped for a quick arrangement and asked for a meeting so they could discuss the project with Maude and agree on a contract. Since they were the U.S. publishers of Barrie's work, "we have therefore a certain special and additional interest in your reminiscences."

Maude responded through her lawyer, Herbert Satterlee, that she would deal with the offer "when the time came." Four months later, Maude received another letter from Perkins asking for a definite commitment to publish, for a royalty of fifteen percent on the retail price of every copy sold. He was quite apologetic about asking her again but reiterated Scribner's strong interest in her material.

In January 1926, Maude answered their letter, enclosing a section she had already written. A few days later, Perkins received a letter from Satterlee seeking a meeting to discuss their offer. Perkins responded by praising Maude's work and enclosed a contract for her to write five, possibly six, pieces, if she could manage it. "The piece has a charm that is peculiarly individual. They could hardly be overpraised."[7]

Did that mean he liked the material or not?

In the meantime, Maude had contracted with the Curtis Publishing Company (*Ladies' Home Journal*) to publish a series of articles that she was in the process of completing. Regarding the Scribner's offer, Curtis indicated they would have no objection to the publication of the articles in book form. Satterlee informed Perkins of the possible arrangement and returned a signed contract to Scribner's.

Actually, the first article of Maude's autobiographical series appeared in the March 1926, issue of *Ladies' Home Journal*, entitled "The One I Knew Least of All." Preparing the material had proven an extremely hard task for her—the Harvard archives reveal numerous revisions—but her articles offered many insights into the personality of an otherwise enigmatic woman. *Variety* noted the publication and expressed astonishment that she had written the entire story of her life in the third person. Throughout the text, she never once used the word "I." They attributed this idiosyncratic trait to her inherent modesty. The series extended through October, six articles in all. It included photographs of her early life, her mother, and her many stage roles.

The articles were a strange amalgam of her early life; several stories, some revisionist, about her life on the stage; and romantic anecdotes about her father and Charles Frohman. She often digressed in the text to offer her opinions on a wide variety of subjects—horses: she was afraid of them but rode well; school: she did not care for school; choices of plays: she did not care for comedy and rather preferred tragedy; swimming: she abhorred swimming; rehearsals: they were very important but tedious and boring; the theater: it was her life.

Throughout the articles, she spoke lovingly of her father—"he was always a faithful ally"—and their time together in San Francisco during her childhood. She loved staying with her grandmother, from whom she had gained her affection for nature. Maude spoke sparingly of her mother, however, mainly about her early years as a child growing up in the theater. She never mentioned that they had worked together in most plays up to the time she had become a Frohman star, nor that they had lived together for many years.

Charles Frohman was viewed as her mentor and "father confessor." E.H. Southern taught her how to laugh. John Drew taught her how to perfect many of her acting abilities. Maude admitted to not much liking children until she played in "Peter Pan." Having grown up with adults, she expressed her fear of children until she acted with them. From that point on, she became their staunch advocate. Maude claimed that she taught herself the human emotions portrayed in her acting by observing people, by learning the parts she took in plays, and by understanding what elements of the play audiences liked. She mentioned nothing about her extraordinary appeal among women, although it represented a substantial aspect of her stardom.

In nearly all of the articles, Maude talked about herself in a self-deprecating manner. She believed she was neither pretty nor strong. She admitted to low self-esteem. She was self-conscious, insecure, and shy. She suffered from a poor self-identity — hence the title of the series, her frequent reference to herself as "the least," and her admissions that, because of the number of male and female roles she had played, she sometimes doubted her own identity.

At age fifteen, she believed her first attempt as a leading lady had been a failure. Even when she became a star in "The Little Minister," she revealed that "the one I knew least had very little confidence in herself as an actress, and her anxiety made her self-conscious."[8] She allowed that she was bad as Juliet, that the arc lights were her greatest enemy, and meeting J.M. Barrie was "a joy." She spoke sparingly of the illnesses that forced her off the stage, except to say that she knew when she was "through." Maude ended the series by relating her experiences at the G.E. Lab and the innovations that had shaped her mind toward motion pictures.

While the series was in publication, Scribner's wrote Maude frequently about a meeting to discuss the book: "the sooner we can publish, the better we shall be pleased." In successive letters, Perkins worried about when the book might come out, that is, when Maude would submit the final manuscript and photographs that she had promised. When they sent her the proofs, she responded by telling them that she would have to work over them "a great deal." Maude also suggested that more material be included in the book, but Perkins rejected the idea because of the need for immediate publication. Maude then postponed the entire project until the following spring, no reasons given, much to Perkins's consternation.

For the next several months, Perkins wrote to Maude, but none of his letters were answered. Perkins begged Satterlee to get answers regarding added material and a final manuscript submission from her. Even Barrie wrote Maude, wondering what had become of her.

> My dear Maudie,
> It is so long since I have heard from you, and I hope it is not from any fault of mine, whether of omission or commission. Certainly never from anything intended, for I think of you often and always with the old regard and affection.[9]

Maude cabled Barrie a response, for which he was quite appreciative. Communicating with Scribner's, however, had become an unwilling task. A letter from Barton Currie, editor of the *Ladies' Home Journal,* to Maxwell Perkins lamented: "The charming and elusive lady has vanished so far, and I am concerned also. I have heard nothing from her for more than two months."[10]

Another letter to Maude from Perkins described, in a diplomatic way, his frustration in attempting to reach her and persuading her to move ahead on the book.

> Is it not possible now for us to get forward with the book? I know you like to do things in your own way and at your own times.... But there are practical considerations which make me feel bound to urge progress now.... Please forgive me if I seem intrusive. I even got your address from one who perhaps ought not to have given it to me. I promise never to use it again if you dislike my doing it this time.[11]

Maude never responded to Perkins's letter, and the book project was summarily shelved. Maude's habit of not answering letters left it to her lawyer to cover for her, for even the most trivial of issues. Maude's reclusiveness now began to take on a new dimension, as it appeared to affect her ability to make decisions.

During 1926 and 1927, Maude saw little of Phyllis Robbins, partly due to the pursuit of her own projects and partly to the declining health of Phyllis's aunt. Near the end of the aunt's life, Maude sent Phyllis a letter of sympathy and unhappiness at not being able to comfort Phyllis in person. Nevertheless, immediately following the aunt's death, Maude visited Phyllis.

Although she had now been nine years off the stage, Maude's artistic reputation had not been totally forgotten. In June 1927, Maude received an honorary degree of Doctor of Letters from the University of Wisconsin. She almost did not attend the festivities but Boynton, Robbins, and Mrs. Alexander persuaded her to face the public, if only for a moment. At the ceremony, Professor Paxson recited the citation honoring the reticent Maude for her artistic integrity and high ideals.

> Maude Adams won the affection of the American audience while the glamour of her girlhood was still upon her. And when she chose to withdraw herself after two decades of friendly contact, she left a model that too few have imitated, and a void that none of her successors has completely filled. The actor writes his record on the passing moment and leaves no monument, unless indeed he leaves it in our hearts. Babbie and Peter Pan are enduring fantasy; but they are also Maude Adams; and while they last Maude Adams will remain with us as the living image of gentle comedy and high ideal.[12]

Both Maude's arrival to and departure from the university were secretive.

For almost a year, nothing was heard of Maude, nor of her projects. When in New York, she could be found at the Colony Club or the Cenacle on 140th Street. For some period of time, she retired to Ronkonkoma. Although it was now owned by the Cenacle, Maude was able to reside in a small, white house on the grounds, with Louise Boynton to protect her from unwarranted intrusions.

When the Ronkonkoma estate was officially turned over to the Cenacle on May 31, 1922, Maude was unable to attend because of illness. In November 1925, ground was broken for a large new building. On August 8, 1926, the cornerstone was placed, accompanied by an appropriate religious ceremony. The new quarters were completed October 7, 1927. As for Maude's former residence, changes made by the nuns included electricity (as opposed to Maude's preference for candlelight) and drapes instead of wooden shades. Ironically, though Maude preferred the atmosphere of a cloister, the nuns opened the building to light and modern conveniences.

Throughout 1928 and 1929, Maude remained in seclusion. Her refusal to appear in public continued. In April 1928, the Philadelphia Forum attempted to get Maude to speak before their group about her lighting innovations for moving pictures. She refused the offer. Later in the year, Maude was invited to participate at a special event in Salt Lake City, the closure and demolition of the old Salt Lake Theater. Local officials believed that Maude would respond to their request because of the significance of the event. Again, Maude declined to attend.

When another of those "unverified reports" arose, suggesting that Maude "had confessed to a desire to do another play," the rumor quickly subsided because no further information was forthcoming. Besides, no one seemed to know where Maude was at the time. Requests from Hollywood for Maude to appear in pictures were frequently made and just as often ignored.

Then, in early 1930, Maude made an unprecedented trip to Southern California and stayed for five months. She was preparing, with playwright John Colton, a play to be called "The Joyous Adventures of Clementine." Supposedly, Maude was in charge of developing the plot; and Colton was assigned to do the writing. After five months of work, only two acts were completed. Maude was reported to be unable to finish sections of the play, rewriting them so many times that Colton had become exasperated and refused to continue the effort. Several years later, Colton would file a lawsuit against Maude because of her inability to complete the work. Maude returned to New York disappointed but, apparently, with a changed disposition toward playacting.

Possibly, the moment had arrived to return to the stage. The timing may not have been ideal — the Depression had impacted the country heavily — but it appeared that Maude's desire to perform again had been rekindled. Where this new interest might take her, she would not speculate; but she now intended to explore her options.

19

Passages

> There'll be a hush at first; a strange, poignant silence. The Erlanger will have become, before the startled eyes of that first-night audience next September, the Empire. And Maude Adams will go on with her "modern romantic comedy."[1]

Douglas Gilbert, staff writer for the *New York Telegram,* so described what Maude's return to the stage would undoubtedly be like. In May 1930, the Erlanger organization announced that, under their direction, Maude Adams would return to the stage "in a modern social comedy by a contemporary American author." They were so confident of her appearance that they began advertisements for the show, claiming that "in this she will match her act against the jazz age blandishments of the current school."

The play alluded to was the same one that Maude and John Colton had spent several months working on but never completed. Instead, Colton, under Erlanger's insistence, had finished the play without Maude. The question remained whether she would accept his completed script. The Erlanger organization believed she would, primarily because she was "hungry" to return to the stage.

At this time, Maude and Louise Boynton were living at the Cenacle residence on 140th Street. The nuns there believed that she would not return to acting because of her age. She was fifty-seven years old and her health remained fragile.

No sooner was the announcement made than the gossip columns took up the issue of who would be selected for the male lead. John D. Williams, from the Erlanger office, was in charge of booking actors and was supposedly looking for a suitable lead, although Maude would make the final decision.

When the new season's shows opened in September, no leading man had yet been agreed upon and rumors indicated that Maude was not entirely pleased with the script. Williams continued to look. Colton became frustrated about the delay in producing his play. Erlanger was unhappy because they had already spent a good deal of money advertising the play and were then forced to make announcements about its postponement.

In early December, *Variety revealed* that the play had been called off. *Variety* reported that Maude and John Williams had disagreed on the selection of a leading man and, therefore, they were unable to fill the cast for the play. Colton was again frustrated and threatened a lawsuit against Maude. Williams expressed his unhappiness about Maude's refusal to make decisions.

In the spring of 1931, after several meetings with Maude, the Erlanger office again announced her return to the stage, which would open the new season in September.

> Maude Adams, who made Peter Pan an immortal being for thousands of Americans, will return to the stage next season to act for the Erlanger office in a modern romantic comedy which is now being completed by a well-known American playwrite.[2]

Williams was now put in charge of selecting the cast, and he was also responsible for booking the entire tour. "All the details of the play and its author are to remain secret until arrangements had been completed," said the announcement. However, everyone on Broadway knew the name of the play and its author, John Colton. Erlanger was again attempting to produce the play and, hopefully, recoup a portion of their expenditures. Rehearsals were scheduled to begin in August but, at the last minute, were delayed indefinitely.

Shortly after, an embarrassed Erlanger had to announce that the play had been shelved, thus putting an unhappy ending to its painful half-life. No special reason was offered; but it was believed that a dispute had arisen between Maude and Williams over who would be in control of the production. Surprisingly, instead of retreating into seclusion, Maude made a proposal to the Erlanger people that they could not refuse.

Maude offered to play and produce Shakespeare's "The Merchant of Venice," and tour with the play. She planned to take the role of Portia; Otis Skinner, her specific selection, would play Shylock. Quickly, an agreement was signed, rehearsals begun in late September, and an opening date in Cleveland, Ohio, scheduled for October. The tour was to continue until May 1932, visiting more than twenty cities across the country. Interestingly, New York was omitted from the schedule at Maude's request. Immediately, she was attacked for not including the big city in her itinerary. New York was the city where she gained her fame and she had been its acknowledged star for two decades. Reporters asked why she was avoiding New York.

Maude was surprisingly candid in her remarks. "I'm afraid," she replied.

"What are you afraid of?"

"I'm afraid they wouldn't like me here," she answered.

"How can they do otherwise, when you've achieved so great a reputation?"

"It's this way," she explained. "When people expect you to turn a double somersault and all you can do is stand on your head, there's reason for being afraid that they will be disappointed."[3]

So obvious was Maude's insecurity and apparent fear of failure at returning to the New York stage that no one pursued her any further on the subject. Her trepidation would not disappear until she entered the stage that first night before a live audience, her official reemergence as a dramatic star.

Ward Morehouse, of the *New York Sun,* traveled to Cleveland to watch the rehearsals for "The Merchant of Venice." His first dispatch informed readers that "she bossed the rest of the cast, even giving Otis Skinner suggestions as to the interpretation of his role."[4]

His observations of the rehearsals were interesting reading. When Morehouse first observed Maude, she was standing in the center of the stage, wearing a bathrobe. On one leg she wore a white stocking; on the other, a brown one. Her hair was tousled. Under the bright lights, her face was worn. She looked all of her fifty-eight years. "Could this little old lady be Maude Adams, the radiant Maude Adams, the mysterious?" he asked. It did not seem possible.

"Yet, when she spoke," Morehouse reported, "when she moved, when she gave her staccato commands, the spell of her came over me."

> She was firm, sharp, nervous, quick, impatient, tense and terse. Also coquettish. Now and then she tried her coquetry upon the greasiest of the electricians, and it always worked.
>
> She was sharp and cross when the stupidity of her crew made her so. Frail and fifty-eight, yet alert and amazingly self-sufficient.
>
> One instant she was pointing up at the flies; another she was crouching at the footlights. She was never still. She paced the stage and raced up and down the aisles, and often I found her, all sudden like, sitting in an aisle seat just across from me.[5]

Maude and Otis Skinner opened at the Ohio Theater, Cleveland, on November 3 to a capacity crowd. She was returning to the stage after thirteen years. Audiences wanted to recapture a grand dramatic moment and renew an improbable dream. No audience could have been more anxious to see an actress triumph or more hopeful

of witnessing an acting miracle. When Maude first appeared on the stage, applause lasted for several minutes. At the end of the trial scene, when the true measure of any actress playing Portia is taken, the applause began again and would not stop until Maude had taken bow after bow, fourteen times in all. After the final curtain, with Otis Skinner in hand, they had another fourteen curtain calls.

Most of the reviews for Maude were complimentary, some for nostalgic reasons, some for

Otis Skinner was seventy-three when he played Shylock in "The Merchant of Venice," one of his last appearances after a career of more than fifty years. It was reported that Maude gave Skinner "suggestions as to the interpretation of his role." (Photo: Stein. Undated. Museum of the City of New York)

her superb acting. Yet, some critics made comparisons with her younger roles or commented on the incompatibility of an older woman playing a younger woman's part.

William F. McDermott, dramatic critic for the *Cleveland Plain Dealer,* was enchanted with Maude's acting.

> There are fine qualities in Miss Adams's Portia, of sweetness and charm, of pauses and words aptly spoken that have in them some touch of the electric. The sheer competence of her acting, so well timed, so deeply calculated, so true in detail, gives a kind of pleasure.[6]

Brooks Atkinson, of the *New York Times,* was sent to Cleveland to evaluate Maude's performance. Her professionalism, said Atkinson, was undiminished.

> Miss Adams goes through her paces like an actress. She trips lightly across the stage. Her arms and hands flutter with bright gestures. There is a simple charm in her smile; she is thoroughly animated. When she comes to the courtroom scene, she plays it with womanly dignity.[7]

Morehouse, too, remarked about Maude's fine acting abilities.

> Some of the old enchantment was there, the quick, broken smile, the caressing voice, the aura of tremulous sweetness, and that quality which Miss Adams's old admirers can only describe as radiance. In the opening scenes the Maude Adams we remembered filtered through in a representation of gaiety and mischief that had the old ring.
> There was a nice feeling, too, in the trial scene, a sense of genuineness, the projection of an individuality which is the opposite of commonplace. She plays this crucial scene differently from any other actress of these times.[8]

Yet, these critics noted that the Maude who played Portia was fifty-eight years old. Her age was apparent; and questions arose in their minds whether she had selected the right role to reenter the dramatic arena.

McDermott did not believe that Maude should have portrayed Portia.

> The choice does not seem a very happy one. The poet's words of ardent young love do not come with perfect appropriateness from this Portia. There is something imperial in Shakespeare's Portia and the quality of imperial is not natural to Miss Adams.[9]

Atkinson was more saddened than critical about Maude's Portia.

> To see her as Portia, however, is to be continually reminded all evening that this lady's little body has grown old with the world. The thirteen years since Miss Adams retired are the years that leave their traces.[10]

Morehouse did not expect a miracle as so many of Maude's admirers were hoping for. "Perhaps we should not expect Miss Adams to be exempt from the ordinary changes made by passing years," said Morehouse, "but somehow many of us do."[11]

Reports from other reviewers reflected many of the same comments regarding

Maude's return and her role as Portia. Yet, capacity audiences filled the theater to cheer her on.

"The Merchant of Venice" played in Boston during the Thanksgiving week. Maude visited Phyllis Robbins suffering from a sore throat that demanded attention. The doctor ordered Maude not to talk during the day if she wished to continue performing in the evening. Maude did not necessarily follow his instructions, but she appeared at every performance. Reviews from Boston critics were similar to those in Cleveland. The same was true the following week in Philadelphia.

An engagement in Newark was the closest Maude came to New York and several critics traveled there to watch her perform. Among them was Alexander Woollcott who wrote in *The New Yorker* of the nostalgia of the moment.

> I found myself yielding to the spell of a music familiar, dear, and ineffably touching. It was the music of a speaking voice I had not heard in years nor ever thought to hear once more. It was the voice — unchanged and changeless — of Maude Adams. And the sound of it filled me with an almost intolerable nostalgia for a day that is not now and never can be again.[12]

Shortly after Maude's successful return to the theater, Perkins of Scribner's renewed his request for her manuscript. "We have all followed with the greatest interest the course of your reappearance on the stage, as Portia, and have been delighted with the splendid success of the production."[13] Thus, he believed, "the precise moment had come" to publish the book. Perkins also sent a letter to John Williams asking him to help persuade Maude to send the manuscript.

In a matter of days, Maude answered Perkins's letter by telegram.

> My dear Mr. Perkins
> I have been working on a last chapter. The book in its present form would be very unsatisfactory to me and I should think of doubtful value to you. I should prefer to buy the rights and make some arrangement about the expense. I am loath to suggest this. You have been so generous and patient. But I doubt the success of the book as it stands.
> M.E. Adams[14]

In several telegrams, Perkins tried unsuccessfully to convince Maude that the time was right for the publication of the book. Finally, on December 11, Perkins acknowledged Maude's refusals and terminated their arrangement, at least until he tried again in 1934.

In February 1932, the company arrived in Chicago, with a great fanfare. Seats for the entire week's engagement had been sold out and newspapers spoke of her resounding return to the stage. They also pointed out that "the lighting arrangements are of Miss Adams' own invention." However, several articles talked more about Maude's past and her association with J.M. Barrie than the current production.

Maude was given excellent reviews for her work: "She is still Maude Adams";

"the old charm is still eagerly at work"; "the Maude Adams that we used to know and dote upon." But said Charles Collins of the *Chicago Tribune* said: "The last word on Miss Adams is that she is not one of the great Portias, but is still a great lady of the theater and a vivid personality."[15]

Demand for tickets were so strong that Maude consented to perform two additional matinees. The company then embarked on two weeks of one-night stands through Wisconsin, Minnesota, Iowa, Nebraska, and Utah on their way to the Pacific Coast. One might question the choice of small towns in which to play Shakespeare for both financial and health reasons, but they were Maude's decisions.

Reviews described the company's appearance at the Columbia Theater in San Francisco as "an unprecedented triumph" and "a spectacle of magnificence," and noted that Maude remained an "idol of the theater." The reviews seemed to be couched in awe of "the great lady of the stage."

> Maude Adams came back last night, back to the stage that needs her; back to a city that loves her.
> Had she changed? Sometimes you thought she had; at others, she was the same elfin, elusive, altogether delightful Maude Adams of the past. At the end of the second act you might have sworn she was Lady Babbie come back with wildflowers in her hair.[16]

The tour ended in May, in Lansing, Michigan. During the final performance, the company's performers and stagehands were especially feted. Maude and Otis Skinner made brief speeches of thanks. The audience demanded a repeat of the trial scene, with Maude and Skinner obliging the crowd. The tour had been an artistic success for Maude and one in which she believed the company had done a commendable job.

Yet, the play's financial success was put in doubt when a suit by John Williams against Maude revealed that the production barely broke even, in spite of its sellouts. Williams blamed Maude for the show's large overhead, her "faulty" decision-making, and her attempts to wrest control of the production from him. A hearing in August was repeatedly postponed as each side claimed they were not ready to go to court. The trial did not take place until 1935.

Maude spent the summer of 1932 at Ronkonkoma to rest after the arduous tour. Rumors suggested that Maude was looking for another play, but nothing seemed to materialize. In December, the Erlanger office had to put out a statement that Maude had denied a return to Broadway.

For most of 1933, Maude remained in seclusion. Newspapers periodically reported that she could not find a play that suited her, which would suggest she continued to look. Maude's only public activity was a fete she gave the end of July at Ronkonkoma as a benefit for the Cenacle. The garden party featured folk dances as part of a total program that Maude had organized.

In late 1933, Maude agreed to enact several of her most successful plays over the WEAF network, in a series of eight radio broadcasts, beginning January, 1934, and continuing to March. The fact that she had been asked to revive her old plays likely persuaded Maude to participate. That she was able to recreate the plays in the privacy of the radio studio also influenced her choice. Not having worked with Maude before, the studio people were quite surprised by her mode of operation.

All visitors were barred from the studio, even broadcasting officials. Maude used no script, reciting all of her lines from memory, along with a generous assortment of gestures. "The Little Minister" was split into two parts, Maude preferring a week's intermission than to a condensation of the drama. Included in the list of revivals were "Peter Pan," "What Every Woman Knows," "A Kiss for Cinderella," "L'Aiglon," and "The Merchant of Venice."

Reviews of her radio work were positive. *Variety* welcomed Maude back with a revival of her plays "as only Maude could render them."

> The glamorous and thrilling voice of Maude Adams, that for these many years has been one of the most potent memories of the American theater, became an incredible reality in radio.[17]

In a little noticed article in *Variety,* buried inside the paper and consisting of only a few terse lines, was the statement that MGM had purchased the screen rights for "Kim" from Maude. The movie would be produced in 1950, featuring Errol Flynn, Dean Stockwell, and Paul Lucas, and shot in the California mountains.

In the spring of 1934, Maude was approached by Walter Hartwig, a New York producer who had led many Little Theater productions, to play Shakespeare again, this time "Twelfth Night," a role she was quite familiar with. He hoped to schedule Maude throughout the East and Midwest in all of the larger cities. Maude had other ideas, however. She quickly agreed to the assignment, but indicated she would perform only in New England, on the summer circuit of small towns and university campuses. Hartwig accepted as long as Maude would supervise the production and technical aspects, select the cast, costumes, and scenery. Maude could not have been more pleased with the arrangements. Setting up a small studio in Ogunquit, Maine, where the play would open, she immediately selected the cast and arranged the play as she wished it to be performed.

Maude's version of "Twelfth Night" was arranged in five acts and twelve scenes. Some dialogue was omitted but the key passages were retained. Her innovative lighting techniques highlighted the stage and performers. She coached the actors in small groups for several weeks before putting them all together for full rehearsals. Only a few hours before the opening performance, Maude called for a change in certain production elements and even altered several of the principal's costumes.

Another surprising decision by Maude was to take the less than leading role of Maria, leaving the roles of Olivia and Viola, the role Maude had performed at the Greek Theater, to younger actresses. By virtue of the revised script, Maria became a character so important to the play that the work of the actors seemed to center about her from the time of her appearance to the end of the play.

To the right of the Ogunquit stage hung a large poster. "There were no theaters in Elizabethan England, save in the city of London," it read, "and strolling players roamed the country side seeking an audience. Tonight you will see a company of wandering mountebanks arrive at the courtyard of an ancient inn, set their stage, hang their arras, and go through their parts in the fashion of Shakespeare's day."

To the strains of simple folk music, the curtains rose and the pantomime described on the poster took life. Players proceeded to hang yards of dark green drapes to serve as a backdrop. Three openings in it provided entrances and exits. Beyond this there was no scenery and only the simplest of props. Placards on an easel marked and described each new scene. This preparation took place while the audience took their seats. Then the play commenced.

"Twelfth Night" opened at the Ogunquit Playhouse on July 16, 1934. The play became a final testimonial to Maude's glorious stage career. After a week's engagement, the play was scheduled to be performed in Camden, Brunswick, and Lewiston, Maine; Conway, Hanover, and Portsmouth, New Hampshire; Brattleboro and Bennington, Vermont; Westerly, Rhode Island; Magnolia, Wellesley, and Cambridge, Massachusetts. Final performances in Cambridge ended the tour in early September.

"It was a performance of the highest quality," said the reviewer of the *Boston Globe* from Ogunquit. "Maude Adams gave spice and piquancy. Hers is a new Maria, less the earthy wench and more the child seeking to make fun."[18]

The *New York Times* praised Maude's efforts, seemingly in awe of what she had accomplished, given her age.

> A capacity audience composed mainly of New York and New England personages thrilled to the acting of Maude Adams and gave the venerable heroine of the American stage an ovation that several times caused the performance to come to a complete halt.
> Her slender voice carrying beautifully to the last rows of this rustic summer theater, Miss Adams's portrayal of the role of Maria made it difficult to believe that she could bear so lightly the burden of sixty-three years.[19]

For more than five minutes after her initial appearance on stage, the audience was on its feet, wildly applauding and cheering, while she took bow after bow. At the conclusion of the play, there was an equally fine tribute of applause and a stage-full of floral bouquets.

A *Literary Digest* article discussed Maude's performance of "Twelfth Night." The writer spoke of her return to the universities, now frequented by the children of those who had so admired Maude twenty years earlier. Even to these children, she represented artistic glamour. They likened Maude to Greta Garbo, for the mystery that surrounded them and their aversion to publicity. They spoke of her eccentricities, for example, her choice to appear in summer theatricals instead of on Broadway. Like Bernhardt, Duse, and Garbo, Maude had managed to remain an independent, privately and professionally.

Plaudits followed Maude throughout the brief tour and every performance attracted capacity audiences. Of course, Phyllis Robbins attended the opening, and visited several other towns. At Cambridge, Robbins brought Maude back to her home for a happy but subdued celebration of Maude's stage triumph. That night was Maude's last performance on the dramatic stage.

In November, the persistent Perkins contacted Maude asking her to reconsider finishing the manuscript for publication. This time, to his surprise, Maude consented. Perkins immediately sent out a contract for her to sign. However, Maude did not return the contract or respond to Perkins for over a month. After several letters asking Maude about the status of the manuscript, she responded by saying it was "progressing." Another letter to Maude in January 1935 reminded her of their eagerness to move ahead.

Unfortunately, Maude became quite ill with influenza, forcing her to bed and preventing her from working on the manuscript. Maude was at Ronkonkoma, being cared for by the sisters, and under a doctor's sharp eye. Her recovery was very slow. She was unable to return to the manuscript until March, at the exact time Perkins wrote that he needed it immediately. Maude sent him the first three chapters. "When can I get the rest?" Perkins asked. There was no response from Maude.

On December 28, 1934, "The Little Minister" was released by RKO Radio Pictures, Inc., starring Katharine Hepburn. Copyright records stated that the film was based on the novel, not the play, but other sources referred to the play as the film's source. Paramount had sold the rights of Barrie's play in exchange for the services of Francis Lederer. The film was shot in Laurel Canyon and the San Bernardino Valley. It was reported that the film's budget was $650,000 and lost RKO $10,000 at the box-office. Maude was not involved in the film's planning or production. The stage play's history of popularity and profitability had been long forgotten.

In April 1935, Maude was reported to be living at Ronkonkoma, still recovering from her illness. Not until July did she reappear in the newspapers, the *New York Times* reporting that Maude had agreed to appear on Broadway, the esteemed John Golden to be her manager. An as yet untitled — and unfinished — script of a play by Adelyn Bushnell was said to be the vehicle. The play was to open October 15 in New York City.

The play was purported to be a comedy-drama with a Maine setting. Maude's role would be of a woman her own age. No supporting cast had yet been chosen nor a director selected. This play disappeared from view when the time came for rehearsals to begin. No finished play; no cast; no director; and no Maude.

As of May, Maude had not returned a completed manuscript to Scribner's. Perkins wrote Maude: "We can't seem to get any answer to our letters and don't know what to do."[20] Maude finally answered, asking for the summer to finish "this immortal work," as she described it, due to her long illness. There were no further letters until April 1936, when Perkins again asked Maude the status of the manuscript. Her response was a request to set up a meeting between Perkins and Louise Boynton, her purpose being to terminate the contract. Perkins asked for a return of the advance, saying how sorry he was that the manuscript could not be completed. "If you still feel doubtful about finishing the book," he wrote, "we think that it would be better to follow the other course."[21]

The court case filed by John Williams against Maude finally began the middle of October. Williams was suing Maude for $200,000 for services assisting her return to the stage. Accompanying Maude at the trial were her lawyer, Herbert Satterlee, Louise Boynton and Phyllis Robbins.

Williams began his testimony by explaining how a play is "ping-ponged," how Otis Skinner was selected for the Shylock role because of the shape of his back, and how a stage director can go "pretty nearly broke" in the process of persuading a star to return to the stage. Williams claimed that he had "her word of honor as a lady" that she would pay him something for his services. Under questioning, however, he admitted that he had never told her he expected to charge her anything directly.

Williams had a contract with Erlanger Enterprises for twenty-five percent of the net profits, $500 a week during rehearsals, and $150 a week during the run of a play called "The Joyous Adventures of Clementine," which was to be Maude's play. He explained that "ping-ponging" occurred when he worked with John Colton, the author, at night, reviewed it in the morning with Maude, and with both of them in the afternoon, handing the lines back and forth until they were satisfactory. Unfortunately, the disagreements that ensued persuaded Maude to turn the play down.

When Maude turned to Shakespeare, she objected to William's fees. She complained to Erlanger. When Erlanger called Williams in, he said: "I've got to drop you or she'll drop us." Williams estimated that his services to Maude were worth $25,000 from 1927 to 1930 and an additional $50,000 from that period to November 1931. He claimed he had a verbal agreement with Maude whom he quoted as saying she was "going to make up for all the special things you have done for me in the past."[22]

On the fourth day of the trial, Maude bowed smilingly to judge and jury as she took the stand. She leaned forward in her seat, alert and attentive to the lawyer's questions, answering in a soft, clear voice. Under cross-examination, Maude returned each thrust vigorously, and sometimes drew the objections of Williams's lawyer, Driscoll, by putting in explanations rather than a yes or no answer. For example, when questioned about her negotiations with Charles Wagner for a lecture tour—which did not materialize—Driscoll asked Maude if she paid him.

"Why should I?" she answered.

"I'm asking you if you paid him," retorted Driscoll.

"And I'm asking you why I should," responded Maude.

"I'm not on the witness stand, Miss Adams," Driscoll replied.

"Oh," said Maude, with a slight toss of her head and a smile.

At another point, Maude objected when Driscoll spoke of "The Merchant of Venice" as a show, insisting it was a play.

Maude talked of the series of aborted attempts to produce motion pictures like "Kim," and seeking plays to meet her desires to return to the stage. When she played "The Merchant of Venice," Maude explained, her contract called for $1,500 a week and fifty percent of the net profits. She had taken her chance with the net profits and "I made less than Mr. Skinner, who played Shylock."

An accountant for Erlanger testified that "The Merchant of Venice" ran for twenty-six weeks, and that net profits were $2,533, of which Maude received half.

Maude declared that she and Williams had no signed agreement and that he told her he wanted no financial arrangement from her. He had also refused the position of "press man" when it was offered him for "The Merchant of Venice."

When asked later about her experience on the witness stand, Maude did not talk directly to the press. Through her lawyer, she said that she was greatly interested in the trial procedure and the legal discussions between the justice and counsel. The newspapers played up her Portia role in "The Merchant of Venice"—"Miss Adams Plays Courtroom Portia" headlined the *New York Times*.[23]

The jury deliberated the case in only one hour and fifteen minutes. They returned a verdict of $25,000 in John Williams's favor. After the verdict had been returned, Maude walked out of the court with nothing to say, although she appeared disturbed. "I am very, very happy," Williams said, "but I'm sorry it had to happen at all."

Maude's lawyer moved to set aside the award as excessive and against the weight of evidence, and the judge reserved his decision. In Driscoll's summation, he had asserted that "all the time Miss Adams was on the witness stand she was the actress, a clever actress, who knows how to play a situation to her own advantage."[24] The jury was reported to have been unanimously in favor of the plaintiff from the start, but had considerable discussion as to the amount of damages.

Six months later, the judge reversed the verdict and ruled excessive the $25,000 awarded to John Williams. He declared that he was setting the verdict aside and order a new trial unless Williams agreed to accept $5,000 in damages within the next ten days. Williams agreed to the revised figure of $5,000. Maude could not be interviewed for her reaction to the lowered charges. She returned to Ronkonkoma for the winter.

The year 1936 found Maude in retirement and seclusion. One moment she was reported to be at the Colony Club; the next moment at her cottage in the Catskills; another moment resting at Ronkonkoma. The only matter of significance was a letter from President James Madison Wood of Stephens College, Columbia, Missouri, asking Maude if she would consider teaching drama at his school.

In their April 21, 1937 issue, *Variety* headlined: "Maude Adams may star in her first film in the fall. Actress is considering offers and is expected to signature a one-pic pact if suitable story can be found."

Of course, the issue of a suitable story remained the primary consideration for Maude. For the remainder of 1937, neither picture nor play was forthcoming.

Sir James Barrie died on June 19, 1937, at the age of seventy-seven after years suffering from various illnesses. When he showed signs of broncho-pneumonia, he was taken to a private residence, supervised by two nurses. Over the next several days, Barrie's mind drifted into vagueness. He was then attended by a doctor, who visited him every few hours. When told he must try to sleep, Barrie answered: "I can't sleep." Those were the last words he spoke.

Barrie was laid to rest in the cemetery on the Hill of Kirriemuir, facing the land he had so often featured in his plays. He was buried in a plot with his mother, father, and younger brother. Tributes came from everywhere, including the King and Queen of England. Columns in the British and American press spoke of his great literary triumphs and contributions to the dramatic stage. When Maude was given the news, she was reported to have retired to her room, where she cried quietly. Barrie had been such an important figure in her life and theatrical career, but it seemed so many years ago.

At the end of August, President Wood of Stephens College proudly announced to the press that Maude Adams had accepted the post of Professor of Drama and would take up her duties with the beginning of the school term in September.

20

The Final Curtain

In August 1833, fourteen leading male citizens of Columbia, Missouri met to discuss the education of their daughters. The Columbia Female Academy was born, its first class consisting of twenty-five girls. In 1856 the school became a full-scale college, the Columbia Female Baptist Academy.[1]

A decade later, James L. Stephens gave the college $20,000. Thanks to his endowment, the school was renamed Stephens Female College. Stephens was named chairman of the College Board of Curators; his son and grandson followed in his path as school leaders.

By the 1930s, Stephens College had developed a national reputation for its innovative educational programs. Under the leadership of James Madison Wood, the college became one of the first institutions to design its curriculum specifically for women. One of its seven areas of academic study was humanities, an integrated program that included art, literature, music, sculpture, and painting.

In 1935, when President Wood approached Maude, he sought the best representative of American theater to head up a new drama department.

At first, Maude was reluctant to consider such a position. She was not interested in teaching students; rather, she wished to teach theater audiences. Nevertheless, Wood pursued her for two years, attempting to convince her that his philosophy of life was similar to her philosophy of acting. Woods' argument was attractive to Maude, who believed that drama played a vital part in all human development. As Larry Clark wrote in his article on Maude's philosophy of educational theater at Stephens, "she was eager for an opportunity to interpret drama in this light to American youth."[2]

When Maude finally agreed to come to Stephens, Wood immediately announced her appointment. The theater world was astounded that Maude had been convinced to give up the one thing she most protected — privacy — in order to teach students the meaning of acting and theater.

In a later news release, President Wood stated that Maude would be teaching at the school during the months of September, October, and November. He expressed a hope that her assignment would lead to a permanent connection with the college. "We are anxious to have Miss Adams's personal influence on the girls," he said.[3]

President Wood also declared that Maude would have complete freedom to develop the drama department. "Her province," he stated, " will include not only the college's little theater and scene shop, but its course in public speaking, radio speech, and its voice clinic, as well as drama." Maude would be working with Professor Louise Dudley, head of the Department of English, in integrating drama as presented in the humanities courses. She would personally direct plays.

When questioned about her agreement to teach, Maude talked about the assignment as being an opportunity to learn about one's own emotions, a long-time topic of hers when discussing the philosophy of theater.

> As President Wood told me more about his plan, I saw that it was not at all the conventional school of acting that he had in mind, but something which would relate the theater and acting to the emotions of everyday life. This idea came very near a long-held belief of my own, that we should know more about our emotions and have a greater respect for them; they are the finest things we have.[4]

When Maude arrived in Columbia, Missouri, she was greeted by hundreds of students who escorted her to the President's residence, where she and Louise Boynton planned to stay for the semester. It was then announced that she would build her first course around the production of Rostand's "Chantecler," because, Maude explained, "it lent itself to feminine parts and because it dignifies labor."

Columbia's newspaper reported on Maude's trip from her "1,200 acre estate" in the Catskills, where she lived in seclusion with her secretary, maid, and housekeeper. They observed that, although Maude was sixty-four years old, she looked twenty years younger, "her face still unwrinkled, her auburn hair showing no trace of gray, and the flutelike voice still as vibrant as it was many years ago." Nor had her manner of dress changed over the years. She still wore a long cloth coat with a large fur collar, a thin muffler, a small box hat with a veil, long dresses, and nondescript shoes, a self-effacing ensemble.

As a complete surprise to the press, Maude made herself available for interviews. Although she restricted the questions to her work at the college, she could not avoid questions about the theater. She hoped that the experiences of the theater would make the students lives fuller, "even though they never step on a stage after leaving school." When asked whether she believed that theater would last, Maude expressed confidence that "it will last forever. Nothing can hurt the theater except bad plays," she said, "and nothing can help the theater but good plays."[5]

When tryouts for "Chantecler" were announced, more than 250 girls applied for the roles. Maude carefully interviewed twenty-four girls a day, explaining the play and having them read sections from it. So many girls were chosen for parts that Maude separated them into four casts, a different cast for each of the play's performances. Maude encouraged each cast to develop their own interpretation of the play. French classes translated the play into English; English classes put it into verse; art classes painted the sets; and music pupils scored the accompaniments.

When Maude discovered that the school had few costumes, little scenery, and practically no stage lighting, she donated a full set of costumes used in "The Merchant of Venice," green velour drapes to replace the front curtains in the Stephens auditorium, the original gauze drops used in the original production of "Chantecler," and two tons of stage electrical equipment, which included a 30,000 watt reflector, six small reflectors and an electric control board. The donations were thought to be one of the largest gifts of stage paraphernalia ever made by an actor (or, for that matter, any theater organization or movie studio) to a college.

The National Broadcasting System agreed to present a forty-five minute program of excerpts from "Chantecler" during the middle of November, with Maude taking the lead and her students in supporting roles. To produce the broadcast, a special line had to be run from St. Louis to the college. The NBS announced that they had chosen Stephens College because of its unusual and unique artistic endeavors. In reality, they sought the honor of sponsoring Maude on radio, acting in one of her signature roles.

Maude had celebrated her sixty-fifth birthday with a quiet dinner at the president's residence. President Wood could not refrain from speaking to the press of Maude's "tireless activity" on behalf of the college. He reported that, when he chided her for working too hard, she had replied: "Leave me alone. I love it. That isn't work to me." Wood talked about Maude waking up at 4:00 A.M. each morning to fix herself some coffee and outline her day's work. From 8:00 A.M. to 12:30 P.M., she trained the girls of her four casts. After lunch, the training continued until 6:30 P.M., when she had dinner in her room. From 7:30 P.M. to 10:30 P.M., she conducted rehearsals on the stage. Then, she discussed the play's operation with her staff, the meetings often going to 1:00 A.M. At 4:00 A.M., she started again. Several years later, Maude admitted that Wood's descriptions of her working style had made her feel uncomfortable and that it took some time for her to accommodate to the public nature of the job.

Another interview, this one by a reporter from the *Kansas City Star*, sounded a bit like an old Frohman office news release.[6] Maude had agreed to the interview with reluctance and delayed the meeting for several weeks. The interview finally took place at the President's residence, Wood likely persuading Maude to go through with it. Maude, in turn, stipulated she wanted no questions about controversial issues about the theater. Maude did talk briefly of her early stage experiences with E.H. Southern, John Drew, and "the most generous" Charles Frohman. She expounded on Barrie and his plays. "I loved the Barrie roles, all of them." Maude called her relationship with Barrie "a very real spiritual kinship." The interview ended with Maude's answer why she had emerged from seclusion to place herself in contact with the "outer world."

"I did want to work, had to work, or be very unhappy," she replied simply. "I've found a lot of splendid, sincere, and talented girls, and it is a joy to work with them and for them." The interview appeared in the Sunday edition of the *Star* and was duplicated in newspapers across the country.

"Chantecler" was performed four nights in a row, with a different cast each night, just before the Christmas holidays. Every performance attracted capacity houses and each cast received accolades for their work. That a play of this complexity was performed so professionally by teenage girls seemed a revelation to both audiences and reviewers. They all recognized it was Maude's doing and, at the conclusion of the play each evening, she was brought onto the stage to receive the audience's appreciation for her work. Many minutes of applause and floral bouquets accompanied bow after bow. Shortly after the final performance, Maude and Louise packed up and quietly left the campus to return to the Catskills cottage for the winter. Would Maude return to Stephens College if she were asked? Of course. The experience was the most pleasant she had enjoyed in many years.

For almost twenty years, motion picture producers had tried in vain to entice Maude to appear in movies. Several times she came close to accepting offers, but lack of good material, as Maude defined it, ended the possibility. Producer David Selznick, who was only a child when Maude was starring on Broadway, was not deterred by her previous refusals. He sent her a script and an offer for her to play the leading role in *The Young in Heart*. Since she did not immediately respond, Selznick was encouraged. As Louella O. Parsons, the intrepid Hollywood gossip columnist put it, "It would certainly be a feather in Selznick's cap if he could induce the shyest actress in the world to come out of her shell."[7]

At this point, Maude was actually feeling uncharacteristically expansive. She had already "come out of her shell" at Stephens and the end result had been gratifying. She had been asked to return to the school for the fall semester, hopefully for the entire school year. A letter from Perkins at Scribner's reopened a dialogue about the proposed book. Calls from several Broadway producers inquired about her interest in returning to the stage.

On April 22, 1938, Maude arrived in Hollywood, California, to discuss the possibility of a film career with Selznick. The initial step, as outlined by the studio, would be the part of the wealthy dowager in *The Young in Heart*. In her

David Selznick greeted Maude warmly when she came to Hollywood for a screen test. But did he really want her for the film *The Young in Heart*? Maude declined to appear in the movie, believing the role unsuitable. (San Francisco History Center, San Francisco Public Library)

discussion with Selznick, Maude indicated a willingness to make limited appearances in films if — that terrifying if — she believed the material to be suitable for her. Shooting for the movie was to begin on May 1, in a little more than a week. The movie co-starred Janet Gaynor, Douglas Fairbanks, Jr., Paulette Goddard, and Roland Young.

Maude agreed to take a screen test; everyone, including Selznick, said that she had done well. Maude herself was not sure. As she was becoming more familiar with her proposed role in the movie, she expressed some discomfort with it. Rumors spread that Maude had not passed the screen test and Selznick was seeking a way to extricate himself from his enthusiasm for Maude.

Whether aware of the rumors or not, Maude nicely solved Selznick's dilemma by refusing the role as not suitable and, instead, suggesting that another stage actress, Minnie Dupree, be given the part. Selznick quickly hired Dupree and shooting for the film began the day that Maude left Hollywood to return to Stephens College where she had been invited to make a commencement address. Selznick claimed that he remained interested in Maude and supposedly had instructed scenario writers to build a picture around her. During this time, photos of Maude and Selznick together dotted the newspapers, all reporting that Maude was about to enter the movies. After Maude departed, however, she never heard from Selznick, or any other studio, again.

In February, a letter from Perkins asked Maude if she was still interested in completing her manuscript and, if she was, when could he expect to receive it. It was a kind but probing letter designed to determine Maude's feelings about finishing her autobiography. He hoped to receive an answer from her since he again offered to publish. No response came.

In April, Perkins wrote another letter to Maude, saying that if she was not interested in his offer, he would appreciate her returning the advance of $1,000 she had received back in 1928. Perkins received a letter from Maude's lawyer, asking for a "few months delay" in paying since Maude was in Hollywood.

There was no further correspondence until September when Perkins demanded, in a diplomatic voice, that Maude's advance was overdue to be repaid. Maude's lawyer responded by asking for a further delay of several months. It was difficult to tell whether Maude was really interested in completing the project or whether she had lost interest in it. When, in December, Perkins suggested that the matter be settled, he was sent another letter from the lawyer offering additional reasons why the advance could not be paid back at the time.

Maude's commencement address at Stephens received coverage from the *New York Times*. The speech was filled with her philosophy of theater and funny anecdotes about her roles in Barrie's plays. More than 1,500 students and more than 2,000 guests sat in rapt attention as she related her adventures, from the first time she met Charles Frohman to her role in "Peter Pan." She spoke of emotions as "being the greatest things we can have" and her remarks on the subject sounded familiarly autobiographical.

> My childhood and girlhood had been spent with older people, and children had been rather terrifying to me. Children remained an enigma to me until, when I was a

woman grown Peter gave me open sesame; for, whether I understood children or not, the children understood Peter.

The acts call to the spirit of man, and in the realms of spirit and the emotions, the theater, with her great traditions and her great history, is not the least among the acts.[8]

Seated in the audience was a booking agent who was so taken with Maude's speech that he asked her if she would be interested in going on a short speaking tour of the country, talking about her love of the theater, with anecdotes, of course. Maude felt complimented but reserved judgment because of her commitment to Stephens College for the coming semester. Still, the proposal was appealing, especially since it paid $1,000 per address plus expenses.

With no second thoughts in her mind, Maude returned to Stephens College for the fall semester. The year's project was a series of short plays adapted from the Greek, and choral readings for the Christmas season. This year, the National Broadcasting System had Maude and her students enact Dickens's "Christmas Carol" over national radio, on Christmas Eve. *Variety* reported that the presentation was "vintage Maude Adams" and the network should be complimented for bringing Maude back to the attention of theater lovers.

The Young in Heart reached movie theaters in late October with Minnie Dupree, in her first screen role, as the leading actress. News items noted that Selznick had originally sought Maude for the role, but that she declined when she discovered the script called for her to die at the end of the film. Preview audiences responded unfavorably to the ending and Selznick recalled the actors to shoot an ending in which the leading lady lived. The picture was *Life* magazine's "Movie of the Week" on November 14, 1938.

In early January 1939, Maude began her lecture tour with an appearance at the New York Town Hall. Accompanying her was Phyllis Robbins who, among other tasks, printed her notes in large, block letters so Maude would not need to use her glasses on the podium. Maude's lecture dealt with her life in the theater and was filled with entertaining anecdotes. It was Maude's first public appearance in New York since 1918. Because hundreds of people were turned away, it was announced that she would repeat the lecture the following week at a matinee. Not surprisingly, eighty percent of the audience was made up of women and, according to the *New York Herald* reviewer, "most of them old enough to have seen her in the days of her greatest glory."[9]

Maude's tour ran to February 4. It included stops in Omaha, Seattle, Pasadena, Santa Barbara, Los Angeles, and finally Cincinnati. By the time they reached Los Angeles, Maude was already fatigued and forcing herself to go through the lecture. Nevertheless, the lectures attracted capacity houses and offered enjoyable performances filled with nostalgia. Maude was often asked how she would compare today's stage with that of yesterday but, except for the mildest of hints, she gave no critical comparisons. Given that plays like "Tobacco Road," "Abe Lincoln in Illinois," "The Little Foxes," and "The Philadelphia Story" represented the new and crisp realism in theater, Maude's only comment was to suggest that plays should be rated either "healthy" or "unhealthy." "Unless actors have real genius, they should leave morbid plays alone," she declared.

After completing her tour, Maude was back at Stephens to prepare the projects for the spring semester. Her $10,000 salary was continued. This semester's play would be a production of "Alice in Wonderland," again performed by several casts.

At another of her now familiar lectures, Maude spoke before the women's literary club at the governor's mansion in Jefferson City, Missouri. She had the rapt crowd of women laughing uproariously or very close to tears, depending on which emotional chord she chose to play upon. Maude was introduced by Governor Lloyd C. Stark, who declared that in her new career as a drama professor "she may be on the road to bringing back another golden age of the theater."

In her speech, Maude admitted that her recent close association with the younger generation had had an effect of restoring her "lost youth." That impetus, she claimed, had given her the confidence to branch out into the lecture circuit. The remainder of the speech was similar in content to those she had given on the tour, including her plea that acting be considered a fine art. As was her usual habit, Maude escaped the after-speech tea to return to Columbia.

For the second year in a row, Maude gave a commencement speech before the graduating students, this time relating the experiences of the theater to learning about living in the outside world. Commencement week exercises featured four presentations of "Alice in Wonderland" to sellout crowds. Again, audiences marveled how Maude had produced such professional shows with such young women.

The ongoing saga with Scribner's took several odd turns in 1939. During the early part of the year, letters from Perkins to Maude became increasingly more direct in demanding the return of their advance. Maude responded to none of these pleas. In the fall, Maude sent her lawyer to meet with the Scribner's people to discuss her proposal for a book of verse lessons she had prepared for her classes. Scribner's turned the proposal down as not being applicable for them to publish. Instead, Maude collected the material and self-published the volume, a mimeographed book of diction lessons and verse selections. For some of the verse copyrights, Maude obtained permissions; for others, she was unable to procure them. Nevertheless, they were all included in the book.

Armed with a text and new play production plans, Maude began the fall semester. She also began a new project, the development of an anthology of excerpts from the great plays in history. Dozens of letters were mailed to publishers all over the world in an attempt to gain permissions to publish these excerpts. Her lawyer had warned Maude about using material without permission, as compared to her book of verse. It would take more than a year to even get answers from publishers and not all of them agreed to Maude's requests. The anthology languished, but Maude copied for her students those excerpts for which she had received permission.

The spring of 1940 found Maude back on campus, in her third successive year as drama professor. The school's reputation for theater had spread throughout the Midwest and at every occasion when a new production was given, people flocked to

Maude brought excitement and expertise to Stephens College's drama students. During her tenure at Stephens, she produced plays, choral readings, and radio dramas, and taught classes in diction and acting. (The Harvard Theatre Collection, The Houghton Library)

attend. Reviews for these shows came from as far away as Chicago. They all praised the actors' work. In a relatively short time, Maude had demonstrated what could be accomplished with young people working in the theater, with the proper motivation, instruction, and materials. Her methods, mentioned in the newspapers, were being copied by other college drama departments. Maude as teacher was becoming as familiar figure as Maude as venerable actress.

The spring semester project was a repeat performance of "Chantecler," with stage renditions made up of four different casts and a special radio production. WEAF again sponsored the radio play, this time coming directly from the auditorium at Stephens College. The play had undergone a new translation by faculty members, especially designed for the needs of radio. Maude contributed to the transmission with special sound effects.

An affectionate article by George Kent, for *Independent Woman* magazine, also appeared in the *Reader's Digest* of July 1940. The article was based on a meeting Kent had with Maude while she was in the midst of preparing for a production. He first discovered her crawling in the attic above the stage to see about building rehearsal rooms.

The sight of that trim, dark figure dangling in the air totally re-illusioned me. All was not lost if Maude Adams, at an age when most of her contemporaries were either dead or retired, was still doing Peter Pan tricks. This time without wires or flying dust but out of some inner compulsion.[10]

Kent observed an "amazing vitality" surrounding Maude. Lights in Maude's bedroom were lit late into the night, her habit of working later fostered by the usual schedule of theater life. Kent reported that when a faculty member apologized for keeping Maude up until nearly two in the morning, she begged him not to be upset: "I have an appointment with the electrician at three," she answered. Prior to and during performances, Kent saw Maude move scenery and furniture, help dress the cast, supervise makeup, and tutor the actors before they went on the stage.

What made Maude so exhilarating a person, according to Kent, was her capacity to change. That she had become "reborn" since coming to Stephens had been a revelation to theater people, who knew her only as a recluse.

Maude talked freely before classes and theater audiences. Her students had easy access to her at all times of the day. She was frequently interviewed. Her productions had transformed Stephens into a center for college drama exhibitions.

When Kent playfully asked Maude if she still believed in fairies, she shot back, in a serious tone, that we need them more than ever.

I think there still are fairies—and that they will save us. An ideal to live and fight for—that is a fairy. Recognition of our limitations is another. When we are young, we all start out to do big things; we are certain we can make the sun rise. If, like Chantecler, we learn unhappily that our work is not so important as we should like to think it, we must remember that it is our work.[11]

Among the students of Stephens, Maude's exuberance for the theater had been translated into sheer affection for their mentor. These feelings made for great learning experiences and enjoyable stage productions.

This unrestrained joy carried over through 1941 and 1942. Maude's productions became more numerous and more complex each semester. In February, 1941, she directed "The Romancers" (Rostand); in May, both "Julius Caesar" and "The Blunderer" (Molière); and she finished the semester with "Alice in Wonderland." In 1942, she directed "The Pretentious Young Ladies" (Molière); "She Stoops to Conquer"; "Patience"; and "Everyman." All of the productions were given due recognition by the press, praise for the actors, and praise for their director.

In the spring of 1941, Maude took more than 600 students to Hollywood to see how movies were made. While there, the Screen Actor's Guild feted her "for distinguished service to the theater." A scroll was awarded Maude at the "Gambol of the Stars," the first time the guild had ever honored an individual actress. Actors and actresses who had played with Maude formed an honor guard at the presentation ceremony.

For the past two years, the Scribner's people had continually pressed Maude to return their advance. Instead, Maude determined what the interest on the advance amounted to, and each year, sent a check for the proper amount. Letters from Scribner's disclosed their frustration over her handling of the issue. Yet they never threatened to sue her.

To celebrate Maude's seventieth birthday, the *New York Times* magazine published a long article, full of vintage photographs, entitled "Her Light Still Glows in the Theater."[12] "Maude Adams still serves the stage," the article said. Only now, she no longer hides herself away. "She has been seen sitting on a high stool at a hot-dog stand; she goes to tea with young things and the faculty; and even goes into town afoot shopping on her own." It is this "woman of spirit," the *Times* continued, that exemplifies a theatrical era in which she was an actress of "unmatched understanding and irresistible appeal."

Maude's past successes were identified and explained. "Peter Pan" was mentioned as her greatest triumph as "it remains true that she is the woman who made real the Never-Never-Land that Barrie created."

> Absence from the stage for a dozen years did not dim the light she had left behind her. And as she goes about that college campus, that light lingers with us still as a reminder that the stage with Miss Adams on it was certainly a force for civilizing — ourselves.

The year 1942 also saw Maude writing for the stage, three short plays: "Jonah, a Biblical Comedy," in which Jewish jokes were featured; "Bengy," the story of a young boy who hates animals but comes to love them: and "Aladdin," for which she also designed the stage settings and costumes. The preparation for "Jonah" precipitated another project, one in which she invoked the Bible as source material, and spent several years working on the script. Unfortunately, by reason of illness, the play was never produced.

On January 23, 1943, the Empire Theater celebrated its fiftieth anniversary with a matinee. Visiting this honored theater, an observer would see large, ornate paintings of its stars, posters announcing its hits, and photographs of its cheering audiences. Standing solemnly in a corner of the elegant lobby, overlooking the crowds of theatergoers, stood the statue of Charles Frohman, the man who had, single-handedly, made all this a reality. The Empire still retained its richly endowed look, never having succumbed to the ravages of age like many other New York theaters. It also retained its philosophy of presenting only the best in theater drama, only "clean" productions and socially redeeming themes. Many of the theater's former actors showed up for the gala event, and brief sketches of old plays were enacted for the worshipping audience.

Of course, Maude was invited to the event but she was unable to attend because of her duties at Stephens. Maude had been one of the first performers to appear at the Empire in 1894. Since she was unable to attend, she was asked to prepare a note about the theater's fiftieth birthday. She sent along a message which was to be read by Alexander Woollcott.

The Empire holds a sure place in so many actors' hearts, she was always such a kind theater and so friendly. She never took one's words and muffled them away in corners; whatever she received the Empire gave again, always in full measure, even a whisper was never lost, and an actor felt there was a friend in front, helping and sustaining him.

What happiness this night would have given Mr. Frohman. His beloved theater! After fifty years she stands, the proof of his foresight and faith.

We are all thankful for her good fortune in the men who have guided her since his time, but perhaps only Mr. Frohman could have realized fully the extraordinary ability and care that have brought her safely through these troubled years. May she look forward to another fifty years of service.[13]

A personal telegram to Woollcott came with the message:

My dear Mr. Woollcott: Will you do whatever you please with this? Lose it if you like, if that would seem best, turn it upside down and make it proper. The Empire is so dear to me it is difficult to speak of her. It seems almost like praising one's mother. I know you will understand.

Woollcott was designated to read the message at the theater. That evening he unexpectedly died while broadcasting on the *Voice of the People* program. In his place, Ethyl Barrymore read Maude's note of tribute to the audience. She had tears in her eyes for Maude's sentiments, the theater's long and glorious history, and the sudden death of its chosen speaker.

It was in the fall of 1943 that Maude became ill with a respiratory condition, the kind that was not easily overcome. She was forced to temporarily retire from Stephens and return to the Catskills to recover. Maude moved from exuberance to frustration and depression. At age seventy-one, Maude's recurrent respiratory problems had drained away much of her vitality. It was almost a year before she had recovered sufficiently to return to her position at Stephens. In the meantime, Maude, propped up in bed and surrounded by mounds of papers, worked on the anthology, prepared notes for future classes, and began a project, hopefully a book, filled with her reminiscences of dear friend James Barrie.

Maude worked at Stephens during the fall of 1944 and the spring and fall of 1945. During this time, she prepared and produced choral readings for her students that were performed at Easter, Thanksgiving, and Christmas. She quickly found that she did not have the strength to mount full productions, as she would have liked. Travel had become difficult for her and she stayed either in Columbia or at her Catskills home during this interval.

Throughout the entire period of the middle '40s, Maude's only connection with Scribner's was to pay the interest each year on her advance. This interaction did not change until 1948, upon the death of Maxwell Perkins, the gentleman who had been so kind and circumspect with Maude. The new editor was not familiar with Maude and treated the ongoing issue of payment like any late bill. He demanded an immediate repayment of the advance or the problem would be turned over to his lawyers. Maude did not immediately respond. Instead, through her lawyer, she sent a proposal to Scribner's for her book on Barrie. In order to ensure their interest in the proposal, so she reasoned, Maude also repaid one-half of the advance. Scribner's categorically refused the Barrie project, but offered Maude an alternative. Since they were Barrie's U.S. publishers, they were planning to issue an anthology of his works. Would Maude be interested in writing an introduction to this anthology? Maude quickly agreed and signed a contract to that effect. No delivery date was mentioned, but Scribner's editor indicated that the proposed book might be ready for publication in a year. Noticeable in the exchange of letters was the fact that Louise Boynton was writing them, although Maude dictated and signed them.

Even though she had not fully recovered from her long illness, Maude returned to Stephens in the fall of 1947. Her efforts, however, were restricted to holding classes in diction, choral readings, and acting. For the first time, she was not involved in any dramatic performances.

Probably due to her decreasing stamina, Maude skipped the 1948 spring semester to stay at her Catskills cottage. Nor was Louise Boynton in good health. Six years older than Maude, she was finding it more difficult to maintain the activity level of even a few years earlier. In the fall of 1948, barely able to walk, Maude returned to Stephens and worked there continuously until the winter of 1949–1950. At that time, immediately after the Christmas festivities at the college, Maude was forced to retire from her position. It was reported that she was too weak to continue her classes. In keeping with her usual exits, Maude left Columbia quietly, with no special "going away" events or school tributes.

In May, 1950, a brief column in *Cosmopolitan* magazine, entitled "What Are They Doing Now?" revealed that "today, at seventy-eight, she [Maude] lives in almost total seclusion in the Catskill Mountains.

"She has a tiny cottage there, decorated with fans and photographs and playbills, all trophies of the past. Those few who have visited it say it seems like Never-Never-Land."[14]

Epilogue

After several splendid years teaching at Stephens College, Maude dejectedly returned to her home in the Catskills. Except for the companionship offered by Louise Boynton and a maid, Maude retired into seclusion. The world of theater was now too far away and too difficult to navigate. Yet, although she might not be able to travel comfortably, she continued to apply her creative abilities.

As was typical of her working habits, Maude juggled several projects at one time. She undertook the task of rewriting her autobiography once again and advanced the project to the point of asking Scribner's whether they were still interested in publishing it. In fact, Maude had enlisted the help of Vida Sutton, a local writer, to help her. She renewed her efforts to finish the anthology of great drama works begun several years earlier at Stephens College. Although Scribner's was not interested in her reminiscences of James Barrie, Maude continued to compile materials for a book on the subject. She also began an ambitious project involving the development of a radio series that incorporated her own career into the background of the country's theater history, supposedly of interest to the National Broadcasting Company. Piles of papers, books, and notes covered her bed, making it impossible for her to maintain a semblance of order. Phyllis Robbins reported on Maude's frequent attempts to organize the materials. The task always seemed to elude her.

Maude continued to be a voracious reader. Thanks to Robbins, libraries in New York and Boston frequently sent books to Maude. Robbins visited often. Except for their drives through the countryside, Maude rarely ventured outside. She continued to enjoy the natural beauty of her surroundings in the Catskills, but primarily from her front porch.

Scribner's answer to Maude's new proposal was understandably cautious. Yes, they would be interested in examining a portion of the manuscript. However, "exactly what terms we might be prepared to offer would have to depend on the book itself as you must realize that times and conditions have changed considerably in the twenty-five years that have passed since the subject was first brought up."[1] Unfortunately,

Maude's plan to complete her manuscript ceased when Louise Boynton unexpectedly died.

As Robbins described the event, it was such a devastating loss to Maude that she likely never recovered.

> Miss Boynton had gone to her room a little earlier than usual, saying she was tired and would lie down, and carrying with her as usual a glass of milk and some graham crackers. When Maude went in half an hour later to see whether she was all right, she found that she had died.[2]

Louise Boynton passed away on March 3, 1951, in her sleep, apparently the result of a heart attack. She was eighty-five years old and had been Maude's companion since 1905. In Boynton's will, written in 1948, she gave all household goods and personal items to Maude, returned a piece of land to Maude that had been given her in 1922, and appointed Maude and Mother Elizabeth Keating of the Cenacle as executors of her estate. Because Boynton had been instrumental in building the original association with the Cenacle and had assisted in donating Ronkonkoma to the religious organization, she was buried at Ronkonkoma, although because she was not Catholic, she was interred in ground adjoining the sacred cemetery. Maude was unable to attend Boynton's funeral and burial at Ronkonkoma due to her weakened condition.

Maude spent her last years in seclusion and died in obscurity. Newspapers across the country wrote of her stage accomplishments, yet the theater had forgotten her. (San Francisco History Center, San Francisco Public Library)

Immediately after Boynton's death, Maude sent for Robbins to offer her comfort. It was quickly decided that Maude could not live alone due to her fragile physical and mental condition. A housekeeper and companion, Mrs. Margaret McKenna, was hired and Maude was moved into McKenna's cottage in Tannersville. As a final donation, Maude gave her Catskills home to the Cenacle, who planned to turn it into a retreat.

Maude took only one trip to New York, to visit the opening of an exhibition at the Museum of the City of New York entitled "Some Wonderful Moments in the New York Theater, 1900–1950." Included in the exhibition were many items related to her stage successes. Maude also brought along a gift for the museum to include in the exhibition, the crown she had worn in her last play, "A Kiss for Cinderella." The headline in the *New York Times:* "City Museum's New Theatrical Exhibit Gets a Gift From a Caller, Maude Adams."

In April 1953, Maude was again stricken with bronchitis and pleurisy, and had to be removed to a hospital. After several days, she recovered sufficiently to return to the cottage. Maude's illness was mentioned in the press and she received cards and letters from hundreds of admirers from across the country. Most prayed for her recovery; a few asked for a photograph or autograph.

The following month, while Maude was recovering, she was invited to attend a special event to be given at the Empire Theater, a tribute to the theater prior to its demolition. "Highlights of the Empire" would be a show commemorating the passing of the famous theater, scheduled to be razed after May 30. The promoters of the event wanted Maude to play a scene or speak to the audience or, barring that, to give a brief statement via a telephone hookup about her experiences at the Empire. However, efforts to communicate with Maude proved fruitless. Of course, she was too ill to attend. But why would she want to participate in another death that, symbolically, spelled the end of a brilliant theatrical era?

Two months later, on July 17, Maude suddenly fell ill. When her doctor was called, he detected symptoms of a heart disorder and ordered in oxygen and stimulants to be administered.

Maude lingered for several hours, drifting in an out of consciousness. "Oh, Mrs. McKenna, I don't feel good," were Maude's last words. Shortly after 12:30 P.M., Maude died quietly; her death was later diagnosed as a heart attack. Only her doctor and Mrs. McKenna were in attendance. Maude was eighty years old.

The news of her death was announced in newspapers across the country and in Europe. According to the press, her fame as a grand actress of the stage who had captivated audiences for several decades was undisputed. A review of her life and career was included in most of the articles, many of them repeating the mythology and speculations that had surrounded her during her lifetime. Included were photographs of Maude in various plays, particularly "Peter Pan." The last photograph of Maude had been taken in 1941.

A few days later, Maude's funeral was celebrated on the Ronkonkoma grounds with simple rites, as she had requested. A community of nearly 100 nuns in their black, white, and purple robes and fifty friends were present to repeat the Lord's Prayer and chant "Ave Maria, Gratia Plena," after which the coffin was lowered into the earth. Mother Elizabeth Keating gave a brief prayer and led a procession past the coffin. The floral decorations consisted of a few simple bouquets of red roses. The burial was just outside the convent's cemetery, adjoining the grave of Louise Boynton.

Representatives of the theater world who attended the funeral included James F. Reilly, executive director of the League of New York Theaters; May Davenport Seymour, curator of Theater and Music Collection at the Museum of the City of New York (whose father, William Seymour, had directed many of Maude's plays); her daughter, Anne Seymour, television and radio actress; Jean Arthur, who had played the Peter Pan role three years previously; Dr. James Madison Wood, former president of Stephens College; Vida Sutton, the writer who had been assisting Maude in her autobiography; Phyllis Robbins; Margaret McKenna; and Robert Adams, a first cousin. Robbins had been in charge of the funeral services.

Several years later, when the Cenacle moved their cemetery to another section of the estate, Maude and Louise's burial sites were included within the sacred grounds. As benefactresses to the Cenacle, they were given special recognition. On a simple, single gravestone, lying on a hill overlooking the Cenacle buildings, shaded by the trees Maude had so graciously planted many years before, Maude and Louise's names were side by side.

Maude's will was simple and short. She had already given all of her property and possessions away and what little remained were to be executed by Phyllis Robbins and Mother Keating.

Many reviewers and critics wrote editorials about Maude, extolling her virtues and accomplishments on the stage and her contributions to dramatic theater. Each gave his own perspective on her life, career, and philosophy. Taken together, they were poignant statements that summed up an unusual and vital voice in the development of theater in America.

Said the *Washington Star:*

> Relatively few American theatergoers can remember Maude Adams personally. Nature gave her beauty, grace, charm of manner, a fine voice, keen intelligence and a peculiar earnestness of spirit which she carried into her work with compelling effect.
>
> Sensitive, shy, and modest, Miss Adams avoided the public on its side of the footlights. She never married, and it may be that she never had any authentic happiness of her own. But there can be no question about the joy she gave to thousands of people who loved her.[3]

From the *New York Times:*

> Miss Adams' faith in clean plays and a clean personal life was a faith she shared with millions of other women. Her attitude was not prudish. She was a gentle, retiring, good woman of intelligence and integrity.
>
> Since her own code saw no reason for separation between her professional and her private life, the public generally required no special generosity to sustain her stardom. Men, women, and children alike, accepted her values; and while the theater, as a whole, during her years of activity in it went in other directions, she continued in popularity because it was part of her code to be as efficient technically as she was upright personally. What we might well add to that reputation is the less known fact that she had developed intellectual qualities which would have assured her leadership in any profession. But the world is richer because she gave all her talents to the stage.[4]

And the *Chicago Tribune:*

> Maude Adams's death does not "mark the end of an era," for she belonged to no era unless it was her own. Though she was born to the stage, she was never what is called "theatrical." Both her stage and private lives were complete departures from the accepted norms.
>
> Into the stiffly stylized theater of the 1890s she brought a fresh and graceful naturalness which immediately won the hearts of all her audience. The charming manners, the appealing grace she brought to her performances were closely linked to the life she led in private. She had a horror of the "fast living stage folk" tradition and felt that only the actress who lived the clean life in private could portray it in public. She was a child of the stage who became queen of the stage.[5]

Regarding Maude, Phyllis Robbins put her final perceptions more simply.

She met the last adventure, which came quietly and swiftly, with the same gallantry with which she had lived.[6]

On October 4, 1953, the residents of Tannersville paid tribute to Maude. They repeated the event on the first anniversary of her death. From that point on, very little regarding Maude reached the public. The era in which she lived, the theater in which she played, and the endearing reputation she had achieved had already been relegated to ancient history.

In 1955, a movement to put Maude on a postage stamp was begun, and as quickly disappeared. When New York newspapers reported that the nuns of the Cenacle were leaving their 140th Street residence for Ronkonkoma, there was only a brief statement that Maude had donated her property to them. In 1976, the Pioneer State Theater in Salt Lake City honored Maude as they received her cradle for their archives.

Phyllis Robbins wrote two books about Maude, one in 1953, the second in 1956. They presented an affectionate and highly romantic version of Maude's life, written by an admirer and close companion. Much of the material had been taken from the papers Robbins had retained from Maude's estate. Robbins later donated Maude's papers to the University of Utah and the Harvard Theater Library. Nothing has been heard or seen of Maude since.

It is unfortunate that Maude Adams and her era are totally forgotten today, or relegated to only brief mention in the history of American theater. This era represented one of the most dynamic periods in the growth of the stage. It was most innovative, setting the foundations for what followed into the twentieth century, and which came to be viewed as an integral part of our culture. That Maude Adams was this period's most talented and recognized exponent cannot be disputed.

Do we believe in fairies? Of course we do. It's what makes our theater experiences most enjoyable and entertaining and our own private dreams so full of hope.

Chapter Notes

Chapter 1

1. *The Mayflower Quarterly*, October, 1953, Vol. 19, No. 1, p. 2.

2. *Latter Day Saint, Biographical Encyclopedia*, Vol. III, No. 37, p. 577.

3. The Story of the Church-Nauvo, http://www.centerplace.org/history/misc/soc/soc31.htm.

4. Ancestry World Tree Project, Ancestry.com, ID: I03408.

5. Kiscadden, A.A., and V.H. Porter, "The Life Story of Maude Adams and Her Mother," *The Green Book Magazine*, June 1914, p. 892.

6. Melville, J.K., PhD, "The Mormon Drama and Maude Adams," *Feminine Contributions to Mormon Culture*, Provo, Utah, Brigham Young University, December 1965, pp. 1–4.

7. *Ibid.*, p. 5.

8. Adams and Porter, June 1914, pp. 898–899.

9. Background on James Kiscadden can be found in the U.S. Census, 1820 to 1880; Mormon Library, Salt Lake City; San Francisco City Directory, 1876 to 1883.

10. Baumler, E., *More Than the Glory: Preserving the Gold Rush and Its Outcome at Virginia City*, p.4, http://www.his.state.mt.us/departments/education/edu_goldarticbaumler.html.

11. *Montana: Its Story and Biography*, Vol. 1, Chapter 14: "Pioneers and Their Society," pp. 335–336.

12. The story of Jack Slade, his wife Virginia, and James Kiscadden can be found in: Jenkins, P.W., "Kiscadden-Slade," *Annals of Wyoming*, Vol. 21, No. 1, January 1949, pp. 88–92, and Clark, A.L, "The Story Maude Adams Never Told," *True West*, May-June 1967, pp. 32–34, 54–56.

13. Salt Lake City Probate Court: Index to Civil and Criminal Case Files, Series 373, October 29, 1868.

14. Adams and Porter, July 1914, p. 12.

15. *Deseret News*, June 9, 1869, p. 209.

Chapter 2

1. Adams and Porter, July 1914, p. 17.

2. *Ibid.*, August 1914, pp. 196–198.

3. For a history of Virginia City theaters and Piper's Opera House, see: "Theatrical Journals and Diary, 1849–1882," 4 vols., Western Room, California State Library, Sacramento, CA, IV, 94.

4. Adams and Porter, August 1914, p. 198.

5. Bordman, G., *The Concise Oxford Companion to American Theater*, New York, Oxford University Press, 1987, pp. 283–284.

6. *Dramatic News*, January 14, 1877.

7. *Dramatic News*, May 26, 1877; June 9, 1877; June 16, 1877.

8. Bordman, p. 146.

9. Adams and Porter, August 1914, pp. 203–204.

10. Adams, M., "The One I Knew Least of All," *Ladies Home Journal*, March 1926, p. 3.

11. Robbins, P., *The Young Maude Adams*, Francetown, N.H., Marshall Jones Company, 1959, pp. 43–44.

12. *San Francisco Chronicle*, March 3, 1878.

Chapter 3

1. *San Francisco Chronicle*, ad for "Uncle Tom's Cabin," November 8, 1878.
2. *Ibid.*, November 10, 1878.
3. *Ibid.*, November 12, 1878.
4. Bordman, p. 85.
5. Adams and Porter, August 1914, p. 206.
6. *The Daily Oregonian*, January 28, 1879.
7. *Ibid.*, January 31, 1879.
8. *Ibid.*, February 6, 1879.
9. *Ibid.*, February 11, 1879.
10. *Ibid.*, February 11, 1879.
11. *Ibid.*, February 18, 1879.
12. *Ibid.*, February 24, 1879.
13. *Ibid.*, February 28, 1879.
14. *Deseret News*, April 12, 1879.
15. Bordman, pp. 44–45.
16. *Ibid.*, pp. 217–218.
17. *San Francisco Chronicle*, September 10, 1879.
18. *Ibid.*, September 14, 1879.
19. *The Daily Oregonian*, March 3, 1880.
20. *San Francisco Chronicle*, September 7, 1880.

Chapter 4

1. Bogar, T.A., *John E. Owens: Nineteenth Century American Actor and Manager*, Jefferson, N.C., McFarland, 2002, Chapters 7 and 8.
2. Robbins, p. 103.
3. *San Francisco Chronicle*, July 24, 1881.
4. *San Francisco Call*, July 24, 1881.
5. *San Francisco Chronicle*, August 9, 1881.
6. Lewis, P.C., *Trouping: How the Show Came to Town*, New York, Harper & Row, 1973, p. 116.
7. *Deseret News*, September 8, 1881.
8. Marcosson, I.F. and Frohman, D., *Charles Frohman: Manager and Man*, New York, Harper & Bros., 1916, pp. 46–113.
9. Brackenridge, R.D., Westminster College of Salt Lake City, Logan, Utah, Utah State University Press, 1998, Chapter 3; The Collegiate Institute name was changed to Westminster College in 1910.
10. *New York Clipper*, April 6, 1883.
11. *San Francisco Chronicle*, September 22, 1883.
12. *Ibid.*, September 23, 1883.

Chapter 5

1. Adams and Porter, August 1914, p. 212.
2. *San Francisco Chronicle*, October 11, 1887.
3. *San Francisco Call*, October 11, 1887.
4. *Chicago Sunday Inter Ocean*, June 10, 1888.
5. *Chicago Inter Ocean*, June 12, 1888.
6. *New York Clipper*, September 18, 1888.
7. Bordman, pp. 389–390.
8. *Ibid.*, pp. 230–231.
9. *Clipper*, March 16, 1889.
10. *Inter Ocean*, November 19, 1889.
11. *Clipper*, January 18, 1890.
12. *San Francisco Chronicle*, May 25, 1890.

Chapter 6

1. Marcosson and Frohman, Chapter 1.
2. *New York Clipper*, September 13, 1890.
3. *Ibid.*, December 6, 1890.
4. *Chicago Daily News*, April 14, 1891.
5. *Chicago Sunday Inter Ocean*, April 26, 1891.
6. *Clipper*, May 23, 1891.
7. *Los Angeles Times*, June 11, 1891.
8. *San Francisco Chronicle*, June 16, 1891.
9. *Ibid.*, June 16, 1891.
10. See: Drew, J., *My Years on the Stage*, New York, E.P. Dutton & Co., 1922, especially chapters 20 and 21.
11. *Chicago Herald*, August 18, 1891.
12. *Chicago Tribune*, August 18, 1891.
13. *Chicago Post*, August 18, 1891.
14. *Chicago Inter Ocean*, August 18, 1891.
15. *Chicago Evening News*, August 18, 1891.
16. *Chicago Tribune*, August 18, 1891.
17. *Boston Globe*, October 6, 1891.
18. *Clipper*, October 17, 1891.
19. *Ibid.*, November 28, 1891.
20. *Inter Ocean*, May 15, 1892.
21. *Clipper*, June 11, 1892.

Chapter 7

1. Marcosson and Frohman, p. 158.
2. Clemens, C. "Theatreana — Some Recollections of Maude Adams," *Hobbies: The Magazine for Collectors*, November, 1953, pp. 127–130.
3. *Chicago Inter Ocean*, September 27, 1892.
4. *Chicago Daily News*, September 27, 1892.
5. *Ibid.*, September 27, 1892.
6. *New York Times*, October 4, 1892.
7. Marcosson and Frohman, p. 146.
8. *Inter Ocean*, March 7, 1893.
9. *New York Clipper*, April 1, 1893.

10. *Boston Globe*, December 18, 1893.
11. *Ibid.*, December 27, 1893.
12. *Inter Ocean*, January 16, 1894.
13. *Ibid.*, January 16, 1894.
14. *Chicago Daily News*, January 16, 1894.
15. *New York Clipper*, February 10, 1894.
16. *Ibid.*, March 24, 1894.
17. *Ibid.*, April 7, 1894.
18. *San Francisco Chronicle*, July 19, 1894.
19. *Deseret News*, August 19, 1894.
20. *Clipper*, September 22, 1894.
21. *Ibid.*, September 22, 1894.
22. *New York Times*, September 12, 1894.
23. Barrymore, E., *Memoirs, an Autobiography*, New York, Harper, 1955, p. 55.
24. See: Davis, C.B. (ed.), *The Adventures and Letters of Richard Harding Davis*, New York, Beekman Publishers, 1917.
25. *Clipper*, January 19, 1895.
26. *Dramatic Mirror*, June 29, 1895.

Chapter 8

1. *San Francisco Chronicle*, August 20, 1895.
2. *Ibid.*, August 27, 1895.
3. *New York Clipper*, September 28, 1895.
4. *Ibid.*, January 25, 1896.
5. *New York Times*, January 21, 1896.
6. *Clipper*, January 25, 1896.
7. *Chicago Inter Ocean*, May 6, 1896.
8. *Ibid.*, May 6, 1896.
9. *San Francisco Chronicle*, June 23, 1896.
10. *Ibid.*, June 23, 1896.
11. *Clipper*, September 5, 1896.
12. *New York Times*, September 1, 1896.
13. *Clipper*, November 28, 1896.
14. *Boston Globe*, January 5, 1897.
15. *Inter Ocean*, April 28, 1897.
16. Marcosson and Frohman, p. 160.

Chapter 9

1. See: Hammerton, J.A., *Barrie: The Story of a Genius*, New York, Dodd, Mead & Co., 1929 and Mackail, D., *The Story of J.M.B.*, London, Peter Davies, 1941.
2. Marcosson and Frohman, p. 162.
3. *New York Clipper*, September 18, 1897.
4. *Ibid.*, October 2, 1897.
5. *Ibid.*, October 2, 1897.
6. *New York Times*, September 28, 1897.
7. *Ibid.*, October 2, 1897.
8. *Clipper*, November 27, 1897.
9. Robbins, P., *Maude Adams — An Inti-*

mate Portrait, New York, G.P. Putnam's Sons, 1956, p. 44.
10. *Clipper*, January 15, 1898.
11. *Ibid.*, October 8, 1898.
12. *Boston Advertiser*, October 1, 1898.
13. *Boston Globe*, September 28, 1898.
14. *Clipper*, January 7, 1899.
15. *Chicago Daily News*, March 4, 1899.
16. *Ibid.*, March 7, 1899.
17. *Chicago Inter Ocean*, April 16, 1899.
18. *Ibid.*, April 16, 1899.

Chapter 10

1. *New York Times*, May 9, 1899.
2. *New York Clipper*, May 13, 1899.
3. *New York Herald*, May 9, 1899.
4. *Boston Globe*, May 22, 1899.
5. *Clipper*, June 10, 1899.
6. *Ibid.*, July 1, 1899.
7. Robbins, p. 53.
8. *Clipper*, November 4, 1899.
9. *Ibid.*, December 16, 1899.
10. *New York Times*, January 10, 1900.
11. *Ibid.*, January 14, 1900.
12. Strang, L., *Famous Actresses of the Day*, Boston, L.C. Page & Co., 1902, pp. 56–57.
13. *Boston Globe*, March 20, 1900.
14. Robbins, p. 59.
15 *Chicago Daily News*, April 10, 1900.
16. Robbins, p. 60.
17. Robbins, p. 63.
18. *Clipper*, October 20, 1900.
19. *New York Times*, October 23, 1900.
20. *Ibid.*, October 23, 1900.
21. *Clipper*, December 8, 1900.
22. *Boston Globe*, January 14, 1901.
23. *Chicago Daily News*, February 23, 1901.
24. *Chicago Inter Ocean*, March 3, 1901.
25. *Clipper*, April 20, 1901.

Chapter 11

1. *New York World*, June 30, 1901.
2. *Chicago American*, August 20, 1901.
3. *New York Herald*, September 9, 1901.
4. *New York Clipper*, August 3, 1901.
5. *Ibid.*, August 31, 1901.
6. Marcosson and Frohman, p. 167.
7. *Clipper*, November 23, 1901.
8. *New York Herald*, November 12, 1901.
9. *Ibid.*, November 12, 1901.
10. *New York Times*, November 12, 1901.
11. *Boston Globe*, February 2, 1902.

12. *Ibid.*, February 3, 1902.
13. *Chicago Tribune*, March 25, 1902.
14. *Chicago Daily News*, March 25, 1902.
15. *Ibid.*, March 29, 1902.

Chapter 12

1. Robbins, pp. 70–71; a similar paragraph can also be found in Adams, M., "The One I Knew Least of All," *Ladies Home Journal*, May 1926, p. 155.
2. Adams, May 1926, p. 155.
3. *New York Clipper*, May 24, 1902.
4. *New York Times*, October 15, 1902.
5. *Clipper*, October 25, 1902.
6. *Ibid.*, November 8, 1902.
7. *New York Herald*, November 9, 1902.
8. Adams, June 1926, p. 22.
9. *New York Herald*, July 6, 1903.
10. Patterson, A., "The Real Maude Adams—A Study," *The Theater Magazine*, August 1903, p. 218.
11. *Clipper*, October 24, 1903.
12. *Chicago Tribune*, October 27, 1903.
13. *New York American*, November 11, 1903.
14. *New York Herald*, November 11, 1903.
15. *New York Times*, November 11, 1903.
16. Patterson, p. 220.
17. *Boston Globe*, February 16, 1904.
18. *Ibid.*, February 16, 1904.
19. *Salt Lake Tribune*, May 24, 1904.
20. *Ibid.*, May 24, 1904.
21. *San Francisco Chronicle*, May 31, 1904.
22. *Chicago Daily News*, December 7, 1904.
23. *Chicago Tribune*, December 7, 1904.
24. *New York Times*, December 28, 1904.
25. *Clipper*, December 31, 1904.
26. *New York Sun*, February 7, 1905.
27. *The Theater Magazine*, February, 1905.
28. *New York World*, February 12, 1905.

Chapter 13

1. Hammerton, pp. 351–359; Hanson, B.K., *The Peter Pan Chronicles*, New York, Carol Publishing Group, 1993, p. 27.
2. Hanson, p. 28.
3. Robbins, p. 89.
4. *Boston Transcript*, October 20, 1906.
5. *Washington Star*, October 22, 1905.
6. *New York Times*, November 12, 1905.
7. *The Theater Magazine*, December, 1905.
8. Robbins, p. 36.
9. *Boston Herald*, November 8, 1906.

10. *New York Herald*, April 23, 1906.
11. *Boston Herald*, October 23, 1906.
12. *Ibid.*, November 11, 1906.
13. *New York Clipper*, December 29, 1906.
14. *New York Herald*, December 25, 1906.
15. *Washington Post*, December 14, 1906.
16. *New York Globe*, December 29, 1906.
17. *Chicago Tribune*, March 5, 1907.
18. *Deseret News*, June 1, 1907.
19. *Ibid.*, June 4, 1907.
20. *San Francisco Dramatic Review*, June 15, 1907.
21. *Ibid.*, July 6, 1907.
22. *San Francisco Chronicle*, August 4, 1907.

Chapter 14

1. *New York Clipper*, January 25, 1908.
2. *New York World*, January 16, 1908.
3. *New York Daily Tribune*, January 16, 1908.
4. *Chicago Tribune*, January 20, 1908.
5. *Ibid.*, April 21, 1908.
6. *Chicago Daily News*, April 28, 1908.
7. *Boston Morning Telegraph*, June 4, 1908.
8. *Boston Globe*, June 4, 1908.
9. *Ibid.*, June 5, 1908.
10. Marcosson and Frohman, p. 173.
11. *Ibid.*, p. 174.
12. *Ibid.*, p. 174.
13. *Clipper*, October 17, 1908.
14. *Pittsburgh Dispatch*, October 20, 1908.
15. *Chicago Daily News*, October 28, 1908.
16. *Chicago Tribune*, October 27, 1908.
17. *Ibid.*, November 15, 1908.
18. *New York Telegram*, December 24, 1908.
19. Robbins, p. 132.
20. *New York Times*, June 22, 1909.
21. *Ibid.*, June 22, 1909.

Chapter 15

1. *New York Clipper*, December 28, 1909.
2. *Chicago Daily News*, March 29, 1910.
3. *Deseret News*, May 6, 1910.
4. *Clipper*, June 4, 1910.
5. *San Francisco Chronicle*, June 7, 1910.
6. *New York Tribune*, January 24, 1911.
7. *Louisville Times*, February 10, 1912.
8. *Clipper*, January 27, 1912.
9. *Chicago Daily News*, March 12, 1912.
10. *Clipper*, July 28, 1912.
11. *New York Evening Post*, December 24, 1912.

12. *Chicago Tribune*, March 2, 1913.
13. *Chicago Daily News*, March 8, 1913.
14. *Boston Globe*, November 18, 1913.
15. *Clipper*, January 17, 1914.
16. *New York Sun*, January 6, 1914.
17. *Ibid.*, February 1, 1914.
18. *Clipper*, September 26, 1914.
19. *Chicago Tribune*, November 17, 1914.

Chapter 16

1. *New York Clipper*, May 15, 1915.
2. *New York Times*, May 9, 1915.
3. *Ibid.*, May 25, 1915.
4. *Ibid.*, May 25, 1915.
5. Gordon, R., "A Great Lady in a Grand Manner," *The Stage*, October, 1936, p. 90–91.
6. *New York Telegraph*, December 22, 1915.
7. *Chicago Tribune*, May 16, 1916.
8. *Chicago Daily News*, May 16, 1916.
9. *New York American*, December 26, 1916.
10. *New York Bulletin*, December 26, 1916.
11. *New York Telegraph*, December 26, 1916.
12. *Chicago Tribune*, December 25, 1917.
13. *Chicago Daily News*, December 26, 1917.
14. Robbins, p. 188.
15. *Salt Lake Tribune*, June 25, 1918.

Chapter 17

1. See: Moore, M.L., *A Time for Hope*, Chicago, Cenacle Retreat House, ND; letter: Betty Sanchez, Cenacle Central Archives, to author, on the Cenacle history and Maude's visits to the convent, April 22, 2003; Maude Adams, Lake Ronkonkoma, New York, Cenacle Retreat House (copy of article, written by Sr. Ellen Frawley, *Encounter*, Spring, 1981).
2. Sanchez, April 22, 2003.
3. Robbins, pp. 196–197.
4. Robbins, p. 199.
5. *New York Clipper*, July 19, 1919.
6. *Ibid.*, October 22, 1919.
7. *Ibid.*, December 3, 1919.
8. *Variety*, April 16, 1920; *New York Times*, April 20, 1920.
9. *Clipper*, May 26, 1920.
10. Letter: Maude Adams to Booth Tarkington, February 25, 1921.
11. *New York Times*, June 14, 1921.
12. Robbins, p. 207.
13. Letters: Bennett Jones to Mrs. John Keiran, March 1, 1956, and March 15, 1956.
14. *New York Times*, January 17, 1922.

Chapter 18

1. Robbins, p. 211.
2. *New York Times*, November 15, 1922.
3. Robbins, p. 211.
4. *Variety*, September 17, 1924.
5. Robbins, p. 234.
6. Letter: Maxwell E. Perkins to Maude Adams, May 18, 1925.
7. Letter: Perkins to Satterley (Maude's lawyer), February 19, 1926.
8. Adams, May 1926, p. 14.
9. Robbins, p. 236.
10. Letter: Currie to Perkins, January 25, 1927.
11. Letter: Perkins to Maude Adams, February 3, 1927.
12. Robbins, pp. 238–239.

Chapter 19

1. *New York Telegram*, May 17, 1930.
2. *New York Times*, May ?, 1931.
3. *New York Herald*, October 15, 1931.
4. *New York Sun*, November 1, 1931.
5. *Ibid.*, November 1, 1931.
6. *Cleveland Plain Dealer*, November 4, 1931.
7. *New York Times*, November 11, 1931.
8. Morehouse, W., "Maude Adams Redivivus," *Literary Digest*, November 21, 1931.
9. *Plain Dealer*, November 4, 1931.
10. *New York Times*, November 11, 1931.
11. Morehouse, p. 20.
12. Woollcott, A., *The New Yorker*, December 19, 1931.
13. Letter: Perkins to Maude Adams, November 10, 1931.
14. Telegram: Maude Adams to Perkins, November 25, 1931.
15. *Chicago Tribune*, March 1, 1932.
16. *San Francisco Chronicle*, April 12, 1932.
17. Robbins, p. 243.
18. *Boston Globe*, July 17, 1934.
19. *New York Times*, July 17, 1934.
20. Letter: Perkins to Maude Adams, May 9, 1935.
21. Letter: Perkins to Maude Adams, September 23, 1936.
22. *New York Herald Tribune*, October 18, 1935.
23. *New York Times*, October 18, 1935.
24. *Herald Tribune*, October 22, 1935.

Chapter 20

1. Stephens College Archives Department, March 1999.

2. Clark, L., "Maude Adams at Stephens College," *The Speech Teacher*, March 1965, No. 2, pp. 123–127.

3. Stephens College Archives Department, March 1999.

4. *New York Times*, September 28, 1937.

5. *Ibid.*, October 20, 1937.

6. *Kansas City Star*, November 28, 1937.

7. *Los Angeles Times*, March 4, 1938.

8. *New York Times*, May 30, 1938.

9. *New York Herald*, January 6, 1939.

10. *Reader's Digest*, July 1940, pp. 23–26.

11. *Ibid.*, p. 26.

12. *New York Times Magazine*, November 8, 1942.

13. Robbins, pp. 282–283.

14. *Cosmopolitan*, May 1950, p. 130.

Epilogue

1. Letter: Charles Scribner to Ethelbert Warfield (Satterlee lawyer), April 25, 1951.

2. Robbins, p. 284.

3. Excerpts from *Washington Star*, July 20, 1953.

4. Excerpts from *New York Times*, July 19, 1953.

5. Excerpts from *Chicago Tribune*, July 20, 1953.

6. Robbins, p. 291.

Selected Bibliography
and Source Material

Archives, Collections, Libraries

California Historical Society
Cenacle Central Archives
Chicago Historical Society
General Electric Archives
Houghton Library, Harvard University
Mormon Library
The Museum of the City of New York
Nevada Historical Society
New York Public Library, Performing Arts Division
Oregon Historical Society
Princeton University Library, Rare Books and Special Collections
San Francisco Performing Arts Library and Museum
San Francisco Public Library, Historical Center
Stephens College
University of Southern California Special Collections
University of Utah
Utah State Historical Society

Newspapers

New York Clipper, January 1870 to July 1923.
New York Dramatic Mirror, January 1880 to December 1910.
New York Dramatic News, January 1880 to December 1890.
Variety, December 1906 to December 1950.
Selected newspaper articles from 1875 to 1953 —*Boston Globe, Boston Transcript, Chicago Daily News, Chicago Inter Ocean, Chicago Tribune, Cleveland Plain Dealer, The Daily Oregonian, Deseret News, Los Angeles Times, New York American, New York Herald, New York Post, New York Sun, New York Telegraph, New York Times, New York World, Salt Lake Tribune, San Francisco Call, San Francisco Chronicle, Toledo Blade, Washington Star*

Books

Barrie, J.M. *The Little Minister*. New York: Dodge, 1922.
Barrymore, E. *Memoirs: An Autobiography*. New York: Harper, 1955.
Bogar, T.A. *John E. Owens: Nineteenth Century American Actor and Manager*. Jefferson, N.C.: McFarland, 2002.
Bordman, G. *The Concise Oxford Companion to American Theater*. New York: Oxford University Press, 1987.
Breckenridge, R.D. *Westminster College of Salt Lake City*. Logan: Utah State University Press, 1998.
Coad, O.S., and E. Mims, Jr. *The American Stage*. New Haven, Conn.: Yale University Press, 1929.
Davies, A. *Maude Adams*. New York: Frederick A. Stokes, 1901.
Davis, C.B. (ed.). *The Adventures and Letters of Richard Harding Davis*. New York: Beekman, 1917.
Davis, S.P. (ed.). *The History of Nevada*. Las Vegas: Nevada Publications, 1984.
Drew, J. *My Years on the Stage*. New York: E.P. Dutton, 1922.
Fields, A. *Lillian Russell: A Biography of "America's Beauty."* Jefferson, N.C.: McFarland, 1999.
Hammerton, J.A. *Barrie: The Story of a Genius*. New York: Dodd, Mead, 1929.
Hanson, B.K. *The Peter Pan Chronicles*. New York: Carol, 1993.
Hughes, G. *A History of the American Theater*. New York: Samuel French, 1951.
Latter Day Saints, Biographical Encyclopaedia. Vol. III, n.d.
Mackail, D. *The Story of J.M.B.* London: Peter Davies, 1941.
Madsen, A. *The Sewing Circle: Hollywood's Greatest Secret*. Secaucus, New Jersey: Carol, 1995.
Marcosson, I.F., and D. Frohman. *Charles Frohman: Manager and Man*. New York: Harper & Bros., 1916.
Maughan, I.F. *Pioneer Theater in the Desert*. Salt Lake City, Utah: Deseret, 1961.
The Mayflower Quarterly. New York: The Mayflower Society, 1953.
Montana, Its Story and Biography. Vol. 1, n.d.
Patterson, A. *Maude Adams*. New York: Meyer and Bros., 1907.
Pyper, G.D. *The Romance of an Old Playhouse*. Salt Lake City, Utah: Deseret, 1937.
Robbins, P. *Maude Adams — An Intimate Portrait*. New York: G.P. Putnam's Sons, 1956.
_____. *The Young Maude Adams*. Francetown, N.H.: Marshall Jones, 1959.
Southern, E.H. *The Melancholy Tale of "Me."* New York: C. Scribner's Sons, 1916.
Strang, L. *Famous Actresses of the Day*. Boston: L.C. Page, 1902.
Who's Who on the Stage. Adams, Miss Maude (Kiscadden), 1910.

Magazines, Pamphlets

Adams, K.R. "The Incomparable Maude Adams Somewhere in Time." *Pioneer Magazine*, January-February 1994.
Adams, M. "The One I Knew Least of All." *Ladies Home Journal*, March to August, 1926.
Annual Circular of Salt Lake Collegiate Institute, 1886-7.
Carpenter, A.G. "Big Mazda Lamps May Revolutionize Studio Lighting." *G-E Monogram*, April 1927.
Castor, R.C. "Maude Adams: No Other Actress Can Take Her Place." *Worth Their Salt: Notable but Often Unnoted Women of Utah*. Logan: Utah State University Press, 1996.
"Charles Frohman, Manager." *The Theater Magazine*, December 1902.
Clark, A.L. "The Story Maude Adams Never Told." *True West*, May-June 1967.
Clark, L. "Maude Adams at Stephens College." *The Speech Teacher*, March 1965.
Clemens, C. "Theatreana — Some Recollections of Maude Adams." *Hobbies: The Magazine for Collectors*, November 1953.
Crawford, M.C. "Maude Adams in Twelfth Night." *The Theater Magazine*, August 1908.
Dudley, L. "Maude Adams' Blueprint for a Campus Drama Workshop." *Theater Arts*, August 1954.
Gordon, R. "A Great Lady in a Grand Manner." *The Stage*, October, 1936.
Gray, D. "Maude Adams: A Public Influence." *Hampton's Magazine*.
Henninger, G. "Broadway Star Ended Retirement to Teach Drama." *Stephens Life*, 1949.
"History of Maude Adams." *Utah History Encyclopaedia*, onlineutah.com, September 2002.

Huguenin, Dr. C.A. "The Cenacle, Maude Adams' Gift." *Long Island Forum*, January 1958.

Jenkins, P.W. "Kiscadden-Slade." *Annals of Wyoming*, Vol. 1, No. 1, January 1949.

Johnston, A. "Wilson Mizner." *The New Yorker*, December 30, 1950.

Kiscadden, A.A., and V.H. Porter. "The Life Story of Maude Adams and Her Mother." *The Green Book Magazine*, June 1914 to January 1915.

Maude Adams. Lake Ronkonkoma, New York: Cenacle Retreat House, n.d.

"Maude Adams as Tannersville and Onteora Friends Knew Her." October 4, 1953.

"Maude Adams in Schiller's Joan of Arc." *The Theater Magazine*, July 1909.

Maxwell, P. *The Stage Story of Maude Adams*. 1908.

McConville, A. "Miss Maude Adams." *Cenacle Retreat House*, July 1981.

Mellon, J. "Peter Pan at Stephens." *The Stephens Standard*, November 1937.

Melville, J.K. "The Mormon Drama and Maude Adams. *Feminine Contributions to Mormon Culture*. Provo, Utah: Brigham Young University, December 1965.

Moore, M.L. *A Time for Hope*. Chicago: Cenacle Retreat House, n.d.

Morehouse, W. "Maude Adams Redivivus." *Literary Digest*, November 21, 1931.

Patterson, A. "The Real Maude Adams—A Study." *The Theater Magazine*, August 1903.

"Register of the Papers of George Dollinger Pyper (1860–1943)." *University of Utah Libraries*, 1970.

Seagraves, A. "Maude Adams, A Delicate, Elfin Actress." *Women Who Charmed the West*. Hayden, Idaho: Wesanne Publications, 1991.

"Some Developments in the Electrical Industry During 1922." *G.E. Review*, January 1923.

Sutton, V. "In Memory of Maude Adams." *Catskills Daily News*, July 16, 1953.

Thatcher, L. "The Gentle Polygamist: Arthur Brown, Ex-Senator from Utah." *Utah Historical Quarterly*, Summer 1984.

Weir, H.C. "Maude Adams," *Human Life*, December 1906.

"Where Are They Now?" *Cosmopolitan*, May 1950.

Whitney, H.G. "The Story of the Salt Lake Theater." *Improvement Era*, Part III, Vol. 18, 1915.

Vinatieri, J.A. "The Growing Years: Westminster College from Birth to Adolescence." *Utah Historical Quarterly*, Fall 1975.

Index